THE
NAME
OF
THE
CAT

Also by Barbara Holland

Mother's Day, or The View From in Here

THE
NAME
OF
THE
CAT

Barbara Holland

DODD, MEAD & COMPANY
NEW YORK

Published by Dodd, Mead & Company, Inc.
71 Fifth Avenue, New York, N.Y. 10003
Manufactured in the United States of America
First Edition
1   2   3   4   5   6   7   8   9   10

Library of Congress Cataloging-in-Publication Data

Holland, Barbara.
  The name of the cat.

  1. Cats—Anecdotes.   I. Title.
SF445.5.H62   1988   818'.5402   88–3685
ISBN 0-396-09175-X

To Sidney

CONTENTS

THE
NAME
OF
THE
CAT

The Conversion of Boston Blackie

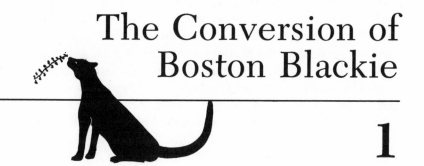

1

You can usually tell by looking at it what's going on inside a dog. Except for the few Thurberian neurotics, a dog wears his insides on his outside, writ large and plain. A cat thinks at the back of its head, and the results can surprise you. No wonder cats were burned as witches; it hurts people's feelings not to know what the lower orders are up to.

Boston Blackie was an outlaw. He was of the tribe known in the city as alley cats, in the country as feral, and in the suburbs as strays, the last word carrying a hint of self-righteous blame; to stray is to wander, ignorantly or willfully, from the proper path. It is the cat who has gone astray, wandered off from domesticity to starve, not the people who have left it behind when they moved or thrown it in a bag with its siblings from a passing car. There are millions of these. They flicker across human paths from time to time, and maybe we say, "Puss, puss," but they vanish as quickly as the shadow of a bird, having no reason to answer. They do not live long, but there are always more.

Boston Blackie was different from most. He was more predator than waif, and his chosen prey was cats. Boston Blackie hated cats; he wanted to kill them, all of them. Coming down out of the woods and fields like the wolf on the fold, he swooped, savaged, and vanished again. My sister Judy and her husband had, at the time, thirteen cats (they now have twenty-three, through no fault of their own) and, weather permitting, these spent most of their time outdoors. Boston Blackie attacked them on their own premises without regard for age or gender, and he beat them bloody. He ripped their ears and gouged their eyes and dealt out deep, suppurating abscesses. Cat after cat was carried bleeding to the vet, cat after cat was dosed with penicillin. Yards of stitches were taken. The vet bills grew.

Sometimes we caught glimpses of Blackie; sometimes we just heard screams. His attack was most uncatlike, with none of the singsong preliminaries to a fight, no foreplay, none of the elaborate adjustment of position and subtleties of eye contact with which normal male cats defuse their aggressions, nine times out of ten breaking off to lick or pretend an interest in some distant object and drift away without a blow exchanged. Blackie just pounced, as on a mouse. Anyone around would run out yelling. Once I beat him with a rake, standing over him panting and whacking, but he went on tearing chunks out of poor Flanagan as if I were made of air. He had no interest in people. I was unnerved by the single-minded concentration of his hatred, like the legends about wolverines. Nothing distracted him from his urge to rid the world of all its other cats; when disturbed by humans he usually drove his victim under the woodshed, out of reach, to go on with the bloodshed. Not even the largest and strongest of our cats landed a blow, and Blackie himself was unscarred. Cats fight by certain rules and ceremonies, and Blackie's bulletlike descent and mad, meaningless hatred disarmed them utterly; they never even had a chance to run. Some of their wounds were on their back legs from trying.

Except for a handful accidentally born on the premises,

all Judy's cats had been strays, and none of them had ever acted like that. Stray cats may be, and usually are, starving, lame, frightened, ill, and in hideous pain from infected wounds, eaten alive by fleas, ticks, ear mites, and intestinal parasites, but they don't go looking for other cats to kill. Since the thirteen had all been neutered, sex could be ruled out as a motive, and Blackie wasn't starving, either. When Judy fed her own she threw a propitiatory handful of food into the forsythia bushes where he often lay in wait, not for food but for blood.

He didn't act like a cat, and he didn't even look much like a stray. The standard homeless cat is a brindled mix of stripes and patches, leggy, with a long nose and close-set eyes and an overall look of skimpiness, as if there hadn't been enough protoplasm to create him properly. Basic out-laws are slat-sided, and almost disappear when seen from above; Blackie was square. He was short of leg and round of ear, with immensely long white whiskers and very small white feet, an outlaw of a different breed.

Conferences were held.

"He's insane," we said. "He's psychotic."

"At least he can't be rabid. He's been coming around for months, since the middle of winter, and if he had rabies he'd be long dead."

"If only the other cats would stick together. Gang up on him."

"Cats don't join armies."

"Besides, they're all afraid of him. It's like saying, why didn't the plane passengers gang up on the hijackers? Who's going to gang up first?"

"If we could just get hold of him somehow and take him to the SPCA."

"You're not suggesting we pick him up? In our *hands*?"

"Maybe if we could catch him in one of those box traps, and then just leave him in the trap and put it in the car?"

The vet, who was sympathetic to our efforts and bored with cleaning and stitching up wounds, lent us a drop-gate

trap and offered to kill the madman if we caught him. Blackie
avoided the trap. It can't have been very convincing; no matter what we baited it with, nothing at all went into it.

Blackie ambushed the smallest and prettiest of the Three
Girls and ripped her ear and slashed her eye.

"We could poison him," said Judy. "I throw food into the
bushes for him. I could poison it."

"That would be the day he was off killing someone else's
cats. One of ours would find it instead."

"We could shoot him."

It kept coming around to that. At first it was a joke. We
weren't people with guns, and God knows we weren't people
who shot cats. Shot *cats*? Judy and Bob were a famous hostel
for needy cats, and bore, they always said, an invisible mark
on the door such as bums were said to make during the Great
Depression, meaning "Here are softies." But summer came,
and Blackie's terrorist attacks continued; no cat had actually
been killed yet, but antiobiotic pills had become a time-con-
suming part of the family routine, and the gun came to seem
less bizarre.

"He's probably in some kind of pain," we argued. "That
could be why he's so vicious. It would be a mercy to shoot
him."

"He might have had a head injury. Something pressing
on his brain makes him berserk."

"Where would we get this gun?"

"Terry's got one. He's got a whole armory, actually, but
he could bring something lightweight that wouldn't knock
holes in the neighborhood."

"Would he do it for us?"

"Sure. We'll give him a beer. I don't suppose it'll be the
first cat he's shot; he's one of those sportsmen types."

"After all, we have to think of our own. They can't live
like this."

"It's agreed, then."

We had sat in judgment on Blackie and pronounced him
miserable, in pain as well as psychotic. Besides, we wouldn't

have to pull the trigger personally, just point out the lurking Blackie and go inside and hold our ears, praying that Terry, not a cat person, could tell one black cat with white trim from the others.

"We're going away for the weekend," said Judy. "We'll be back Tuesday. Let's do it Tuesday night at feeding time."

"Tuesday night." We all nodded, feeling that we should prick our fingers and seal the decision in blood, to share the guilt equally.

Judy and Bob went away for the weekend, and I fed their cats. Feeding their cats was not child's play. The assortment of battered tins and dishes covered half the backyard, and protocol had to be observed. Muffie, senior cat and major-domo and sergeant-at-arms, followed me into the kitchen to supervise. It was one of his duties to see that meals were served on time, and to find and chivvy the feeder if they were late. Muffie was getting old, but he delegated no responsibility, had no lieutenants, and no other cat seemed ready to take over and let him retire. He was looking a bit careworn and heavy in his mind. Poor Muff, he would have loved more frequent laps, or a word of appreciation, but in households so crowded the attention goes more often than it should to the young, the cute, and the pushy.

I dumped a large can of cat food into a kettle of dry chows, poured water over it, and mashed and stirred the mess vigorously while Muffie watched and the others took up their stations on the lawn.

Zachary was fed on the back step, and first; at the time, Judy still considered him the baby of the family, though she's had an accident since that wiped out his title. He is a curious-looking cat. His sharply crossed eyes are Siamese-blue and his body is buff, but his legs and tail are striped. Judy loyally insists that he's a tabby-point Siamese, a recognized creature in English show circles, but nothing about his shape or voice suggests Siam. Was he the product of a misalliance, or the result of some misguided breeding experiment? Apparently his owners had been dissatisfied with him and cut off his whiskers and threw him away in a patch of steep, rocky woods; he was too small to have wandered so far from human habitation on his own, half starved and screaming lonesomely to himself when Judy found him.

The Three Girls—Stubby, Gray, and beautiful Marzi-pan—eat together out of one rusty pan, and care must be taken that their mother, Mehitabel the witch, doesn't chase them away from it; she never could stand them, even when they were tiny. She was found, pregnant, in a dumpster at a construction site, and Judy and Bob often said, "You can take the cat out of the dumpster, but you can't take the dumpster out of the cat."

Throw a handful at the bushes for Blackie. Like throwing salt over your shoulder to ward off evil spirits.

Ferdy, whose teeth are bad, eats last and gets the soft-ened juicy dregs at the bottom of the kettle. I never come out quite even and have to hustle around snatching back some from the other dishes, but when you've finished feeding Judy's cats you've accomplished something, and can stand back and survey the seething lawn with pride.

I had gotten as far as, I think, Porky, when Boston Blackie came out of the bushes.

The other cats froze, and then the ones closest to the woods began to slip away. Marzipan broke and ran, like a fool, followed by her sisters, and Muffie edged backwards to-ward the kitchen door. I stood still.

Where had Judy left the cat carrier, in case someone had to be rushed to the vet? Why hadn't we called Terry at once, on Thursday, as soon as we decided on the gun? Could I call him now? Would he get here in time?

Blackie walked steadily across the grass toward me, and I backed against a tree. I had never heard of a cat walking up to a human and attacking it, but I've learned to be wary of generalizations about cats, and this was no common cat.

He moved purposefully, without haste, and ignored the other cats melting away, ignored their abandoned dishes.

In front of me he stopped and looked up, and I looked

down, hugging the kettle as a kind of bulletproof vest. His tail was high in the classic greeting gesture. He opened his mouth and gave a ridiculously small hoarse mew.

It was the first time he had ever noticed any of us. It was absurd to think of it, but could it be a trick? A trap? "Are you hungry, Blackie?" I asked in nervous falsetto. "Help yourself. The others lost their appetites." I could reach down and grab him, if only I had steel gloves on. Throw him loose in the car and drive hell-for-leather to the SPCA's gas chamber.

He lifted a front paw and curled it, and mewed again.

"You mean you want a plate of your *own*?" I asked.

Apparently he did. I went and got one, and filled it, and he settled quietly to his dinner without glancing around, tail down and stretched out in the classic gesture of satisfied dining. One by one the others crept back to gulp a few bites from their own plates, never taking their eyes off the guest, but he paid no attention. He ate daintily and slowly, and when he was finished he washed his white paws and whiskers and then went over to the daylily bed against the sunny wall and found a patch that hadn't already been marked off by other cats and stretched out and closed his eyes, crushing daylilies.

He's called Basil now, and sometimes Bison because his head and shoulders have grown to enormous size, and he purrs like a helicopter. He's been known to cuff an unruly kitten, but otherwise peace is his whole desire, peace and for pure heaven a little rubbing under the chin until his purr amplifies to the gurgle of a Boeing with a sea gull in its throat.

I have coaxed wild cats in from the woods before, and this is not how it's done. It's a long process and full of setbacks. First the dish at the edge of the lawn is ignored completely or falls to a raccoon. Then the food is eaten, but secretly, at night. Then if all goes well and no one slams a door, no far-off dog barks, no phone rings, maybe there's a glimpse of cat at the dish at dusk. Emboldened, you move the dish six feet in from the woods, onto civilized grass, where it stays untouched for three days. You may never see the cat again, or it may eventually reappear to snatch a morsel and race with it back to the woods.

With Rupert, I began in July, and by the time leaves were falling in October he would suffer me to sit on the back steps and watch him eating from twenty feet away. After that I had to go away and my mother took over. By first snowfall she had him in the house, but now after twelve years of domestic life he's still twitchy about it. He still disappears for hours at the sound of a strange voice. He accepts food from no one but Mother. Two years ago he took to sitting beside her on the couch in the evenings; if he lives long enough he may someday sit in her lap, but he's still terrified of my brother. More than once he's mistaken me for Mother, and when he realized I wasn't, squawled with horror and fled.

Rupert was coaxed with infinite gentleness for months; Boston Blackie, who had known only shouts and occasional beatings from us, converted himself between morning and evening.

What happened? We argued it over. Dr. Jekyll and Mr. Hyde? But there had been no Jekyll moments in his outlaw days, and months passed and Mr. Hyde never returned.

Sometimes desperate circumstance will force a feral cat to ask for help that it hates. Once, in the country, a nursing female came to my back door in bitter January and asked for food. I don't know how she knew to ask, but certainly she knew she had to have help or she and the kittens would die; it's unwise, when you're on your own, to have kittens in zero-degree weather. There was something terribly proud and bitter in this little cat, who didn't pretend to be friendly but only showed me her desperation, her hat-rack hipbones and dry, dangling teats. I put out food and water, and then followed her to the kittens, in the semi-shelter under a shed. They were very young, with their eyes still sealed shut. The little cat growled at me when I reached out a hand, and scratched me when I tried to gather her young up to take them someplace warmer. She had hated having to ask for food, and as soon as a break came in the steely cold she and the surviving kittens disappeared.

But Boston Blackie wasn't hungry, and to a cat who'd survived the long Pennsylvania winter these June days with their meadows full of mice must have seemed very endurable indeed. People who extol the independent, solitary nature of the cat would have considered his life ideal.

Maybe he had had a spell of madness, or perhaps amnesia. Maybe, since there was a respectable strain of protoplasm in his shape, some racial memory had risen in his brain like a bubble. Maybe he had once belonged to people, and been a house cat, and then lost his sanity or his memory and somehow that Saturday it came back to him. "Maybe," Judy suggested, "he'd had a blow on the head, and then he had another blow on the head and it brought back his memory."

"Like in the cartoons."

"Exactly."

It was a silly idea, but it was the only one we could think of, or the only one we could admit to without making fools of ourselves.

The unmentionable answer was, of course, that Blackie had made a decision.

A cat will stand for a long time at an opened door and consider the immediate sensory arguments for and against going out: wind in the ears, rain, cold, snow on the ground, dogs, planes, sunshine, squirrels, and the condition of the litter box inside. The weights of these matters nudge the cat in one direction or the other, or, more often, in both directions until a human foot pushes him firmly out onto the steps. If the decision is negative, an experienced cat will go back to bed, sometimes for the whole month of February, while a young cat may ask to have the door reopened twenty times in the course of a single rainy day, to see if things have changed, but the decision process is the same. It's a decision we can allow a cat to make, simple and physical and based on observable factors: it is raining and in the past when I went out in the rain I got my feet wet; I don't like rain so I will stay in. This is no more complicated than deciding whether or not to scratch an ear—and I've seen cats undecided about that, too. If we're going to admit independent volition in animals, and Descartes begrudged them even that, insisting that all animal behavior was as automated as digestion, then we have to allow them to act on past experience and what they can see and hear at the moment.

But a cat does not make New Year's resolutions. A cat does not sit in the bushes one day and decide, without pressure of any kind, to stop being a vicious renegade with a price (we were going to give Terry a beer) on his head and turn himself into the mildest of house cats. Precious few humans are capable of this decision; our habitual criminals tend to stay criminal, and even our own simple resolutions, such as spending more time with the children, tend to fade by Groundhog Day. But leaving aside the effort of will involved in changing one's whole personality and behavior instantly and permanently, the intellectual leap is beyond him.

We know perfectly well that a cat doesn't have the kind of brain that could conceive of itself as a different creature from the one it is now, and take steps to become that creature. We are, surely, the only animal self-conscious enough to inspect our behavior and wonder if life would be more satisfying if we changed it: a cat can't imagine life as a different sort of cat any more than it can imagine life as a rhinoceros.

Even a very young human child can say to itself, "Maybe if I were a better boy my mother would be nicer to me and this would make me happier." No animal can say this. A dog can learn that if he sits when he's told to sit he'll get a pat on the head, but he can't suppose it before it's ever happened; dogs may want to please, but they aren't supposed to suppose.

Blackie cannot have thought things over and decided to become Basil.

What, then, did he think—or should I say "think"? What did happen? As swiftly as a werewolf changing back into hu-

man form with the blood of his midnight rampages still wet
on his claws, he became a different cat, a cat of peace and
sofa cushions, and in time even the other cats forgot his outlaw days and allowed him to curl among them in a patchwork
heap, and no outsider, looking them over, could have
guessed for which of these a man was coming with a gun.

Smart Like Us

2

When humans address the question of nonhuman intelligence, what we ask is, "How close is this creature's mind to ours?" Naturally it can come only so close and no closer, but our mind is the standard of perfection against which all imperfect, lesser minds must be measured. Then we make up tests to see just how far inferior cats are to humans at solving human puzzles; when the cats pose us feline puzzles we are not obliged to solve them, nor to call it failure if we fail to. Our tests measure the kind of persistence and cleverness valuable to humans in a modern, human world, because if not of use to us, then of what use at all?

We do not test for adaptability, or consider it a form of intelligence, because we're in charge here: humans don't need adaptability because humans call the shots, and adapting is the necessity of those below. We don't test for the capacity for contentment, because contentment is the enemy of progress; a contented human, if there were such a thing, would be useless to society, even a threat. We don't test for physical competence, because next to the warthog we're the most incompetent creature alive; therefore it simply doesn't count, an odd notion in a society that makes millionaires of its ballplayers.

Top criterion for true humanoid achievement is the use of tools. We feel that using tools is pretty fancy stuff, possible only for smart people like us, and it never enters our minds that it might be smarter still if we were so sufficient in ourselves that we didn't need to use separate tools—if we were our own tools. In 1950 a four-month-old kitten climbed the Matterhorn with a group of mountaineers. It was the only member of the party without climbing and safety equipment. Is it, in the eye of eternity, really nobler to have invented the crampon than not to have needed the thing in the first place?

Besides tools, we admire as intelligence the concept of work. Being so ill-equipped for the world, we have to do a good deal of work just to survive, and since we do it, it must be a sign of intelligence, this submersion of natural inclination in order to accomplish a task. In animals, this usually boils down to working for us, at jobs we want done. Dogs understand work, and often seem to take the same self-important pleasure in it that we do, enjoying it as much for its own sake as for the praise attached. The bird dog brings us the bird, never thinking to eat it himself, and takes pride in the job well done. The elephant, considered an animal genius, seems to understand working for us and even to enjoy it, its little eyes twinkling merrily as it helps us destroy the forests that shelter its fellows. It even helps us trap wild elephants, herding them into stockades and then disciplining and instructing them in their future duties to man. Most people find this charming as well as intellectual.

The cat, a lesser being, does not work for us. It catches mice, but not for us, not as a job, though it may bring us one as a gift, freely offered and not because we asked. Task and obligation are not catly concepts. In the building of Grand Coulee Dam a cat was useful, taking a string tied to its tail along a winding drainpipe so that the engineers could pull a cable through it; what cat could resist exploring a winding drainpipe? No one supposes it wanted to be useful, or took any interest in dams; our separate interests, just for a moment, happened to cross.

They don't often. I have read, though I'm not sure I believe it, that in Vietnam the United States Army undertook to make cats on leashes lead foot soldiers through the night jungles, using their magical eyes to help us win our war. The project had to be abandoned because the cats kept playing with the pack straps of the soldiers in front, stopping to strop their claws on the soldiers' boots, and knocking off work altogether when it rained. It's rare that the cat's concept of fun coincides with the human concept of work; when the human tries to do paperwork, all the cat sees is a person wasting on a sheet of paper valuable attention that might better be spent on cats; when the human digs a row of holes in which to plant daffodils, the cat follows along using the holes for feline purposes and then filling them neatly in again.

We never ask—it would be sentimental to ask—what the purpose of intelligence is to its user, how successful the cat is to itself as a cat. We ask how successful it would be as a human. We ask it to prove that it could build a better mousetrap, perhaps forgetting that it doesn't need to; it is a better mousetrap. It never seems to occur to us that a cat, if it were human, might not want to learn to program in COBOL but instead to compose songs or dance with the Bolshoi or translate its dreams into numbers that win the lottery. We're disappointed in it when it doesn't bother to solve our puzzles, or push the right buttons to get out of a cage in which, contrary to instructions, it decided to take a nap.

One thing we used to know for certain about the lesser forms of life: they can't talk. Speech, human speech, we ardently believe, is the one utter necessity for abstract thought and the crowning glory that distinguishes the human mind from all other "minds." Lacking speech, an animal cannot entertain concepts. It's impossible, for instance, that both the Siamese Morgan and the new little black cat, being young and inexperienced, tried to play with the letter O. Both of them, on separate occasions, saw it, one of the big decorative capitals used to break up a page of print, and tried to roll it off the page. They ignored the F, the L, the T, as being too angular, but they pawed for quite a while at the rollable O before they realized they'd been duped and gave up. Without the word *round*, they cannot entertain the thought "round," and this can't be allowed to have happened.

Without speech nothing can exist but the here and now, the concrete, the immediate sensory impression. Speech *is* thought. Without it, an animal's world is reduced to heat and cold, hunger and thirst, sex and reproduction: the rest is silence.

Consider Betsy, a most unremarkable cat. My daughter brought her home, a wretched scrap of alley flotsam with patches of white and patches of gray stripes, and she ate, washed up, and stayed. A nice enough cat and immaculate in her personal habits, but not the kind that impresses itself on a cat household; I more or less ignored her.

One evening I was scraping carrots into the sink and Betsy jumped up onto the counter. This was surprising; unlike all my other cats she never jumped onto counters or the dinner table, having apparently made herself a set of rules for household behavior that never occurred to anyone else, least of all me. She stepped delicately into the sink, gazed greenly up at me to be sure she had my attention, and squatted and urinated.

"*Betsy!*" Betsy the prissy, Betsy of the perfect manners— in the *sink*? I raised my hand to smack her and she sprang onto the floor and raced toward the laundry room. I chased her. Glancing over her shoulder to see that I was still on her trail, she led me to the cat pan and stopped in front of it and looked up at me. She lifted a curled paw in disgust. It was a mess. I had been busy. I had neglected to change the litter.

I apologized, I cleaned the pan, I went back to the carrots. But I was shaken.

Consider the necessary train of thought, or "thoughts":

1. The woman changes the litter pan.
2. It needs changing badly, so she must have forgotten.
3. If I remind her, she'll change it.
4. How can I remind her? Just pacing back and forth meowing, or scratching the furniture, or nipping her ankle, will direct her attention to me but not to the litter pan.
5. How can I say, specifically, "litter pan" to her in a way she understands?
6. With a symbolic gesture. I will get her attention, and then demonstrate the problem to her.
7. Then she'll change it.

I don't know whether my chasing her was part of the plan, so she could lead me to the laundry room, or a spontaneous addition when she saw she had overestimated my intelligence and further explanation was necessary.

Those who have spent time in a country where they didn't speak the language know the difficulty of conveying a problem not in the same room, an invisible problem, even with hands to gesture with. Your car has broken down, but how to explain a car when there is no car in sight? Even given pencil and paper and hands to draw with, how to explain that the car won't run? It takes very little genuine intelligence to say "My car broke down" to someone who understands the words; inventing a symbolic demonstration is high-order effort.

When a cat wants a door opened, it pantomimes opening the door, reaches for the doorknob or hooks a paw under the edge and glares around at the people. But the door is there, and means door, directly, as refrigerator means food, while urinating in the sink only symbolizes a dirty litter pan, the way setting fire to a piece of striped cotton means "Americans go home." We like to think we hold a monopoly on this symbolic reference to the intangible; in fact, we insist on it.

Roger Brown, in *Words and Things*, says, "Most people are determined to hold the line against animals. Grant them the ability to make linguistic reference and they will be putting in a claim for minds and souls. The whole phyletic scale will come trouping into Heaven demanding immortality for every tadpole and hippopotamus. Better be firm now and make it clear that man alone can *use language and make reference.* There is a qualitative difference of mentality separating us from animals."

The italics are mine. Betsy couldn't use our spoken words, lacking the vocal setup, but she used what physical equipment she did have. And if she wasn't "referring" to the litter pan—if I were a scientist it would be worth my diploma to suppose she was—then we have to assume that this cat of almost irritatingly hygienic habit once in her life suffered from an aberrant impulse, a kind of psychobiologic twitch, that made her risk a beating by jumping into the sink and committing an unheard-of indecency right under my hands. When screamed at she coincidentally ran toward the litter pan; the fact that it needed cleaning is inadmissible evidence, since I couldn't retest her to prove that she *wouldn't* run toward a pan that *didn't* need cleaning; science is hard work.

Always ascribe intelligent behavior to coincidence, however bizarre. Anecdote is not evidence, and no valid results can be taken from a test set up by the animal itself and not by us; only human testing is conclusive.

In the animal laboratory of the Department of Psychology at Columbia University, Audrey M. Shuey worked with eighty-two kittens for nearly a year and a half, during which time they grew into eighty-two deeply confused cats.

She constructed a cage within a cage. The inner cage had the food in it, and a door; the outer cage had three electrical pressure plates in the floor, programmable by the operator to open the door to the food when properly stepped on.

In the beginning the door opened whenever any one plate was stepped on, then if any two plates, then any three. Each kitten was given five minutes to pass the test, and to Shuey's apparent surprise they didn't all buckle down to work immediately, but frittered away the precious minutes "sitting or washing, playing with tail, pawing at shadow, jumping, rolling over, rubbing against the walls." Sometimes they simply curled up and went to sleep, indicating a lack of ambition repulsive to the human mind.

It took them anywhere from nine to 136 sessions to learn to step on one plate to get dinner. To step on two plates took from one to seventy tries, and to step on all three from one to 121. The kittens that came out best were "facing the inner door as they touched the plate accidentally and probably saw the door slide back." Shuey doesn't seem surprised by this, but it bears thinking about.

A cat knows nothing of electrical impulses that open doors from a distance, any more than Betsy, when she was shot by a neighbor a year after the sink incident, could have understood murder from thirty feet away. The fact that the kittens made the connection "step here and that door opens over there," though it was irrelevant to Shuey's question, seems rather clever. If I rub my ear and a fire truck passes by outside, I don't assume I've produced the fire truck by rubbing, but only because I've been told of the habits of fire trucks. Some of the kittens made an assumption and happened to be right.

They could have been wrong. A French writer reports on a cat and her kittens who always ate lunch with the family, on the table. One day, just as the platter of pork chops was set on the table, there was a loud explosion in the gas pipes, frightening everyone. No damage was done, and the people resumed their lunch, but the cats stayed in hiding. Some weeks later, with peace long re-established, pork chops were served again, and when the platter was set on the table the cats panicked and scattered. Pork chops do not cause explosions, but given that the cats' ignorance of gas pipes is greater even than mine, the assumption was sound enough.

Understanding cause and effect isn't really the high-level thinking we've made of it, and doesn't depend on knowing exactly how the effect is caused; if I answer a ringing telephone, I expect a voice at the other end, though I couldn't explain how it gets there. When Blueberry and I lived in a third-floor walkup, the snarl of a buzzer meant that someone was coming to visit: I pressed the button that released the catch on the downstairs door, and after a suitable interval company came in, gasping from the climb. I didn't tell the cat that a fellow tenant had lost her key, and I had promised to let her in when she rang. She did, and I did, and thought no more about it. Blueberry sat by the door and waited. Nobody came. She paced. She glowered at me. She hooked her paw under the door and rattled it angrily. Buzzer means company; where the hell is company?

Cats have less trouble than we like to think with this much thinking.

Meanwhile, back at Columbia, Shuey pressed on. In the next phase of the exam, the cats had to step on all three plates and then go back and step on one of the first two a second time. Then on all three once and the first two twice, then on all three twice but without repeating the immediately previous plate. Shuey then added a fourth plate, so that getting the food required the proper stepping-on of plates twelve times. Then she arranged to have the door open only if the plates were stepped on in a preprogrammed order.

The natural way for a cat to get its dinner is to lie in wait, to stalk, and to pounce; putting up with this electronic dance seems uncommonly good-natured of them if not necessarily intelligent.

Four of the cats did brilliantly and one poor dodo took 271 tries to get through the first basic series. (Perhaps the food in the inner cage was something he hated. One of my cats hates kidneys, another won't touch liver.) The study, when Shuey finally ran out of plates and quit, proved conclusively that some cats are more intelligent than others. Or hungrier. Or less interested in alternative activities like chasing their tails.

Since she noted that eighty percent of the cats stepped on the plates with their front paws first, it also proved that more cats walk forward than backward.

It's interesting to consider that Shuey's intelligence, or even sanity, was not under question at any time, nor was she asked, as a control, to pass a test of the cats' devising. Crossing the room without stepping on the floor, for instance.

In recent years studies of animal intelligence have shifted from the ability to manipulate traps to the ability to use language. Not to communicate, which is primitive, but to use *real* language. *Our* language. Words. Cats are off the hook, primates are on, and gorillas and chimpanzees are crowding our solitary superiority by talking to us in the human sign language. Where now is our "qualitative difference of mentality separating us from the animals"? Not only do they learn to make the signs, which really would seem a simple enough intellectual feat, and the hand sign "hunger" not too far above a cat scratching at the refrigerator door, but they also learn to put the words together into groups that, when we use them ourselves, we call "thoughts." They ask for comforting hugs when things go wrong, and asking for them in a language *we've* invented seems very much classier indeed than, for instance, a cat asking for a comforting lap in the language natural to a cat.

These primates say insulting things about each other. And they tell lies.

Lucy, the famous signing chimp, was asked by her trainer if she was responsible for that pile of feces (for all their brilliance, they're as hard to housebreak as a human) in the middle of the floor. She said no. She said the trainer had done it himself.

A lie is a sophisticated concept. First to learn the words, then to arrange them in groups, and then to use them to say something contrary to fact in order to blame another for one's own crime—now, *that's* human. That's getting uncomfortably close to home. Carry this thing much further and it could raise all sorts of questions few of us are pure enough to face.

Luckily we're dealing only with primates here, since nothing else has fingers, and if we have to move over and make room in the intellectual community we won't have to make very much room.

It may really be that primates are smarter than other animals because they're the most like us; certainly we like to think so, having had to swallow the theory of a common ancestor. And certainly they are like us. Meeting, through smudged glass, the eyes of a gorilla in the zoo, we feel the quivering shock of recognition that runs through every fiber: an animal not ours but *us*. The endless fascination of a cat's eyes lies in the difference. A cat is not us. The cat is inside there, and its mind is working, but how?

We've never even considered inventing a practical speech for animals with neither hands nor voice boxes, and if we did, how would we teach it to a cat, or answer, since we lack a cat's movable equipment as much as it lacks ours? Our deficiency in the matter clinches the cat's inferior mentality.

Speechlessness doesn't stop the cat from telling lies. Derek Tangye's cat Monty lied. In *Somewhere a Cat is Waiting*, he tells us that he and his wife were packing to go on a trip when Monty came to them with a painful limp, hobbling on three legs, unable to touch paw to floor. They called the vet, the vet came and examined the cat and said there was nothing at all wrong with him, and Monty stalked huffily away on all four feet.

A horse, no intellectual giant, who has gone lame and been let off work because of it, may fake going lame again, but this is only cause and effect at its simplest. Suitcases are only cause and effect: all cats know that their appearance means the people are going away, and some cats sulk, or hide, or hunker down inside the suitcase to make it impossible to pack. But apparently Monty, to whom it had never happened, supposed, like Boston Blackie supposing a reformed life, that if he were ill the people would cancel their trip. And apparently he also knew when his bluff had been called. And certainly he told a deliberate lie.

The naturalist W.H. Hudson said, "Cats are mentally near to us; their brains function even as ours do." Somewhere in there beyond the language barrier.

Lately it has occurred to our researchers that, if we can't

teach cats a real language, at least we can write down their own unschooled and primitive utterances and assign them meanings. On a recent Public Broadcast special I admired a massive computer console digesting a program that analyzed the sounds of cats; each sound was recorded and broken down and assigned a meaning, and when the project is complete we will have a written language for the cat. It's simple enough, according to this research, since the cat has only fifteen different sounds to be combined into twenty-five different vocalizations. "Meow" is actually two words, "me," a greeting, and "ow," meaning "keep your distance," used more with people than with other cats.

Unfortunately, in a recent book, *How to Talk to Your Animals*, Jean Craighead George says that "meow" with the accent on the "ow" means "follow me," while the same word drawn out and unaccented is a whine of protest.

And of course in order to carry out this translation we'll have to search out cats that say "meow" at all, though I did meet one once. It was unnerving, like having a rooster walk up and say "cock-a-doodle-doo." And having compiled a glossary of terms for cats that use the sounds that English-speakers think of as cat sounds, we can turn our attention to other countries, since the Chinese think their cats say "ming" and what we hear as "purr" the French hear as "ron-ron." In the end the cats will be no better than the humans, separated from cats in other lands by separate languages.

My own unscientific feeling is that the language of the cat is as individual as fingerprints, and the wonder of it is that it's understood by us and by other cats without anything resembling a commonly agreed-on vocabulary. And, being more music than word, it cannot be transliterated. We can represent the opening of a symphony with "da-da-da *dah*," but that isn't at all what it sounds like, and the only reason we recognize the syllables is that we've heard the thing the way it belongs, as music. We cannot decipher what Beethoven "meant" and proceed from there to assume that other composers would mean the same thing from the same notes.

Some cats use their voices rarely and some never stop

yammering except in sleep; are we to suppose that the silent ones aren't communicating and the noisy ones are? Not necessarily. I have here a young Siamese female who, since she was neutered, says almost nothing. When she speaks, it's a syllable somewhere between "mah" and "wan," and it means "want." She has a high opinion of my intelligence, and never goes to the cupboard for food or the door for out; she comes to me and says "want," and I'm supposed to understand. The Persian Barney speaks even less frequently, his single "meh" being forced up from his very toes with obvious difficulty, and depending on location it means either that breakfast is late or he wants the tap in the basin turned on.

Neither cat is unintelligent or uncommunicative.

The new little black cat never opens her mouth to say anything, but speaks in her throat, to herself, trotting up and down stairs and in and out of closets chirping and murmuring and exclaiming in a kind of watered-silk pattern of sound that can make the possessor of mere English feel as mute and flightless as a turnip. This is interior monologue, though, intended to communicate with no one but herself; for speech she has a long, wavery, pointed tail of such expressive grace that it must be a perfect poem for those with the sense to understand its voice.

Then there's Corvo, a stout elderly Siamese, who speaks in deep chest tones, as if from a bellows, in an infinite variety of yet-to-be-invented vowels, comparable maybe to an unmilked cow or a French horn with a sore throat. It sounds consistently gloomy, and is capable of roaring amplification, but it's used mostly as a greeting, or to suggest the making of a lap, or to inquire after missing members of the family.

Sidney, probably the least intelligent, has the largest vocabulary. He believes that a cat can penetrate a windowpane with a bird on the other side of it by standing on his hind legs and swimming violently on the glass with his front paws, and he has believed this for seventeen years in the face of overwhelming evidence to the contrary, but he has a marvelous range of vocal expression. Some of it means something. A booming spectral moan means he doesn't like riding in cars, and a cantankerous "a-yow" means he's about to use the litter pan. A sharp nasal "yan" means it's twenty after three in the morning and time to get up; this is followed by duck-like food cries of "skwap skwap" as he hustles down the stairs urging us to follow and serve breakfast. (The fact that he keeps on hoping, though he never has been fed at that hour and often gets things thrown at him, speaks poorly for his learning ability, and if he'd had to step twelve times on electric pressure plates to get his food he would have starved.) However, most of what Sidney says is apparently meaningless, a kind of feline skat or do-wap with dozens of different grunts, squeaks, cries, and murmurs that seem to be just Sidney talking to hear the sound of his own voice, as a human might sing in the shower. Sometimes he goes down in the basement and sings to enjoy the hollow concrete acoustics.

There is no cat "language." Painful as it is for us to admit, they don't need one.

We depend quite woefully on speech to understand each other even slightly. When the leaders of great nations get together to sort out the problems of the world, they have no way of knowing what's in each other's minds without an interpreter, and if the interpreter has to duck out to go to the bathroom, the great leaders are left sitting there twiddling their key chains and avoiding each other's eyes until he comes back. We've been talking to each other for so long that our more efficient lines of communication have withered away. Granted, cats can't discuss the future deployment of missiles, but consider the advantages of not needing to discuss them.

A cat can tell us infinitely more than we can tell a cat, and certainly more than the great leaders can tell each other across the language barrier. A cat has, for instance, thirty different muscles in its ears, making them expressive of the subtlest shades of interest and disapproval, while we have only six and most of us can't use any of them. If we live with a cat, and the cat holds its ears in a certain position, we know without thinking about it that the cat is cross, or that it hears something across the room. How do we know? We just do. Perhaps we aren't so dense after all.

The whole cat is an instrument of communication. It has forty more bones in its flexible body than we do; the bones of its spine are connected by muscle instead of ligament, so that even its back communicates. Its movable whiskers inform us, and the pupils of its eyes expand and contract with mood as well as with light. The hairs of its back and tail rise up for threat or fear, accompanied by the international Esperanto of growls and hisses. A sound that Colette spells "Mouek mouek mouek, Ma-a-a-a" and B. Kliban spells "wacka wacka wacka" means "I see a bird, and I wish I could catch it, but birds are hard to catch, not worth making a fool of myself over, and that makes me furious."

Without trying to decipher the meaning of "meow" we can understand a good deal of cat. How does the cat understand us? No mere human can begin to realize the scope of smell for animals that can use it; it's a whole lost language for us. Through a haze of cigarette smoke, garlic, bath soap, and cologne the cat can smell on our skin subtle pH changes from fear or anger and heaven knows what else. Any illness changes our scent, grief changes it, and the cat reacts, sometimes with motherly comforting and sometimes with panic and anger. Posture, energy level, tone of voice; all this is easily read. And language? Words?

Does not being able to speak them mean not being able to understand? Conservative science holds that human speech in the cats' ears is only a formless river of intonation and inflection, and no cat can make the intellectual connection between the sound itself and the indicated object, only learn from long experience, from the speaker's body language and tone, to make a few tentative inferences: "Bad!" doesn't mean "bad" but is only a sound, like a growl, that comes from the human when you rip up the couch. "Here, kitty, kitty, kitty" is a sound preliminary to dinner. The dog that comes when called doesn't understand his name as meaning *him*, only as a sound that means his owner wants him, accompanied by subtle tonal qualities that help him identify it; he may not even recognize it in another's voice. A name is a word. Animals can't grasp the concept "word."

Gone with the Wind was playing on television. Barney was sound asleep. The little girl was riding around on her pony, about to break her neck, and for several minutes the set rang with cries of "Bonnie! Bonnie!" The cat woke up and looked at the television, but nothing on the set related to him. "Bonnie!" they cried, and he turned and looked at me, first inquiringly, then angrily. Someone, somewhere, was teasing him. "Bonnie!" He got down off the couch and left the room in a huff, and I remembered his first owner and her soft southern voice. "Bahney," she called him. "Baahney." If I hadn't had the spellings in my mind, I couldn't have told the sounds apart. And in Barney's ears it was a word, and meant whatever he thinks of as "him," and had nothing to do with recognized inflection or tone; he has never even met Clark Gable.

If "Barney," then what else? I'm not suggesting we can explain physics or calculus or the Roman Empire to a cat, because there's no way to make a cat care enough to want to learn about them, a problem shared with many humans. But what indeed are the limits? If we say often enough to a cat, "Do you want to go *out*?" and then open the door, many cats I have known learn to go to the door and say, even if it's a sound they never use elsewhere, "Ow." Are they saying "out," or is this pure coincidence?

If the cat wanted to learn, how much could we teach it? But why should it want to learn? A cat is different, a cat is not us, a cat is satisfied to be a cat and speak as a cat.

I've known only one cat that seemed to long for human speech, and in this I'm being outrageously sentimental and subjective. His name is Flanagan and he's one of my sister's horde, a beautiful cat with the softest blue-gray fur and round yellow eyes with an intense, yearning expression. A cat of passionate moods, when he feels loving it's not enough to watch a human from across the room and squeeze his eyes shut; laps are not enough. He scrambles straight up toward the face, clawing his way up trousers and shirt and throwing his forelegs around the neck in a desperate hug, his body pressed against the chest, and purrs raggedly and nips and licks the face in a fit of thwarted passion quite awkward for a human to accept from a cat. Even in his less emotional moments there's something urgent and frustrated about Flannie in his human contacts, and even the most pragmatic among us struggles with thoughts of reincarnation and princes enchanted into toads.

Not that he doesn't enjoy other cats. He used to come down to my house every day to sing with Sidney. These sessions were enormously satisfying to both cats; he and Sid faced each other off on the porch and yowled and yodeled after the manner of the pregame show of rival tomcats. Both were neutered, and unthreatened, and secure in their territories; it was a combination of concert and the war games of little boys. Flanagan had a fine talent for swelling up, not just the fur but the entire cat, like a blowfish, to astonishing size and weaving his head gruesomely while he yowled. No blows were ever offered. After twenty minutes or so, Sidney would come back inside and Flan would go on home.

Unhappily, after several months Sidney got bored. He stopped going outside when Flanagan gave his invitational calls. He is old, and would rather sleep than sing.

Then Flanagan would hook his paws into the screen door and stare beseechingly in at me, trying to leap out through his own eyes and tell me how badly he wanted Sidney to come out. I would drag Sid from his chair and throw him out the door; Flanagan would moan hopefully, and Sid would turn his back in silence and ask to come inside again. It was very sad.

Then I had to move away from the little house. The furniture left in a truck, the cats and pictures in the car, and the next day I went back with a broom and a bucket for the final cleanup.

Flanagan heard my car and came hurrying down the driveway and across the porch and hooked his paws into the screen door. I let him in. "He's not here," I said. "He's gone." Flanagan scattered in panic through the empty house and ran around every room and closet, over and over. Nothing. He came back to me and stared up, searching my face.

He wasn't looking in my face for Sidney; he was looking for an explanation. He was straining to split open his limitations and ask "Where is he?" and understand the answer. Yet how can a cat, who has never heard an explanation, want one so badly?

I could only shake my head and gesture vaguely at the empty room.

There was always something embarrassing in my dealings with Flanagan. Once or twice it flicked across my mind to offer him a pencil and paper: if he couldn't say it, maybe he could write it down. It was hard to fend off the sense that inside that gray fur a frantic human was waving his arms and pointing to the adhesive tape across his mouth.

Able to limp only the smallest distance into the minds of the speechless, we comfort ourselves with the thought that there can't be much to find in any case. A twitching collection of nerves and reflexes. A dark hole illuminated only by flickering reactions to stimuli like heat and food.

With the signing primates we feel we've made some progress into the darkness, and admire the apes being slow and clumsy as humans over cats being competent as cats. Probably there's a distinction, though it's hard for the unscientific to see, between teaching them sign language and dressing them in funny hats to photograph them eating birthday cake. Probably we've learned something. Probably they're almost smart like us.

A cat sits on our rug with its tail wrapped around its feet and its eyes focused on a point in the middle air, and we tell ourselves that its mind is an emptiness unimaginable to the clever human, who, we like to believe, spends its idle hours musing on political economy, existentialism, and the lesser comedies of Aristophanes. Take away our words and we wouldn't be able to think of anything at all, so it stands to reason that a cat, having no words, thinks of nothing.

Our real need of speech is just to tell each other about the far-off times and spaces that distract us so: over there, back then, last week, next year, Washington, Syria. But to a cat space is easy, space is only territory, contained and known; and time is easy, time is where the cat is sitting now. Spring speaks to its loins, breakfast time speaks to its stomach, but time past is a flicker of dateless memories without perspective and future time doesn't matter at all. At the point where time and space meet the cat sits on the rug, cupped in the immediate moment like a single note struck on the piano, and what we call intelligence is of less importance to its life than the dust motes in a shaft of sun.

T. S. Eliot says the musing cat is contemplating his secret name, the name that contains the compact essence of the individual cat, the kernel of his unknowable self. Mr. Eliot was being whimsical, but he was right just the same.

People With Cats

3

Very few people have no opinions about cats. Even those who have never known a cat personally, scarcely even spoken to one, feel strongly and sometimes hysterically on the subject. Consider Buffon, the great eighteenth-century naturalist, and his cool scientific detachment: "Many people ... raise cats solely for their own amusement, which I find utterly abnormal ... a malicious streak in [cats], and a naturally perverse dishonest character ... ruthless ... fawning and opportunistic ... the same devious techniques as any human thief ... shifty eyes ... seek human company exclusively for their own benefit ... mothers occasionally become unnaturally cruel and eat their own dear offspring alive ... systematically malicious ... "

It's rather a compliment, really; we can hardly imagine him working up such a lather about, for instance, sheep.

Equally detached, the zoologist Scheitlin rhapsodizes, "The forehead has a truly poetic curve; indeed, the whole of the skeleton is beautiful and suggests a highly mobile animal, particularly well suited for all graceful and undulating movements." We have all known cats so graceless they could barely undulate across the floor without tripping over it, but there's no arguing with a man who finds even their bones enchanting.

People who hate cats tend to be proud of the fact, and brag about it as if it proved something honest and straightforward in their natures. Nobody brags about hating dogs. To hate dogs would be mean-spirited and peculiarly unpatriotic; dogs are a very American concept, fraternal, hearty, and unpretentious, while cats are inscrutable like the wily Oriental and elitist like the European esthete. In advertising, cats turn up selling perfume (wily) and expensive rugs and furniture (elitist), while dogs sell such solid family values as station wagons, life insurance, and sporting goods.

Men who hate both cats and women say cats are like women, and refer to even the most swaggeringly potent tomcat as "she."

Cats are held to be sneaky. They earn their livings sneaking. Dogs in the wild catch their prey like good old boys, outnumbering it and running it down in broad daylight, and they can make as much noise as they please in the process. Cats in the wild don't hunt in packs, though lions may cooperate, and they can't outrun their prey; they're fast, but only in the short sprint. They have to surprise their dinner by creeping quietly, waiting patiently, and springing accurately. Sometimes they hunt by night, too, which is manifestly unfair. None of this is very attractive to the human mind. The human mind may even remember Smilodon with his six-inch saber teeth, who could probably sneak as softly as any house cat in spite of being fourteen feet long, and his dinner might have been a friend of ours. When he isn't hunting, the domestic cat is anything but sneaky, and a pair of them in a hurry down a flight of uncarpeted stairs makes as much noise as a pair of adolescent male humans on the same journey. Hunting, he has to sneak; you don't catch mice by stamping your feet and shouting about your intentions. And since they say we took him on in the first place to catch mice, it seems ungrateful to complain about his *modus operandi*.

It's commonly said that cats are never attached to their people and hang around only because they're fed. The phrase "cupboard love" was coined for cats. This is odd since cats are notoriously finicky eaters, easily put off their feed by emotional upsets, and often better able than dogs to supplement their diet with a catch. And every cat household has known a cat that blatantly preferred a member of the family who never fed him to the one who did. Pet dogs, presumably, get fed, and goldfish, and gerbils, and no one accuses them of cupboard love. It goes with the legend of the independent cat; if not for food, why would nature's freest spirit stay at home?

Konrad Lorenz, pioneer animal-watcher, says in *King Soloman's Ring*, "All other domestic animals, like some slaves of ancient times, became house servants only after having served a term of true imprisonment, all, that is, with the exception of the cat, for the cat is not really a domesticated animal and his chief charm lies in the fact that, even today, he still walks by himself. Neither the dog nor the cat is a slave, but only the dog is a friend—granted, a submissive and servile 'friend' ... "

It's a strange notion he has of friendship, with one party doing all the commanding and the other all the obeying, and we might wonder how he'd feel about his dog if it started ordering him to sit and heel and fetch. It's a strange notion of slavery too, which remains nonetheless slavery even when the slave enjoys it thoroughly.

"The cat still walks by itself." Ah, yes, we do cherish the thought. The undomesticated cat, free as the wind, beholden to no one, waving his wet wild tail as he moves on down that lonesome road. The more our own lives are fenced around with obligations and family ties and jobs to show up for, the more we dwell on the dream of the unfettered cat. Cat-haters hate him for it, cat-lovers love him for it. Like the jolly miller on the River Dee, he cares for nobody, no, not he, and nobody cares for him. When things get sticky he can simply leave town like the beloved imaginary cowboy of the Old West, riding away toward the blue hills and leaving only a puff of dust as a forwarding address.

We could pick genuine wild animals to envy, eagles and wolves and mountain goats, but they live remote from our houses, and besides, we sensibly see their lives as pretty arduous. Not free like cat and cowboy but beset by blizzards and hunters and young to rear. We see the cat as needing nothing, in spite of the fact that the actual independent cats we run across are wretchedly thin and miserable, with an estimated maximum life expectancy of two years. That has nothing to do with it; the *spirit* of the cat, like an invisible flame hovering over its starving body, is independent and rides away into the sunset the way we would ride if we could, singing nonchalantly of the girl we left behind.

It's curious that throughout our history together, with no apparent effort, people have been able to think of the cat simultaneously as the guardian spirit of the hearth and home, and as the emblem of freedom, independence, and rootlessness.

Capriciously, we keep them at home as guardian spirits or abandon them as independent. People otherwise decent and kindly throw away countless thousands of cats and kittens to die slowly of hideous hardships; cats, after all, can take care of themselves, cats are not domestic animals at all.

The cat is neither cowboy nor spirit, but flesh and blood, a small predator adrift in a world of garbage cans and highways, domestic now for thousands of years. Unknowable, maybe, but ours. Under modern conditions it survives on its own only briefly, with pain and difficulty. The fact that it treats us as equals rather than gods doesn't mean it can find its way in our world without help.

We owe them help. In spite of all they've suffered at our hands they seem to like us, of their own free will, a compliment our rapacious bullying species can't afford to ignore. What other animal sits with us because it chose to?

Wild dogs live in groups and give their leader, until the time comes to challenge his leadership, an unquestioning military loyalty; domestic dogs offer the same religious devotion to the human they consider their leader. According to Lorenz, dogs of primarily coyote extraction spread this feeling out over most of the humans that cross their paths, while dogs with more wolf in them concentrate on one. Either way, it's natural for humans to applaud this taste in idols.

I've been lucky in being loved by some cats, but I've never had one who seemed to think that, aside from my presumed ability to improve the weather if only I would, I was any bigger, stronger, or smarter than I am. Cat people find it soothing to be loved in spite of their faults; dog people find it even more soothing to be considered faultless.

Because of their instinctive reaction to leadership, dogs are forced to like us, whoever we may be; they have no choice. The cat can choose and, having been chosen, we have a right to be pleased.

Many of us aren't. Something in the cat's attitude, or in its eyes, disturbs us, and we invent all sorts of plausible-sounding excuses to explain our uneasiness.

One prime reason cat-haters give for hating cats is that they kill birds. Even people who can't tell a nuthatch from a raven complain about it. To listen to them, a cat barely needs to stroll outdoors for birds to keel over in midair for miles around. Catching a bird isn't easy, as anyone knows who has ever chased a loose canary around the living room, and if the canary has the whole outside world to fly around in it's simply impossible. Let the bird-lover just try it himself and see. Cats may cull the elderly and the genetically incapable, the way wolves weed out the caribou, but this makes life easier for the healthy remainder, since shrinking habitat is much the fiercest pressure on bird populations.

Wildlife managers estimate that birds kill more birds than cats do. I believe it, having watched a blue jay murder a nest full of baby wrens outside my window. The wrens had successfully routed the cats from their whole end of the yard, but they were helpless against the jay. They darted back and forth shrieking; I ran out yelling and waving my arms. The jay, for no reason but wantonness, pounded the babies to bloody shreds and flew away cawing. I never saw the parent wrens again, and the cats were once more free to walk across that part of the lawn.

Birds know more about cats than bird-lovers do. The sedentary robin, checking the grass for worms, flies only eight or ten feet when he sees the cat approaching and then goes on with his search, removing himself from time to time until the cat gets bored and leaves.

I hung the bird feeder over the back steps, just over the cats' heads. The old cats enjoyed watching and made no move, but young Morgan wanted one badly. She could hardly stand it, the fluttering toys, just barely out of reach; it was maddening. Once in a while she made a fool of herself leaping into the air and trying to catch one by clapping her paws together. Then they all flew into the maple tree and waited for five minutes while she chattered with frustration. But when a hawk made a pass at the feeder they vanished instantly and completely and the feeder stayed birdless for days, as if his passage had left a stain of terror across the air: it takes wings to catch wings.

We had a cat who got adopted by a bird. George the Second had once been chased and bitten by one of my sister's white mice, and this may have shaken his confidence or confused his sense of his role in life, and he was one of the peaceable grays to begin with. When the baby blue jay started eating out of his bowl on the porch George just backed away into a corner, looking baffled, and waited till it was finished. It was a very young bird, probably fallen from its nest and abandoned, and certainly it was a very resourceful one. It stayed on the porch, waiting for George's twice-daily bowl of cat food, and it ate first, and George twitched his tail and looked put-upon. It grew. It took to following George everywhere, on foot. Birds apparently learn their identities from their parents, and identify their parents as parents because they supply the food. George supplied the food, therefore he became father to a blue jay child, which presumably thought it was a cat.

What George thought was obvious. He was embarrassed, horribly embarrassed, to walk across the lawn with a yeeping, gaping baby bird trudging after him clamoring to be fed. He tried to be invisible, bending his knees and huddling his head down into his shoulders, and he lashed his tail with impotent disgust. In theory he could have turned around and atomized the cheeky little thing, but it wasn't acting very much like prey, and besides the white mouse had bitten him quite hard.

In time the jay grew up and went off to find its own food, but we always wondered what kind of life it had later, and whether it continued to think of itself as a cat, and how this would affect its chances for a sane and normal married life. George was enormously relieved when it left.

Every so often a state's bird-lovers will band together and try to get legislation enacted that will keep cats under control, duly licensed, and on their own property. In vetoing such a bill in Illinois, then-Governor Adlai Stevenson wrote, "It is the nature of cats to do a certain amount of unescorted roaming ... Moreover, cats perform useful service, particularly in rural areas, in combating rodents—work they necessarily perform alone and without regard to property lines. The problem of cat versus bird is as old as time. If we attempt to resolve it by legislation, who knows but that we may be called upon to take sides as well in the age-old problems of dog versus cat, bird versus bird, or even bird versus worm."

Cats give legislators a lot to worry about. It's illegal in Natchez for a cat to drink beer, and illegal in Morrisburg, Louisiana, for a cat to chase a duck down the city streets.

Another common complaint is the cruelty of cats. They not only kill mice, they torture them first, apparently for the sheer pleasure of seeing them suffer.

Actually, the business of playing with the catch has to do

with the education of kittens in mouse work, and however it may look from a distance, the cat isn't mangling the mouse, except psychologically; if it were a robin's egg it wouldn't break. Killing, when the time comes, is swift and immediate, with a quick bite to the base of the neck that severs the spinal cord, and until then the game has the secondary effect of giving the mouse a sporting chance. I've seen quite a lot of them escape from the dallying cat to the safety of their holes. When, in our relentless pursuit of hamburgers, we herd the gentle steer in terror to the abattoir to knock it on the head, it doesn't have the shadow of a chance, any more than the bull in the bullring after we've finished our game.

Not all cats play with their mice. Corvo the battling Siamese is the most efficient mouser I've ever watched. He springs from incredible distances, lands with pinpoint accuracy, and kills on landing. Then he hunkers down to eat. Corvo comes from a cattery, and his businesslike approach finishes off the widely held theory that a cat whose mother never showed it how may chase mice but can't kill them: no mice volunteered as demonstration models in the cattery.

The Siamese Morgan, on the other hand, *only* plays with mice. She's fond of things that move when she pats them, and keeps a supply of pecans under my desk for the purpose. Vacuuming, I gathered them up and put them in a bowl on the desk, and then forgot to put them back. Morgan found them, and had to scoop them all out one by one and knock them to the floor and roll them, muttering crossly to herself, back where they belong. She's a cat with a strong sense of order and the rightness of things, and would have made an excellent secretary.

She seems to think of mice as an outdoor pecan supply. She'll chivvy one out into an open space like the gravel driveway and pat it till it runs a few feet and then freezes. She follows it and with velvet paw pats it to make it move again. After a few minutes she begins to lose interest, her mind wanders and she looks away, and the mouse runs like hell. She looks back at the spot where it was, but it is gone,

so she yawns and goes off to see if I've left the car windows
open so she can take a nap.

Granted the mouse's nerves are probably shattered, but
we can't worry about everything.

Still, the charge of deliberate cruelty is a heavy one, if we
can believe the cat understands the mouse's sufferings, and
we've all been comforted by cats who understand ours. But
we are people, the cats' people, and a mouse in the cats' eyes
is only a mouse. In *Hen's Teeth and Horses' Toes* Stephen
Jay Gould quotes from St. George Mivart's *Genesis of Species*; Mivart holds that animals feel little if any pain, because
physical suffering "depends greatly upon the mental condition of the sufferer. Only during consciousness does it exist,
and only in the most highly organized men does it reach its
acme. The author has been assured that the lower races of
men appear less keenly sensitive to physical suffering than
do more cultivated and refined human beings."

The British scientist feels himself as far superior, in his
delicately nurtured nervous system, to the uneducated races
as the cat does to the mouse. If primitive humans feel no
pain, how much credit shall a cat give a mere mouse for sen-
sitivity? The only charge we can pin on the cat is that it has
advanced in empathy no further than a nineteenth-century
scientist.

The defense rests.

And in any case it's pointless to argue; cat-hating is
visceral.

We have a cat around the house in a different sense from
having, or owning, a dog. Even the law recognizes this, and
considers the dog as property, and subject to property laws of
damage and recovery, but no rights attach to cat ownership.
Domestic, yes; property, no.

The cat doesn't bolster our self-esteem, and we can't pretend it works for us; it is *around*, in the nonspecific way all
animals used to be around. We've grown so wildly successful
as a race that we've managed to set a wide space between
ourselves and the rest of the creatures. Pouring cream into

our breakfast coffee, we are far, far from the cow, and except for occasional parasites like the pigeon most of the creatures most of us see in our normal rounds are human. A dog, since it's come to live with us, is hardly an animal at all, but a cat flits across the back of the couch and, in defiance of orders, leaps to the top of the bookcase and flips her tail at us, an animal nearby but not totally under our control. Hardly under our control at all except as she pleases, the way once the plains and forests all around us were full of animals nearby and uncontrolled. Many people dislike being reminded of the past and our humble, sometimes precarious, place in it, but it may be good for us.

Cat-keeping nowadays is almost always pure self-indulgence; very few cats are essentially employed. Only a little while ago cats were working wherever we went, as they still are in Europe; the butcher had to have one, and the fishmonger, and all proper groceries had two, one for the shop and one for the cellar. But America, being fond of science, progress, and hygiene, passed laws saying cats were unscientific and unhygienic and can no longer live in or even stroll through places where food is kept or sold. The plump and cozy grocer's cat has been replaced by the sickening stench of rat poison and, occasionally, of poisoned rat rotting its heart out in some inaccessible corner. The farmer with his barnful of cats has been replaced by food production on a scale so dizzyingly vast and automated it's hard to imagine where the humble cat could fit in; perhaps they have giant robot cats.

Now the only working cats we see are in bookstores and antiques shops, where they sprawl in the display windows to strike the proper note of cultivated leisure.

It has been said that to respect the cat is the beginning of the esthetic sense, and at a stage of culture where utility governs all, mankind prefers the dog. We have time here for esthetics now; we can stop sleeping with our boots on and use our cats for subtle, impractical purposes.

We keep cats now for their otherness. A dog, a well-trained dog, can feel almost like an extension of ourselves, responsive and familiar as our own hands. A cat is not us; a cat is the Other. It's a mark of a mature civilization to be able to accept an other, and respect its differences without feeling threatened; it would do wonders for world affairs.

Some people are more temperamentally suited to cat-keeping than other people. In general, those whose souls rejoice in the power struggle and the conquest of nations get along badly with cats. Genghis Khan hated them, and Alexander the Great, and Julius Caesar, and Hitler is said to have thrown fits at the very word. Shortly after the battle of Wagram, Napoleon was on his way to bed when an aide-de-camp heard him screaming for help, and rushed to his bedroom to find the victorious commander half undressed and slashing his sword wildly at the wall tapestry, behind which a cat was hiding.

It's the statesman, not the conquering hero, who has a cat. Thomas Jefferson was fond of cats. Winston Churchill's ginger tomcat sat in on cabinet meetings, and the Prime Minister insisted on personally carrying him to the shelter during the London blitz. Louis XV's big white cat was the first visitor in his bedroom every morning. Queen Victoria's White Heather became a well-known personage, and Abraham Lincoln rescued three young cats he found half frozen in General Grant's camp.

Those who observe rather than control are the natural companions of the cat. Charles Darwin, Victor Hugo, Honoré de Balzac, Samuel Johnson, Montaigne, Thoreau, Matthew Arnold, Petrarch, Verlaine, Wordsworth, Sir Isaac Newton, and Sir Walter Scott loved cats. Henry James wrote with a cat on his shoulder. A catless writer is almost inconceivable; even Ernest Hemingway, manly follower of the hunting trophy and the bullfight, lived waist-deep in cats. It's a perverse taste, really, since it would be easier to write with a herd of buffalo in the room than even one cat; they make nests in the notes and bite the end of the pen and walk on the typewriter keys.

Mohammed had a cat named Muezza, which means "fairest and gentlest," and as we all know he cut off the sleeve of his robe where she was sleeping rather than disturb her. Jean Cocteau said the cat was the soul of his home. Alexandre Dumas said, "The cat, an aristocrat, merits our esteem, while the dog is only a scurvy type who got his position by low flattery." Mark Twain wrote, "A home without a cat, and a well-fed, well-petted, and properly revered cat, may be a perfect home, perhaps, but how can it prove title?"

Revered, yes. Revering a cat is by far the easiest way to get along with it on a day-to-day basis. You do not order a cat around, as this has no discernible effect and makes you feel like a fool, like Canute shouting at the tides. You respect a cat as an honored guest. This makes the least amount of work and frustration for you and minimizes stress in the relationship. The lazier you are about disciplining your cat and trying to impose your will on its ways, the happier you both will be.

It is the nature of a cat to do as it pleases. In the days before we met each other, the cat made up its own mind and took orders from no one, and obedience was never built into it. Many of the books on cat-keeping find this alarming, and warn us that a cat that gets its own way will grow up spoiled and disagreeable.

Certainly some cats, like some people, are disagreeable, but not because they're spoiled. I know a woman with a cat that bites her savagely if she infringes on its space or sleeps on the wrong side of the bed or breaks its rules, which it keeps changing. This is just not a nice cat. It may not have all its marbles. Any attempt at discipline might turn it totally savage, and I would give it away to my worst enemy and get a better cat. There are too many deserving kittens in need of homes to waste food and shelter on a monster. On the other hand, she's had this cat for many years and it's been biting her all along, so maybe they've worked out some sort of neurotic symbiosis; maybe we get the cats we want.

There are various books on the subject of "training" cats, and if you read too many you get the unsettling feeling that the authors have never laid eyes on a cat and are making the whole thing up, or else don't recognize a cat when they see one and are actually working with a kind of horizontal monkey or meowing dog. One book describes teaching a cat to roll over on command by harnessing it with a leash to a hook on the wall and pulling until the cat is dragged over onto its side, repeating the words "roll over" all the while. After an unspecified interval, the book claims, the cat will roll over when told to do so, instead of laying back its ears and leaving the room, and the house if possible, with all deliberate speed. This is clearly not a real cat of which he speaks. It may look like a cat to him, but closer inspection will reveal the slot where you push in two C batteries.

By and large, people who enjoy teaching animals to roll over will find themselves happier with a dog. Once, though, there was an Englishman named Leoni Clarke who made quite a good thing from a troupe of fifty performing cats. They walked across the stage on tightropes, stepping carefully over arrangements of mice, rats, and canaries, and they jumped through flaming hoops and parachuted down from the ceiling. Clarke billed himself as "The King of the Cats," and he must certainly have had some peculiar rapport with them. Perhaps he'd cracked the language barrier. It doesn't happen often.

There's a kind of elegance and poetry to the trained horse or dog, the Lippizaner and the working sheepdog, and the relationship between horse and rider, dog and shepherd, is enhanced until it glows, and illuminates the animals' lives by realizing their natural talents in a higher form. This simply isn't true for cats. We do not train a cat in anything that is useful to us or natural to the cat; you don't teach a cat to catch mice any more than you teach a hen to lay eggs. Teaching the useless and unnatural isn't training, it's pure trickery, and despicable in a way. Mr. Leoni's cats weren't herding sheep or carrying riders, they were entertaining paying customers with purposeless and undignified antics, and this is an unpleasant way to use an animal.

If we are to be friends with a cat, we must treat it with an egalitarian courtesy inappropriate for the dog and the horse, and make room in our lives for what is natural to the cats'.

Philosophical exception could be made for showing the cat how to use the toilet instead of the litter box, since it's useful to us and no more unnatural than using a litter box instead of a flower bed. Instructions are available, and several cats, all of them Siamese, turn up in the literature as having figured it out for themselves, presumably by imitation, which is much the easiest way to teach things to a cat. To explain the matter to the cat, first you put the litter box beside the toilet for a week so the cat gets used to the area. Then you start slipping things under the box to raise it an inch or so at a time, until it's on a level with the toilet seat. Now you replace it with a box designed to clip underneath the toilet seat; nobody says where to find such a thing, and I suppose you have to create it yourself. Obviously, you have to leave it in place there, since cats take care of these matters on erratic schedules of their own. The books don't say what the humans are using in the meantime or how to explain it to visitors. Anyway, once the cat is using this device regularly you replace the box with one-inch wire mesh, to keep the cat from falling in. No cat likes to crouch on one-inch wire mesh, so it crouches, they say, on the toilet seat instead. Remove mesh. Mission accomplished.

I think it's on the last step that I'd lose my own cats; they would simply find it uncongenial and use the floor or the bathtub instead. Also they're in the habit of drinking from the toilet, and the dual-purpose aspect would be abhorrent to any right-thinking animal. But who knows? It might appeal to to some, and certainly it's a swell conversation piece, and most cats would enjoy the cries of surprise and admiration from passersby.

The really basic books on educating cats begin with teaching him to use the litter box itself (hold his paw and make scratching motions in the litter; lock him in the room with the box), but I've never had to do that, merely show him where the thing is located, as one would with any guest. His mother taught him.

Most of the books say that a cat should know its name and come when called, and that would indeed be convenient. Kittens, unless they're very busy, come when their mother calls, especially if they're hungry, but then a hungry cat comes even when it isn't called. If you have nothing to offer that interests it, it doesn't, but this doesn't mean it doesn't know who it is.

I walk into a room where three cats are sleeping and speak the name of one, and it opens its eyes. It doesn't jump to attention, exactly, but it opens its eyes, cross at being waked for nothing.

We "train" it to know its name by using its name when we speak to it, especially while opening a can of cat food. Committed dog people will insist that unless it comes running when we say, "Charles, come here," then it can't actually *know* its name, but that is the way committed dog people think, or "think," confusing obedience with understanding.

Sometimes a name for a cat will spring to mind at once and stick with the cat forever; sometimes you can't decide, or the family disagrees and everyone calls it by a different name; sometimes you pick a name that sounds good at the moment but somehow slips off the cat later and falls into disuse, leaving it to go through life as The Siamese or The Black Cat. Children are easier, as we have to keep filling out tax forms and applications and documents with their names, and even if we're dissatisfied it's too late from day one.

From the cat's point of view, strong vowels are useful. It's a mistake to have Morgan and Corvo in the same house here; while they can distinguish between them, they both look up at the "or" sound. I'm trying to call the black kitten Spider, which won't fit her if she fills out later, but we need the long "i" sound in a house full of soft-vowel cats. This is no reflection on the cats' powers of discrimination. English is not their native tongue; even those of us who have studied a bit of French and can read it printed down may have trouble sorting out the Parisian taxi driver's opinions from his flow of sounds.

They know their names. They do not come when called.

Cats are not just not obedient, they are actively disobedient. Gillette Grilhé, in *The Cat and Man*, says, "His pride forbids him to obey, or—if he does—he will do so only when a sufficient amount of time has passed after the order to make the full weight of his disdain felt, reacting only as a gesture of condescension."

Happily, by reason of its intelligence, modest size, delicate and cleanly habits, and general goodwill the cat may be considered to come preassembled and ready for use, naturally adapted, all uneducated as it is, for life in the homes of man.

Except for one small matter.

Some people care more than others about their furniture. Some have valuable and elegant couches, some are content with the effluent of attics, but nobody really wants to live among furnishings with woolly gray stuffing leaking from the sides and backs. It looks slovenly.

Cats scratch to hone their claws and keep them clean and exercise their backs and legs and mark their territories, and for various other reasons cited by the authorities, and because they like to. The books tell you to get a scratching post. It should be solidly based so as not to fall on the cat, and tall enough so he can stretch up full length to attack it. If you make it yourself and cover it with carpeting, glue the carpeting on inside out, with the tough, coarse backing material on the business side. Put some catnip inside it.

The authorities insist that the cat will gladly use the post instead of the armchair. Not just when he's passing by, but always. This has not been my experience, but then, as previously noted, the authorities have some strangely docile cats.

In spite of their confidence in the post, the books include methods to make your cat stop using the furniture anyway, such as crying "No!" and clapping your hands or swatting the couch with a rolled magazine to make a loud noise, which will frighten the cat away.

Once, maybe. The second time, a cat of any spirit will enjoy the fuss, and pin its ears back and scratch harder, watching for your reaction. Cats feeling bored, neglected, or ignored will head for the couch just to stir up some action and get some attention. Many cats, especially Siamese, rather enjoy being beaten a bit, and will scratch anything they can get their claws into to achieve this pleasure. Cats who don't want to get hit will scratch only until you drop what you're doing and hasten across the room with your hand raised, and then spring away just as the blow is falling to slip under the couch or up onto the curtain rod, out of reach. In the cats' eyes, it's the world's finest game.

You can spray a cat with a plant mister; this, too, comes highly recommended. By the second try my cats had figured out to the microsecond how long it takes to find the plant mister and pump it up to working capacity, and for the cat to be gone from the target area before the spray lands. The couch got wet, the cat stayed dry and hugely entertained.

In *The Siamese Cat*, Phyllis Lauder recommends growling at the cat the way its mother would if she were displeased with it. I tried this just once, and the cat seemed so confused and upset, and avoided me so nervously for days afterward, that I must have gotten the intonation wrong, or said something I didn't really mean. It's unwise to try to swear in unknown tongues.

One problem with all these methods is that they involve quitting your job and staying awake and in the living room twenty-four hours a day. Leave, and all bets are off.

There are products on the market, said to be feline repellents, for spraying on the furniture. My cats seemed not to notice them, but they made my guests sneeze uncontrollably.

The claws of an indoor cat grow out into a long curve like a miniature upholstery needle, ideal for slipping under threads; clipped claws do less damage. Some books recommend having your vet do this, but it isn't really that delicate a matter. You buy a clipper designed for the purpose, and do it in stages. Press on the paw pad to shoot the claw out of its sheath, and cut only the curved part, not the thin red line above it that hurts and bleeds. A cat that's fond of you will let you do three or four claws before he gets bored and leaves. Do the rest another time.

Or you can decide that by the time the couch starts to un-ravel you'll be tired of the blue velvet anyway, and it will do you and the living room a world of good to have it re-covered.

Or you can get different furniture. Leather, real or imita-tion, can't be clawed. A tight fabric like chintz doesn't unravel like wool, or offer a good hold. The modern unstruc-tured things that are basically piles of pillows feel unstable to a cat, as if they might fall on his head, as well they might.

Or you can get the cat declawed.

Elizabeth Keifer in *Wholly Cats* writes that her veterinar-ian heartily approves of declawing, which, he says, gives nei-ther pain nor psychic distress. Indeed, the cat never misses its claws at all, and its pads, he says, become so callused af-terward that it has no trouble climbing trees.

He doesn't explain why the pads should get callused; a cat's claws are retractable, and the cat walks on the same pads before and after the operation. Nor does he explain how to climb a tree with callused pads. Would he care to put on some stout hard-surfaced mittens and scramble up to demon-strate?

A friend of mine had a little black cat named Siam and needed to leave it for the summer with her parents, but they insisted on having it declawed first, front and back, perhaps with visions of its standing on its head to slice upholstery from the rear. The next time I saw my friend, her parents, alas, were still unsatisfied. Siam cried night and day and kept them awake; she bit and chewed frantically at her paws so they didn't heal, and everywhere she went she left little rose-buds of blood on the precious upholstery and rugs.

Patricia P. Widmer, in *Pat Widmer's Cat Book*, recom-mends, almost insists on, declawing as a basic routine proce-dure like neutering, adding parenthetically that her cats are somehow managing to destroy her furniture anyway, but that fore-and-aft declawing is necessary to keep the cat from scratching people. I'm not sure I'd want to keep a cat that wanted in its heart to scratch me, front claws or back. Widmer doesn't mention trees, but she seems to live in Manhattan and probably, like most New Yorkers, finds it hard to entertain the possibility of intelligent life elsewhere.

Dr. Susan McDonough, vet of final authority, says the world is full of cats kept locked away from normal life in kitchens or basements or bedrooms out of deference to the living room furniture, and claws are a reasonable price to pay for release.

My Persian Barney has been declawed. A cattery stud for his first ten years, he lost his claws when the cattery closed and the owner planned to take him to an apartment full of new chairs and couches. On an impulse, she gave him to me instead.

We lived in the city together and he learned a whole world of new things, refuting the scholarly theory that cats can learn new things during only a few brief months in their first year. He rejoiced in his retirement, and in having a person of his own.

After a couple of years, life being unpredictable, we found ourselves in the country instead. In the new place there was another cat, and Barney watched Sadie, and learned from her to sit on laps and ask for tidbits from the table.

Outdoors, for a clawless cat, was dangerous, so I kept him company on small excursions to the back porch. One day we sat there and watched Sadie climb up the willow tree, sit on a branch for a while, and climb back down.

Barney trembled all over. Racial memory sprang to life in this twelve-year-old cat who had never in his life before seen a tree up close. He whisked down the porch steps and trotted across the lawn with his tail on high and fluttering like a helmet plume. He put his paws on the tree and gave a little spring.

Using his clawed back feet for push, he got about three feet up before he toppled and fell over on his back on the ground; I heard the thump.

He wasn't hurt, but the cat that came back across the

lawn was a different cat, and smaller than the one who had rushed to climb a tree at his ancestors' bidding, and his tail dragged in the grass.

Claws are central to a cat, to his ego, his sense of himself and his competence in the world. He sees himself as a creature with claws; they're as much a part of his inner image as arms are to us. When he raises a warning paw to an adversary, claws are what he means; when he signs a tree by scratching it, he was there, he left his mark; when he hooks open a cupboard door he is master of his world. He's a small animal, as predators go: claws are his stature in his mind's eye.

Oh, well. It's a fairly simple operation, and routinely performed now by all veterinarians, even those who hate it.

Tidy people make another problem for themselves from the matter of cats getting up onto tables and kitchen counters. The easiest way to deal with this is to tell ourselves the cat washes itself as diligently as we wash the table, and then throw it off only when we need the space for our own purposes. Perhaps our mothers won't agree, and it may not even be true, but it's certainly convenient to believe, and we aren't the first to hold a conviction from convenience.

My own cats sit on the dinner table, which I use—or try to use, among the cats—more for working than for dinner anyway, and when I bring out the plates and forks they get down, grumbling. Even cats who customarily sit on the table and watch while their person dines alone seem to realize that company alters the case. Or else company crowds the table unacceptably, or else they just don't like the company. In France, the cats of many famous statesmen and literary luminaries have always been welcome on the table, some of them with places regularly set for them. Germs are not a French obsession.

The uncharitable tell us that cats get up on counters because they want to steal food, but a properly treated cat who is fond of its people isn't anxious to steal their food. A purely functional cat, barely on speaking terms with its people and scrambling for enough to eat, might feel all food is fair game, but a personal cat will usually leave your chicken for you and wait by its dish. A cat knows the uses of food: when I tried to introduce a kitten into Blueberry's household she tried to starve him right back out again. A naturally dainty and desultory eater, she took to wolfing her dinner and then shoving the kitten aside and eating his too. She was going to get rid of that kitten if it choked her; as one's parents used to say, "If you don't feed it, dear, it won't hang around." What happy cat wants to starve out its people?

As the feline narrator of Paul Gallico's *The Silent Meow* says, "Stealing is for dogs. We are above it."

Exception must be made for cats that have conceived an unreasonable passion for food not on the ordinary menu. Jenny stole hot biscuits; Mai Tai snatched mushrooms from the refrigerator; Shibui will grab an ear of corn even from the diner's hand. The new black cat is frantic for pistachio nuts and French bread. Colette's mother's Long-Cat raided the garden for strawberries, asparagus, and melons, which last he slashed open with his claws. The literature also mentions freshly ground coffee, olives, broccoli, grape jelly, and cinnamon Danish. Probably these exotic items aren't considered nourishment in the ordinary sense, and a cat that will steal our olives wouldn't steal our steak, or our mouse.

Why, then, if not to steal food, would a cat go up on the counter? Why did George Mallory try to go up on Mount Everest, which was quite a lot more trouble? Because it is there. Because of the view from the kitchen window. To lick the drips from the tap in the sink. To try to pry open the cupboards and see what's inside them, maybe to squeeze in among the glassware. Or, on a rainy day, to look for small objects to knock off onto the floor and see if they roll. And because it is in the nature of the cat to get up on things. Cats enjoy height. It makes them feel safer from nonclimbing things, and superior, and they can see farther. If our eyes were only six inches from ground level, we'd want to get up on something, too.

If we have a decent sort of cat to begin with, and have always treated it courteously, and aren't cursed with meddling, bullying natures, it's a pleasure to let it do as it pleases. With children, this would be wicked and irresponsible, so raising children involves a lot of effort and friction. They need to be taught how to tie their shoes and multiply fractions, they need to be punished for pocketing candy in the grocery store, they need to be washed and combed and forced to clean up their rooms and say please and thank you.

A cat is our relief and reward.

Cats With People

4

It's part of the great body of cat lore that cats like their homes more than they like their people. If we move and take our cat along with us, tradition holds that its paws must be buttered to keep it from going back to the old place; the cat licks the butter off and decides to stay, perhaps because nobody ever buttered its paws in the old place.

The purely utilitarian cat, kept for reasons other than personal, might well feel more attached to place than to family, and find familiar faces and voices a poor substitute for familiar hunting grounds, but mostly a personal cat makes do with wherever its person takes it.

I move a lot, and no cat of mine ever suggested going back. They inspect the new quarters warily, checking baseboards and marking the edges of doors with their cheeks, and then curl up in their accustomed places on the accustomed furniture. Still, Sidney, in the move before last, was disappointed in the outside of the new house. It was in no way equal to the old outside; it had streets and cars instead of woods and fields, and he asked to have the door opened twenty times a day for weeks, and looked out, and then up at me, hoping that presently I would surround the new in with the old out. The others clearly understood that new houses mean new yards, but Sidney kept waiting and asking. With such a confused notion of place, it's doubtful he could ever find his way back home or much of anywhere.

Some cats do find their way. They do this by means that are totally mysterious and clearly superhuman, and consequently pretty annoying. Salmon and hummingbirds find their way too, but they're retracing, in the company of other salmon and hummingbirds, a journey they've made before under their own powers. A cat that was taken away by car or plane, locked up in a carrying case, can make its own way back again if it wants to badly enough, sometimes dying of exhaustion shortly after arrival. We don't know how it's done. The *Encyclopedia Britannica*, which has some curious notions about cats, thinks it's done by purring; a cat's purr, which has "no specific emotional connotations, . . . seems merely to be a homing device." They don't explain how it works, though, nor why a cat half asleep in its own living room would need a homing device. The *Britannica* may have cats confused with bats, who use a kind of sonar to find their way around.

Another theory holds that it's done by the position of the sun in relation to the exact time, which sounds more reasonable, especially if the differential is east-west and not north-south, and the cat is wearing a really accurate watch.

An investigator anesthetized a quantity of cats and put them in a car and drove them, completely unconscious, far away and dumped them; when they woke up they all went back home. Another investigator, however, proved they don't do any such thing. Under the auspices of Yale University, Donald Keith Adams conducted a series of experiments on eighteen cats that were kept, when not being investigated, in a bare stable and fed on a paste made principally of flour and water and alfalfa meal. He took one of them, in a box, two and a half miles from the laboratory and turned it loose to see if it could find its way back. The cat inspected the immediate area for a few minutes, and then moved quickly and purposefully off in a direction at right angles to the correct one and was never seen again. Some homes are hardly worth finding.

Every cat person knows a tale of a returning cat. Friends of mine were in a car accident while driving back from the New Jersey shore with their cat, and in the ensuing confusion the cat escaped into the woods; the people were treated for minor injuries and went sadly home, catless. Some weeks later the cat appeared on their doorstep on the far side of Philadelphia.

Philadelphia is a long, dreary, dangerous city to trek through on foot, and the bridges over the Delaware River from New Jersey are few and far apart; how would a cat, or even a person without maps or signs, know which roads led to bridges? How would it have the courage to cross those roaring vibrating metal spans? For how many days did it crouch in the weeds and stare at that rumbling high horror before setting foot on it? Or could it, maybe, swim? Cats are fair swimmers, but the Delaware there is a mighty stretch, open to international shipping, and poisonously filthy, full of rushing flotsam, sewage, oil slicks.

However many times we hear the stories, there's something moving about them. Even for a human on wheels, speaking the language and armed with street maps, it's not a light journey, along those highways and across that river and through that city; what a thing to require of a small speechless battered creature, thrown from a wrecked car.

And, of course, how did it know the way?

The unpalatable truth is that cats have ways of locating things that we can no more imagine than we can imagine inhabitants of another planet breathing methane gas. We're limited by our personal experience, whatever our pretensions to abstract conception.

At a cat show recently, two Siamese kittens escaped from their cage and vanished completely; the doors were locked and the building searched; no kittens. Some time later they were found out in the parking lot sitting on the roof of their own car, waiting. As a person who has more than once climbed into the driver's seat of a car like my own and tried futilely to turn my key in the ignition, a person who has many times, with eyes placed far above tire level and a rudimentary knowledge of automotive makes and models, searched vainly for my car in a parking lot, I find this just as mysterious as homing. It seems to be a sense of the uniqueness of a thing, so that there can be only one right car, only one right road, and these right things call to the cat, and are not to be confused with other, identical, cars and roads. The sense works in unfathomable ways, and fails just as unfathomably: a cat who has seen your briefcase a hundred times in your hand or in the closet may be terrified of it on the living room floor, fluff up its tail, approach it cautiously, ready to turn and flee, and then, inches away, recognize it and feel a perfect fool and have to sit down and wash or pretend to be interested in something else across the room.

How can a creature who can find its own car in a lot or its own home across three states fail to recognize a briefcase in the wrong place? We'll never know. We see things, not as themselves, but as members of classes and categories, and that leads us to use different equipment. Maybe we never had this sense of things from the beginning, or maybe we've been relying too long on crutches like reason and maps.

If stories about homing cats rouse the sympathies, and the impulse to reach a hand across time and space to help, stories of psi trailing simply make us nervous.

Psi trailing is the scientific name for the unscientific act of finding people who went away into the unknown.

Friends of my family gave their cat to a kind neighbor in Washington, D.C., when they moved to Ohio. The cat, who had never been out of Washington before, took five months to find them. The man of the family still staunchly insists that it can't be the same cat, only an identical cat with identical habits that came to their door clamoring to be let in, emaciated and with serious clinical evidence of hard traveling, five months after their own cat had vanished from her new home. I know how he feels. Veterinary and dental evidence be damned; things like that can get on your nerves.

Dr. J. B. Rhine, former director of the famous Parapsychology Laboratory at Duke University, investigated and substantiated some of these stories. In two of the best-documented cases, a veterinarian's cat found him in California after he'd moved there and left it behind in New York, and a part Persian named Sugar took fourteen months to find her family's new home in Oklahoma after they'd left her in California; small but distinctive bone deformities clinched both identifications.

Cats, says Konrad Lorenz, will never love you the way a dog does, but what unimaginable longing could force a cat out of a comfortable home to risk its life on such a desperate trip? And what molecular evidence has our passage left in the air to be followed; what recognizable tracks did our tires leave on I-95? What unique vibrations are we emitting from our new house two thousand miles away?

Best not to think about it.

And on the other hand, George the First quite deliberately left his home and family and moved to another house two blocks away. Our house was full of noise and small children; he put up with us for several years and then disappeared. He was searched for and mourned, and then months later my mother saw him, sitting on his new front porch looking sleek. "George!" she cried, outraged. He answered at once, and trotted over to rub her ankles and be patted and speak in his distinctive polysyllabic voice, and then he went back up his front steps and settled down again. The house looked quiet and comfortable and there was no evidence of children.

In the matter of homes, a cat can decide to better itself.

Caroline bettered herself.

Caroline was born in a part of the world where the dogs are treated more tenderly than the children and live in pampered luxury, while the cats live outside and remain name-less. Since no cat is ever vaccinated, vast numbers of them die of enteritis in infancy; but since no cat is ever neutered, there are always more. They're attached to the property in the same sense as the birds at the bird feeder, and to wonder about the quality of their lives would be considered senti-mental; to keep one as a household pet is a sign of senility. They are wild and shy, but they stay where they are, half fed, unpetted, untreated for wounds or parasites or diseases; it takes an exceptional cat to dream of something better without evidence that it exists.

The striking thing about Caroline's arrival was that she seemed to know exactly what she was doing as she came across the yard toward the house; she moved like a cat com-ing home in time for dinner. She seemed, in retrospect, like some healthy, hopeful, immigrant girl approaching Ellis Is-land with a shabby traveling bag and a determined light in her eye. She didn't pause or detour to inspect the trees and rocks; she headed straight for the door, and I opened it, and she came in. I had the uneasy feeling that I must have in-vited her somehow, or hired her, and forgotten, and here she was at the appointed hour.

Only the sudden appearance of our dog, Vicky, confused her, and she fluffed up and jumped onto the mantelpiece; ap-parently she'd seen the whole place clearly in her mind ex-cept for the dog. After watching closely for a while, she saw that the resident cats ignored the dog, so she jumped back down and went over to Vicky and with the prettiest possible gesture walked under her chin, arching her back against it, as a sign of friendship and perhaps apology.

The other cats accepted her as if they'd known for weeks that she was coming. She had naturally sweet manners; per-haps intercat civility is essential in the marginal world she came from, or life would have been chaos. She never forgot the little niceties, like the lick that asks permission to join an-other cat in its patch of sunshine. She was also the only grate-ful cat I've ever known, and in foul weather sat for hours on the windowsill and looked out, and then turned and looked in, surveying the warm room, the soft furniture, the cat dishes on the kitchen floor, and then looked at me and half closed her eyes and flexed her paws.

Because of a kind of modesty in her she never became a major cat around the house; she wasn't shy, but she never pushed her way into people's affections or laps and seemed always to remember that the others were there first. And maybe she'd accomplished what she set out to do. Maybe the comfortable home was what she'd come to find, and affection was beyond the scope of her plans.

What brought her, my immigrant girl? Did she see it all in a dream and go out and follow it, like a biblical figure obeying the voice of the Lord? How did George find the childless house on Primrose Street? It's unlikely he went there begging for food; he was indecently well fed. What brings cats to my sister's sanctuary; what changed Boston Blackie's mind? Why did Rose, a city stray, sit for three months on Patti's windowsill and stare compellingly in at her until finally, tired of hiding from her, Patti, who had never liked cats, let her in? Rose was right, and it turned out to be the perfect home, but how did she know this before Patti herself knew? How did Gloria, another city stray, know the exact moment Elaine and Vic began recovering from the death of Jemima, and arrive to climb screaming insistently up the back door? Is is possible that cats, so long revered as the demigods and protective spirits of the domestic hearth, can foresee a new home as well as locate an old one?

It might be.

Certainly cats, or some cats at least, have a strong sense of the home as place, as walls enclosing something more than furniture and people. In the country the Siamese Corvo went abroad to look into other people's houses. He sat on the windowsill or perched on a low branch and looked in the window, and the people, going about their business, ironing clothes, playing Scrabble, fidgeted under his scrutiny. He didn't want to go inside, or to be petted or fed. With miles of woods and hunting grounds at his disposal, he wanted to look into a human house instead, and absorb the sense of it. Barney, when we lived in an apartment, visited the other apartments in the building. He wasn't visiting the people, as a dog might; he took an interest in the apartments for their own sake, scarcely glanced at the residents, and walked around in their rooms like a prospective lessee. Is there more under our roofs than we know?

Some cats people their own places with imaginary spirits. Sidney has for weeks now been very angry with the wall forming the side of the staircase at the back of the living room. Not the whole wall, but a section about a third of the way along it. He sits glaring furiously at it. He can't pass by it without a malevolent glance, and sometimes he attacks it and tries to rend its bland unmarked surface with his claws. My cousin's cats, Thing One and Thing Two, spent a substantial part of their lives peering nearsightedly at an area just above the baseboard of the wall in the hall, an occupation they seemed to find endlessly satisfying, like reading a good book. Colette, in *The Cat*, speaks of "the fixed attention she gave to things swimming about in the air in front of her eyes . . . 'What is that cat staring at? Tell me. There's nothing where she's looking,' 'Nothing . . . for us.' "

In *The Good Cat Book* Mordecai Siegal says cats stare at the wall so people can make fools of themselves trying to figure out why.

Efforts at scientific thought are caught in a bind here. We can't very well allow ourselves to believe in actual invisible spirits in the home, nor can we allow a cat a human imagination, so we're left believing that some cats, normal in all other respects, are subject to psychotic delusions that manifest themselves only inside the cats' own homes. Even at that, it's a strain to allow something so presumably simple as a cat something as sophisticated as a delusion. A delusion of *what*, for heaven's sake? What shape does it take for them, what does it mean? Why are some delusions enraging and others merely interesting? Is it a form of religion? A chemical imbalance in the brain? How is it related to the physical house itself, so that a cat with a delusion in one house has none when it moves to another, and if it is house-connected, is it part of what calls a cat home across long distances?

And can a bored cat summon up a delusion for entertainment, the way we turn on the television? Should we replace this possibly unwholesome recreation with real television?

Some cats, I'm told, watch a lot of it. Maybe they have larger screens and better reception than my cats do, or maybe, like our children, they find it easier than summoning genies out of the imagination. It would be interesting to know if they have any preferences in programs, if the content makes any difference to them. Does what a cat sees on television make any narrative sense to it? Most cats recognize their reflections in the mirror as being cats, so presumably people on television look like people, but would they understand, for instance, a chase?

Barney once watched an entire program about caribou. It was one of those hypnotically peaceful public broadcast programs that all seem to be about a hundred years in the day of a sandhill crane, only these were caribou. Caribou walking back and forth, moulting and migrating, eating and giving birth, accompanied by the singsong drone of narration, and Barney watched each caribou's every step, utterly absorbed, only his eyes moving as it crossed the screen. When it was over he got down off the table and went out to the kitchen to check his dish.

He has never watched anything since, or shown the slightest interest in subsequent nature programs.

Why caribou?

Morgan also watched just once. This program was about birds, a twittering flock of them, and she watched until they all flew upward and vanished from the screen. She raised her head and looked up over the television, and then turned to inspect all the corners of the ceiling; no birds. She was displeased: not real birds at all, then, but a trick, a joke to play on cats. She left the room and has never again even glanced at the television; if she sits on my lap while I'm watching, she closes her eyes. She seems to me an earthy, sensible, pragmatic sort of cat, and has no delusions and no use for unreal birds.

The ways in which they share our lives and occupations and accommodate themselves to our households vary from cat to cat. Some cats listen to music, or to certain kinds of music, with every sign of enjoyment. Some are indifferent to it and some, like my Blueberry, find it all excruciatingly painful. Morgan hates guitars. My aunt had a cat named Simke who hated Caruso. She ignored all other vocalists, but Caruso's opening notes sent her yowling across the room, throwing herself against the door to get out. In *Are Cats People?* Paul Corey mentions playing a Caruso record that always brought a neighbor's cow galloping across the field to lean over the fence and moo. Perhaps investigators could spend a couple of grants analysing Enrico's vibrations.

Sidney, though not intelligent, is musical. A lot of his vocal expressions seem to be musical in intent if not in effect, and he used to play the piano. He played in the classical kitten-on-the-keys fashion, by walking on it, but he stepped thoughtfully, and paused, and sometimes crouched to produce chords with his haunches, all with deliberation and obvious enjoyment. He's an insomniac, and from time to time I woke up in the dark house at four in the morning to the unsettling notes of a piano in the empty living room below.

Then one day Sidney watched my husband playing. He sat on the floor and stared and stared, apparently never having noticed before: the man sat on the piano stool and used only his two hands. When my husband vacated the stool, Sidney hopped up onto it. He sat and looked at the keys. He lifted a front paw and reached out tentatively and touched one. Nothing happened. Presently he got down and went away, and never again went anywhere near the piano.

Sidney has always shown uncatlike signs of feeling inferior to people, or that people were somehow doing things the right way and cats the wrong way. At dinner he sits on the extra chair, not on the table, and watches the people eat. When he accepts a tidbit, instead of putting his face down and eating it cat-fashion, he hooks at it a while with his paw, as if wishing he could use a knife and fork on it, correctly. It seems fair to suppose he felt that my husband was playing the piano correctly, and since as a cat he couldn't do it that way, then he wouldn't do it at all. I don't think he envied the actual sounds produced—he'd always seemed pleased with his own efforts. It was only the method he couldn't master.

Cats give up quickly. It is not in the nature of the cat to struggle for accomplishment against heavy odds. A cat that has tried a difficult jump and fallen, or failed to make sense of television, or to play the piano properly, will not persevere. It will turn its attention elsewhere. Cats dislike failure, especially in public, and prefer doing the things they're good at and dealing with things they understand; the incomprehensible they simply turn their backs on, and wash. Perhaps the human race would be in more peaceful circumstances today if we weren't so proud of our passion for solving riddles and conquering obstacles.

There are usually enough things to do that a cat is good at to keep it busy, and many more things for two cats. If we keep our cat closed in, in house or apartment, and especially if we're often away, it's only humane to have two or more to ward off boredom and loneliness and too much communing with the spirits of the wall. Two cats take up very little more room than one, and the games of two cats are more fun for humans as well as for cats.

To the restless, ambitious human mind the normal occupations of a house cat seem idle and frivolous. Except for persuading people to open doors and cans, they are not what career counselors call goal-oriented. They include lying in the sun, eating house plants, many of which are poisonous, squeezing into boxes too small for them so that folds of cat hang over the edges, looking out the window, rumaging in bureau drawers, and watching their humans.

How do we appear to our cats, that so many seem so interested in and even so deeply attached to their people? In *Cat Behavior*, Paul Leyhausen says that the cat's dependent life with people is a kind of extended kittenhood, so that it transfers its affection from its mother to us, and we stand to it in her place while it accepts our care, though from time to time it's seized by a fit of adulthood and asserts its independence. Living, in short, like a permanently thirteen-year-old human, an appalling thought. I've been pushing this theory around for a while, but I'm still not sure about it. It doesn't quite ring true; it's too easy. All right, once in a while a cat will behave like an adolescent person, but only under stress.

When I had pneumonia, Boy, the black supercat, the major cat of my life, spent his days and nights by my side, watching me. Then I went away, to the hospital, for ten days. There can be no connection in a cat's mind, unless just possibly death, between a person's illness and subsequent disappearance. For ten days he lived an apparently normal life in his own home among familiar things and people; he was fed regularly and ate his food. When I came home he refused to greet me or even meet my eyes. I reached down with an apologetic pat, and pulled back my hand: his fur was disgusting. He was filthy. He was so dirty he was almost sticky to the touch. Always a vain cat, he burnished his slick black coat till it flashed blue glints in the sunlight, but since my disappearance he obviously hadn't given even the most cursory lick. Now he walked a few feet away and sat down with his back to me. He was very angry, but I had finally come home, and he began to wash. He spent the remainder of the day washing; it was a long, disagreeable job—he was a perfect Augean stable of a cat; he even smelled bad, my flower-scented Boy—but when he was finished he glittered as before. He still didn't speak to me, though. It was days before he forgave me and things were the same between us.

That was adolescent of him, a thoroughly adolescent revenge, not washing because I'd abandoned him. But who among us, caught in a painful and incomprehensible position with no way to fight back, hasn't stooped to unworthy reactions at some time in our adult lives? Given the helplessness of their small size and limited communications with the masters of the house, a cat may be driven to expressions of frustration that seem childish to us. Childish and sometimes repulsive. Without a common language, a cat who must tell us something is limited to the use of its body and the functions thereof.

The most obvious form of expression it has is what I suppose I must call defecation. Cats invest heavy emotions in their toilet functions. A cat outdoors finding the right place to use, and using it, is a busy and seriously involved creature. Indoors, the litter pan is an important element in life. Sidney even has a special noise, or song, he makes when he's about to use it, and another, victorious song that means he's done so; sometimes he tears around the house afterward ruffling up the rugs with a wild light in his eye.

In my unfeeling youth I kept a lone and lonely cat in my apartment and went off to work every day. Sometimes I went out after work and was gone all evening as well, and when I did this the cat would leave me a small pile on the floor directly beside the litter pan, no more than half an inch from it, to underline that this was no thoughtless accident but a deliberate message of anger and loneliness.

My grandmother's Siamese went further. My grandmother was old and ill, and a nurse-companion was hired to live with her. Nurse-companionship isn't a very desirable career, and the people who go in for it are not always the best and brightest. This woman was slovenly, cross, and disagreeable, and resented the extra work of feeding and opening doors for a cat. No one knows in what ways she revenged herself on the cat, but the cat retaliated with the only weapon she had to hand. She slipped into the room where the woman slept and left her weapon on the pillow, not once but several times. Maybe it was only simple vengeance; more likely she took it a step further and hoped that the woman, rather than sleep in a pile of feces, would simply go away.

She didn't, of course. Nurse-companions, even horrid

ones, are hard to find, and it was the cat herself who went
away to a shelter.

A cat who uses secret, hidden places as a toilet has some
other and deeper problem, but a cat who leaves the matter
in plain sight has something important to say. No matter how
thoughtfully we care for it, there is always that element of
helplessness in communication that forces the cat into infan-
tile behavior, but I don't think we need to interpret this as a
relationship of childish dependence.

In fact, it sometimes seems quite the opposite, and the
cats, especially females, treat their humans with the worried
protective bossiness of anxious mothers, and fret inordinately
over illnesses or accidents. Blueberry used to try to rescue
me from the bathtub, lest I drown. When my children were
young, their cuts and scrapes and howls of pain drew cats of
both sexes, distressed and fussing and interfering with the
first aid. Many are the stories of cats watching tirelessly at
sickbeds, of cats alerting their people to fires or choking babies, even of cats hunting and bringing back small game for
people trapped or in wartime peril or famine: are these dependent children, or responsible adults in the family?

Few things about the cat can be exposed to the daylight
of reason, least of all how it stands, in its own eyes, in its relationship to us.

Why do cats bring us things? Country dwellers are accustomed to the rows of corpses on the morning doorstep, mice
and moles and the occasional bird or baby rabbit. People in
apartments whose cats don't go out may wake up in the morning beside a row of small objects, socks and matchbooks and
the like; a friend of mine woke up with a dead rat on her
chest. My daughter's cat Hector, living illicitly in a college
dormitory, foraged around and brought things back to her in
her room, underwear and earrings and, once, a dollar bill.
Blueberry, an apartment cat, never showed the least interest
in hunting even when taken to the country, but she brought
me a dead crow once, an enormous crow half again as big as
the cat, struggling down the driveway and up the walk to lay
it at my feet with every sign of pride. She didn't kill it, it had

been shot by hunters, and I'm not sure whether I was supposed to think she did, or only be pleased because this is the kind of thing humans want.

They don't expect us to eat what they bring, apparently, any more than the gods of primitive religions are expected to actually eat the sacrificed sheep or bullock or virgin. Cats show no other sign of regarding us as gods, and religion, even primitive religion, is held to be one of the immovable barriers separating humanity from the lowly beast, but what *are* these offerings? I have heard of a cat, rescued in wintertime as a stray, who was deeply concerned with keeping warm. His house had a basement furnace that sent heat up through a floor grating, on which he luxuriated. When the furnace went off he anxiously rounded up all his toys and carried them to the grating and laid them out. A sacrifice? A trade? A bribe?

Sometimes there's a sexual element in the relationship, and cats attached to a human of the opposite sex will be sharply jealous of a spouse or lover. With Barney, in the beginning, the relationship was obviously sexual, but then, life as a cattery stud doesn't teach a cat much about other ways of feeling. From time to time he would scramble onto my back and try to hold me by the neck with his jaws, as he used to do with his Persian clients. He had strong feelings about me, and this was the only thing he knew to do about feelings. Later, after he'd had a chance to watch other cats with people, he learned the sadly limited repertoire at his disposal: the flexed paw, the purr, the stomach exposed for rubbing, the half-closed eyes. Dogs can show their devotion by a glad submission, but cats and people can only signal a little to each other across the gulf, like lovers in adjacent prisons.

Cats enjoy our company, compete for our attention, and often seem to love us deeply, and we don't know why; we don't even understand its simplest expression.

Take the matter of purring, a mystery so impenetrable that entire books are written about cats without mentioning it. We assume that purring means affection, but a number of authorities say no, and cite the fact that cats will purr when frightened. I don't think this reaction is all that common; in a long life among cats I've heard it only once, from a vet's examining table; I thought the cat had gone mad. Perhaps it was a plea for clemency. Perhaps it was a kind of hysteria; laughter in humans is supposed to mean pleasure, but a frightened human may laugh from pure nervousness.

How can we doubt, with the *Britannica*, that purring means what we think it means? Recently at the zoo I watched a pair of tigers in amorous dalliance; between matings the male threw himself down on his side with a thud and gazed at the female and purred until the sidewalk shook under my feet. An affectionate cat purrs when patted or spoken to by its human or nestled into a lap, and a cross cat will refuse to purr. Paul Gallico in *The Silent Meow* calls this The Withheld Purr, a useful form of communication. You speak kindly to the cat and rub gently under its jaw with your finger, and the cat should purr; you expect it to purr; you can almost hear it purr; but it doesn't. The silence bursts on you with its information: you have displeased this cat somehow.

From a scientific viewpoint the problem of the purr is that by the time the investigator gets inside to search out the mechanism the cat has stopped purring. The great naturalist Gilbert White said parts of its windpipe are "formed for sound." The *Encyclopedia Americana* offers two theories— vibrations of the false vocal chords that lie above the true ones, or of the hyoid apparatus, which are small bones between the skull and larynx. *The World Book Encyclopedia* leans toward a theory of blood vessels with vibrating walls inside the chest, while Elizabeth Keifer in *Wholly Cats* says it's made by vibrating the soft palate and resembles snoring in humans, which raises various questions, such as how they purr when awake and can they, unlike the rest of us, vibrate the soft palate at will? *Pat Widmer's Cat Book* makes the inarguable statement that "purring is a noise made by the cat while breathing." Therein lies the investigator's dilemma: a cat that stops breathing stops purring.

The most recent report, in *The Compendium on Continuing Education for Veterinary Medicine*, is that cats can control the air pressure through the glottis, the opening of the larynx, both inhaling and exhaling, as if we could produce a continuous "hummmm" sound breathing in as well as out. *Veterinary Aspects of Feline Behavior* says that kittens begin to purr at the age of two days, using the vibration to locate important landmarks like their mother, and then after their eyes open they extend the purr's purpose to include a call for food or attention. And Public Broadcast television says the purr, a consistent twenty-five vibrations per second, means the cat wants a contact to be continued: if you're holding me, go on holding me.

Don't stop. Don't leave.

We do leave, though. Perhaps so much fuss is made over the loyalty of dogs because we ourselves are capable of such treachery, and can terminate a relationship without a backward glance, breaking our contract with an animal whenever it seems convenient to do so. Many are the classified ads and notices on bulletin boards: "Free to good home; moving." From the frequency with which we abandon our friends you'd think a cat was more trouble to crate and transport than a breakfront full of grandmother's china. It's not likely we'll find a good home, not for a grown cat, and what, from its point of view, is a good home? Perhaps anywhere, any motel room, as long as we were there. Let's not be too easily satisfied with a roof and regular meals for our old companion; it may be we have broken his heart. When our own hearts are broken we can rationalize them whole again, or pull our pride over the wounds. A cat can't. He may go on living in the new home for many years, and listen for our voice and footstep every day of them.

We made a contract, and the fine print is in a language we can't read. There are connections here we don't know about, or how can a cat go find its person half a continent away? Honore Balzac's cat asked to go out every day in time to meet him coming home from work, but when the man silently changed his plans and wasn't coming home, the cat stayed curled in its chair and didn't bother to go out.

Of course it's also possible to have a cat around on a totally impersonal basis, to catch mice or decorate the living room sofa, as long as you're sure you both understand the terms.

Jane kept Esmeralda to catch mice. The two of them lived alone together in a big house on a windswept hill, and Jane complained often of loneliness, and invited me over. Esmeralda got to know me (I slipped her bits of cheese from the cocktail table; "Stop it," said Jane, "you're giving her ideas above her station") and the sound of my car, and always waited in the hall to greet me. The three of us sat in the living room, and Jane complained of loneliness.

"You have Esmeralda," I offered.

"Huh. Esmeralda."

At the sound of her name the cat gazed adoringly at Jane and flexed her paws deeply into the rug.

"She loves you," I said. "Look at her. She's asking to sit in your lap." Esmeralda reached out a polite paw and touched the couch by Jane's leg, asking.

"She does not love me. She only wants to sit in my lap so she can scratch me."

"*Scratch* you?"

Jane nodded emphatically. "That's what she wants to do. I let her sit in my lap just once, and she dug her claws right into my leg like a savage."

"Oh, Jane, she didn't mean it that way. It means love, and pleasure. It's because kittens do it to their mothers when they're nursing, kneading their paws like that."

"I'm sorry for their mothers, then. And if that's her idea of love, no thank you."

Esmeralda slitted her green eyes at Jane and purred hoarsely.

"Let her sit beside you, then. Invite her up."

Instead Jane scooped up the cat and carried her to the basement door. "She can stay down there. She's a useless cat and I've got a good mind to get rid of her. I got her to catch mice. The people said her mother was a great mouser, and does Esmeralda catch mice? Hell, no. She plays with them.

She's made friends with them, I caught her sharing her food with them."

"*What?*"

"You heard me. I opened the basement door and there they were, there she was by her dish and there were two or three mice with her, and they ran away when they saw me. She was letting them eat out of her dish. I'd just like to give her back to those liars who gave her to me, it would serve them right."

The stairs down to the basement were steep and long, and Jane had a bad knee, but every day she carried Esmeralda's dinner dish down those stairs and set it next to the litter pan, an uncongenial arrangement to say the least, rather than share her big bright kitchen with a cat. Alone in her living room Jane watched television and complained of loneliness. Alone in the dark basement the cat, desperate, made friends with mice like prisoners in the dungeons of song and

"Damned useless cat." Jane slammed the basement door. "I expect she does it just to spite me, she knows I hate mice."

And so they lived together there for several years, woman and cat, until Jane died of the various complications of loneliness and relatives drove Esmeralda to the vet to be "put to sleep," as we like to call it.

If we don't expect to love a cat, we should be careful to find out what the cat expects. And if we don't plan on a personal relationship, we must at least arrange for it to have some company, some friendship. The cat goes hunting by itself, because that's the way a cat has to hunt, but it doesn't choose loneliness. It seems to contain great secret lakes and continents of generous affection, much of it, surprisingly, for us, and it shouldn't have to pass its days in such miserable solitude that it shares its food with mice.

Cats With Cats

5

Relations between cat and cat are as complex and stylized as Chinese ideographs. It's easier, really, for cats to get along with people. Friendships between cats and people come naturally and are simple enough, sometimes dangerously simple, to establish. Just leave the door open a minute too long on a dark and catless night, then turn back into your house and it has a cat, like a puff of fog blown in, and it turns out you've met before in an earlier life. The cat was born knowing how to arch its back under your hand, and your hand knows how to smooth itself along the cat in a gesture clinically proven to soothe you both. The cat will settle down with its paws folded under its breast and accept you with its eyes, and be perfectly at ease in your presence. You are natural companions.

Getting along with other cats takes teaching. Cat manners and communication are taught positively by example and negatively by direct, sometimes very direct, instruction from any other cat close enough to aim a slap. Some of it does come built into the cat; a kitten with a safe and happy mother never saw her fluff her tail and hiss, but surprise this infant in its box and it swells into a spitting pincushion. The smaller the kitten, the more thoroughly it can fluff itself to look bigger. A grown cat expands its tail and a ridge of fur along its arched back, turning sideways to the enemy to show the full effect, but the kitten bristles all over. You can say a lot with fur. Lions, instead of turning sideways, face the threat head-on to show the splendid intimidating mane and hide the absurdly unimposing leonine rear. Dogs' hackles are confined to the back of the neck and frontal spine, and raising them means the same thing. A friend of mine has a Rhodesian ridgeback whose hackles are permanently raised, stiff as a hairbrush even in her sleep, and this gets her in trouble, as if she were a human waving a loaded shotgun. On her most peaceful country strolls, farm dogs see her and react by either slinking away or taking up the challenge.

Tails communicate, too. They may possibly help a cat right itself in midair, but they aren't for balancing with; they're for conversation, like a dog's tail. The vertebrae of the cat, from skull to tail tip, are flexibly connected so the cat can contract and expand its length, curve its back upward as well as down, or ripple it along the spinal line, and my mother's cat Tadger can roll up his tail like a stuffed anchovy. The language of the tail raises questions about the tailless cats that turn up here and there through history; are they semimute in the cat world, or have they found another, invisible way to communicate, maybe with a wider range of scents?

A kitten running to greet its mother carries the tail straight up but relaxed at the end, so the tip flutters like a waved hand. In later life it will use this position to greet its human and to trot in to dinner. Put the dish on the floor, and if the food is acceptable the tail drops slowly until it lies straight out and flat on the floor, ready to be stepped on, while the cat eats. If the food is no good the tail drops only to half mast while the cat makes scratching motions on the floor around the dish, meaning that this smells so foul that it will bring enemies from far and wide unless we bury it, or, metaphorically, this shit belongs in the litter box. Some sources maintain that the cat is trying to bury it for safekeeping, to return for it later, but my cats never go back.

The fluffed tail held up stiff clear to the tip is a threat; up and arched forward it's defensive. Then there's the inverted U, an anxious sign seen in the pursued cat during a rough game of tag, and the fluffed inverted U, half offense, half defense.

These matters are pretty well standardized, though as usual with cats, not universal; I knew a pair of white cats who always carried their tails resting comfortably between their ears, and what other cats made of this unorthodoxy I can't imagine. Turkish Angoras do the same, and presumably understand each other.

Fur and tail combined with the hundred variations of body posture, of ears, whiskers, pupil dilation, and verbal comments make up an intercat vocabulary not demonstrably smaller than that of the average American high school student. Making friends is another matter.

Friendships between cat and cat are a luxury, born when the cat of civilization no longer needs solitary hunting grounds in order to survive. Cat friendships are a gift we can give them, a subsidiary of guaranteed meals and sexual cancellation.

Hunting animals are never automatically at ease with each other the way plant-eaters are. Cows in a field, antelope on the plain, finches in a flock, need each other deeply and mutely, and except for the squabbles of mating season draw great comfort from knowing there's another of the same kind around. They think communally, a single idea flowing like water through the group. On catching sight of a neighbor grazing nearby they don't need to have any special reaction or establish any specific relationship between themselves and this other; a cow is unsurprised to see another cow, and never has to ask if this cow is stronger or braver than she is, or is chewing a better bite of grass. Either there is grass to eat or there is no grass; one doesn't compete for grass.

Meat-eaters need more space, and their food comes singly, meal by meal. An eagle can't afford to ignore another eagle nesting next door, and a cat moving into the hunting grounds is a rival cat. Among cats every chance meeting is an encounter, and needs alert consideration; a cat pretending to ignore another cat is playacting. He looks at the sky, he licks a perfectly clean spot on his side, the feline equivalent of shoving your hands in your pockets and whistling. He yawns, and almost, but not quite, closes his eyes; let the other cat make a move and all the lights snap on at once.

Outdoors, cats have a home territory, to be defended, and beyond it a home range, an area full of special spots for hunting or resting or watching, all connected by invisible pathways, and this they'll share with other cats, avoiding direct encounter when they can. Bobcats in the wild cover extensive tracts of land, and a study showed that they all circled through the territory counterclockwise, so as not to bump into each other and have to make a scene. Domestic cats using the same range may work out a time-sharing schedule. Sometimes it's prearranged by time of day—morning cat, afternoon cat, evening cat—and sometimes they lay messages like the Occupied sign on a public toilet; the first cat into the field leaves scent markers on the path, and the next cat, sniffing, can tell whether they're fresh and he should turn aside and go a different way, or whether they're several hours old and their creator finished his hunting now and out of the way.

Scent is sophisticated communication for cats. All of us, coming home, have been checked out by our cats and wondered if the cat may not know as much about where we've been as we do. Between cat and cat, smell is raised to an art form. Scent glands are stationed along the tail, on each side of the forehead, and on the lips and chin; a cat that rubs its face against you is marking you for its own. A possessive cat like Morgan marks everything she can reach, especially when it isn't hers; at my mother's house she claimed all the doorways and furniture and my mother as well, to the indignation of Mother's own cat. Even the pads of the feet leave messages, as the cat walks through the world like a graffiti artist leaving his name on bridges and buildings.

Most cat marks are subtle, and invisible to the human nose, but spraying is something else again, a gross message even humans can read, though all it means to us is "cat." Sniffing it, the cat opens its mouth in what looks to us like an expression of angry disgust, but what it's doing is opening an auxiliary nose. This is the "flehmen reaction," and it gets the smell's information to the ducts behind the upper incisors that channel it to the vomeronasal organ for decoding. Some researchers believe a cat may leave a record, not just of its presence, but of its age and sex and status, emotional state, readiness for love, and individual identity. As much, in short, as a human can pack into a personals ad, and far more likely to be true.

A leopard, most solitary of cats, adds a postscript; he sprays a tree and then stands on his hind legs and claws the bark as far up as he can reach, meaning, "Back off; an enormous cat with very sharp claws lives here."

Recent studies suggest that even we are more sensitive to smell than we realize. Maybe because we smelled so personally unpleasant for so much of our history we came to suppress olfactory information as both impolite and disgusting. Cats never smelled bad. They buried their excrement and cleaned their fur with a saliva that contains a cleansing and deodorizing agent, and left themselves open to the educational symphony of smell. Lend your cat carrier to someone else, and when it's brought back your cat can spend twenty minutes with it, learning who knows what richly detailed nuances about your friend's cat and its life and secret name. We'd consider it rude to sniff our friends for news, because until very recent times indeed one's friends didn't bear close sniffing; instead we stand well back and say, "How have you been? Are you feeling better? Are you happy?" and very likely get a lie in return. Cats can't lie to the noses of other cats.

Once full identification is made the cats decide, on the evidence, whether to fight, or threaten, or separate, or pursue the acquaintance.

In a large household, a colony really, the size of my sis-

ter's, there seem to be few close friendships or strong enmi-
ties, as if the sheer numbers re-created a solitary state; they
are part of a whole, like soldiers in an army, and used to each
other, but except in very cold weather they maintain air
space in between. The disappearance of one or the arrival of
another causes little comment. This seems sensible. Cats are
not cattle, to huddle blankly together, and to have to take
sharp emotional notice of so many others every day would be
exhausting; easier to remain aloof.

After breakfast they fan out like the spokes of a wheel.
Zachary goes down the driveway toward the woods, Flanagan through the neighbor's yard and around the north side of
my house, Ferdie through the back hedge, Marzipan across
the vegetable garden; their paths neither cross nor conflict.
(Basil, having found his home, stays by it, pressed heavily
against its wall to pin it down.) Indoors, no one has made an
effort to stake out a particular chair or rug; presumably it
would take so much defending there'd be no time for sleep.
But outside there's space enough for each to have his own,
established by custom and mutual consent rather than confrontation. It's recognized that these paths and areas are not
property, to be defended, but rights-of-way only. It would be
bad manners, not trespass, to use Flanagan's path by the leaf
pile; Morgan, who has very bad manners, used it often.

Close trespass is another matter. Mehitabel sat on the
roof of the sheep shed to make sure Morgan didn't come up
the driveway into the space where Mehitabel is queen
mother. For years she was the only female here except for
her three cowed daughters, and while she ignored Barney's
and Sidney's encroachments she stood guard against Morgan's. Gender is important to cats. Morgan sat across the
drive on a woodpile, on her own side of an imaginary line
drawn straight across from Mehitabel's fierce, beautiful owl
eyes. Morgan understood; she and Mehitabel are birds of a
feather in this lust for power and property.

Mehitabel's will stretched across the driveway like an
electric eye, and I crossed it apprehensively as if it might be

carcinogenic, though she wasn't hostile to me. Quite the contrary. She courted me lavishly, shamelessly; that would have been the final victory, to take me away from Morgan, to supplant her, move into her house and order her cast onto the dung heap for the crows. From the woodpile Morgan watched her, on the alert for any temporary failure of will or loss of nerve that would slacken the line and let her cross. Once, to see what would happen, I picked her up and carried her past Mehitabel; she struggled and scratched me, leaped down, and dashed back to the woodpile. In the interplay of cat and cat, humans simply don't count. We can't, like the Greeks' gods, hang around the battlefield helping out our favorites; it's a breach of etiquette and our favorites wouldn't thank us and any victories we scored would be scrubbed from the record.

In a group as large as my sister's there is no pecking order. It would be mathematically impossible to keep track of, especially since these rankings have a way of shifting for no apparent reason. As in any group, though, there's always the last and least, usually the newcomer or junior member, but in this collection it's Snipe. All of us knew a kid like Snipe in school. If Snipe were a human eight-year-old he would come from the wrong side of the tracks, whine a lot, and smell of sour milk. He would wipe his nose on his coat sleeve all winter; the nurse would send home notes about things living in his hair. His ears would be full of scabby stuff, and when it came to choosing up teams the captains would come to blows over which had to take Snipe.

He's a narrow-chested, rat-faced, black and white cat with a hacking cough, made of poor protoplasm poorly put together, and no amount of nourishing food or veterinary attention has been able to improve on the hand nature dealt him. No matter who comes or goes in the household, Snipe is last, and knows it.

Among more primitive creatures like chickens or eight-year-olds, the others would simply fall on him and destroy him as a blot unworthy of existence, but Snipe goes unscathed. He is the opposite of threat. In a feline society where status is based on self-confidence, Snipe's well-founded humility is a *laissez-passer* and makes him invisible, crawling beneath everyone's notice like a low-flying plane avoiding radar. It's the cocky cat who may be asked to prove himself, though not if he's cocky enough.

For years Barney never had to prove a thing. His cockiness was so immense that no cat questioned it. Before he was neutered and set down among common cats he lived like a sultan in his cattery; not for him the wearisome searches and the pleading serenade from the fence, the backyard skirmish and the torn ear. He never knew the meaning of failure or even competition, and year after year beautiful eager females were put into his cage without his even needing to ask. No other cat challenged his right to them. Success followed success. A life like that gets into the blood, literally. In groups of apes with a dominant male who gets all the best females, the subordinate male grows more and more subordinate, his confidence withers, and the testosterone in his blood sinks lower and lower. But take away the leader and he perks right up, his testosterone leaps, he beats his chest, chooses the prettiest mates, snatches everyone else's bananas, and becomes dominant himself. Barney, always the one and only, must have been pure testosterone by the time he retired.

He was castrated and disarmed into impotence, and it made no difference at all. In *The Fur Person*, castration reduces May Sarton's cat to humility overnight, but Barney's supercharged blood took years to cool down. Past the same line where Mehitabel's burning gaze kept Morgan at bay, Barney sauntered unconcerned. He kept right on going, through the garden bristling with astonished cats on their own property, and up to the front door, where he stared at the nearest human to open it. He rarely uses his voice; he has rarely needed to. He walked into the house and through the kitchen, and the resident cats parted for him like the Red Sea. He never even glanced at them. God knows what they thought; perhaps they felt like the unfortunate Aztecs at the time of the Spanish invasion: they had always had a legend that invincible white gods were going to show up one of these days, and by golly, here they were.

It was an appalling piece of effrontery, walking in like that without asking, but he clearly didn't feel the need to ask: does the sultan ask? His assumption of invulnerability stunned the others into belief, and he came and went when it pleased him, looking neither to left nor right.

Very slowly the elixir drained from his blood. It seemed to be a natural chemical process; there was no evidence that any other cat ever challenged his godlike status. Vulnerability crept up on him little by little. Within two years he stopped going there unless I went with him, and then he stopped going even with me. He began to defer occasionally to others, and sometimes even foolish Sidney pushed him away from his dinner. The world was no longer his; he stayed closer to home. When the kitten Morgan bothered him, instead of grandly ignoring her or staring her down, he stooped to hissing and sometimes backed away or changed his path.

Deposed by his own chemistry, the sultan had become just another one of the eunuchs. Still, he had had a grand time while it lasted.

He has made no friends, though. Friendship in a cattery is complicated by sex and the currents of protectiveness and territoriality among so many unaltered cats and kittens, and studs live in cages. For Barney, learning human friendship came quickly and easily, but cat friendship never came; no cat snuggles up to him, and he washes no cat's ears. He avoids interaction, and if he finds a cat in his favorite place, instead of asking permission to join it, or cuffing its head, or squeezing in on top of it, he simply walks away.

While challenge and strife may spring up among equals, in groups the hopelessly incompetent like Snipe are *hors de combat*, and the young or unfortunate are often tenderly protected. Derek Tangye describes a moving father-and-son relationship, with the father licking and cuddling his kitten and taking it for instructive walks. In *My Five Tigers* Lloyd Alexander documents the painstaking education of a new kitten by his two older, unrelated male cats. In *How to Live with a Cat* Margaret Cooper Gay mentions three abandoned starvelings she called the Joes, brought home to his own refrigerator by her cat Charlie. Another writer mentions a country tramp cat who was fed one day at a farmhouse and came back the next day with twenty-nine deserving friends. Colette's Long-Cat jumped into a cold and rushing stream to swim after, rescue, and drag back a drowning kitten, no relation of his. And then there was the Gray Cat.

The Gray Cat was an unaltered teenage male who came over regularly to play with my friend's small male kitten. This was in the city, and the Gray Cat, who plainly had a home, shouldn't have been allowed to travel around like that, but that's another story. The kitten's house was in a courtyard off the street, and he was let out to play there, with supervision from a window, and the Gray Cat played sweetly with him and taught him tag and wrestling.

There's a law in our city about dogs on leashes, but the only people who obey it are the owners of tiny fluffy dogs like animated dusters; people with Danes and Dobermans let them gallop on ahead, and stroll after them carrying the leash looped over the wrist with casual grace as if, like the riding crop, it existed mainly to decorate the owner. The gate of the courtyard was open and the Doberman, passing, saw the kitten outside alone. He sprang for it with the speed of a panther and the teeth of the great white shark.

From nowhere the Gray Cat flashed into sight and leaped straight into his face. My friend, watching from a window, screamed simultaneously and rushed out waving her arms, but even so the dog had plenty of time to close his steel jaws just once and crush the Gray Cat to a pulp; that he didn't must have been due to his slow-wittedness in dealing with the unexpected. His owner arrived and, after inspecting his friend for scratches and delivering himself of a few words on the unwisdom of letting cats out into a dog's world, they departed.

Saved from the literal jaws of death, the kitten crept out from under a bush still fluffed, and the Gray Cat licked him on the head and shoulders before settling down to wash himself all over.

We can dismiss the heroism of a mother cat as mainly instinct, a blind urging in her nerves and muscles that she has no choice but to obey, but what can we say about the Gray Cat? If it had been a human that he saved, a deed of a quite different and far higher order, of course, no doubt he would have been invited to the White House and given a medal and it would have been on the evening news, but the kitten was only a kitten, and so the Gray Cat was allowed to go about his business.

If in a colony cats seem largely to ignore one another, among individuals and in smaller families they often go beyond tolerance to develop genuine personal affections for each other. All proper behaviorists base cat relationships firmly on dominance and submission, but the closest inspection of my family of five shows no evidence of it at all. Even in his sultan days Barney imposed his will on no other cat, and took no other cat's space or food. No cat here is in charge, no cat here submits; they all have their personal crotchets, but no one seems to care who's first. Maybe the behaviorists have studied too many families of a mother with grown children. Mothers tend to maintain their sway. Or maybe my cats are simply lazy; with more than one or two other cats around, upholding a superior position is a lot of work, which cats avoid, and involves contention, which unsexed cats avoid as destructive of peace and naptime.

My group seems to have melded itself into a family of such wordless solidarity, and to take such evident comfort from each other, that I sometimes suppress a twinge of envy. There are chronic washers and washees among them, but this is personality, not dominance; Sidney never did learn to wash himself. Barney sits apart from the others, but he's one of them, a member if not a friend. When the little black cat was sick and got well again and came back from the vet with her bandages finally off there was a spontaneous rejoicing of great giddiness all around the house and up and down the stairs, more like a dance than a game, and even Barney joined in.

They parcel me out among themselves in my different times and places. At the typewriter I am Morgan's, to climb on my shoulder and bite my face and stand on the repeating keys. Reading the Sunday paper I am Barney's and sometimes the little black cat's; she's new and still pushing herself into place. Barney also waits on my bed at night to claim those first few minutes before Corvo takes over. In my sleep I am Morgan's from the collarbone up, Corvo's from collarbone to waist, and Barney's from the waist down, while the black cat free-lances. My daughter is Sidney's, and no one questions his possession. Behind this sharing there's no grand abstract notion of fairness, only a reasonable cooperation to minimize stress.

There's a basket here that sits on the table under a lamp, and it's the premier cat place in the house. There's room in it for only one of the big cats, though the two smaller ones can squeeze in and share. The basket would belong to the dominant cat if we had a dominant cat, but its occupants rotate regularly and peacefully; the cat in possession is never challenged or chivvied, and when it leaves possession passes to the first cat to notice the vacancy. Perhaps I've just made an accidental lucky selection of feline equals, or perhaps cat society isn't as ambitiously human as it's been painted. Perhaps scientific laboratory conditions are the wrong place to inspect the cat.

Cats who are friends will lick each other, with special attention to the head and ears, wrestle, stalk each other from behind the furniture, and conduct noisy games of tag up and down the stairs and through the bric-a-brac. They will play a noncompetitive form of hockey or billiards with a ball or a walnut, with a lot of strategic cat-positioning behind chair legs and a hunkering of haunches for the spring. It takes two cats to play the bag game properly. You drop an empty grocery bag on the floor so the top is open, and one cat gets into it, rustling interestingly. The second cat pounces on the bag, the first cat springs out from ambush, and both pretend to be surprised. Then the second cat gets in the bag. Repeat steps two through four. There are no winners. There are rarely winners in a cat game. When it gets too rough or one cat gets bored, the game stops by mutual consent; it's enough to stop any game just to sit down and wash.

The sterner authorities insist that cats don't actually *play*, that only humans have the concept of play and all the games of cats are merely to keep themselves in training for hunting mice, but this view is narrowly based on human experience, in which all games are merely to keep ourselves in training for business competition or war. Maybe only cats have the concept of play.

The *Britannica* warns us that having two young cats of the same age may make training and discipline difficult. It doesn't say what it was trying to accomplish in the way of training, or what happened, but I have a vision of, instead of one obediently intimidated kitten, two of them, adolescent confederates, crouched giggling together in a corner while the *Britannica* stamped its foot and bellowed commands in a rage of impotence and fired warning shots into the ceiling. Perhaps the *Britannica* isn't temperamentally cat people. And if we have no cat and want two cats, two from the same litter will already be friends and need no introduction.

There are authoritative instructions for introducing a new cat to an established cat or cats. You can set up a screen door or baby-gate between rooms to separate them while they get acquainted. You can keep them closed up in separate rooms, and then switch rooms, giving them a chance to get used to each other through the residual scent markers, but I'm not sure about this; it wouldn't work with me. I'd feel much worse knowing an invisible stranger was lurking around the premises, like lying in bed listening to assassins downstairs that turn out to be only an errant brother blundering around in the dark.

I've always just dumped the cats on each other, with varying results. Probably no matter how it's done there'll be a certain amount of hissing, but I've never had a conflict that lasted more than a couple of days. Maybe some of it's in our minds. Our civilized tradition of hospitality is outraged, and our feelings ache vicariously for the one received so brutally in its new home, like an orphan out of Dickens. The cats don't feel that way, though. It's normal to them, this defense of home and privilege against strangers, and then the gradual acceptance of stranger as resident, and the new one has never read Dickens. It knows full well it's intruding, that its entry-level position is on the bottom, or even in a closet or under the bed, and its job is to cringe and ingratiate, proceed slowly, and look for room for advancement later, seizing small opportunities to encroach.

When there might be real bloodshed, we can put it away somewhere, let things simmer down, try again, keep an eye on developments.

The more cats, the easier; for a longtime only cat a new one is a darker threat than if there have always been plural cats, as a new baby is more upsetting to an only child than to a houseful of children. And young cats are easier. Cats, sometimes grudgingly, are careful of the young, and probably the resident cat will eventually, with some grumblings and backsliding, admit the kitten's claim on care and lick its head. Especially if we ourselves aren't taking terribly good care of it. A kitten sobbing in a corner for its mother is a lot more appealing to our cat than a kitten purring on our lap. This seems hard on the kitten, but it doesn't have our sentimental overview, our dual mind in which we both suffer and redouble our sufferings by watching ourselves suffer, and comparing our condition to the happiness of nonsufferers. It will feel better soon. Pat the old cat, let the new one cry awhile.

Not all cats take to group living. Cats vary. Cats vary so widely that all data is meaningless and the professional classifiers gnash their teeth trying to come up with even a single fact common to all.

Some cats, for whatever reason, are as solitary as their reputation would have them; some strike up close, enduring friendships with other cats and mourn bitterly when they leave or die; some have no use for cats and care only for their humans. There is even unnerving evidence that some nonfamilial cats gather in groups for social purposes.

This goes against everything we think we know. Aside from impromptu gatherings around females in heat, which are marred by loud noises and occasional warfare, a cat should not be a joiner, should disdain bylaws and secret handshakes and cocktail parties. His independence from social entanglements is part of what we like about him. Dogs, yes; dogs hang out together in groups on street corners, socializing and sniffing each other's rear ends, but they're pack animals; it's their tradition to do so. Cats, no.

Just the same, the literature of superstition is full of secret cat meetings. The cats in these tales are usually witches or demons in disguise, or accompanied by actual witches and/or devils, and nobody is up to any good. In the ancient story "The King of the Cats," the traveler comes across a funeral procession of cats, en route to bury their leader. Since the cat is known to be a solitary, where did these tales come from; what terrified peasant came upon a group of them, and did the unlikeliness of it make it all the more sinister?

Lloyd Alexander claims that his cat Rabbit joined a local club and attended its meetings in an outbuilding in a nearby field; there were perhaps a dozen members, he says, and meetings lasted until two or three in the morning, with occasional all-nighters. Later his young Siamese David formed a group of his own that met in the basement, coming in through a broken window, and these seemed to be the younger cats of the neighborhood. They were neither fighting nor making love, the two accepted social activities of cats. They were just *there*, apparently taking some unfeline pleasure in the company.

I would have assumed that all the members were male, like Shriners, but animal psychologist Dr. Michael W. Fox thinks not. In his splendid book *Understanding Your Cat* he says, "Gatherings of cats, which have nothing to do with mating, often occur at night. They are purely social . . . Male and female cats will congregate at a meeting place not far from their home range where they sit quite close, even engaging in mutual grooming and licking. Occasional hostility may be seen, such as hissing and ear flattening, but these gatherings are generally peaceful and, interestingly, occur *outside* the mating season. Around midnight the meeting may quietly disperse and each cat will return to its sleeping quarters."

And these are the same creatures that go to such lengths to avoid even crossing each other's paths in the woods?

Boy had no interest in other cats and gave his undivided attention to me. As other household cats came and went he walked among them apparently barely distinguishing one from another, and washed his own ears.

Then we rented a house in a seaside town for a month in the summer, and took Boy with us. I let him out, and he sniffed the premises and presently came back. Within a few days, however, something had happened. He had to go out, urgently, every evening at nine o'clock, and he returned promptly at five in the morning, somehow scaling the side of the house and scratching at the screen of the window over my bed. He slept most of the day, and in the late afternoon began prowling the windowsills, looking out. It rained a lot that month, and whatever it was was canceled if it rained. If it was still raining at six or seven he seemed quite frantic, checking the sky from every window as if he had planned a picnic for forty people that might have to be moved into the living room. If it was still raining at nine he gave up and slept that night on my feet, where he had always slept before. Otherwise he hardly noticed me.

I was hurt. This was my major cat, my close friend, and he had never before followed any routine but mine, going to bed when I did and getting up with me in the morning, and now something in this temporary town was more important to him than I was.

I have no evidence that a group of cats, probably many of them vacationing transients and strangers to each other, met every night in Stone Harbor, New Jersey; that Boy, a lifelong loner, was invited to join, and did; that they met by prearrangement at a certain hour and broke up just before five in the morning; but I haven't got any other explanations, either. On previous vacations in the country he'd gone out only casually, and slept in my bed at night. He was not equipped for making love, and there was no evidence that he went hunting; he never hunted. Sometimes a cat will take on a second home, and two families, unknown to each other, will feed him and consider him their own, but why visit so late at night when most humans are sleeping, and who would let him out again before dawn? Besides, he was my cat as no other cat has ever been, and I can't suspect him of disloyalty with other humans. But something out there took him away from me every night unless it rained.

And it was important to him. Instead of strolling out the door, pausing to consider the prospect and inspect objects of interest, he hurried away like a man with an appointment, and always in the same direction. He was black all over, and he would have been in deep trouble in the fifteenth and sixteenth centuries; it would have been my duty, anyone's duty, to kill him instantly if he'd hastened away like that on St. John's Eve, or the second Wednesday in Lent, or All Hallows' Eve, or most of the nights in between.

At the end of the month we went back to the city and took up our normal lives, and he slept in bed and never even glanced out of a window. Still, there had been that month, and I thought about it. I assume that, if there ever really were demonic cats out covening, by now and in a sleepy little American beach town they must have degenerated from their unholy purposes to the sort of beery conviviality associated with Elks and Moose, but I'll never know. However long you have a cat and however plainly he lays his life open before you, there is always something hidden, some name he goes by in a place you never heard of.

The French psychologist Leyhausen compares cat relationships to those of a paranoically unsociable human, and Fernand Méry, agreeing, adds that even the friendship of siblings ends the moment they're able to hunt and fend for themselves. But environment does affect sociability, and when the struggle to survive eases off, surely a cat, most adaptable of creatures, can lay down the sword and indulge in the luxury of a friend, even a club full of friends?

There are also reports of ownerless cats living free in communities with a kind of social structure, or government.

Most of the stories come from Italy, especially Rome. Cats there, they say, live in a colony or federation of colonies and submit to a sort of law or code of behavior. If a cat commits a heinous crime—and no one has been able to report on what constitutes a crime among cats; kitten murder, perhaps—that cat is expelled from the colony. Ostracized; shunned, as among the Amish. And it is further said that a cat so shunned falls into despair and may commit suicide by running under a moving car. Given the nature of traffic in Rome, it seems a bit thick to attribute intention to a run-over cat, but that's the story.

In *Rome and a Villa* Eleanor Clark reports that the Roman cats seem not to be wandering freely around the city but keep together in a clearly defined asylum area. In a market square, Piazza Vittorio, she watched a group of about 150 going about their business and sunning themselves on the remains of a great ruined fountain, completely relaxed and at home, washing each other's heads. They were well-mannered and there was no fighting, no scars or chewed ears. When a sudden rainstorm struck they all dashed for shelter, but not for the closest shelter; apparently each had a prearranged niche under an eave or in a cranny and made for it in an orderly fashion, with no confusion or squabbling. They weren't thin, being fed on a kind of semiofficial basis, and they enjoyed a life midway between childish dependency and the perils of utter wildness.

Maybe we're being presumptuous in assuming that there

is even such a thing as cat "behavior." Opportunistic, flexible, perhaps almost reasonable, maybe a cat can behave in any way at all that seems consonant with its own best interests. Unlike the confused, neurotic human, bewildered by guilt and aspirations, a cat can usually assess its choices and act accordingly.

They have few prejudices. A cat that lives with different creatures learns to explain itself to them, if not with subtlety, then at least well enough to build a relationship, and affectionate friendships have sprung up between cats and horses, roosters, goats, rabbits, guinea pigs, wild foxes, and even canaries. More than half the households with cats have dogs as well, and everyone usually gets along. Sometimes it's only a guarded neutrality, but often they're deeply attached, and a well-disposed dog will defend its cat from other dogs. One cat in the literature required her dog to move her kittens for her from place to place in the house. She was a restless mother, constantly looking for better nests for her babies, and when she found one she went to the dog, and he followed her to the kittens and picked up each one very gently by the scruff of the neck and followed her with it to the new site.

People worry that a cat raised among dogs will be too trusting of strange dogs, but even the dimmest cat distinguishes between family members and outsiders, and all cats consider the circumstances. A cat in a safe place may tease a dog unmercifully; a cat that knows a dog is chained knows the precise circumference of the chain; turn the dog loose and the cat retires discreetly up a tree.

A cat of ours was regularly chased by a neighborhood dog, who dropped by almost daily for the purpose, until she had kittens. The next day the dog trotted into the yard as usual, and she sprang at him and scrambled onto his head and clawed his eyes and nose and rode him howling up the street. She had been chased by consent only, and now the game was over. Forever after when the dog had to pass our house he left the sidewalk and detoured widely into the safety of the street.

In an area with nothing to climb and loose dogs prowling in pairs or teams, we might worry. But indoors, within the family, as often as not it's the dog who gets bullied. Poor scruffy Vicky was intimidated by cats all her life until the kitten Gregory came. She'd always admired cats, and here finally was one that didn't scorn her company. A childless dog, she took him for her own, and held him between her paws and washed and washed him, crooning, until he was sopping wet. When he'd had enough he escaped to barricade himself behind a row of cookbooks for a nap, while Vicky sat in front of the shelf and mooed lonesomely for him. Alas, when he got older he realized it was an undignified relationship for a cat, and scorned her like the others.

Cats and dogs rarely fight like cats and dogs. Beyond a temperamental difference, there's no real reason for war; cats and dogs aren't items in each other's diets, and they aren't rivals in the hunting field like cats and owls. (Cats can be an item of owl diet, which is why a wise cat checks the sky before leaving the house, and why a nervous cat likes to be under something, and why the approach to a strange cat is from its eye level instead of from on high.)

It's natural for a dog to chase small animals that run away, but the dog may not be thinking "cat," as distinct from "rabbit" or "squirrel." Since nothing else chases a cat on foot, the cat may be thinking "dog," and Morgan is categorically afraid of them, though that might be maternal teaching. The others stand their ground: if they run the dog will run after them. It's traditional.

In the town of Chanhu-daro in India, a dog chased a cat across some fresh-made bricks before they dried, and their paw prints are still there, the pursuing dog's pressed in over the fleeing cat's. They've been there for four thousand years.

The Cat's Early Years

6

Nobody seems to know for certain what a cat is or where it came from, though everyone has a theory.

Pliny tells us that, some six hundred years before the Prophet, Arabs worshiped a golden cat and believed that there was such special cleanliness and purity about cats that their origin must have been distinct from that of ordinary creatures. One Arab version has it that one of the lions on the Ark sneezed and brought forth the cat to control the shipboard mice; another, less ethereal, holds that the male monkey got bored with his watery confinement and took to playing around with the lioness, their relationship producing the first two cats.

In classical mythology Apollo created the lion to scare his sister Diana, and to tease him she mocked his invention by creating the cat.

In the West of Ireland they say that at some turning point in the world's history the snakes turned into cats, which is why the cat's bite is venomous.

More prosaically, in the beginning was Miacis, a weasel-like creature of the Eocene age some 40 or 50 million years ago, who branched out into various specialties; some of them were small cats. Cats developed early in mammalian history and guessed right the first time; they looked like cats back when most mammals' ancestors were still unrecognizably experimental. Between 7 and 40 million years ago, depending on which book you read, a cat was already a cat.

That much seems widely believed. But when we narrow it down to the present-day house cat, all is confusion.

The first famous cats were Egyptian, which proves only that imperial gods leave records that endure for five thousand years and house pets don't.

Was the Egyptian cat the same as our cat? Were there *two* Egyptian cats? Some scholars insist that there are two types in the paintings and carvings, one with short ears and a blunt nose, one fox-faced with a sharp nose and pointy ears. All were short-haired and ginger-colored or tawny, with black markings.

In 1907, an expedition into Egypt sent back to the British Museum a box of 192 cat skulls from the cat burying grounds at Gizeh, dating from around 600 to 200 B.C. Some years later, when he got around to opening the box, Dr. T.C.S. Morrison-Scot said the skulls were of two types, one resembling *Felis chaus* and one *Felis libyca*, both small wild cats still around in North Africa today. *Libyca* is long-faced and big-eared, with ticked fur like our modern Abyssinians. It has white toes and is familiarly known as the Gloved Cat; tribes in the eastern Sudan still tame it from the wild. *Libyca* is a desert cat, *chaus* a jungle cat, more Asian than African, sandy brown with black tufts on its ear tips and very shy. Somehow, so late in the day of the Egyptian cat cult, they were still distinct enough for Dr. Morrison-Scot to tell apart, and hadn't blurred together over a thousand years of close association. There were fewer of the *chaus* type. Most of the skulls he examined were of the *libyca* type but somewhat bigger than normal, and bigger than our house cats' skulls but smaller than *chaus*'s. He thought these might be a separate strain, and tried calling it *Felis libyca bubastis*, but the idea never caught on.

The *Encyclopedia Americana* throws us an alternative to *chaus*, *Felis ocreata*, another African. (Unless, of course, they're two different names for the same cat. The naming of cats, as T.S. Eliot points out, is a difficult matter.)

Some authorities say cats weren't originally from Egypt at all, but were brought in from Ethiopia; several state firmly that they were brought by Sesotris after his conquest of Nubia. Méry suggest that they have no true wild ancestors, that the Egyptians discovered a mutation, something different that interested them enough to cosset and breed it, effectively inventing their own cats.

At different points in history we start to run across the sturdy, round-faced cat of Europe, a slender, long-faced cat in Thailand, and chubby, fuzzy cats and tailless cats in Japanese and Chinese paintings. And what of the blue-eyed jungle cats of Southeast Asia, and the chunky, long-haired Persian and the slim long-haired Angora, and the Siamese with its knobbed tail, raucous voice, and different estrous cycle? How many cats are there? Science would prefer to name a single cat, a single point of origin, a single ancestor; it would be unprofessionally messy to have various cats developing here and there from various genetic material.

To compound the problem, British authorities feel that, since Britain is the only part of the world that really matters, no merely North African cat can be a real cat, a proper cat, and therefore *Felis* as we know her must be descended in part from *Felis sylvestris*, the European wildcat and a British subject that some say is still common and widespread and others say is almost extinct. Linnaeus thought he had disproved this conclusively in 1736, but many scholarly modern sources still state the connection as a recognized fact—Egyptian cat + *sylvestris* = proper cat— and add that our house cats still breed freely with wildcats. Other authorities, equally positive, say this rarely happens, and when it does the kittens are sickly and sterile. Some claim *sylvestris* has a very different bone structure from puss, and can't be related.

We could almost conjecture that some of these science people aren't making a clear distinction between *sylvestris* proper and puss herself in the woods, homeless for generations and hissing and scratching when grabbed up by marauding scientists, but still genetically one of our own.

It seems safest to go with Linnaeus on the wildcat matter. In its pictures *sylvestris* looks quite dauntingly savage and morose. It's said to be untamable even when taken in infancy, and it grows up to be a burly and powerful opponent; in Scotland's surviving tales of man versus wildcat, the wildcat often wins. This doesn't seem like a promising basis for a friendship. Surely an amiable inclination to get along with mankind brought puss to our hearths in the first place, and the self-confident Gloved Cat and shy *chaus* seem more likely to have bequeathed it.

Alas for eurochauvinism, the evidence of origin seems weighted in favor of North Africa, though Darwin said Asia, and another source says *libyca* is as much Asian as African. And domestic cats were mentioned in Chinese and Sanskrit writings from several thousand years ago, though they may not be quite the same cats we're talking about. There's a modern domestic cat in India, small and spotted, that looks a lot like *Felis ornata*, a desert cat that still runs wild there and interbreeds with house cats.

Cats of one kind or another, large and small, are native to all continents except Australia and Antarctica; many of them, though visibly different, are cross-fertile. I don't see why we need to narrow it down to a single, historically verified, proto-house cat, especially since no one seems able to. Many small cats can be tamed. No one knows why.

The business of tamability doesn't much interest historians; no one wonders what it means, this inclination to our society, or why it should happen at all. It's quite reasonable that so many wild creatures can't be tamed even when caught young and gently treated; it seems vastly strange that some are naturally pleased to share their lives with us even under circumstances, as must have happened often, when their own world was just as comfortable as ours, or more so. Scholars who believe that humans have only to will a thing in order to accomplish it say we "tamed" cats because they caught rats and mice, but who among us has an owl or a blacksnake asleep on our couch? There must have been some give-and-take, a willingness on the cat's part, or we would have had a prisoner instead of a friend. Northerners like Kipling make much of fire and warmth as a lure, but the first tame cats of record lived in mild and pleasant climates.

Cats are the only domestic animals that came to us from independent lives of their own. All the rest of our retinue arrived with innate traditions of pack or flock or herd, of follow-the-leader, of submission to a superior or to the common law of the group. Only the cat had always made its own decisions. It decided in our favor, for reasons we will never know.

All we know for certain of the early days is that some millions of years ago cat-type animals appeared, and then some five or six thousand years ago the Egyptians were tripping over a cat in the kitchen, and calling it "mau."

Why did they call it "mau"? You'll never guess. *Mau* is also the Egyptian word for seeing or for light, and because of the reflecting layer of tapetum behind a cat's eyes that makes them glow in the dark, and the way the pupils contract and expand, cats came to be associated with light, and more specifically with the changeable moon that hoards the sun's light for us during the dark hours; hence "mau."

This is an example of scientific reconstruction at its finest. Not for scientists the offhand supposition that they might have called it something *before* they decided its eyes were like the moon; not for them the humble domestic scenario:

"There's something at the door that says 'mau,' and it wants to come in."

"Is it dangerous?"

"No, it's quite small. Sometimes it makes a humming sound, then it rubs against my legs and says 'mau.'"

"Let it come in, then."

"Come in, Mau."

No cat ever came to the door and said "cat." It's a most unfeline syllable, and its origins are another flurry of confusion. It shows up in Latin and Greek around the first century A.D., although one source tells us Herodotus was using *kattos* four hundred years earlier, and said it was an Egyptian word. An ancient writer says the Latin *catus* is from *cattare*, which in turn is from *captare oculis*, "to catch by seeing." In 1658 *The Historie of Four-Footed Beastes* said it came from the Latin *cautus*, meaning "cautious." Untouched by Latin, the Zoroastrians called it *gatu*. One scholar says the Latin comes from "African languages" by way of Arabic, Syrian, and Greek. The *Oxford English Dictionary* offers us "catt," "catte," "kat," and "katte," but says it's of unknown origin.

"Puss," on the other hand, comes from Bastet, or Bast, or Pasht, the Egyptian cat-headed goddess. The pleasant thing about feline scholarship is that anyone can play; your guess is as good as theirs, and I'd like to submit "puss" as coming from "Pss!", the sound you make when you'd like a cat to stop ripping the furniture. Because it approximates the hiss of a hostile cat, your cat will probably glance up at you, if not actually desist from ripping, as even the Egyptians may have noticed. I admit it doesn't sound very scholarly, but I submit it anyway. It's better than "to catch by seeing."

Even the scientific classifications are subject to argument. The *OED* calls puss *Felis domesticus* and the wildcat *Felis catus*, but the *Britannica* admits of no *domesticus* and uses *catus* for house cats and house cats only. Some authorities call the wildcat *sylvestris*; others consider it the same as a house cat and call it whatever they're calling her. The American bobcat is sometimes set apart as *Felis rufa* and sometimes lumped together with *Felis lynx*. The problem seems to be that classifications are based on skulls and teeth, an area where all cat-creatures are so similar that science has trouble telling one from another, except for the cheetah, which has nonretractable claws and likes to go for walks on a leash and is arguably more dog than cat.

In paintings and statues the Egyptians' cat, whoever she was, sits tall and narrow and stately with her back very straight, as befits divinity.

In the early days there was nothing cuddly about the Egyptian cat gods. The Book of the Dead is said by some to have been already ancient at the time of the First Dynasty in 5650 B.C., though others move it up to 3500; a papyrus copy of it from 1580 B.C. offers us an early glimpse of the Great Cat Ra, the male cat, the sun-god cat. Sir Ernest Budge's translation begins, "I am the Cat which fought near the Persea Tree in Heliopolis on the night when the foes of Neb-er-tcher were destroyed." The illustration shows a ferocious-looking cat slicing into a huge snake with a knife; the snake is Set, the serpent of evil and darkness. Eclipses of the sun in Egypt became re-enactments of this primal battle between the snake-forces of darkness and the cat-forces of light; everyone turned out into the streets to cheer for the cat. The cat kept the world safe from darkness. The cat slept curled in a circle like the moon, clearly showing that it was also in charge of tides, weather, and crops. With connections like that the cat was to go far.

At Thebes, on the royal tombs of the Nineteenth and Twentieth Dynasties, an inscription reads, "Praise be to thee, O Ra, exalted Sekhem, thou art the Great Cat, the avenger of the gods, and the judge of words, and the president of the sovereign chiefs, and the governor of the holy Circle, thou art indeed the bodies of the Great Cat."

The female cat represented a mother-goddess called Mut, later Bastet, Bast, Pasht, Ubastet, or Bubastis; the Egyptians were easygoing about names. Some say Bastet was the offspring of the sun god Osiris (or Ra or Horus or Ptah) and his wife Isis, while others hold that Isis was a later evolution of Bastet. Somehow Hathor, goddess of pleasure, was involved in it too. Maybe the Egyptians could keep all this straight in their heads, or maybe they didn't bother and just let the priests worry about it.

The earliest portrait of the cat-headed Bastet is in a Fifth Dynasty temple dating from around 3000 B.C. Mut/Bastet was in charge of motherhood, and sex, and fertility, but in another aspect she was connected with Sekhnet, the lion-headed goddess of war, death, and sickness. She also supervised good health, and music and dancing, and crops, and hunting, and wisdom, and happiness.

Some scholars suggest that, though sacred, the cat wasn't necessarily domesticated much before 1500 B.C.. But there's a picture from 2600 B.C. of a cat wearing a collar, and it isn't easy to put a collar on a cat you're not personally acquainted with.

Certainly from 1500 B.C. paintings and carvings show the erstwhile ferocious warrior cat Ra and the great mother Bast now very much at home in Egyptian family and social life and living well, jeweled and pampered. That was the year a temple was dedicated to Bastet at Beni-Hassan on the Nile, and from all over Egypt people sent their cats to be buried there, embalmed, spiced, and mummified, with turquoise collars around their necks and cloth ears and painted eyes. In the nineteenth century, excavation of this site yielded three hundred thousand cat mummies, along with some mummified mice as food for the long journey. They were shipped to England and auctioned off as fertilizer, the auctioneer, according to a newspaper report, using a stiffly mummified cat as a gavel. They brought around eighteen dollars a ton. Considering the extensive Egyptian curses invoked by even the accidental molesting of even a single cat, it would be interesting to learn what happened afterwards to the fertilizer entrepreneurs and the auctioneer, and their descendents.

Sacred as they were, Egyptian domestic cats were no mere decorations. They were companions. In 1400 B.C., we see a cat retrieving a duck for a hunter, and in another picture a man whose name is given as Mutsa has taken his family and his cat fishing and duck hunting; the cat is eagerly poised to leap in and bring back the duck. There seems to have been a doglike tone to the relationship: the cat gets taken along. In a New Kingdom (1570–1075 B.C.) carving, Queen Tiyi is in a canoe with her daughters, sitting on a chair, and a brisk-looking striped cat sits under the chair and enjoys the outing. Any modern apartment cat would envy it.

The cat came to banquets. In one scene, the woman has tied her cat to the leg of her chair, where it's trying to unfasten itself to get to a bowl of food just out of reach. In another, a cat with a ring in its ear sits under the woman's chair while the man holds a kitten on his lap; the kitten plays with his sleeve. At another banquet, the cat under the chair is eating a fish. Under a chair has always been a good place for cats; it keeps them from getting tripped over and offers access to dropped fish.

In the temples the high priests watched the temple cats day and night for the omens and prophecies spelled out by how they slept and woke and stretched, and held their tails and whiskers. The expression in their eyes told whether or not the sick would recover. In the street, a man who found a dead cat had to run away screaming and lamenting, lest someone think he had killed it himself, even by accident; killing a cat was punishable by death from stoning. In the house, if the family cat died the family shaved off their eyebrows and went into deep mourning, and the body was mummified at all possible expense. If the house caught fire, the cat had to be rescued first. At adolescence, children had a cat's silhouette tattooed on their arms to call down the blessings of Bastet on their lives. At human funerals, the deceased held an ivory wand with a cat's head to guard him on his trip to the land of the dead; various later traditions in other countries took up the cat as guide and protector of the soul after death.

The Egyptians seem to have had no trouble connecting the powerful supernatural goddess with the cat curled up at the foot of the bed or begging scraps in the kitchen; they were the same, and not the same, a difficult concept for us whose deities have been centralized and invisible for so long. Religion was tangible and flexible, and divinity flickered like an antic lightning from host to host. Priests wove their own colors into the rationale. First causes, if there were any, were not only lost, they were unimportant. Perhaps in the beginning cats had something to do with lions; the dangerous cats have always been nervously respected, and jaguars were worshiped as gods in pre-Columbian Mexico, Guatemala, and Peru. A cat could have originally represented a lion, been a sort of ambassador from lionhood to be propitiated, and its cultivation a symbolic truce with lions, or a kinship with their powers. (I hasten to add that this is just me talking to myself, and the notion has no basis in any sort of scholarship whatever, but the historians' insistence on the practical benefits of cats seems almost too simple to be true. Mouse hunting is reason enough to keep cats but not to worship them.)

Bubastis, center of cat worship, became the capital of all Egypt, and in April and May some seven hundred thousand pilgrims gathered there for the yearly festival of Bastet. By most accounts it was the kind of party that in modern times would have ended with tear gas and fire hoses. The annual religious duty of the faithful around 950 B.C. was to spend the spring drinking heavily and making public love to one and all to set an example for the season's crops. Those who were unable to make the pilgrimage heard the roistering boats go by on the Nile and began their own sacred duties in the streets of their home towns.

It all sounds a bit rowdy for a cat's taste, and probably the objects of this devotion were glad to take up their customary positions under chairs while the party raged.

In 500 B.C., the Persian king Cambyses invaded Egypt and laid successful seige to the city of Pelusium, giving birth to a tale that turns up in various versions from various scholarly sources, each solemnly represented as historical fact. In one version, the Persians threw live cats over the walls of the city, which blasphemy so panicked the Egyptian defenders that they ran distracted till the city fell. A second version says the Persians carried cats instead of shields, and naturally no Egyptian could touch them for fear of harming a cat and incurring the death penalty himself. Version three says simply that the Egyptians refused to engage in battle at all lest a cat in the city be accidentally hurt, and so surrendered without a blow exchanged. The fourth version says that Cambyses ordered his soldiers to search the area and collect all the cats, and then attacked the town driving a horde of cats before him, each soldier carrying a live cat, and the Egyptians surrendered to protect them.

Somehow the whole episode seems odd. Even in those far-off times cats had claws, and a natural aversion to being thrown over walls or snatched up and clutched as shields by strange soldiery. And as for rounding up hundreds of cats for this base purpose in an area where they were held sacred, how did the Persians manage that? Were they starving strays; were gods allowed to wander loose and starving? And even if they were, consider the problem of the average Persian foot soldier chasing a stray cat across fields and down alleys with which the cat was more familiar than the man. And what of the populace, the Egyptians outside the besieged city; what were they doing while an army chased their cats? Did the soldiers burst into their houses and kidnap their personal cats, when a cat is so small and easy to hide and an Egyptian would fight like a tiger to defend it? And how do you drive a horde of cats before you? Cats are not sheep. The vision of a Persian army organizing a mass of angry, terrified cats and moving them in a forward direction toward a designated goal is hard to entertain no matter how deep one's respect for historians.

It all sounds a little like a contemporary joke, translated and solemnized in later centuries, as if one of our political cartoons were unearthed and reported as gospel: see, their president held hands with a bomb, or see, a donkey sat in their Senate. Maybe after the fall of Pelusium some local wag made it up to tease the defeated commander, or maybe he made it up himself as an excuse, and the versions developed by word of mouth for a while before anyone wrote them down. I for one don't believe anything except that Pelusium fell to Cambyses, while the local cats went padding about their apolitical purposes underfoot.

Still, Egypt's strong feelings about cats were clearly beginning to affect international matters. There were cat troubles with Greece. Egypt had passed laws making it illegal to sell cats out of the country, so the Greeks, bothered by rats and mice and weary of dealing with the voracious and disagreeable weasels they used to catch them, stole cats. They supported a regular pirate trade in cats, with severe diplomatic repercussions. Egypt even sent missions around the Mediterranean ports trying to buy back her cats, with only moderate success. A Greek bas-relief from the fifth century A.D. shows a cat on a leash about to attack a dog, so clearly some very tough specimens were leaking out to the larger world. (An entirely different line of thought holds that the Greeks had no domestic cats, valuing them only for their fur, which was widely worn by the poor, and the cat was on a leash to keep it from escaping an arranged fight with the dog.)

In the first century B.C., during a delicate period in Egypt's relations with Rome, a Roman soldier killed a cat by accident and was mobbed by the Egyptian crowds in spite of frantic official attempts at intervention. According to one report, he was killed and his body dragged through the streets, and the incident led to a series of reprisals and rebellions that plagued international relations all the way to the suicide of Cleopatra and Egypt's decline.

Cats continued to spread. The Phoenician sailors, mobile traders of the eastern Mediterranean since the tenth century B.C., probably carried them, deliberately or accidentally or both; sailors have always had a soft spot for cats, and Phoenicians always had a sharp eye for trade goods. Some say they carried them as far as England. Some say cats found their way through Europe by way of Greece, and others that the Roman legions took them, part of the "impedimenta" Caesar was always complaining about; cat remains have been found in Roman villas in Britain.

In Rome, where today officially protected cats sleep in the sun on Keats's and Shelley's graves, the cat became a tutelary spirit, no longer a reigning deity in charge of all the major aspects of life and death, but a humble hearth watcher. With the mental split we still manage today, the Romans considered her both a protector of the home and an emblem of liberty. They were a cleanly people for their time, and no doubt admired the immaculate cat, but probably their straight-edged military minds were never deeply tuned to the feline.

It's said that the Greek general Galsthelos, who commanded Pharoah's army, fled to Portugal after his defeat when the Red Sea parted. He took along his wife Scota, the Pharoah's beautiful daughter, who naturally brought her cats. Centuries later their descendant, Fergus I, became ruler of a northern kingdom he called Scotland after his ancestress, and introduced to Britain the descendants of her cats.

Accepted opinion puts cats in Gaul in the fourth or fifth century A.D., by which time they were catching mice as far away as China, but there's a statuette and a table pedestal from the first or second century that shows them already comfortably established there. The statuette wears a collar and looks entirely domestic; the cat on the pedestal is held by a small boy and wears a bell to frighten off evil spirits. All the early Gallic cats look cuddlier than the Egyptian, rounder and fatter, and are shown being clutched and carried in awkward positions, often by children, gods no more.

The pragmatic historians keep reminding us that the cat spread around the world following the spread of rats and mice, and was taken up by humans solely to protect granaries—or, in China, silkworm cocoons—from rodent teeth. They tell us that back when man was a hunter the cat was hated as a rival in the hunting field (though I've found no early paintings of men hunting mice for the table), and that as farming and grain storing spread the cat became accepted as an ally.

No one will admit of cats as self-indulgence.

Maybe history exaggerates the utilitarian. Maybe we're attributing too much common sense to our ancestors. We assume that, since their lives were harsher than ours, or seem

so from our complacent viewpoint, they had no time for sentiment, and no one would invite a pretty cat indoors on a cold
night or carry home a cheerful two-months kitten without an
eye to usefulness.

Of course, we like to believe we're nicer now than people used to be, more sensitive, imaginative, generous. And
it's true we've been through, or cats have been through, periods of hideous cruelty in the embarrassingly recent past. It's
comforting to tell ourselves we're getting better all the time,
in a straight line through history, and if people three hundred
years ago tortured cats without regard for their pain, then
people a thousand years ago must have been inconceivably
crueler. Unless favored by superstition, as in Egypt, cats
must have been suffered to live at all only under mouse-
catching covenants.

And again, we look backward through the glass of Victorian scholarship, when everyone believed that Creation was
placed here for us to eat and wear, and all we had to do was
find out how God intended us to use its lower elements. But
were they really so businesslike, these ancestors of ours?
Surely well-treated cats were no less affectionate, kittens no
less endearing, and there were children a thousand years
ago, and monks, nuns, widows, prisoners, sailors, and people
in isolated hamlets and fortresses who may have needed affection as much as rodent control.

We can't know. After Egypt the cat begins to slip underneath history, at knee level. In feudal times the master's favorite hawks, hounds, and horses all had their quarters, and
the Great Hall was heaped with snoozing dogs; where was
the cat? Was an individual cat a farm tool rather than a friend,
out in the stable treading a nest for kittens in the hay? Or was
it asleep on the mistress's bed? Or in the kitchen watching
the meat turn on the spit?

Probably it was better off in England than in northern
Europe. In 1205, the English Nuns' Rule stated, "Ye shall not
possess any beast, my dear sisters, except only a cat." In the
fourteenth century, Chaucer wrote, "Or take a cat, nourish it

well with milk / And tender meat, make it a couch of silk . . . "
English etiquette books of the fourteenth and fifteenth centuries forbade the feeding of cats under the table. Certainly some cats were appreciated as much for themselves as for their granary work.

There's a great psychological gulf between corn crib and lap, between farmhand and friend, and very few of our useful creatures have taken the leap, or wanted to. Probably many cats didn't. Certainly some did. Came inside, small and with cleanly habits, perhaps looking for a safer place to kitten, and looked into people's eyes and purred when touched, and stayed. Or were brought in, because of being lame or sickly or orphaned, and cosseted by the kitchen fire, and stayed. Whoever made the first move, cat or human, probably people far from Egypt became attached to their cats then as they do now, mice or no mice.

The surviving written word concerns itself with practical matters. For instance, the Welsh king Hywel Dda in 936 organized the tribal laws that had been established by long custom. A newborn kitten's value, or the compensation payable to its owner if you killed it, was one cent. When its eyes had opened it was worth two cents, and after it had killed its first mouse it was worth four cents, which would also buy you a sheep or a goat. To clarify the matter for barter, a calf, an ordinary filly, and a cat were of equal worth, unless the cat was one of the many that watched the king's own granaries and so worth a lot more. If you stole one of the king's cats, the fine was a pile of grain equal to the length of the cat, including its tail. The cat was held up by the tail and grain heaped around to its full length, which can't have done either the cat or the tail holder any good.

In order to enjoy legal status as a hamlet, a Welsh settlement had to include nine buildings, a plow, a kiln, a churn, a bull, a cock, a herdsman, and a cat.

If husband and wife separated, the wife got the cat.

Clearly the cat was a person of consequence in farming country, a creature with a legal position, and worth stealing.

But no document mentions its emotional status. No one bothered to record that in the year 400, or 600, or 1000, such-and-such a fisherman or shepherd or farmwife dearly loved an old striped tom with a torn ear.

It seems likely that they did, though, and even continued to do so through the dark times that lay ahead.

Cats and the Church

7

The cat is useful for catching mice, and affectionate toward affectionate people, but there's something else, something odd about the cat, something more than meets the eye. Everyone's noticed it.

The cat, always and everywhere, has been a means of getting in touch with something unreachable by humans—the Egyptian Land of the Dead, the Norse World Serpent at the bottom of the sea, the future, the Christian Hell, spirits good and bad, and uncontrollable factors like the weather, love, shipwrecks, and wealth. A cat has always been what the computer people call a "communications tool."

In one of the sections in *A Certain Lucas*, Julio Cortazar announces his realization, in the middle of a business meeting, that cats are telephones, cordless telephones, who have been trying since antiquity to communicate messages to their biped subscribers. Unfortunately, even if humans do discover that the cat is indeed a telephone, we have no way of understanding the message it has to convey or its origin, but the cat continues to try. Sometimes its silken discourse and sentences as smooth as glycerine concern hunger, at which times the cat is simply a cat, but at other times the cat has no personal needs to explain and is speaking purely as a telephone from elsewhere. "Clumsy and pretentious, we have let milennia go by without answering the calls, without wondering where they were coming from or who was on the other end of that line which a twitching tail grew tired of showing us in houses all over the world."

A stable and self-confident society can take a few domestic animals walking around like open lines to another world; a society in transition is touchier. A society of innumerable major and minor deities among which the citizens may pick and choose can take their come-and-go in stride, but monotheistic Christianity, jealously exclusive, marched across Europe hand in hand with patriarchy and brought bad news for cats, goddesses, and the unofficial mysteries.

In the fourth century the Emperor Constantine established Christianity as the state religion of a good deal of the civilized world. His nephew, Julian the Apostate, made a rebellious effort to restore pagan tolerance, but it didn't last; after his death his heirs decreed uniform Christianity and launched the long campaign to stamp out competition. The Roman Empire fell, but the Christian empire grew and spread.

At the same time, in Arabia, Mohammed was building up another monotheistic religion, but this was a less ominous one for cats. The Koran stated that while dogs were unclean creatures, cats were the very essence of purity. At Bab-el-Nasz a cat hospital was established, and contributing food to its patients was an act of piety. Cats were most especially never to be chased out of the mosque. In a recent television program on Islamic Africa, rows of the white-robed faithful are prostrating themselves in the mosque as a fine striped cat with white gloves strolls past the camera and on beside their bowed heads, tail on high and fluttering with confidence, a traditionally welcome guest.

Christianity's specific horror of cats came on slowly and sporadically. In the sixth century Pope Gregory the Great had a cat he was deeply attached to, and Saint Jerome kept a cat as well as his more famous lion. Saint Agatha, back in the third century, was a kind of patron saint of cats, though she may have inherited a sanitized version of an older cat cult; her day is February 5, and in later centuries cats found abroad in the month of February were considered witches, and killed.

Moving across Europe, the Church wrestled everywhere with the entrenched customs of paganism. Under pressure, they were to fragment and go underground, and debased forms of them, still connected with animals, resurfaced everywhere as sorcery and diabolism.

Northern Europe, which had maintained contact with Egypt through the Amber Trade Route since a thousand years before Christ, worshiped a major goddess named Freya (or Freyia, Frieda, Feyda, Frigga, Freja, or Frigg), with noticeable overtones of Bastet. In Greenland, women worshiping Freya wore gloves of white catskin with the fur side inside, a haunting glimpse of white-gloved *lybica* back in the homeland of sacred cats.

Freya was originally a three-way goddess, in charge of sex, motherhood, and destruction, with the power to give and take away life, and the cat was closely associated with her in all these aspects. In the early Norse mythology her chariot was pulled by two cats, and by the fifteenth century in Scotland their numbers had increased, as cats' numbers will, to twenty. Gradually her motherhood jurisdiction withered away and left her with the two opposing aspects of sex and destruction, of love and marriage and of disease and death. She was the foremost of the Valkyries, and she and her cats prowled the battlefields deciding who would die, and escorted them to her underworld.

On the other hand, Friday was the preferred day to get married because, being her sacred day, it promised fertility: Freya was always promiscuous. In the myths she had affairs

with most of the male gods, and her festivals were public orgies that may have seemed more prurient in the iron-gray
north than under the blue skies of the beneficent Nile. What
the Church could not abolish it tried to adopt, but it found no
equivalent to Freya. She and her cats were clearly unassimi-
lable in the new religion, and a basic and surprisingly dura-
ble enemy.

The Church had better luck absorbing other matters. The
two main celebrations of the pagan year, the winter and summer solstices, were converted to the respective birthdays of
Christ and John the Baptist, but they brought with them to
their new respectability their raucous old ceremonies, dancing, feasting, games, improper songs, and bonfires. Regretta-
bly, some of the bonfires were made of live cats.

The cat's association with fertility had always been a
mixed blessing for the cat; cat sacrifices in the interests of a
good crop had sprung up in many cultures. With the absorp-
tion of pagan practice into Christian ceremony the custom
flourished under new auspices, and the Church set up official
cat-burnings of its own to underline the message that these
were basically Christian, not pagan, occasions and had nothing to do with crop magic.

The druids seem to have patented the wicker cage that
held live cats over the flames, and later iron cages came into
fashion for their greater durability, prolonging the excitement, but more casual sacrifice needed only a good fire and
some cats.

Cats were burned alive at the beginning of spring, which
was now called Lent, or buried alive in the fields to protect
the crop from evil spirits. In southwestern France a kitten
would be buried alive to clear the weeds from a patch of
ground, a horticultural practice I can't recommend as I don't
think it would work, and cats were buried alive around apple
trees to increase the yield, which might indeed work. In Russia, Poland, and Bohemia a black cat was buried alive in the
freshly plowed fields. Shrove Tuesday and Lent's first Sunday were popular occasions for burning cats, but on all Len-

ten Sundays and Wednesdays it was especially pleasing in the eye of Heaven, culminating in some areas in an enormous Easter Sunday cat fire. In Denmark a live cat was put in a barrel on the eve of Shrove Tuesday, and horsemen tilted at the barrel with spears to run it through. In parts of England a cat had to be whipped to death on Shrove Tuesday, and in Roxburghshire one was put in a barrel of soot and the barrel beaten with sticks until it fell apart; the maddened cat, trying to escape, was caught and killed by the excited crowd.

Perhaps the most successful Lenten ceremony, Cat Wednesday, took place in France, at Metz. Held on the second Wednesday in Lent, it was first mentioned in 962, not long after King Hywel Dda had established the high value of Welsh cats and Henry I of Saxony had decreed a fine of fifty bushels of corn for killing a cat. Cat Wednesday became the heart of a famous festival that continued until 1773, with a grand bonfire attended by the governor and chief magistrate; all the civil and military authorities helped in the burning of thirteen cats in a wooden cage over a fire while everyone danced. The cats were said to be disguised witches, and this seems to be the first definite mention of cats in connection with anti-Christian sorcery. Worse was to come.

Midsummer, now called the Eve of St. John, occasioned the greatest cat fires of the year, and the most persistent; the event wasn't discontinued in the province of Meurthe until 1905. In Paris great numbers of cats were packed into a barrel or basket and swung from a pole over a roaring fire in the Place de Greve; afterward people took home scraps of ash and scorched bone for good luck and protection from lightning. A specialized vocation was the collecting of cats for the fire, and the record shows that a Lucas Pommerieux was paid a hundred Paris sous for supplying, over a period of time ending on St. John's 1573, all the cats "necessary" for the Paris fire plus a large canvas sack to contain them. The king attended the event; in 1648 Louis XIV lit the fire wearing a wreath of roses.

Midsummer still had its unsettling ambiguities, though.

At Aix-en-Provence, up until 1757, the area was scoured for the very finest tomcat, who was wrapped in swaddling clothes to represent the infant Jesus, adored at a special shrine, and taken on procession in a litter with flowers strewn in his path. Then at noon on June 24 he was put in a wicker basket and thrown into a large bonfire in the city square, while bishops and priests sang accompanying anthems.

After St. John's, the next important cat event was the harvest, now All Saints' Day. Throughout France and Germany a fine plump cat would be decorated with garlands at the beginning of the growing season and pampered until the harvest, when it was eaten. In France a cat was buried under the last bundle of wheat before it was threshed, and when the threshers' flails had killed it, it was roasted, to be eaten on the following Sunday. It's hinted that even today in remote places a cat is ritually burned alive to celebrate the last of the harvest home, or buried alive at the entrance to the barn; getting in the last of the crops is still called "killing the cat" in some countries. The cat, a male cat here, descended from the Great Cat Ra, had assumed the duties of a kind of corn god, and it had to be propitiated for the next year's growing season by decking it in ribbons and worshiping it, or by killing it, or both.

The effort to assimilate and sanctify the season with All Saints' Day was never entirely successful; the end of October retains an unhallowed air, and the witches of the night before seem more present than the saints of the day. The truth is that Christianity was never as deeply concerned with field crops as the pagan cults were, and had nothing solid to offer as a substitute, so cats continued to be more involved than priests in farming and fertility matters.

Least important for cats was Christmas, and sometimes only a single cat sufficed to celebrate it, usually tied alive to a stake and roasted slowly. In parts of central Europe black tomcats were buried in the fields on Christmas Eve to keep evil spirits away from next year's crops, but in general it was a time of truce until February, when witch-cats associated with Saint Agatha were killed for appearing abroad, perhaps on the assumption that any cat not sensibly in front of the fire at that season must be driven by demonic business. Then it was Lent again.

Throughout the eleventh, twelfth, and thirteenth centuries the identification of cats with sorcery spread and grew, and the ceremonial nature of cat sacrifice began to degenerate into free-for-all torture. It was never sufficient for the cat merely to die; considerable suffering was part of the point. Cats were burned, boiled, impaled, hanged, skinned alive, gutted alive, buried alive, dropped from towers, stoned, scalded, and stabbed. An added touch to the traditional bonfire was a mast or pole in its center; cats fought each other in the flames to scramble up it to brief safety, extending the ceremony until the last screaming victim fell back to its death. In 1231 Pope Gregory XI set up the Inquisition, and the owners or befrienders of cats, accused of worshiping the devil, were burned as well.

Very likely the cat in Europe would have been completely exterminated during the Middle Ages if it hadn't had an ironically lucky break from the enemy Church itself; returning Crusaders brought back a new kind of rat in their ships, the black rat. This Palestinian import was smarter, hungrier, and more prolific than the few native rats, which it quickly supplanted, and within fifty years it had swept through Europe, spreading plague and destroying as much as half the harvested grain. Cats were badly needed for their ancient purpose in farming areas and around mills; sheer common sense in the countryside saved enough of them to keep the populace from starving and the cat itself from vanishing.

Not all cat killings were connected with the Christian calendar and anti-Christian sorcery. A particular highlight of the coronation of Elizabeth I was the burning of a huge wicker effigy of the Pope, stuffed with live cats to provide appropriate sound effects. Throughout northern Europe and the British Isles cats somehow retained their benign connection with hearth and home, so that when you built a house it was wise to bury a live cat under the threshhold, and when you moved into a house it was customary to roast a cat on its hearth, to ensure domestic happiness. In the footings of the walls and towers of castles and churches cats were buried alive as guardian spirits and to make sure the building would stand stoutly; even august Westminster, during later repairs, gave up its withered feline body. Cat sacrifices attended the building of bridges; cats were particularly associated with bridges, and all sorts of odd and complicated stories survive about cats and bridges and the devil.

A bright cat would have done well to emigrate from Christendom altogether. Eurocentric scholarship shapes the records, but Buddhists do not torture animals, and Hindus have always been instructed to keep and feed at least one cat in the home. In Japan, the killer of a cat was to be cursed by ill fortune for seven generations. The Islamic world kept its traditional respect for cats, and in 1280 the Sultan of Egypt and Syria left provision in his will for a garden for homeless cats, where they were to be freely fed and cared for. Ghet-el-Quoth, it was called, or Orchard of Cats.

It's restful to the mind to turn away from the agonized feline screams of six hundred European years and think of the Orchard, and sleek cats in it lazily watching butterflies in the sunshine, licking their shoulders and looking forward to dinner. The cat will endure, even in Europe, though just barely.

Devil worship in Christendom was not a myth. The Church was not utterly paranoid. It was battling the remains of a tradition from prehistory that found animals spiritually important, and trying to supplant it with an invisible manlike God who paid no attention to the ancient preoccupations of birth and farming and held that only man was possessed of spirit, or soul, or immortality, or any sort of meaningful reality at all. Back in the fourth century, Saint Ambrose had protested that the doctrine of animal soullessness was leading to frightful cruelty, but the Church's main concern was its war against pagans, and spiritual animals were a pagan concept. Cats harked back to Freya, whose underground cult was still very much alive. They harked back to pagan preoccupations like fields and sex and weather, and were therefore a direct line to the Devil, his incarnation and representative.

The Devil in the Middle Ages was a main character in life. Everything unexplainable or unlucky or theologically unorthodox was his doing, and in his carvings and drawings he got increasingly ugly. He had cat's ears. He rode on a black cat. Devil cats held dances, and a black cat led them. The head cat was always black, the color of evil. Witches under torture confessed to worshiping the Devil in the form of a black cat.

Witches were not a myth either. They existed all over Europe, and met in secret covens, and worshiped in bizarre rites that were a surviving corruption of the more formal pagan ceremonies. Cats, especially black cats, were important in their rituals. Goats and cocks were involved on a regular basis too, and authorities point them out as equally demonic, but it's worth noting that nobody held them responsible for their connections; no goat or rooster burnings were recorded. They were victims or accessories; cats were principals.

Men as well as women took part. In 1305 the Archbishop of Coventry was arraigned before the Pope for worshiping the Devil in the form of a cat. He was too important a figure to be burned at the stake, but my own feeling is that he was guilty as charged; you don't accuse an archbishop of Devil worship without *some* evidence.

The fragments of decaying religions, practiced in secret, rot into unpleasant forms. There were complicated sexual orgies, and disagreeable rites in which the elect were allowed to kiss the anus of a black cat, animal blood was used extensively, and peculiar refreshments, like cat soup, were served.

In 1484 Pope Innocent VIII issued a papal bull, "Against Sorcerers," designed to stamp out these rotten scraps of paganism, and the witch hunt gained momentum.

As the modern concept of the witch began to take shape, old and unattractive women became strongly suspect. Spinsters were likely witches because in some of the myths

Freya's attendants were virgins. The young and the married were not exempt, however, and many a man turned in his wife for suspected midnight rambles. Dozens of stories tell of women who slipped out of their husbands' beds to take part in diabolic rites, usually having changed their shape to a cat's. It was no longer necessary to own or be seen with a cat, since it was well known that any witch could turn into one simply by rubbing herself with an ointment made from the fat of a black cat. In many of the stories, the errant woman gets hurt while in her cat form. A man or group of men stumbles on the cats at their wicked revels and wounds one, usually in the paw, and in the morning a local woman is seen with a limp or a wounded hand and burned as a witch. (Cats could change themselves into women, too, often for love of a man, but usually betrayed themselves by chasing mice.)

In the sixteenth and seventeenth centuries, over a hundred thousand witches were executed in Germany, and seventy-five thousand in France. America, coming late to the game, convicted a mere two thousand of cat-related witchcraft. The dead cats were long past counting.

The Church found a new ally in the medical profession, which joined enthusiastically in the witch hunt. Witches and sorcerers, when in their human forms, claimed to cure diseases with herbs and spells, and given the state of official medicine at the time were probably safer and more effective than the doctors, who resented the competition.

Basically, any cat might be and probably was a witch, but certain tests could be made. A cat that showed reluctance or alarm when confronted with holy water or a crucifix was a witch, as was any cat that didn't die immediately when you tried to kill it. A cat connected with or seen around a house where there was illness or injury, or even soured milk, was a witch. A cat found near fields where the crops were doing poorly was a witch. Any trouble involving a human baby was witchcraft and a death warrant for the nearest cat. In Hungary all cats between the ages of seven and twelve were sorcerers. A cat near a deathbed was a sorcerer waiting to seize the victim's soul, and a cat near a baby was a witch waiting to kill it by sucking its breath.

Witches and sorcerers had made a contract with the Devil, their souls in return for favors, usually money, making the possession of money questionable in itself (though the lack of it didn't exonerate you; you might have it hidden). The Devil was invoked by various chantings, and appeared in the form of, naturally, a black cat, to work out the agreement by which he would be your servant in exchange for your soul. The contract was signed by a mark on the new witch's body, generally a cat's paw print in blue or red, reminiscent of the guardian cat tattoo in Egypt. This mark was insensitive to pain. Inquisitors looked for it on witches, and if it wasn't visible it could be located by stabbing the suspect all over with needles until, perhaps exhausted, she stopped screaming, which meant the Devil's mark had been found.

The Devil's access to money made him a popular figure to invoke. Pious folk tortured and killed cats to please God, but the impious did it to summon the Devil. Since the cat was his own creature, if he heard its screams of pain he might appear and offer you gold and silver to let it go. He can't have done this very often, but a surprising number of people kept trying. Their faith seems a bit irrational in hindsight, but everyone must have heard of the cousin of a friend of a friend to whom it had actually happened.

The most tiring diabolic invocation appeared in the Scottish highlands. The Devil was to be summoned in the form of an enormous black cat, and the summoners were ordinary black cats. The ceremony began at midnight on Freya's Friday. The supplicant roasted a black cat alive, turning it on a spit, as slowly as possible to prolong the howls of pain. The tricky part was that the instant the cat mercifully died and stopped howling it had to be replaced by another black cat, and this procedure had to be carried out over four full days and nights, ninety-six hours, during which the petitioner paused for neither food nor rest; "keep the cat turning," as they still say in the Hebrides. The ritual must have used up an enormous number of cats, no matter how slow the fire. If it was astonishing that cats survived at all, that the black genes endured and there are still black cats around today seems nothing short of miraculous, or perhaps diabolical. The last recorded performance of this rite was undertaken in 1750 by two brothers named Maclean, and according to the record it worked; at the end of the fourth day the huge black cat appeared and gave the brothers wealth and heirs.

It was scarcely necessary to sell the Devil one's soul if he could be blackmailed into doing one's bidding, and the notion was enduringly popular. In York County, Pennsylvania, during a witch alarm in 1929, a newspaper reported that you could bully the Devil into leaving you in peace by plunging a live black cat into boiling water and, having cooked it down, keeping the last bone of its tail as a protective amulet.

The connection of the black cat with money from the Devil lived on more benignly after the Devil had lost his grip; even in the Middle Ages money cats turn up without satanic connections. After all, cats had once been in charge of the prosperity of good crops, so why not the prosperity of cash in a cash society? Puss-in-Boots, who made his master rich beyond imagining, is a tale of ancient and cloudy origins that first surfaced in sixteenth-century Italy, and surely no one doubts that Puss was black. In the fourteenth century Dick Whittington, thrice Lord Mayor of London, doesn't seem to have recorded the color of the cat who made him rich, though contrary to legend he wasn't poor to start with; being real, she may have been a perfectly ordinary gray tabby with a white bib. Stories of cats that bring their masters fortunes go back at least a hundred years before Whittington, in places as far apart as Denmark and Persia. And in parts of twentieth-century France, a kind of godlet black cat is called the matagot, and brings its household great fortune as long as it's always served the first bite of every meal. One version holds that you must keep your matagot cat in a chest, and every morning you will find a gold coin in with it; I suppose if you let it out it would be stolen immediately, and no wonder.

In Brittany, the lucky black cat is called a Silver Cat, because he goes out by night and brings home money to his people. He can serve nine masters and make each one rich. (Seven and nine are the cat numbers. Everyone knows they have nine lives, and in Sicily if a black cat serves seven masters it will take the soul of the seventh to hell. In Russia, all black cats turn into the Devil at the age of seven.)

The cat's connections with eyes and seeing, in addition to money, held fast in the underground culture. In *The Once and Future King* T.H. White offers us a recipe used by the sorceress Morgan le Fay. It called, as most such recipes did, for an entirely black cat without a white hair; the cat must be boiled very slowly until all the meat falls from its bones, and a certain small bone, when held in the mouth, makes the cook invisible. In a simpler process from *L'Evangile du Diable (The Devil's Bible)*, invisibility is produced if you only put the cooked meat in a new dish and throw it over your shoulder.

The flesh, bones, blood, brains, ashes, and fat of black cats all had magical properties. Even the afterbirth was useful; the Talmud offers a complicated long-range plan for seeing evil spirits, in which you take the afterbirth of a black female that is the first-born kitten of a black mother who was also the first-born of her mother, and burn it and rub the ashes in your eyes. In Cornwall, a sty can be cured by stroking your eye with the tail of a black cat, which, mercifully, can remain attached to its owner. Topsell's 1606 *Histoire of Foure-Footed Beastes* has a recipe that cures blindness and all eye diseases with a powder made from the burnt head of a black cat.

On the other hand, if you intend to cheat or steal from someone, the ashes of a blind cat thrown in his eyes will blind him to your plans. In the British Isles if a cat has jumped over a corpse, or even been in a room with one, the next person who sees it will go blind.

If black cats were in charge of black sorcery, it seemed reasonable to some that white cats were good magic, though this didn't always work to their advantage: evil spirits could be warded off by throwing the head and tail of a white cat into the fire.

White cats were always popular in the Orient. In the early Middle Ages in Japan, a whole cat cult grew up out of the mystical occasion when a white cat, imported from China, produced five white kittens on the tenth day of the fifth moon. They were cosseted like princelings, and the fashion spread. For centuries cats were spoiled and kept indoors or walked on leashes and tempted with delicacies, while mice wrought havoc among the silkworm cocoons. Unsuccessful attempts were made to frighten off the mice with pictures and figurines of cats, until, regretfully, in 1602 decrees were passed sending the cats back to work.

In World War II, when the Allies entered Burma they found the local population hostile after intensive Japanese propaganda until a resourceful British colonel had white cats stenciled on all the Army's jeeps and trucks; the Burmese were so impressed by this powerful talisman that they abandoned their Japanese connections to cooperate with the Allies.

Three-colored cats also enjoy a special position in the East, and Japanese ships have always carried them for their usefulness in predicting storms, succoring the souls of the drowned, and guiding ships to safety.

The cat's sovereignty over storms, weather, and the sea continued. In the British Isles and other seagoing northern countries, shipwrecking storms could be created by throwing cats into the sea. A witch-cat washing its ears could cause thunderstorms; in modern times it still means rain or frost is coming. The way a cat sleeps predicts warm or cold weather, reasonably enough, since even the least clairvoyant cat sprawls when hot and curls when cold. In Java rain can be induced by washing a cat or, better, a pair of cats.

The cat's jurisdiction over matters of sex, marriage, and home life also persisted. In the Middle East black cats have always had aphrodisiac powers. In Europe Freya's lusty powers moved easily from orgies to marriage. A black cat is a lucky wedding present. A girl will be lucky who hears a cat sneeze on her wedding day. A black cat around the house ensures that all the daughters will marry well, but a girl who steps on a cat's tail won't marry for at least a year. In France, it rains on the weddings of those who have mistreated cats, and in the Netherlands it's bad luck if the cat sits by the door on the day of the wedding, meaning it wants to leave because the bride hasn't treated it with proper respect.

So the cat emerged from its centuries of diabolic association and Church persecution with quite a lot of its Egyptian and pagan powers intact. Death and eternity had been taken over by the Church, sickness and health by doctors, and the sun and moon by men with telescopes, but the cat remained the open line to money, crops, eyesight, weather, and sexual and domestic felicity.

Through the sixteenth and seventeenth centuries the cat fires raged, but there were breaks in the gloom here and there. Cardinal Wolsey, who became Henry VIII's lord chancellor in 1515, was powerful enough to keep any pet he pleased, and carried his cat to the dinner table and to the cathedral when he officiated at services. A hundred years later Cardinal Richelieu, chief minister to Louis XIII, had fourteen cats that he was deeply attached to, and let them sit on his desk and play with the wigs of his distinguished visitors. He made generous provision for them in his will, but unfortunately when he died in 1642 his Swiss guards, more typical of their time, collected and burned them all.

In the 1660s in England, Samuel Pepys kept a cat, and was no crosser than the rest of us when he had to get up and let it out at night; nor did he wonder where it was going. It's hard to imagine Pepys dancing around a fire of cats, much less worshiping a cat-shaped devil. He was an educated man of active scientific curiosity, fond of theater and pretty women and making money; his religion was confined to thanking God at the end of every month when he totted up his accounts. A God with a personal interest in one's profit-

and-loss ledgers has changed somewhat from One who liked cats burning. Cats still burned, but Pepys was the wave of the future.

It would be nice to think that the Church recognized the error of its ways and absolved the cat of evil, but more likely the torturing of cats was simply, finally, going out of fashion. In the European cities of the late seventeenth century, education was becoming less clerical and educated men more visible. Scientific experiment was a fashionable hobby; superstition was for country folk, for crones, for the ignorant and old-fashioned. The pagan threat had withered. The old gods shriveled into fairies with gauzy wings, wee folk in funny hats, goblins to be tolerantly ridiculed in cities; the corn god shrank back into his shrinking fields. Like witches, these rural sprites can still do mischief if displeased, but it's a mild bucolic mischief, souring milk or borrowing your horse by night and bringing it home muddy. Although these gods have become quite separated from the feline, it's still taken for granted everywhere that they can be placated and made into useful guardian spirits with regular saucers of milk or porridge left on the kitchen floor or on the doorstep by night.

The cat and the Devil were parting company, and by the middle of the eighteenth century Christopher Smart could write:

> For I will consider my cat Jeoffry.
> For he is the servant of the Living God, duly and daily
> serving him.
> For he keeps the Lord's watch in the night against the
> Devil, who is death, by brisking about the life.
> For in his morning orisons he loves the sun and the
> sun loves him.
> For he is of the tribe of Tiger.
> For the Cherub Cat is a term of the Angel Tiger.
> For he has the subtlety and hissing of a serpent, which
> in goodness he suppresses.

For he will not do destruction, if he is well-fed, neither
will he spit without provocation.
For he purrs in thankfulness, when God tells him he's
a good Cat.

Of course Smart can hardly be considered typical, since he was an alcoholic, and insane, and at the time was locked up in Bedlam with only Jeoffry for company. Still, no one suggested burning either of them for his sentiments.

Toward the end of the century Dr. Johnson, as sane as Pepys and not a man given to exercise for its own sake, was going out in person to buy oysters for Hodge, lest the servants take a spiteful dislike to the cat from being put to the effort.

By the beginning of the nineteenth century, the cat has so far lost its evil connotations as to be patronized by the likes of Robert Southey, Poet Laureate of England, who burbled, "A kitten is in the animal world what a rosebud is in a garden." The cat may have been relieved not to be made into bonfires, but one can imagine a quick twitch of irritation at the tip of the tail for being called a rosebud.

Cats were in for a sentimental spell. True, Baudelaire in midcentury wrote respectfully in *Fleurs du Mal*:

Stretched pensively in noble attitudes,
Like sphinxes dreaming in their solitudes,
He seems to ponder in an endless trance;
With magic sparks his fecund loins are filled,
And, like fine sand, bright golden atoms gild
With vague and starry rays his mystic glance.

But Baudelaire was French. In Victorian times a suffocating wave of coziness settled over the English-speaking world, all mysteries lost their darkness, and the cat became as tame as a teapot and, to judge from the paintings, shaped rather like one. Saucers of cream and the company of women and children became its lot; no parlor scene was complete without an overfed cat. Kittens played with balls of yarn.

Pretty girls fondled them. We descend from Jeoffry, servant of the Living God and term of the Angel Tiger, to

I like little pussy,
Her coat is so warm,
And if I don't hurt her
She'll do me no harm.
So I'll not pull her tail,
Nor drive her away,
But pussy and I
Very gently will play.

The fierce and lordly Ra-cat had become a young lady, Freya's lusts had been sanitized into family life, and even the valuable hunting instincts had fallen into disrepute; it was considered not quite nice of cats to kill, a deplorable sideline to their proper role as cuddly toys on lap and cushion. Since neutering was uncommon, one wonders how the always noisy and explicit personal sex life of the cat fit into the parlor portrait; nothing is more educational for the young to observe than the magic sparks of those fecund loins, and nothing was less appealing to Victorians than sex education.

We may safely assume that the cat was no cozier in 1880 than it was diabolical in 1380; the cat is not malleable to human opinion. In the Middle Ages when it got the chance it sat on laps; in the nineteenth century when it got the chance it howled on rooftops and ripped open mice.

The twentieth century has been a mixed bag. Veterinary medicine sprang up from virtually nowhere, and eventually turned its attention to cats and began to distinguish their diseases from those of dogs. Vaccines were developed against the great killers like feline enteritis, though they're no use unless someone pays to have them actually administered to the individual cat. Antibiotics arrived for the same privileged few. Cat food, at first an unwholesome, inadequate brew of ground fish scraps, caught the eye of commercial enterprise and improved, and the domestic cat's previous diet of cold noodles, applesauce, fat, and gristle, scraped from a plate, passed into history for the lucky; whole books were to be written on cat nutrition.

On the other side of the balance, the twentieth century brought the car.

The car has changed the cat's life as much as it has our own, killed far more than the Inquisition, and made prisoners of cared-for cats in populous areas. Signs are taped up on every post and wall: LOST. Missing since 9/3. Gray and white tabby. Orange tabby. All black female with flea collar. Answers to Rusty, Samantha, Tuffy, Tigger, Angela . . . Reward. Owner heartbroken. Child grieving. Large reward, call any time.

Cats that can find their way across the continent are not likely to get lost around the corner; cars have done for Rusty and Samantha, Tuffy and Tigger, as they went about their catly business and refreshed their ancient spirits under the moon that used to be theirs.

Here in the city my cats are prisoners. No more the smells of evening or the joys of the chase, no more trees to climb, bushes to nap under, holes to dig, or even strolls down the alley in search of friendship or a fight. The books all say it's best. The books all say cats adjust to it perfectly well and never miss freedom, learn to watch the world from a window and go to bed at night domestic as a hen.

They're healthy here, and as safe as cats can be. They have each other, and they're fond of me, which may be some compensation, if cats think in terms of compensation, but who can doubt that they're diminished? Did they come this far, having been worshiped as gods, having saved the world from rats, having survived European Christianity, in order to be ornaments for my couch? The old ones sleep more here; there's only dinner to wake up for. Morgan paces and whines and searches my face for the answer.

I think about living in a place where cars are as rare as ostriches, and opening the door, and the cats departing one by one across the garden with their tails up, toward the dark woods where only cats and owls can find their way, swaggering like the cat that walked by its wild lone through scent-scapes of night and rustlings in the grass.

Here we are in the city, though, and everywhere I go along the streets cats behind glass watch me from their windowsills, many of them alone in there all day, and certainly many more without even access to a window and only the motionless furniture to watch. A square of sunlight creeping across the rug. Their minds must be dulled and fogging over, and their spirits shriveling.

Cats are not likely to outlast the car, but cars are not likely to outlast the cat, either, only limit the lives of some and shorten the lives of others. Shortening the lives of strays is a mercy, but the car isn't going to wipe them out. Nothing will.

The underworld of cats will continue, thanks to their resolute sex life and skill and devotion as mothers. All over the world in their millions cats still slip past the hazards of history and between the ankles of adversity and survive, even if only for a year or two, tenacious of life, searching out what they need to stay alive for long enough to nurse their young. And in the intervals of survival, they find a sunny ledge on which to wash, and contract the pupils of their eyes to slits, drawing the iris like a luminous silk curtain almost closed across what it is they know.

There's a notion common to many cultures that you can tell the time by looking into a cat's eyes. Baudelaire looked into his cat's eyes and said: "Yes, I see the time; it is eternity."

A Choice of Cats

8

Not so many years ago in America, the purebred cat was considered a snobbish and specialized taste. Even the word *purebred* was suspect, and smacked of an elitist European reverence for aristocracy. These weren't real cats, they were designer cats, man-made cats, interior decorator cats, probably fragile and neurotic, owned by a small band of fanatics who exhibited them in shows and a larger group who acquired and discarded them according to the color of their furniture. Among the rank and file there was a distinct feeling that they were artificial somehow, created by genetic meddling to please the kind of show-offs who shouldn't be allowed to keep cats in the first place.

It's true that some of the breeds have been produced or at least encouraged by meddling, crosses like the Himalayan, and genetic sports like the Scottish Fold that would have been absorbed again by nature if we hadn't found them interesting. But the major types we've all heard of are natural breeds, just Eastern rather than Western, and no more artificial than an Oriental human. In their early days in the West the small genetic pool may have deepened mental and physical flaws, but bolstered by imports and widely established now they aren't any more fragile and neurotic than the rest of us.

Cats, like women, should be respected as individuals rather than admired as decoration, but there's no harm, given a choice, in taking up with a strikingly attractive specimen of either.

A long time ago, I drove across the United States with a Siamese cat and drew incredulous crowds in the small towns and crossroads where I stopped for gas; many gapers refused to believe it was a cat at all. No one would be surprised to see one now, but a certain suspicion persists. The Siamese is widely considered to be unfriendly, perhaps because of its voice, and neurotic, possibly insane; everyone has a tale of a mad Siamese.

The Siamese is different from other cats, or, since generalization is dangerous and some Siamese are dull as clay, *most* Siamese are different. More intense. They're generally conceded to be highly intelligent, but many people do not feel intelligence is an advantage in a pet. It makes them uncomfortable. Not every Siamese is a genius, either. I had one once with the brains of a potted plant. Son of champions, he had trouble locating his breakfast dish every morning, and spent a lot of time sitting bolt upright in corners with his eyes crossed, apparently trying to remember his own name. In general, though, whatever we mean by intelligence in a cat, they do seem well endowed with it, and the French statesman Poincaré said his Siamese Gri-Gri was "as intelligent as any man."

Properly treated, Siamese develop a deep, single-hearted devotion to their people and overreact to competition, absences, and infidelity like an adolescent in love. They need attention, and think nothing of pulling the books out of the bookcase and the pictures off the walls to get it. They demand notice in a raucous, echoing voice that many people and some other cats find alarming; the sound has been compared to that of a giant sea gull in distress. Taking on a Siamese is rather like getting married.

Show cats are rewarded for being "typey," or slightly more like whatever they are than the next cat. The Siamese is supposed to be a long slender cat with a wedge-shaped head and a thin pointy tail, so the breeders keep working toward longer, slenderer cats with wedgier heads and thinner tails, and the results have come to look something like ferrets. The best Siamese in a cat show is one you could pull through a wedding ring; I'm sure they're perfectly charming cats personally, but they don't look very cozy. For those of us not planning on the show circuit, there's a kind of Siamese underworld. The second- and third-class and no-class Siamese, found in disreputable places like casual classified ads and supermarket bulletin boards and small family catteries and even, if we're a bit wary and inspect carefully, pet shops, are generally considered disreputable indeed. From the better breeders, they're called "pet quality," meaning they're good enough for the likes of you and me but not something a breeder wants hanging around lowering the tone of the neighborhood. They're less serpentine. Their heads are too wide, their eyes too round, and they harbor endearing small imperfections in their tailbones, the knobs and kinks all Siamese used to have. In fact, these rejects look much more like the pictures of the first nineteenth-century imports than any modern ribbon winner does. They may even, in middle age, develop a spreading belt line and a double chin, just like ordinary folk. I recommend them. They cost about as much as dinner for two, with wine, in a fairly good restaurant, and they last longer.

The beginnings of the Siamese are lost in the jungle, and we don't even know for sure which jungle. The *Encyclopedia Americana* thinks they originated in China; the *Britannica* says nothing is known of their ancestry and "there is no living species of Oriental cat that would serve as ancestor."

The sacred cat of Burma is descended from a cat named

Sinh the Oracle, who was white but with ears, tail, nose and paws "the color of earth." Its eyes were yellow, but turned blue while it was defending the temple from Siamese invaders, after which all sacred temple cats had blue eyes. This is the long-haired, white-gloved Birman, though, proudly claimed by the Burmese, while what we call Burmese are said to be common in modern Thailand. The Thais say that any Siamese seen in their streets nowadays have been imported from the west, and that *their* cats are Korats, natives of the Korat province there and, though always rare, one of the oldest recorded breeds; they're silver-blue with green or amber eyes. On the other hand, there's a drawing of a seal-point Siamese in The Cat-Book Poems in the Bangkok Museum, and the book came out in 1350.

Jungle boundary lines between countries have never much bothered cats.

The story that arrived in the West with them was that they could be owned only by priests and royalty, and lived jealously guarded in the temples and palaces, and that to steal one was punishable by death. Early imports often had crossed eyes and kinked tails, attributed to watching over temple treasures, staring fixedly at them and wrapping their tails around them for safekeeping. They're said to have attacked thieves. Perhaps they merely spoke, and frightened them off; perhaps they jumped onto their shoulders. Siamese have always liked shoulders. In a Victorian photograph of a pioneer Siamese collector, one of her overweight cats is draped awkwardly but contentedly over her shoulder. Siamese find it amusing to come quietly up behind you and spring from the ground to your shoulder or, failing that, your back, where they hang suspended from your clothes and flesh. Corvo gives a little cry of warning before he jumps; Morgan doesn't. Once settled, they will ride happily around on you, purring with satisfaction and nipping your ear and jaw in the sharp Siamese way of saying "love." Certainly this would disconcert a burglar, but the cats do it only to intimate friends.

Or maybe they tripped the temple thieves; tripping is another Siamese trait. They enjoy pushing ahead of you on the stairs and then hunkering down on the bottom step to see if you will fall over them, the Siamese notion of a joke. Corvo in his wild youth used to trip cars; he lurked in the woods by the road until the car was almost level with him and then danced giddily across in front of it. After he finally succeeded, and lived to tell the tale, he quit.

Perhaps there's nothing but public-relations hype behind the sacred-temple-cat, royalty-only story; at a thousand turn-of-the-century dollars per kitten, the least a buyer could expect was an exotic romance to go with it.

Whoever they were originally, our Siamese did come from Siam. The first pair arriving in England were brought from Bangkok in 1884 by a Mr. Owen Gould; he had been consul-general there, and they were a gift from the king. Their names were Pho and Mia and their kittens won prizes at the Crystal Palace Exhibition in 1885, the same year Miss Forestier-Walker brought in Susan and Tian O'Shian, and the French resident minister in Siam sent a pair to the Jardin des Plantes in Paris, which probably lacked the right emotional atmosphere. The kittens were proving tricky to raise, and enteritis losses were heavy.

In 1900 Mrs. Clinton Locke of Chicago registered Lockhaven Siam and Lockhaven Sally Ward, and the following year she signed up two chocolate points.

All the immigrants carried the genes for chocolate points, with its lighter body color, and the elegantly pale blue point; a blue point named Rhoda was registered in England in 1894. The recessive blue color is said to have been introduced by an all-blue jungle cat of Malaysia, a cross that was entirely the cat's idea. Two seal points with recessive blue genes will produce one blue for every three seal kittens. Blue and chocolate together produce some lilac points, and lilac to lilac will breed true.

All real cats.

Breeding out to plain cats, known as European cats in

Europe and American shorthairs in America, has produced some offbeat points like red and tabby, considered Siamese in England and Colorpoint Shorthairs in America. The English seem to go in for more vivid colors than the Americans, and in their pictures the English red points are a startlingly fiery red-orange and their blue points almost blue, rather than the dove color common here.

It seems to me there's a temperamental difference between the male and female Siamese, rather like the difference I imagine between lion and lioness. The male is lordly and swaggering and pleased with himself, laid back in his life-style and grandly demanding in his affections; he strolls into a room and expects to be applauded, he stretches in the sun with admiration of his splendid self. When living at home with his own female, he takes a nobly tolerant interest in his kittens and an affectionate, if casual, pride in their accomplishments.

The females, like lionnesses, are busy and responsible and fussy, and behave like loving but competent secretaries constantly reminding you of appointments. Morgan cries to be let into my desk drawers to sort through my papers, and keeps a close eye on the other cats and their health and behavior, and rounds them up in time for meals. She wants me out of bed on the tick of seven and back in it again at eleven, and paces back and forth across my book muttering discontentedly if I linger. Corvo thinks I'm well enough the way I am; Morgan is half distracted trying to whip me into shape. She is, however, a tireless and conscientious nurse to ailing man or beast, and would have made a model mother.

Siamese are considered among the best warriors and ratters, and kill snakes too; it's a pity more of them don't have an outdoors. They suffer very much from boredom in small spaces. It isn't a question of exercise, they always get plenty of that; they just long for the unexpected, the new, the odd encounter, the changing scene. Sameness gnaws at them.

Several sources claim that they don't get along with other breeds. This libel probably arose from their jealous passion for their people; the Siamese may have his problems, but he's no snob, as legions of half-breeds will testify. Indeed, the Siamese is a genetic factor in a whole swarm of breeding inventions: Balinese, Bombay, Colorpoint Shorthair, Havana Brown, Himalayan, Lilac Foreign Shorthair, Si-Rex, Manxamese, Oriental Shorthair, and Tonkinese. He enjoyed every minute of it.

Occasionally I see evidence in my two of a vague sense of kinship, and the younger will sometimes watch the older to see what he does so she can do it too, but they seem equally fond of the others.

The Siamese female goes into heat oftener and stays in it longer than anyone else, and makes an unendurable noise about it. Screaming, writhing, and prowling, she bellows with rage at the unarriving prince and wears herself down to the bone with exhaustion; neighbors, even quite distant neighbors, call the police. Her gestation period is longer than a house cat's, and her litters smaller. The kittens are tiny, pure white, and look like larvae. Often their eyes are half open at birth, but in other ways they're slow to develop and need a long childhood.

Siamese cats have been known to eat wool; I heard of one that ate a couch. One theory is that the lanolin in the wool reminds them of the scent around their mother's nipples, and it seems reasonable to guess that the wool eaters left home too young.

In the dark, blue Siamese eyes burn red as rubies instead of green or gold.

I can't leave the Siamese without considering that nameless breed of black cat usually associated with Siamese blood. It is not recognized. Officially, there is no such cat, and those of us who have known one, and we are surprisingly numerous, constitute an exclusive underground cat club, nameless by necessity. We refer to them as *those* cats, as in, "Oh, you have one of *those* cats! I had one once."

There's a recognized cat called the Oriental Shorthair, billed as a knowledgeable blend of Siamese, American

Shorthair, Colorpoint Shorthair, and other judicious ingredients, and it comes in exotic colors like Silver and Cameo Smoke, but that's not what we're talking about at all. The cats under consideration are black, and accidental. One source refers to a "royal cross," a splendid black sometimes produced from careful Siamese/Burmese mixing. That's not it either. I had a black Siamese/Burmese cross once, and she was so abysmally dull I finally got rid of her. Jean Cocteau adored a cat, "a kind of black semi-colon," the grandchild of his Siamese and his blue Persian, but that can't be it either.

Most owners of the magic black cats take it for granted that they're half or part Siamese, but in not one single case have I found a person who could prove it or even reasonably assume it. On the contrary; both my daughter and I, on unrelated occasions, found black kittens born to Siamese mothers and seized on them as certain to be those cats, and both grew up to be as ordinary as cats can be. The magic blacks are all changelings in the cradles of commoners. They come from the shelters; they come in off the streets, ripping furiously at the back door and shouting for admission; they are born among ordinary kittens. The little black cat who lives here now was born in a section of the country where no Siamese genes could be supposed to float among the population; dog and horse country, where any human owning a Siamese would be stoned clear to the county line. Her mother is a dumpy, fluffy, round-faced little person in gray stripes; she herself is one of those cats.

They stand out in a litter. Their ears are large and open, with a bald patch running down to the eyes, and their tails are long and thin. At an age when other kittens look like stuffed toys, they look like six pieces of oiled black string. They seem to mature early. The expression on their faces is extraordinary. They stare into your eyes with peculiar intensity, as if recognizing you in some more penetrating way than you have ever been recognized before. If this is a common mutation or a throwback to an extinct wild type, and if it's been around for a while, no wonder the Church chose the black cat as a supernatural emissary. Whether or not they're interested in buying your soul, they're certainly looking straight into it.

I went to the SPCA to get myself a kitten, and was shown a cage full of them, dozens of them napping and washing and wrestling together. Only one noticed me, and gave a piercing shriek, and climbed the wire of the cage to get as close as possible to my face, screaming all the while and staring steadily into my eyes with that extraordinary recognizing look: where had I been, what had kept me so long? I fell over myself in haste, apologizing, to get the attendant to let him out. That was Boy.

Those cats are exceptionally alert, brave, bossy, curious, and agile, and figure out ways to get into trouble that never occurred to the other cats in the house. They're clever with their hands, and use their mouths as an extra hand. While still quite small they take over the sacred places of the other cats. They eat like young wolves and get longer and heavier but no rounder; their flesh has a hard, spare, uncuddly quality, lean as cheetahs but weighing like bricks. When the baby fluff gives way to proper fur they look like wrought iron and shine like polished coal. Sitting up straight they have the long back and peaked breastbone of Egyptian statues. Their paws are small ovals on which they balance down the path like tightrope walkers.

With the right person, when they grow up they develop an exclusive, passionately possessive relationship, not always demonstrative but unmistakable. It's risky to leave them for long periods and criminal to give them away. Laps are not their milieu; they lie on the chest and neck and bite the chin, or simply sit and look at you. To other members of the family they're barely civil.

Sometimes the object of their love proves unworthy. I met a woman at a party, and we fell to talking of those cats. She had one; it had been her constant companion for six years, until she got another cat. When the new cat came, the black cat went down to the boiler room in the cellar and stayed there. The woman hopes she will die soon, as it's a nuisance going down there in the musty dark to feed it and change the litter. It's been eight years.

To the Siamese cat person the Persian is bland; to the Persian person the Siamese is noisy, demanding, and neurotic. Persians are noninvasive, and never shout. While the Siamese is bellowing for your attention, springing onto your shoulder and biting your cheek to get noticed, the Persian simply pats at your arm, over and over and over, and looks pained. They're gentle, though not nearly as gentle as they look: round eyes and long fur impress people immediately as the essence of gentleness, though the genetic connection would be hard to work out. People who dislike cats or are slightly afraid of them like Persians. Strong, great, lumbering men come to my house carrying refrigerators and such on their backs, and pause nervously on seeing the other cats. Then, on seeing Barney, snow-white and blue-eyed, they melt at once; now, there's a cat they could like. A *gentle* cat. From the emphasis, you'd think the average shorthair was a leopard balanced on the branch overhead.

Actually, even without claws Barney has strong jaws and sharp teeth and can use them to good effect when needed. When he was first mine, and we lived together in a ground-floor apartment, he attacked a police dog he thought was trespassing. The back door was accidentally ajar; the dog, attached to a policeman, was patrolling the alley, and Barney shot out and sprang on him without hesitation. I rushed after him; dog and policeman were both in shock. I apologized, I tried to detach Barney, and he turned and bit deeply into my hand. He was sorry about it, of course, but I was interfering in his guard duties.

Other cats aren't fooled by those cream puff looks. A friend of mine in difficulties parked her cat, an enormous black tom named Butcher, on me while she straightened out her life. Barney knew at once that this wasn't an addition to the family, only a passing guest. He never growled or hissed at Butcher, he never raised a paw, he simply sat on the bottom step of the staircase that led to the room where he and I slept and he looked at Butcher with his round pale eyes, and Butcher understood. The message was that Butcher could stay, as long as he stayed under the couch in the living room. All the way under the couch, out of sight. Since the litter pan was upstairs, and Butcher was under no circumstances to use the stairs, when he needed toilet facilities he could creep out at night while Barney was asleep and use the flowerpots in the kitchen. He could eat, but only if his bowl was shoved under the couch for him. All these instructions passed soundlessly through the air, and Butcher, his whiskers full of dustmice, obeyed.

Persians are fond of their homes and defend them, don't pine for adventure, and make good apartment cats.

The usual confusion obscures their roots. For a long time, "Angora" was considered a rather ignorant synonym for Persian, but current thinking holds them to be two separate cats, and the Turkish Angora one of the oldest recognized natural breeds, the name being a corruption of "Ankhara," and once the privileged pets of the harems of Constantinople. The Persian is variously claimed to be a mix of Angora and a longhair from Afghanistan, or the descendant of the central Asian Pallas's cat, or manul. One source mentions them in India. Turkey, Persia, Afghanistan, and even the near edge of India spread out in a long contiguous reach, and nationality can't have made much difference to native long-haired cats prowling through the centuries looking for mice and sex. Perhaps what we've come to consider local varieties would depend on what was locally admired, and cherished, and bred. Which king's harem took a fancy to which type.

Longhairs appeared in Europe in the late 1500s. Cardinal Richelieu, in the early 1600s, had an elegant black one named Lucifer among his feline retinue at court. The usual stories about Eastern royalty came with them, and if there were originally two distinct types they were freely mixed after they came west.

Concerned about the purity of what they felt was the true

Angora type, officials at the zoo in Ankhara recently undertook a breeding program with several pairs in what they felt was the authentic color, pure white, with blue or amber eyes. It was from these that an American army colonel brought back two pairs in the early 1960s, and breeders are working from their descendants. This authenticated Angora is longer and slenderer than the Persian, and its head is quite different, wedge-shaped, with a long foxy nose, slanted eyes, and big pointed ears. It carries its tail up over its back.

The Persian, on the other hand, is square and solid, deep-chested and short-legged, with short ears and nose on a big square head. It has big round eyes and an expression defined by some as "sweet" and by others as "mournful" or "imperious." The extremest type, the peke-faced, with a nose so short it's said to have trouble breathing, must have its admirers, though I can't think why.

The assertive, inquisitive, imaginative breeds enjoy a reputation for brains. It's harder to tell with the sedate Persian, but the ease with which Barney understood his new uncaged life at the age of ten speaks well for him. Curiosity may be a sign of intelligence, but contentment shouldn't be considered stupidity.

Dignified and affectionate, well-behaved and a bit lazy, the Persian has only two drawbacks: it seldom provides its owner with funny stories to tell at dinner parties, and it sheds. Some shed more than others. Friends of mine have a dark tortoiseshell with coarse, full-bodied fur that stays with her; she rarely has mats of hairballs, and doesn't create housekeeping and dry-cleaning problems. Barney's weightless fluff seems to be everywhere but on Barney in every month of the year. Where it does stay on him, it makes mats; he needs brushing and vacuuming. He much enjoys being vacuumed, and rushes over when I turn the thing on; it's one of his few pleasures now. Confined to quarters here, he sleeps a lot.

A Persian looks dramatic, but there's nothing dramatic about his temperament, and he wouldn't be first choice for people looking for an exciting relationship and major person-age in their lives. He's a fine choice, though, for those of us busy and away a lot. He'll wait, and be glad to see us when we do get home, unlike Siamese, who, when we come back, rage and sulk until it's time for us to leave again, and Abyssinians, who will have dismantled our closets and pulled all the papers out of our drawers and probably made a lot of long-distance calls on our bill.

What's called a Himalayan in these parts and a Colorpoint Longhair in England and a Khmer in France is just what it looks like, a blend of Siamese and Persian. Why, you may ask, when we already have the ancient and sturdy originals, each with its own distinct character, muddle around with a mix of the two and satisfy the aficionados of neither?

A.C. Jude, in an older book, *Cat Genetics,* called them merely "interesting," speaking as a geneticist, and doubted they would ever become popular. He was wrong.

They have been said to be delicate, perhaps due to inbreeding; one authority mentions a sixty percent mortality rate. Their fanciers say they have the sweet dispositions of Persians, though in this case we may have sweetness confused with imbecility. The only thing Siamese about them is the coloring. The few I've known seem shy and rather tentative, as if astonished by themselves, and why not? On the map we can see the unbridgeable miles between their two homelands; this isn't a blend they could have thought up for themselves, and they seem uncomfortable with it.

A breeder friend of mine had trouble with her Himalayan stud, who was chastely in love with his sister and had eyes for no other. Perhaps he was doing his bit to put a stop to the whole experiment. Just because a thing can be done doesn't mean it ought to be done.

Off the record, cat professionals warn against the taut and elegant Abyssinians. It's their ceaseless busyness; it makes them hard to manage. They pull the stitches out of their incisions and unfasten their splints and bandages. They take the house apart piece by piece and leap easily onto the curtain rods. "It gave me a headache just watching them," said an anonymous breeder. "Made me want to go and lie down."

Going and lying down is what they don't do. If part of the purpose of other cats is to teach us the blessing of peacefulness, the lesson of the Aby is industry.

A wide body of belief holds them to be the direct lineal descendants of the sacred kaffir cats of Egypt. One source says they were brought to England from Abyssinia, now Ethiopia, by returning British soldiers in the 1860s; another says firmly that they're unknown in Abyssinia. The English writer Grace Tabor, who wrote a book about her Aby Amber, says the Phoenicians originally took them to Egypt.

Another writer plainly considers them non-domesticus and says, a bit dubiously, that they have been tamed in parts of Europe.

They don't look tamed.

The distinctive thing about the Abyssinian is its ticked fur. Each hair is ruddy brown or red (or, now, blue) for three quarters of its length, and then ticked at the end with a double or triple bar. The underparts are solid cream or tawny. The ears are tufty. Altogether the effect is far from domesticated, the kind of creature that, if you saw it in the woods, would make you hold your breath and inch forward, careful not to startle it, to get a closer look.

They're generally considered to be the closest domestic cat (if you believe they're domestic cats) to the authentic, ancient, wild original (if you believe there was once a single original). Tabor says they've been called water cats, and were used to catch fish back in the dawn of things. They're strongly psychic, and see ghosts. Loving, rather timid, tirelessly curious, they have an uncontrollable passion for secrets, for the half hidden, the half closed, pocketbooks, bureau drawers, briefcases, the insides of cupboards and refrigerators. Flinging things over their shoulders, they rummage with the anxious intensity of a man who has lost something small but priceless in the laundry basket. When you yell at an Abyssinian, it gives you a look of utter, astonished innocence: Abys cannot be blamed.

If you live in close quarters, an Aby will have to keep itself busy by dismantling them. Two Abys will make twice as much mess but entertain each other.

Remember you were warned. They're happy cats, though. To have missed the joy is to have missed all.

Very recently, a cattery in Michigan, looking for an Aby-pointed Siamese in the usual dissatisfied way of catteries, crossed a Siamese and an Abyssinian, bred one of the kittens back to the Siamese, and to their astonishment came up with spots. The spots run horizontally along the cat, not at all like the vertical pattern of interrupted tabby stripes. Much as I disapprove of this kind of tinkering, the Ocicats are dazzling to look at, with the alert, affectionate faces of anyone's favorite puss and the wild spots of something that leaps for the jugular. They're expensive, scarce, and as artificial as possible, but they're certainly electrifying to see. In 1986, the CFA gave them provisional, or wait-and-see, status.

The friends of the brown Burmese insist that no one is more affectionate and loving than a Burmese, and it may be that they are right and I am wrong; stranger things have happened. My own feeling is that it's a question of heat. Burmese are heat freaks. To the standard query "Hot enough for you?" the Burmese answer is no. Burma, if that's really the country we're dealing with here, is famous for its swampy warmth. If the air in your house rarely gets above eighty degrees, and you sit there being ninety-eight point six, you will have a Burmese on your lap, and that Burmese will stay there until the room temperature reaches ninety-nine. If you're trying to work or eat or sleep, you can throw the Burmese on the floor, and it will be back almost before it hits bottom, and you can keep on throwing it till you're sobbing with rage and frustration and still it returns. They're enormously stubborn, and it's impossible to insult them or hurt their feelings; their golden stare defies you to penetrate their self-absorption. By night they sleep heavily across your throat, over the warm pulse point, and give you nightmares.

When the Siamese cat lies down heavily on your person, he is claiming your flesh as his personal property; when the Burmese does, he is warming his feet.

Bossy with other cats, they fret themselves unless clearly top cat, and may develop respiratory diseases if they don't get their own way.

Recently they've started appearing on the market in a rainbow of colors, red, lilac, blue, cream, and so on, which is confusing since their brownness was the point of them to start with, and it's odd to see their boxy little faces looking out from under cream-colored fur.

All American Burmese are descended from Wong Mau, who came from Burma and was taken up by a Dr. Joseph C. Thompson of San Francisco in 1930. With the help of the Siamese, Thompson established the breed. Wong Mau had powerful genes; Burmese are not Siamese at all.

If you want a cat on your lap and in your bed at all times, winter and summer, go Burmese. Don't get two of them, though; they will ignore you and sleep with each other, because a cat's normal temperature is around 101 degrees.

The Maine Coon Cat is a great big longhair. People love it. It would be dangerous to criticize it, and what is there to criticize?

They're considered the indigenous American cat; since America's history is so brief a hundred years makes an indigene. The notion of their part-raccoon heritage is charming, and if such a cross were possible I'd be first in line for a kit; but alas, it isn't. The accepted theory is that they're the result of plain short-hairs, brought from Europe by settlers, mixed with Persians or Angoras brought by seafarers, perhaps a Captain Coon, in the 1800s. I can't quarrel with authority, but it seems odd that this doesn't happen anymore. Cross a Persian and a house cat and you get a fluffy house cat. You get Sidney, round-eyed, lazy house cat. The first official Maine

Coon, Captain Jenks of the Horse Marines, surfaced in 1861, not giving the genes much time to change in response to the environment. Besides, why were they all outside in the environment, these sons and daughters of Persians and house cats?

A romantic but unofficial theory implicates the Norwegian Forest Cat, a similar creature domestic in Scandinavia for centuries, and just possibly left on our northern coast by Vikings long before Columbus. British experts sniff, and say the Coon is a recent and artificial breed, while the Norsk Skaukatt is ancient, pure, and natural, and not an ancestor because its back legs are longer, but it seems clear they're jealous; no British cat has such panache.

Inspecting a generous sampling of both, and all unversed in anatomy as I am, I found them very hard to tell apart.

Along about the time of the Civil War and after it, Coon Cats grew in popularity, attracted national attention, and won ribbons in shows until the Persian invasion at the turn of the century, when people lost interest in the mere native. Because they faded from the show circuit, show people thought they had become extinct, but of course they were doing just fine back home.

In the late 1920s, the naturalist Henry Beston spent a year on Cape Cod, writing his classic book *The Outermost House*. "Twice during the winter," he says, "I saw a wildcat of domestic stock hunting along the edge of the marsh, and marked how savagery had completely altered the creature's gait, for it slunk along, belly close to the grass, like a panther. A large brown cat with long fur and an extraordinarily foolish face."

Leaving aside the naturalist who thinks domestic cats stalk their prey standing up straight and tall, and the scientific description of its face as "foolish," surely he saw a Maine Coon Cat rustling its breakfast on the Cape, not in the least extinct and, foolish or not, at least as capable and independent as Mr. Beston, who kept bumming rides into town to buy his groceries.

Maine cats make splendid instructive parents, and the

kittens, who adore them and mature slowly, shouldn't leave home till they're twelve weeks old. They grow into considerable cats, weighing eighteen pounds and up, and rather clumsy on their big snowshoe feet, with brushy raccoon tails, loud purrs, merry dispositions and a grand self-possession. They like water, and that bushy coat is protected by a water-resistant oil for swimming; even when soaked, a Coon Cat is said to dry in fifteen minutes.

I went to a party in the suburbs. At exactly eleven o'clock in the evening a guest said, "There's someone at the door." Our host opened the door and stood staring blankly out into the empty darkness at eye level while an enormous cat stalked in around his feet. It marched across the room, ignoring the guests all reaching to pat it and crying "What a beautiful cat!", and stopped in front of George and Pat, and looked at them. It did not meow or rub against their ankles; it stood there and looked at them. They jumped up and made their apologies, found their coats and said goodnight and left, following the Coon Cat, who led them out looking neither to left nor right, for all the world like the father of errant teenagers come to fetch them home.

Fine fellows.

The Manx cat is not part rabbit, though the *Britannica* does hint mysteriously at a possible derivation from "another species." As far as we know, rabbits mate only with other rabbits, and are looked on by cats more as dinner than romance, and the notion is only slightly more probable than the story of how they arrived late at the Ark and Noah slammed the door on their tails. They seem to come from the Isle of Man in the Irish Sea, but since this is an insignificant area of only 221 square miles, various theories are put forth as to what larger place they arrived from. Some say Spain, swimming ashore from a shipwrecked galleon of the Armada. Some say China or Japan, because there's a tailless cat of long history called the Japanese Bobtail, considered very lucky when it turns up in three colors, though actually it may have been Korean to start with. The most recent investigations, however, conclude that it's genetically quite a different cat, and the Manx may come from Man after all; one source observes that there are tailless dogs on Man.

A single stubborn authority maintains that there is no Manx cat, and taillessness is simply a genetic freak that can turn up in any breed at any time.

Some Manx cats have no tail at all, just a dimple at the base of the spine, and some, called "stumpies," have part of a tail, and some have proper tails. My sister's Mehitabel, long-haired and of unknown origin, has half a tail; two of her daughters have real tails, and the third has a two-inch downward hook of a tail like a spit curl.

Among the Manx, only the quite tailless cat is eligible for showing. But breeders need to keep a few stumpies around for breeding, because there's a lethal factor in the missing tail; in the mating of tailless cats, the third generation will be weak and sickly and the fourth will be stillborn. There's something a bit skewed in the human encouragement of such a suicidal trait.

Manx cats have plushy undercoats and long hind legs like rabbits, and they swim well, as befits islanders.

Gray cats are nice. All gray cats, recognized or not, are nice; when they're recognized they're called blue cats. Each nation claims to have its own, and though to the untrained eye they look remarkably alike, each nation feels its own is best.

Malaysia has its blue jungle cat, and the light gray cat of Cyprus has black pads on its feet. Malta has its Maltese cats, and American gray cats with no exotic connections were once always referred to as Maltese, giving them status above their littermates to the human eye.

The Korat, native of Thailand, is silvery with green or amber eyes. For centuries it could not be sold, only presented as a gift to a deserving friend because of its great luckiness, signifying wealth and crops and happy marriages.

The Russian Blue, in the more exalted version, came straight from the Imperial Palace; more prosaically, it came to England on cargo boats trading with Archangel in the far north, on the White Sea, a charming place for a cat to come from. They have dense, double-layered fur suitable for such northern cats, and graceful, delicate, long-boned bodies with long tails and big pointy ears. Their eyes are green. Saha, in Colette's *The Cat*, was a Russian Blue, exquisite, sensitive, and adoring, whose master had to choose between her and his bride, and chose her.

Colette's own last cat was a Chartreux. The Chartreux is a French gray, and a country sort of cat, good-natured and simple, Méry says, solid and stocky and round-faced, with short legs and woolly fur and great enthusiasm for mousing. It's been around since the Middle Ages, and is said to have come from southern Africa with Carthusian monks who named it for their first monastery, La Grande Chartreuse.

The British Blue is a British citizen type, neat and sturdy-looking, with orange, yellow, or copper eyes. Some English experts think it's the same as the Chartreux, a notion patriotically ridiculed by the French. And some writers refer to both the British and the Russian as Icelandic cats.

Georges I, II, and III were all gray; Flanagan is gray; Al and Leila and their kittens are gray. Gray alley cats, American cats, melting-pot cats. Not blue, because born at random to cats of great ordinariness working plebeian breeding ranges: gray. Gray with a plushy density of fur, all the same length like sheared beaver. Gray with silvery edgings and highlights about the paws, the ears, the twinkling testicles. Gray with eyes as yellow as suns. Loyal. Cheerful. Enormously *likable* cats, cats for the daily living, the long haul; cats as sound and friendly as a loaf of good bread. Solid cats, but with a touch of delicacy as they come toward you across the morning grass, putting one foot tidily in front of the other like Siamese, tail high, happy to be there.

Geneticists would scoff, and say there is no gray cat, only a genetically diluted manifestation of black, but this isn't true. Grays are good for you. They make you feel better about life.

They're easy to love. Teddy Roosevelt's gray cat Slippers was always allowed at important diplomatic dinners, and the sixteenth-century poet du Bellay wrote in anguished mourning:

> *My heart is almost breaking in me*
> *When I speak or when I write*
> *For Belaud my small gray cat.*

The Sidneys of the world, the random patches of black and white, represent an interesting genetic battle in which the white moves in an orderly progression. First the locket under the chin, perhaps a bikini-pants crescent, then the bib, then the white toes. The bib spreads down along the stomach and the toes creep up into stockings. Fingers of white extend up the sides, broadening into peninsulas. It always moves up from below; we never see a cat white on top and black or gray or striped below. A cat in the next block to me represents a late stage, white all over but for four or five roundish black spots along the spine, more doggish than cattish. And in a pet shop I saw the very last stand, a white cat with a single brush-stroke of black on the top of the head, between the ears; in the genetic chess game of black against white, white has won.

Black-and-whites come in some pleasant patterns, like Sidney's big clear butterfly over the head, and in some cluttered and unappealing ones, and the cats themselves are various. In Judy's colony they form an astonishing majority, their arrivals all quite unrelated, and their only common trait is that they either love their home, or are inordinately fond of food, or dislike adventure: all day long the cats of other colors are invisibly off about their catly business in woods and fields, and all day long there are six black-and-whites disposed about the lawn where the feeding dishes are, not communing with each other, each at least eight feet from the next, but there. At dinnertime they will not need to be called.

Sidney too is a trencherman, never called for dinner or before an approaching storm; he was already home.

They're comfortable cats, the black-and-whites, and will never run up the grocery bill by demanding designer food. Mr. Eliot's amiable uncomplicated Jellicle cats are good examples.

So many blue-eyed white cats are deaf that an impressive weight of authority holds that all blue-eyed white cats are deaf, even that white kittens born blue-eyed whose eye color changes later stay deaf for as long as their eyes stay blue, miraculously developing hearing only after the color turns.

Barney is a blue-eyed white cat.

Barney can hear a cat chow drop three rooms away. Barney can hear the difference between milk and water being poured into a bowl.

He can hear his name whispered a block away. He can hear paint drying, grass growing, hair turning gray, time passing. He can hear words that have never been spoken and songs that no one else will ever hear.

He can hear me thinking about him.

I hope that clears up the matter.

Striped cats are basic. Stripes are so essentially cat that they're the bane of breeders, and come creeping forward out of the buried generations to flower in shadowy bands down the legs of cats that aren't supposed to have stripes. Stripes are the irresistible jungle that keeps on whispering in the well-bred ear.

Striped cats are satisfying to look at, with their elaborate, inscrutable details, the lavishment of necklaces and bracelets, the *M* for Mau inscribed on the forehead, and the infinitely pleasing shades of cream and tawny around the eyes, the nose, and the whisker pads with their dark freckles marking the base of each hair. Striped cats are household hieroglyphics, undeciphered messages washing their paws after dinner and waiting to be read. Is it our fault or theirs, or the strange language they're written in, that no one seems to have a deep personal relationship with a striped cat? The experts, agreeing for once, say that the striper is closest to the wild; several say that of all the colors of cat this is the best able to survive on its own, and that it's noticeably more independent and predatory than its siblings, and makes the best mouser. Is it true? It sounds about as scientific as that blondes have more fun. Could it be that we believe it ourselves, and treat the striper differently, more respectfully but less intimately, because this is serious cat here, not an extra child to be cuddled but the Cat by its Wild Lone, and the cat reacts aloofly? Or did it start out a bit more distant, a bit less cheery and loving, than its solid-color littermates? All I know is that none of the striped cats in my life have ever been intimates, just respected associates.

Not that they're unfriendly. There's a photograph of the older Ernest Hemingway sharing his dinner and apparently conversing with a striped cat on his table; it's just that it was probably Hemingway and not the cat who started the conversation, or else the cat was merely listening, or pretending to listen.

As to whether they survive better on their own, proving this would involve getting a number of cats of the same age and different colors and dropping them off in the woods, and coming back some months later and rounding up the survivors and weighing them. It sounds impractical.

They are very wonderful to look at, though. The sheer luxury of their design and shadings puts all human attempts at personal decoration to shame. And even considered as the humble necessary mouser of the millennia, the unassimilated cat of barn and kitchen and cellar and granary, is that an unworthy calling? The striped cat is first of all a *cat*.

I'm looking at a photograph I took of two cats that I met, if "met" isn't too strong a word, in an isolated village on the Pacific coast of Mexico. They were a mated pair and they lived around a beachside restaurant specializing in fish; the restaurant was open to the world on all four sides, so they came and went as they pleased. People fed them from the tables, though they never asked for food in any way we know as asking. They would sit near a table, looking at nothing and no one, gazing indifferently into space, until a piece of fish was dropped at their feet; they ate it without acknowledgment as if it had fallen from the sky.

Whose cats are those? I asked. A shrug and a laugh. They were no one's cats. They were their own cats. They lived there, that was all.

To the best of my limited knowledge, they were Egyptian Gloved Cats, the image of the cat in the temple I'd seen on television. Broken stripes of black on gray, tawny cheeks and ears, barred legs and tail, white toes. Long cats, with long, long tails that had a curiously massive and imposing shape, like a cheetah's, narrowing as it joined the body, with broad assertive bands.

They were in splendid shape, elegant and strong. What were they doing here, these North Africans, half a world away in this scruffy, mountainous, appallingly poor stretch of western Mexico, where occasionally in the night bigger cats could be heard coughing in the hills? A pet cat here, if anyone could have imagined such a thing, would have starved along with its people.

When I approached and spoke to them, their indifference rebuked me. They didn't respond, and they didn't run away; they ignored me so utterly I felt rather drafty, as if abruptly disembodied, mixed with air. This is unsettling to humans. We're used to animals who either greet us or avoid us, or in some cases attack us, not animals for whom we simply don't exist. I felt diminished and a bit embarrassed, as if I had slapped the back of a stranger in a crowd.

This is how it was, then? Back in the beginning, with the first of people's cats? The only animal that showed us no fear, no hostility, and no acquiescence, that simply came to eat our fish and stare past us into space? No wonder we were fascinated. No wonder we searched out the hidden kittens and cuddled them, trying to coax some acknowledgment from those remote yellow eyes—if not thanks for the fish, then at least some hint that we were there, and seen.

We succeeded. Now we have only to ask in order to have one of our own, in our house, blinking affectionately at us and purring with pleasure in our company.

Traveling by various means, sailing with Phoenicians, jumping ship in strange ports, coming west with returning Crusaders, strolling across national borders in Southeast Asian jungles and Himalayan passes and East African deserts, traded for bananas or silk or amber, mating with the locals and moving on, cats cover the earth and spring up in such infinite variety it's a wonder any of us can be content with just two or three when there are so many others waiting to be known; a cornucopia of cats.

Show Business

9

The hall is arranged with rows of cages across its middle, seven judging rings along the sides, and things for sale at the ends. In the aisles between the cages exhibitors have set up housekeeping on folding tables and chairs and boxes and fallen to eating, napping, reading magazines, and playing cards, like a band of travelers in an airport waiting out a storm. It's hard to push past them, hard to see into the cages to the cats. But of course that's not the purpose of the thing; no one cares whether I see cats or not. These owners and breeders are dressed in a motley assortment of garments, as if there'd been a fire in the hotel, or all their luggage had gone astray. At dog and horse shows the people seem as much on view as the animals and size up each other's tweeds with covert glances, but these cat people give off a thorny intransigence and have scarcely bothered to comb their hair. After all, this isn't the big one. Madison Square Garden has already come and gone, leaving all hands with tales of its blizzard, and airports and highways closed; perhaps they dressed for that one, and have made their effort for the season.

This is only the second cat show of my life, and all I remember of the first one is that I took my impulsive little sister and she spent three weeks' salary on a rather self-centered Persian kitten named Mokey, leaving me with the impression that they were dangerous events to attend, and of dubious purpose. Watching hunting dogs at field trials or horses racing, horses cutting cattle, or horses in the Handy Hunter Over Fences or the Knockdown and Out, it's nice to see what animals can do. They seem to like it too, and why not? It's satisfying to do things well, whether or not they appreciate the competitive point of view and the ribbons afterward. But cats are shown only for their looks, and how their looks conform to standards inexplicable to the cat or even the uninitiated human. The catliness of them is not at issue; they might as well be framed and hung on the wall.

Here I am, though. Stepping warily. Prepared to sneer.

The program says the exhibitors will be happy to explain and discuss their cats with me, but the program is wrong. Even people with signs saying "Kittens for Sale" are laconic and suspicious and go on laying out a round of solitaire. Maybe they were up too late last night, or got up too early to polish fur and backcomb tails. They barely chat among themselves, and no one greets another with cries of recognition; this is not a social occasion. They sit, blocking the view, in front of their cages, each of which has a sign saying "I'm Friendly But My Owner Bites," or "Touch Not the Cat," or "Don't Touch Me Even if I Ask," or "Your Kind Affection Could Result in Infection." Some cages are fronted with plastic wrap. I feel a bit leprous, my hands aswarm with invisible poisons.

Most of the cats are sensibly asleep.

One of the cages in the first row contains a patterned dollhouse rug on the floor, an elaborate standing lamp, and a four-poster bed with chintz bolsters and matching ruffled coverlet on which a Persian kitten is asleep. It's a pretty kitten in one of those pale Persian designs I can't keep straight,

Cameo maybe, and doesn't seem at all affronted by life in a dollhouse. Other cages are fitted with curtains for withdrawing behind, or triangular ledges in the corners for lolling on, and one cat has retired into a drawstring bag and left only an ear showing. Ribbons, I suppose from earlier shows, hang across the wire like medals on a military chest: Second Best in Division, Best in Class, Fifth Best Kitten.

Many people have invested in pipe-cleaner tarantulas to hang from the ceilings of the cages, and several cats have already hooked them down to chew on.

A number of cats are sleeping in their litter boxes, paws decorously curled under chests.

Later a prize will be awarded for the best-decorated cage. A stand at the end is selling cage decorations.

The stands are doing a brisk business in sacks of scientific cat food, stuffed plush cats, coat conditioners, silvery cat bracelets and pendants and cat-shaped plastic earrings, mountains of pins and T-shirts and bumper stickers and mugs and decals and dish towels saying "I (heart) My Cat," ". . . My Burmese," ". . . My Manx," and so on, carpeted posts and platforms called Custom Cat Houses, kitty candies, collars, books, toys, toys, toys. A genial girl has set up a stand featuring home-grown catnip and toys thereof; already she's sold out of the pots of growing catnip. I buy a plastic bag of the straight stuff, to be assured later at home that it is indeed the real thing.

An official-looking woman strides by with a blue-point Siamese on her shoulder, an incongruous Siamese of the old-timey, chunky, round-faced type; I try to speak to it, but the woman hurries on.

The standard of manners among the cats is high. No one yowls, no one rips its cage apart, no one seems angry or nervous, and only one of a pair of Burmese kittens is frightened to see me and tries to hide behind his sister. The rest are old-timers. All but the Household Pets are unneutered, but no cat seems interested in its neighbors or the cats passing to and from the judging rings.

People are eating from paper plates what looks like cat

food; in their cages cats are not eating what looks like the same stuff.

I come to a pair of young Singapuras and stop to stare. I've never seen one before, and they give the whole hall a momentary zoolike feel. They have slick lion-blond fur, ticked like an Aby's, and cross-looking dark lines running down beside their noses like cheetahs. Natives of Singapore. Small but dangerous-looking; something you'd bring home as an orphan from the jungle only to have it turn savage later and eat your left arm. They're asleep, but they sleep alertly. If I woke up to find one of these curled on the pillow beside me, I expect I'd scream.

Shorthair kittens are being judged in ring 3, a ring being a stainless steel table in front of a bank of cages. The judge is holding up a white Oriental Shorthair by each end, like a length of ribbon, and discussing it quietly to herself; I think she says she'd like to see it lose a quarter of a pound. How? From where? Cut off one of its enormous ears? There's no cat there to reduce; it's narrow as a newt, an albino snake with albino bats for its ears. It's hardly wider than its own tail; where does it put its dinner? Every mouthful must leave a lump. Its head is shaped like a log-splitting wedge; its legs are thin as pencils. I try to imagine it taking its place in the semicircle of barn cats around old Mrs. Reid, who was Finnish and milked by hand, and catching its squirt of milk when its turn came. Try to imagine it catching a mouse, or even a spider.

The judge puts it back in its cage next to a black sample of the same thing, the insides of whose ears are pure white, like a black satin smoking jacket lined with white silk. All these cats are like something else besides cats, exaggerated beyond cathood into artifact.

In the next ring a judge returns two Persians to their cages, held on high in each hand like a giant's orange fur mittens.

My judge picks up a plumey feather and walks along the cages waving it at the bars. Some jump for it, gaining points,

I suppose; others merely stare and look offended. The kitten in the last cage screams like a rusty gate: a Siamese. The only Siamese in the class. She continues to yowl after the judge moves on, as if suddenly fed up with the proceedings, reminded by the feather maybe that there are better things to do.

Once focused on her, my eyes don't want to leave, and I stand there gaping and tracing over her shapes, drawn in brown-black ink on cream-colored paper; the precise coil of her thin, dark tail against her creamy hip could not be improved by all the calligraphers in Japan. As she sits there shouting at no one, her furious little profile is a bone-and-fur reconstruction of what every unborn creature must hope to look like, sooner even than a swan or a luna moth. Probably she was a saint in some earlier round of things, as the Birman cats are said to embody the souls of dead priests, and the purity of her first life, dedicated to constant contemplation of some single perfect truth, is reborn in these lines and colors. There's nothing luxurious about her, nothing lavish or extra; she's an ink drawing, not a painting, and I lace my hands behind my back not to accidentally touch and smudge it. If she were mine, I'd probably forget to feed her, or feed her on drops of honey like a hummingbird. Herb tea in a painted porcelain cup.

It dawns on me that one of the two men standing beside me owns her. I slide him a sideways glance: an ordinary mortal sort of man. His companion is saying, "I remember you said you were pleased with her refinement."

"Refinement"? Well, yes, if that's the best word we can find. "Refined," as in gold.

The two men have their catalogs folded back and make marks in them, apparently understanding something from their pages. I open my own copy. To me it's an Arabic train schedule, a Coptic stock-market report. "JB MC PM BM, AB AB AB AB. BR/OW. (NE) 0.11. SGC TYPHA NITE SPRITE." Where am I? I search for the same page they have. All right, if this is really the page, and this is the only SP kitten, then her name is Soroko Forever Amber. Preposterous, there's nothing amber about her; if he must name cats from his bookcase, why not Soroko The Jungle Book? Soroko Anna Karenina? The man's unworthy. The man, if I have the right page and the right cat, is listed as a doctor. Not even a Buddhist priest. And why isn't she looking at him? She shouts, but she's glaring off somewhere to the left.

I don't really want his cat, though; it isn't because of her that I've left my checkbook safely at home. There's no place to put her where I live. Be she ever so adaptable, there is no corner in my house, no chair, no windowsill, that she wouldn't disgrace by her presence; nothing I own would be a suitable place for Soroko Forever Amber to sit. And what of the doctor? He's listed as BR/OW, which must mean breeder/owner, which must mean he has a houseful of these, or a catteryful; does he keep them in cages, rows of them in patient captivity, with the thin white flames of their holiness waiting for rebirth or liberation to nirvana?

He seems discontented. Listening, I learn that if the show had been just one day later she would have been eight months old and eligible to show as an adult. This kitten class counts for nothing, doesn't accumulate the right kind of points; it's practice only, a waste of his time. He scowls and ruffles the pages of his catalog, his karma roiled and seething.

The judge hangs ribbons from the cages, the doctor goes to get his cat, and I turn away, remembering only later that I hadn't noticed if she won anything. I think one of the Chartreux kittens beat her, handsome chubby fellows. It doesn't seem to matter.

Needing solid earth, I go to visit the Household Pets, and speak to them in normal, irreverent tones. There are fewer vigilant owners on guard here, so they're easier to see. Unburdened by family standards to uphold, they look well fed, these normal cats, and unremarkable, and I'm secretly pleased that none is as stylish as my little black Spider, and none of the black-and-whites has Sidney's sweet nose and outlined eyes, or his whimsical markings. A spark of competitiveness darts through me; it must be in the air here: I should have brought Spider. Spider would win. I leaf through a booklet they've given me to the piece on Household Pets. They're judged, it says, giving 25 points for their looks, 15 for personality, and 60 for "condition." A health contest, then. That must be hard to gauge; it's easy to see how sick a sick cat is, but how do you measure its healthiness on, say, a scale of one to ten? Sickness is relative; health, unless they've planned a rope climb and some footraces to assess it, is health. I won't bring Spider; this is patronizing, a contest for schoolchildren, complete with lecture on nutrition afterward. I can see the point, in a way, of judging how good an Aby an Aby is, how like the perfect Aby, but there's no way to judge the goodness of a Household Pet; that's a private matter between pet and person.

The woman with the blue point on her shoulder hurries past again, cat swaying, and I realize to my chagrin that this isn't a hefty old-time Siamese at all, but a Tonkinese, a new Burmese-Siamese blend. After all the years of narrowing and shrinking the Siamese and sharpening its angles, people must have been nostalgic for the old ones, and turned them backward with Wong Mau's blood into meatier cats again, with softer fur and gentler faces.

I don't belong here; I'm out of my depth; I don't even recognize half what I'm looking at.

I look for and don't find the highly publicized California Spangled Cat, something new that's been rather a celebrity and appeared on television. Somebody dedicated almost beyond the point of sanity took eleven generations to produce it, working with a Siamese, Silver Tabby, Manx, Abyssinian, Cat of the Nile, Brown Tabby, Malayan Tropical Housecat, and a Spotted Silver Longhair: a veritable cat stew. It has spots. It was featured in the Neiman-Marcus Christmas catalog as "a leopard for your living room" and sold for fourteen hundred dollars; they had dozens more orders than kittens, and the waiting list is years long. In spite of its price it hasn't been recognized as a breed yet, so it gets to stay home in the living room instead of traveling around in a box.

Someone has taken a Scottish Fold from its cage for a

quick touch-up, and I've never seen one of these before either. The fancy-cat world moves too fast for me. They're one of the genetic accidents, descended from a farm cat named Susie born in 1961 in Perthshire with her ears folded down. This struck the neighbors as interesting, and they put her into the kitten business. Breeding from only a single, accidental cat, they ran into problems and some of the Folds were born with skeletal deformities and some were born deaf, but the breeders, so fiercely do we lust for peculiar cats, persevered, and they're well established now, with fifty or more catteries doing business in the United States. They're said to be gentle and playful cats who like to sleep on their backs and to sit around on their haunches with their tails stuck out behind like beavers.

Now I hear we're about to have something similar of our own, the American Curl, whose ears bend inward as if it were standing in a private eddy of wind.

This Fold submits to a small plastic blade that scoops and peaks up the fur on its nose to a jaunty ridge, visible at close quarters and lasting only until the first paw swipe. The folded ears alter its expression so much that I can't tell how it feels or what it's thinking. What do other cats make of it? It looks a little like an owl and a little like a Beatrix Potter cat wearing a bonnet; Tom Kitten's mother, maybe.

One problem, I understand, is that the female's ears straighten out when she goes into heat, and may or may not fold up again afterward. While I'd love to be around at the onset of estrus to watch the ears unfurl with longing, it still seems less cat than conversation piece, and I always worry that there may be a God somewhere who doesn't like us fooling around with His cat like this.

At least it wears fur, though, fur like a cat. This show has a generous share of curly Rexes and wrinkled, naked, suede Sphynxes; it even turns out that there are two kinds of Rex, Cornish and Devon. "Elfin" is the word the booklet uses, and perhaps elves are what they look like, elves from outer space. I study them with quick glances and look away again as my mother told me to: "Don't stare, darling, it's rude." They're tiny cats with ears bigger than their heads and bulging out sideways like loaded saddlebags. How did we make them look like this in such a short time, starting from a farm in Cornwall in 1950 and an accidentally curly kitten named Kallibunker? And, of course, why? From the corner of my eye I stare at a cat intended to be black and white but actually, thanks to our tireless efforts, black and pink; the rows of short, soft, poodley curls are so sparse that pink skin shows through. Its face is a tiny dog's face under the absurd ears; we're ambivalent about ears, apparently, so that Persians and Folds are admired for having almost none, while these poor creatures must need guy ropes on a windy day. Its whiskers are gnarled stubs, as if a wicked child had singed them with a match.

Embarrassed for it, I go off to watch the judging of Norwegian Forest Cats. Now, these are cats, real cats, these Norsk Skaukatts, an honest armful of cat with honest whiskers and long, solid fur. For some reason we humans were pleased with them just as they were, and no effort has been made to make them twice as much like themselves. I check my pocketbook to make sure I have indeed left my checkbook at home.

There's one in particular, a female (even I can see that some of the numbers are on pink cards and some on blue) whose mix of cream and dark fur, whatever it's called, is pleasing to look at and whose charm and cheerfulness flow from her cage. Behind the judge's back she has hooked a prize ribbon from outside her cage and brought it inside with a delicate curled paw, and pats it around the floor and chews on its string. When the judge takes it away and fastens it up more firmly, she turns her attention to the male in the next cage, reaching her paws out to play with him, standing up to show us the waterfall of fur down her stomach. A feminine cat, the creamy ruff and flowing bib showing off her sweet face like a hat on a pretty girl, and she likes the young man next door. I will have them both, then, and have kittens.

The checkbook is safely home on the bureau.

The judge gives the feather test; only this judge uses an orange ball on a bouncy wire, and one cat cringes and hisses at it. My cat reaches out for it with both arms to the shoulder through the bars. A happy cat. I try to look her up in the catalog, but I can't find my way through the pages.

The judge passes out ribbons, but I don't know what they mean. Cat shows are not a spectator sport. Any fool at a horse show can see Number 27 refuse the In-and-Out, or hear the bonk when a hock clips the top bar, but in this place you have to belong to know what's going on. Or, I suppose, to care.

I pick my way back through the card tables, down the row of Rexes. The black-and-pink has been taken from its cage by its owner, a motherly-looking woman in a low-cut blouse seated on a folding chair. I smile nervously down at it. I'm told they feel warm to the touch, like puppies, because of the short fur. I try not to notice its whiskers.

As I pass, it worms its way up the woman's front and buries its face in her neck, nuzzling and licking, and begins to purr. I stop to listen; yes, it's purring. *Purring? That?* I'm as shaken as if a frog had said "meow." Distorted, monstrous, warped by human meddling till God Himself wouldn't know it as a cat, it thrusts its head against its human's neck and purrs as if it had a right to purr. It's a *cat.* I suppose it must eat its dinner and wash its paws, sprawl on the rug in the sunshine, all those things, as if it didn't know or humbly accepted what we've done to it. All our long, expensive efforts to turn cat into not-cat have been in vain; strong as wire, catness still runs humming through the generations of increasingly uncatlike cats, and just like Kallibunker's mother on her Cornish farm, this thing can purr. Leave it alone for a few generations and it would cure its own monstrosity, flesh out, grow fur, have real ears and whiskers. Persians that snuffle like bulldogs would grow their noses back; Siamese that look like strings would broaden, and catch mice.

The cat triumphant. Cats 10; people 0.

Satisfied, I get my coat and leave.

Medical Matters

10

Cats feel pretty good most of the time. They rarely indulge in the ailments so popular on television: the common cold, flu, headaches, insomnia, sinus pain, indigestion, lower back pain, hangovers, coffee nerves, sore throats, and sunburn. On any given day they probably feel better than we do. They live the way we should, and while they may eat an occasional button or length of thread, they never go out and buy junk food full of salt, fats, and sugar, and they don't need exercise clubs to keep the muscles taut; an occasional dash up the curtains and a little stretching does it.

Their talent for sleeping anywhere and any time is enviable. Their capacity for contentment keeps the heart and nerves and gastric juices in the pink. If they've eaten unwisely, and even sometimes when they haven't, they vomit swiftly and easily. They do not stress their systems with office politics, nuclear war, the stock market, or whether their children are using drugs, but live contained in the savored moment, an example to us all. And the lucky cats of responsible people have the advantage of dizzying recent progress in feline veterinary medicine.

It's as well they don't get sick often, because a sick cat is a discouraging creature to nurse. We go to the grocery store and buy a lamb chop, get down the heating pad and the cashmere shawl, sit beside it, and speak gently; it turns its head aside. A cat friend licks its head and ears and curls up next to it; it turns its head aside. Struggles to its feet and staggers off the heating pad, out from under the shawl, steps over the bits of lightly broiled lamb chop and crouches on the cold bare floor with eyes averted: it will not take comfort. Cats can sicken with terrifying suddenness, and in this as in other things they do not persevere; like the American Indian of cherished legend they compose themselves for death. Love and kindness cease to matter, and they avoid looking us in the eye, lest we learn what they have in mind.

A cat in extremis will manage to get to the front door, even if it has never been outside, and scratch at it, begging permission to go away and be alone with dying. Go out and meet it halfway.

All the more urgency for professional medical care, with cats; for doctors to grab the departing cat by the scruff of the neck, so to speak, overrule its decision, and snatch it back to us.

Sometimes. Not always, of course. Not forever.

Sidney is sick. Sidney, who has never been sick for a moment in his seventeen years, has one of the swift and sudden cancers of feline leukemia virus. One day he was playing with the kitten and wolfing down his dinner, and the next day he sat hunched between his elbows looking at the floor. The cancer can be treated to a certain extent, but only until the kidneys go.

The kidneys go.

Two Siamese cats, kindly young Morgan and cross old Corvo, sit one on each side of him and lick him tirelessly. His white patches have never been so clean.

You'll know, the vet says; his back legs will give out.

His back legs give out. Flopping and staggering, he makes his way to the front door and asks permission to leave.

Morgan, Corvo, and my daughter sit up with him all night. He sighs, he moves from one position to another, uncomfortable everywhere. He goes back to the door and hooks a paw under it. Morning comes. Wrapped in a bright red towel, he makes his last trip to the vet.

It's a decision often described as harrowing, but not now, not here. It's almost a joy, and a fine thing we have in our hands here for our cats, to shorten the hard journey. Lift them over the last bad mile.

We can't do this for people we love, but we can do it for our cats and rejoice. We can't give our children a good life, either; all we can do is start them on their way and hope: we can give our cats a good life. We cry, of course, everyone cries, but we keep saying to each other, Didn't he have a grand time of it, though? Didn't we spoil him, the old slob? He was always petted and babied, even the other cats babied him, in all his life he never once washed his own face. He was an uncomplicated cat, and easily content. He loved to eat and to sit in the sun. He had a fine time.

The saddest note is young Morgan, who searches the house for days, upstairs and down, wearing herself to a rag and pausing only to stand in front of me and shout angrily into my face; she seems to think I have lost him, and forgotten about him. All she knows is that he was sick and she was taking care of him, and now he's nowhere to be found; perhaps in the basement, weak and forgotten behind some boxes? Perhaps up on the third floor accidentally closed in a closet? How can I sit there, and not join her in looking? She is furious with me and will not be touched.

I hope someday there will be a pill for home use, and that last frightening trip not be necessary, and the cats and people gather around the familiar couch to say good-bye, and the cats know what became of a friend.

After a week or so she stops looking. Life goes on.

The first rule of cat ownership is to protect ourselves

from guilt. "Well, we did everything possible ..." is sad enough to have to say, but it doesn't sting like "If only we'd ..."

When things end badly, it helps to know we had the world's best vet. It's important to be sure. Most of them are conscientious, but some are more skillful surgeons, and better informed. Some are principally interested in dogs and don't make the steady effort to keep up with fast-breaking developments in cat treatment. A cheerful, confident, friendly bedside manner with the human client is no indication of anything, any more than it is with car salesmen. Not being doctors ourselves, the best we can do is ask around. Ask as many people as we can think of, all the cat owners we meet, breeders, shelters, local cat clubs, everyone. Bring the subject up at the office and at parties. People who are pleased with their vet are more than anxious to tell us about it; it's a kind of one-upmanship: "Oh, you don't go to *him*? You have to go to *my* vet, mine's the best." Tabulate the answers. Consider the circumstances. If we hear that Dr. A is a murderer, ask what happened. Did he overdose the cat, miss an easy diagnosis, leave a pair of dirty socks in the incision? Or did his patient die of lymphosarcoma at the age of twenty-three? It's a delicate matter, losing your cat, and everyone feels that more should have been done, up to and including miracles. On the other hand, if several otherwise sane people tell us Dr. A killed their cats, we'd better check Dr. B.

There's an undeniable charm about holistic medicine and the idea of curing disease with old-fashioned, gentle, sweet-smelling teas and baths of herbs and flowers and wholesome natural things like yeast and garlic. Lots of these naturopathic remedies, inspected under controlled conditions, turn out to be beneficial. Mildly beneficial. The problem can lie in the mildness, and a vet wholly dedicated to this kind of care may go on treating a cat with vitamin C, rosemary, and pennyroyal long after strong intervention with cold heartless antibiotics is called for. Gentle is good sometimes, and sometimes modern, fierce, unnatural, invasive, sudden, surgical or chemical attacks will save the small life; an abstract conviction is worth only so much. Probably, from the cat's point of view, very little; cats aren't given to convictions. Those of us personally committed to natural medicine should at least look for a vet who's not too proud to admit its limitations, and one who is indeed a VMD and not just a kindred spirit with a book about herbs.

All praise to preventive vaccines. There was a time when sensible persons held back a bit before taking a young cat to their hearts, because it was almost as likely to die as not. Now our standard essential package protects against enteritis, rhinotracheitis, and calici virus, making it far safer to get fond of a kitten. (If we get a kitten billed as having "had his shots," it's best to find out exactly what shots; it was probably just early temporary protection, needing reinforcement.) A cat who goes outdoors needs a rabies shot, required by law in many states, with boosters every one to three years as recommended by our vet or insisted on by our state.

The best news in recent years is the Leukocell vaccine, available since 1985, that protects against the number-one killer, feline leukemia virus, known in cat circles as FeLV; I don't know how they pronounce it.

The leukemia virus destroys the cat's immune system, leaving it open to cancers, most commonly lymphosarcoma, respiratory diseases, feline infectious peritonitis, and thymic atrophy. It's contagious from cat to cat, though not from cat to person, and the virus is passed in saliva from licks or bites. It can infect unborn kittens through the placenta, and born kittens through the milk. The commonest age of onset is around two or three years, and the common signs are malaise, anorexia, weight loss, fever, lethargy, and enlargement of the lymph glands.

When a cat's been exposed, various things can happen. It may not be infected at all. Or it may get infected but neutralize the virus somehow, and wind up not only healthy but resistant to future infections. Or it may be infected but not sick, and carry the virus in latent form. Or, finally, it may get infected and develop one of the related diseases, with a death rate around eighty percent. It can take a while to show up; the official word is from a few weeks to a few months, but Sidney hadn't seen a cat outside the family for eight months, and all the other cats tested negative.

The tests aren't absolutely accurate. A negative answer means only that the cat wasn't carrying the virus at the time the blood sample was taken, and it may even have been in the earliest stages of infection. It's a good idea to do a second test later. Positive answers don't show whether it has or may get one of the related diseases, but even if it doesn't, it will shed the virus and shouldn't hang around with other cats until they've been innoculated.

Negative cats who may have been exposed should have the series of three Leukocell vaccinations. It's a nuisance, but it beats the possible alternatives.

More good news: in 1987, cats with the killer heart disease called dilated cardiomyopathy, curable only by heart transplant, were found to have inadequate amounts of an essential nutrient called taurine in their bloodstreams. Its addition to their diets cured the condition, which had killed tens of thousands of cats a year in the United States.

Pet food makers were alerted, and moved quickly to add taurine supplements to products that tested deficient in it. (This breakthrough may eventually prove to be good news to humans with congestive heart failure, if a correlation can be found.)

On the bad-news side stands hyperthyroidism. The first cases of this surfaced in 1980, so the older books don't mention it, but it's showing up more and more frequently among the senior cats.

The early signs can even look cheering to the cat's people. When a torpid, overweight old cat begins to perk up and spring around the house ruffling the rugs, eats more enthusiastically and yet slims down, it looks like a whole new lease on life, but it might be hyperthyroidism. It's caused by a thyroid adenoma, an enlargement of the thyroid gland that makes it secrete too much thyroid hormone. This sends the cat's metabolism into the racing mode. Fat and muscle tissue are consumed, high blood pressure can lead to heart and kidney failure, and circulating immune complexes get trapped in the kidneys and damage them further. Things to look for in the cat over seven or eight are weight loss, increased appetite, hyperactivity, increased drinking and urination, heart murmur, vomiting shortly after eating, diarrhea or larger stools, and difficulty breathing. If you spot more than a couple of these, take him in for a blood test.

The best treatment, as of now, is what humans get, with radioactive iodine taken up by the tumor tissue and destroying it. But unfortunately, it's expensive and not widely available for cats. It's also possible to remove the abnormal gland or glands surgically, a fairly tricky procedure but the treatment of choice right now. There are also medications, propylthiouracil or tapazole, that control it to an extent but have some side effects. Dr. Susan McDonough, vet of final authority in these parts and a kind of feline Surgeon General, currently uses them only as a preparation for surgery.

Most recently, cases are beginning to crop up in more than one cat in a family, meaning that there may be some infectious agent involved, or a culprit in the environment. Dr. McDonough thinks it might hinge on diet, and hopes that thorough research on cat foods may pinpoint it.

In the meantime we have to cast a skeptical eye on the magically rejuvenated older cat.

Back to good news: nonsurgical hope for the cat with Feline Urinary Syndrome, familiarly known as FUS to vets and cystitis to the rest of us. It isn't cystitis; that's an inflammation of the urinary tract. With FUS, the urine forms crystals in the bladder or urethra that make urination painful and difficult or impossible. It happens only to males, and without quick treatment it can lead to uremic poisoning and death. The cat makes frequent sad trips to the litter box, and strains and cries, and produces little. Boy was a martyr to it before much could be done for it, and notified me of attacks by going to the bathroom and pulling down all the towels and sprinkling each with a few agonizing bloody drops. A vet with a catheter relieved the immediate problem, and then there were little red pills that may or may not have helped, and then it would happen again.

Some cats never get it, and some cats, on the same diet and leading the same life, do; they're called FUS cats by their vets, because once it's happened it's very likely to happen again. It's a sad problem. With an old or chronically ill cat you always have the option of ending his troubles, but what to do with a fine young friend in perfect health except for these spells of dreadful pain and danger?

Diet was always suspected as a factor. More than one doctor blamed the use of cereal in cat foods. Ash was considered a major villain, and pet food manufacturers made great news of their low ash content. We were told never to feed male cats fish. We were told never to feed FUS cats dry food. We were told to feed them anything but to salt it heavily, so they would drink more water and dilute the urine. Now, finally, they seem to have gotten it right, and put the finger on the acid/alkaline balance in the urine. Acidic urine won't let the crystals form; alkaline will, and happily it's no great matter to lower the urine pH to the desired 6.2 to 6.4.

At Dr. McDonough's Cat Hospital of Philadelphia, the cat arriving with his first FUS attack is given a quick urinary-tract acidifier plus ammonium chloride for long-range management, and put immediately on Prescription Diet c-d, from Hill's Pet Products, one of the delicately compounded designer cat foods available from vets and pet shops but not from supermarkets. As a preventive measure, the hospital recommends Science Diet Feline Maintenance, and both are just fine for the other members of the family. If the condition recurs, and Dr. McDonough believes it extremely unlikely if the people in charge of the can opener stick to the diet, the cat's second attack is followed by urinary bypass surgery.

The very thought will make the sympathetic human wince, but it's now a safe and standard operation that repositions and widens the opening of the urethra so that the crystals can slip easily through. Its only drawback is the slightly increased risk of urinary infections because of the wider opening, but at that the risk is no greater than females run to begin with. Still, if the problem can be wiped out by controlled diet, it's madness to put a cat through surgery.

Dr. Shelley Blum at Blum Animal Hospital in Chicago does ongoing independent research on food for the FUS cat, and his list of canned food goes: Prescription Diet c-d and Science Diet Feline Maintenance, Friskies and Fancy Feast beef and liver, and 9 Lives country chicken and gravy, choice cuts and cheese, tuna and chicken, savory stew, and beef and egg.

A spokesman for the company that does research for Carnation products says their dry foods, Friskies, Chef's Blend, Fish Ahoy, and Bright Eyes, create a most acceptable 6.2 pH urine. Iams, a rapid riser in the special-foods world, makes a dry food with a low magnesium content that's becoming increasingly popular for FUS management. Purina, at this writing, feels the whole concept of urinary acidity is still too new for comment.

Dry food for the FUS cat was under a cloud for years, but Dr. McDonough suggests that this may be from the way it's fed. After eating, she says, an alkaline tide is automatically released and raises the cat's pH. Dry food is usually left out for whenever the cat feels peckish, and the frequent snacking keeps the alkalinity coming. Serve it as a meal, then take it away.

This seems like rather a lot on the subject of a few tiny crystals, but anyone who's been through it with a sufferer, even if the good news comes too late, rejoices in it.

On the subject of normal diet for normal cats, much is written, much of it contradictory. Books from Britain confuse the American reader with recipes; British cat food, if it exists, must be a disaster, and proper cat owners cook. Not that they agree with each other. Some feed only raw food, darkly hinting at the effects of cooking; pregnant females fed cooked food, for instance, have but few and sickly kittens, often still-born. Their colleagues hotly maintain that raw food is virtu-ally poisonous for cats, leaving us to imagine cats in less protective times grilling their mice over tiny outdoor barbe-cues. One says nothing but raw beef, the perfect food; an-other warns of the dire effects of pork; another says one-third of the meal should be such cooked vegetables as leeks, aspar-agus, lettuce, carrots, and endive. Cat-keeping in England is hard work. One writer's cat "makes a habit / Of eating noth-ing else but rabbit," prepared fresh daily. Another says the diet must be supplemented with boiled oatmeal and milk. Europeans pour their cats a lot of milk, while the American feeling is that it's bad for adult cats. The fact is, digesting milk is related to an enzyme that some cats lose when they grow up and some don't. If our particular cat doesn't get diar-rhea from milk, there's nothing wrong with it.

Americans are blessed with a busy and competitive pet-food industry. To watch the television commercials you'd think they didn't have a brain in their heads, but in truth they're backed by professional research teams as much con-cerned with nutrition as with talking cats. American cat food is good stuff, at least the recognized brands; we're warned against generic cat food as lacking quality control and possi-bly containing whatever was cheap and handy at the moment.

The disciplinarians say it's sentimental to suppose our cats need or want variety in their meals, but Dr. McDonough recommends it; there may be things we haven't yet learned about nutrition, and it's safest to touch as many bases as pos-sible. Besides, the single-food cat can be a problem. A cat fixated on tuna, for instance, may develop kidney troubles and have to give up tuna as too high in phosphorus, and then compound its problems by refusing to consider anything else. (A few years back, tuna cat food made feline news as the villain in steatitus, a particularly vicious inflammatory dis-ease, but the addition of vitamin E has eliminated the prob-lem, and the only steatitus victims the Cat Hospital sees now have been eating human tuna, without the supplement, a most mistaken kindness.)

Controversy rages over canned versus dry food, with a heavy weight of authority on the side of the dry, often with a noticeably puritanical ring to it. Those who favor strict rules and discipline for cats seem to insist on dry food as well, as if canned food were a wanton luxury, a dietary satin cushion guaranteed to produce whining, spoiled, demanding children. It isn't. However, chewing dry food is a kind of feline toothbrush, and may help prevent some dental problems. At this house, having no FUS cats, we have our saucers of dry food topped off with small amounts of our favorite canned stuffs for excitement; the topping is eaten at once and the crunchy part picked at later.

The "soft-moist" foods in their convenient packets are poorly regarded and often referred to as junk food. I looked up some of the ingredients once in a king-size dictionary and found that one of them is also used in embalming corpses; probably there's nothing wrong with eating it, but it isn't something you'd order from a menu if you had a choice.

Dr. McDonough offers no people food to cats at all, but most of us don't see the harm in sharing an occasional treat. Some cats get quite excited over it; Sidney, admirer of human customs, was delighted by scraps of this and that, but only at the table, where humans ate. Others will accept them only in their dishes, where cats eat. And still others glare, suspect poison, and scratch imaginary dirt over anything that isn't cat food. Those of us lazily given to canned or frozen human dinners will get a dismaying look of reproach if we offer to share; perhaps we'd be better off sharing theirs.

I've always felt an egg yolk, fork-beaten with a dash of milk, was a wholesome small luxury, but we should throw away the white.

The puritanical experts are also severe about overweight, and to be sure it's no better for him than for us to get fat, and a cat without enough to occupy his mind may get obsessed with meals and overeat just for something to do. But with a busy, healthy cat I don't see any sense in fussing around weighing him, and measuring out his tablespoon of breakfast. The fattest cat I ever knew, a neighborhood gent named Junior Reynoldson, was reputed to weigh thirty pounds, and died under a lilac bush at the age of twenty-four, having enjoyed an excellent life. Perhaps if he'd been severely dieted he would have lived to be thirty, or perhaps he would have lost interest in life and died young. It was his vocation, his calling, to be an enormous cat.

A cat that goes off its feed may be sickening with something, or there may be another problem, requiring thought on our part. Corvo, for instance, refused his food for several days and sat in the kitchen doorway watching the others eat. Before I rushed him to the vet it occurred to me that he wanted to be *fed* in the kitchen doorway, as a mark of distinction from other cats, a sign that, while the others, of whatever breed, feeding in a row under the table, were only cats, he was *Corvo*. It's a great nuisance stepping over his dish in the doorway now, but he eats well.

All books tell us to keep a bowl of clean, fresh water available and change it daily, and of course we should. I do, and sometimes, when there are no foul-smelling marigolds rotting in a handy vase, no muddy puddles, leaking faucets, damp bathtubs, or melting ice in a whiskey glass, and someone has put the toilet lid down, they are forced to drink some of it.

Cats eat grass. Nobody knows why. Some claim it's because they need it in their diets, and instruct us to keep a pot of it growing in the house in winter and for indoor cats. They don't explain what possible nutritive use it is if the cats are going to keep throwing it up on the rug the way they do, unchanged and only slightly marked by teeth, since cats are not cows. It's also been put forth that they eat the grass because they need to throw up; but how is it, then, when you open the door on a sunny May morning, that every cat in the house suddenly needs to throw up and runs out to eat grass?

Contrary advice claims that eating grass is bad for them

and fills them with parasites and we should prevent it, an athletic job if we have several outdoors cats; we'll need to hire assistants. Nutritious or not, they can't stop themselves.

I've been told that when cats eat grass it's a sign of rain. Perhaps that's it. They eat grass to tell us it's going to rain, and come to throw it up at our feet to make sure we noticed and will take our umbrellas.

Cats eat grass. There are always some mysteries left.

Whether or not they're eating grass, they do get uninvited guests from time to time. Roundworms are the commonest. They can arrive in kittens via their mother, or be passed on in the litter pan or just from the great outdoors. They produce flatulence, diarrhea, pot belly, retching, and vomiting; the worms themselves appear in the vomit, curled up into little spirals; hence, roundworms. Tapeworms are most commonly transmitted by fleabites, and advertise their presence with little white rice grains around the cat's anus. As usual, we're discouraged from using supermarket medicines for them without consulting our vet.

Ear mites pass easily from cat to cat, and strays come fully equipped with them even more often than with incipient kittens. They itch. I've seen a cat kick its ears to bloody shreds from a particularly bad mess of them; with a lighter infestation the host just sits around with its ears at half-mast and an inward expression on its face, scratching moodily from time to time. Mites prefer the short and furry ear to the naked, drafty caverns of the Siamese, and are said to be at their happiest in the lop-eared Scottish Fold. You can get drops for them from your vet, but it's best to let him do the initial scrape-out, since most of us are too timid, and rightly so, to be sufficiently savage and thorough.

Fleas are among the most successful inhabitants of the earth. If, as we're told, there will still be cockroaches around after the nuclear holocaust, the cockroaches will probably have fleas.

One cat book says, reproachfully, that the well-cared-for cat seldom "catches fleas," but I don't see why a bright flea wouldn't actually prefer a tender, plushy cared-for cat to a slat-sided, thin-coated stray. Surely the attention of fleas is a compliment?

Some cats have an allergic reaction to their bite and some seem hardly to notice them, but all can get tapeworm from them. And in a suitably welcoming environment, a happily married pair of fleas can give us six thousand youngsters within a month.

Some years seem to favor them. One summer, in the country, the whole county had fleas. Even people with no resident livestock had them, and people with cats and dogs beggared themselves with collars and sprays and bombs, and still they came. Only Rachel and her two cats had no fleas. Rachel put brewers' yeast in their food. There wasn't a flea in the place; it was a refuge for the flea-bitten neighbors, and as we sat there scratching our ankles and brooding we noticed there were no screens in the windows and no flies in the house. Rachel planted tansy under the windows to keep out flies.

I don't know about the tansy, but scientific tests prove that brewers' yeast has very little effect on fleas. My private feeling is that it had something to do with the faith and personal goodness of Rachel herself, and if *I* relied on yeast and tansy the cats and I would be bare, bleached bones by morning.

Garlic doesn't help either, they say.

Once you've got fleas, there's no use just tackling the cat's, you've got to do the house. A recommended fogger is Siphotrol-Plus, with both instant and long-range action. Spray areas the fogger doesn't reach, and put some mothballs or a flea collar in the vacuum-cleaner bag and vacuum daily for a while, to catch the eggs before they hatch. For the cat, there are collars and tags, sprays and roll-ons, powders, shampoos, a whole arsenal. The collars are all right if the fleas aren't too many and the cat isn't sensitive to them; they give Barney raging sores. Get collars from the vet instead of the supermarket. The sprays have the drawback of hissing like a hostile cat; the new Supra-Quick roll-on rolls on quietly, and it's safe for kittens too. A cat with battalions of fleas or a severe allergy to them should have a medicated shampoo; it takes the flea allergens away as well as the fleas, and leaves a repellent residue.

We all have better sense than to use a dog flea product on a cat unless it says on it, loud and clear, that it's safe to do so, but a cat can have a reaction even to a cat product, with foaming and drooling, trembling, or contracted pupils. He can even go into convulsions and coma. A swift and thorough bath should help, and if it doesn't, off to the vet.

At this writing, the oral flea killer Proban isn't licensed for cats in this country, though several other countries have okayed it. The Cat Hospital sometimes cautiously dispenses it in a crisis, but feels there must be some reason behind the hesitation.

There's an electronic flea collar on the market. It works on something called "pulsed, modulated, burst-circuit sound"; only a flea can hear it, and he hates it, and leaves. He can hear it up to four feet away, so he goes clear away and, presumably, starves. The collar runs on batteries, and it's entirely safe. The one available through The Sharper Image catalog is said to be twenty percent lighter and smaller than competing models, and thus more suitable for cats. It's expensive; if you have half a dozen cats it could run into major money, though perhaps if the cats spend a lot of time within four feet of each other one collar would do for all.

All proper books contain long lists of substances, from mothballs to marijuana, that can poison a cat, making the human dwelling sound like a feline deathtrap, but actually the Cat Hospital says it sees very few cases of poisoning. It's true there are plenty of things that could poison a cat if the cat ate them, but mostly the cat doesn't. What does happen is that something gets on the paws or the fur and the cat licks it off: whatever goes outside on a cat will get inside. Garden sprays and dusts, weed killers and insecticides are especially lethal, and we might ask the neighbors to let us know when they're going to be killing things in the vegetable patch or on the lawn so we can keep our cats indoors for a few days, or until it rains hard. And there may be spilled things in our own basements or garages, like engine oil or kerosene.

Poisoning is instant illness: the cat, well a few minutes ago, suddenly retches, slobbers, totters, and dilates or pinpoints its pupils. Unfortunately, it's hard to ask a cat what it ate. A half teaspoon of ipecac will make it vomit, or a teaspoon of hydrogen peroxide and water. (Many books suggest salt on the back of the tongue, but salt can have a toxic effect and is very strongly disrecommended by vets.) However, as with humans, we do *not* induce vomiting for petroleum-based products: paint, paint thinner or remover, kerosene, gasoline, benzene, fuel oil, floor wax, lighter fluid, or furniture polish. Or with corrosives like lye, washing soda, Drano, ammonia, metal polishes, or grease solvents. Or for strong acids or pine oil. For these, give milk or water.

If it might be insect repellents or the neighbors' garden poisons, carbon tetrachloride, or moth flakes, give water only, no milk.

For car anti-freeze, mysteriously appealing to cats, Sterno, and windshield de-icers, one source says vodka in milk is the treatment of choice.

If you spot the culprit on the paws or fur, plunge the cat into an immediate bath.

And, of course, you rush to the vet. Only, as with small children, these things happen with diabolical regularity on Sundays, late at night, or on Christmas morning, and finding the vet who's on emergency standby, or even rousing your own vet's answering service, can take a lifetime. A cat's lifetime. Those of us in the centers of civilization can at least hope that someone, somewhere, can be found to help. Country folk, though, should keep first-aid supplies on hand and fresh, remain alert, stay calm, think fast, and, when possible, drive like hell.

We should remember to think external for cat poisoning. To clean up spills. To lock cats away when disinfecting or polishing or painting or exterminating or dealing out death in the garden.

The list of poisonous plants is dismaying, and most lists make little distinction between leaves that kill at a glance and those that, if the cat eats the entire bush, roots and all, may give it a stomachache. Every Christmas we're warned that the whole festival is poisonous, the holly and the ivy, mistletoe, poinsettia, Christmas cherry, the works. (The tinsel on the tree is bad news too.) This year the little black cat ate some poinsettia to no ill effect; Dr. McDonough says it's really more an irritant than a poison. Mistletoe berries, though, fall readily on the floor and make intriguing toys, and we might just shuck them off before we hang the spray.

Bored cats indoors may take up plant eating for entertainment or, some say, because they need vegetables. Toss them a sprig of parsley or a carrot top and get rid of the ivy, the philodendron, and the avocado plant (which is probably dreary-looking anyway; they usually are). Replace with ferns. Cats and kittens that gleefully use the dirt in the pots as an in-house outhouse are sometimes discouraged by stockades of matches, toothpicks, or sharp sticks, and perhaps a mulch of stones.

Occasionally a vet will recommend a minute dosage of aspirin, but otherwise we may consider it cat poison; it hits their livers. If you drop one on the floor, or Tylenol, or ibuprophen, pick it up.

Pick everything up. More cats than get poisoned swallow, in an experimental way, unsuitable small objects. Threaded needles are lethally appealing. String in the intestine can be a killer, and rubber bands. The little black cat loves rubber bands, which appear all over this house without human agency; she hooks them over her lower teeth, pulls them down with her paw, and lets them go with a snap, a game so charming and harmless-looking that I feel like a monster snatching them away. Buttons. Paperclips. Safety pins. These otherwise adult creatures have no more sense than a two-year-old.

Open the mouth of a choking cat to see if you can see the problem and grab it with fingers or tweezers. If not, hold cat upside down and shake. If that doesn't help, try the Heimlich maneuver: holding cat upside down, pressed to your chest with your arms if you're alone, put a hand on each side of the chest and upper ribs and give a sharp squeeze. Get to the vet for help if possible. Even if the item goes clear on down, get to the vet; a small, smooth object might complete its journey, or it might not.

As with two-year-olds, when we see a cat playing with something, we go find out what it is.

Burns: Ice, cold compresses, or a twenty-minute cold bath.

Convulsions: Caused by various things, including simple stress. Just try to keep him from hurting himself, and if it lasts more than five minutes or he has another one within the hour, to the vet.

Heatstroke: Panting, weakness, staggering. Cool cat instantly with hose or basin of cold water, and think shame to have let it happen. Even with the windows open, a cat in a carrier can easily die in a hot car.

Wounds: Clip the hair from around it and clean with mild soap and water, no disinfectants. Abrasions and scratches usually heal by themselves, but bites and other punctures go to the vet, because they abscess. Actually, we often don't know they're there at all until they do.

Bleeding: Pressure bandage. If it bleeds through, hold it there and slap another on top. Tourniquets to be used only in darkest emergency and with great care, releasing frequently.

Broken legs: A dangling broken leg can be splinted with a pencil, table knife, squill of rolled paper, anything stiff and handy, to prevent tissue damage on the way to the vet. Tie it above and below the break, gently.

General injury: Wrap cat in towel or jacket or whatever and put it carefully in a box or slide in onto something stiff for carrying to the vet.

Electrical shock, from biting through lamp cords: Mouth-to-nose respiration. Close cat's mouth, take a breath, place your mouth over its nose and exhale very gently, then let the air back out. Proceed gently and slowly, ten to fifteen breaths per minute. Coat electrical cords with vinegar or Tabasco.

Diarrhea: Half a teaspoon Kaopectate after each trip to the box. If it persists or the cat seems otherwise ill, you can guess where to go next.

Constipation: A dab of Vaseline on the nose, to be licked off.

Hair balls: A splash of olive oil in the dinner.

Vitamins: From the vet, not the medicine cabinet, for pregnant and nursing mothers. Not to pop them in indiscriminately; too much is poisonous.

Other pills: When the vet says give him all of them, give him all of them. Resist the temptation known to us all to save out a few of those broad-spectrum antibiotics for an emergency, now that the cat is well again and howling for its dinner.

One popular book on cat care recommends regular doses of Valium for nervous or aggressive cats, but let's discuss it with our own vet first before sharing our tranqs around.

As the years begin to pile up on our cat, he may lose his relish for dinner. His teeth may need work. Probably they need cleaning. Or his sense of smell may be clouding over; he won't eat what he can't smell. A topping of something aromatic like tuna or sardines, or garlic if he likes it, may perk up his interest.

We should check him for tumors. Give him a thorough feel from time to time. Palpate the breasts, males as well as females, and most especially females unspayed or spayed late in life. Under the last pair toward the rear are two normal fatty pouches, but these feel smooth; what you're looking for feels nodular, like grape seeds. And check in his mouth for abnormal swellings or strange smells.

And make sure he can get up to his favorite places. Arrange steps and bridges. The view from the window is even more important in old age, and it's sad to jump and miss and be confined to the floor because no one's noticed you can't make it anymore.

Some say all cats should have their ears washed weekly and be given thorough and regular baths. These, again, are the sterner sources, who may be recommending baths just to remind the cat who's boss around here. It seems to me a bath should be considered therapeutic intervention, for fleas, or poisons on the fur, or an accidental deluge of filth like the time Sidney went up the chimney, rather than routine hygiene.

A cat, after all, is a very workable item just as it comes from the package, and to feel that we should be constantly adjusting and tinkering with it to keep it in working order is hubris. It doesn't much need our advice on staying healthy. It's clean, it's sensible, and it doesn't drink or smoke. Its only really deplorable physical habit is a relentless passion for making kittens.

Sex and Kittens

11

Cats are famous for sex. Lion couples have been clocked at 120 matings in a day. All that sex, all those kittens, are rarely in the best interests of either the mother or the unwanted young, but what cat resists?

Although there are perhaps 56 million cats living under American roofs, there are somewhere between 15 and 25 million homeless, living hard, and the shelters kill over three million every year. It's irresponsible of the cats to keep adding to this tragedy, and irresponsible of us to let them.

"Neutering" is an unfortunate word. To neuter is to make neutral, to send to the sidelines, to make pale and wishy-washy, to negate, disarm, remove from the game. It sounds as if our bright, brisk cat were about to fade into a shadowy half-life more vegetable than animal. And even the most enlightened humans identify with this sexual obliteration, deep in their own organs, and shudder at murdering nature in their cats.

Men especially find castration hard to face, and when

their loved Timmy or Charlie goes far afield in search of sex and gets killed by a car at the age of three, they console themselves with the natural, free life he led. They have lost their friend, and the cat has lost twelve or fifteen years of living, and the kittens he fathered probably led brief, desperate, and painful lives; the price is high.

There's also a widespread feeling that the neutered male turns fat and sleepy and becomes a blob of a cat, neutral indeed, but this isn't true. An intelligent cat will take up a number of peaceable, non-sexual pursuits and have time for all his hobbies; if he lives confined to an apartment and his hobby is food, he may indeed gain weight, but so would we all.

For the female, sex leads to what Don Marquis's Mehitabel called "just one damned kitten after another," but unspayed and unbred, her periods of fruitless yearning can lead, especially in the Siamese, to cystic ovaries and other female complications. They start young, too. At least one cat on record was pregnant when she was four months old. Between six and twelve months is more usual for the first heat. ("Heat" is considered vulgar, and nice people say "in season," like shad or asparagus, while scientific types say "in estrus" because it's always more delicate-minded to use words no one understands.) From then on her life, if unsupervised, consists of pregnancy, kittens, and pregnancy.

In truth, neutering is a wonderful release for a cat's life. Up till the age of sexual maturity a cat's world is wide and various and alive with rich experiences and discoveries and games and interesting things to do and ponder on; after maturity, all is sex. The sexual cat is like the human alcoholic or drug addict, its vision narrowed to a pinpoint, its mental landscape contracted to a single thought. The neutered cat expands again. Released from the blind all-absorbing monomania of making more cats, it can look around, rediscover human friendship, feline friendship, butterflies, scraps of paper, patches of sunshine, mice real and imaginary, humor, play. It's the neutered, not the "whole," cat that lives a full life exploring its potential. And of course it has more time for us; an unneutered tomcat is away on business a lot, and a producing female has little energy for human conversation.

All this said, and wicked as it is to add to the oversupply of cats, fairness forces me to admit that a litter of kittens is by all odds the solidest entertainment value known to man. What can stage or screen offer that will keep us watching for weeks, cause us to neglect all else to watch, and make us laugh until the tears come, not just once but every evening for months? And all in the comfort of our own homes, all for the price of a little cat food.

And perhaps a stud fee. To be cynical, it helps to have purebreds when it's time to look for good homes. People who would turn up their noses at the most charming litter of blacks and grays and stripers will stand in line for our Persians or Siamese, and take good care of them too. People respect monetary value, and they like to think they're getting something valuable for nothing. The ordinary shorthair is not valuable, because of the aforementioned oversupply. It's common as dandelions, common as water, or bread, or sunlight, and any Tom, Dick, or Harry can have all he wants for the asking. When the neighbors' children come knocking with a carton full of kittens to give away, we are being pestered, not offered a gift beyond price. If the market could be cornered, if we could control the supply and pass restrictive ownership laws like the Egyptians', a litter of common kittens could make us richer than Whittington, but barring some disastrous epidemic it seems unlikely to happen.

The other advantage to purebred kittens is that you know roughly what you're going to get. The domestic shorthair, no matter how personally attractive, can surprise you with kittens God himself wouldn't adopt.

The female cat doesn't ovulate until copulation; copulation stimulates the ovaries to release the ova, which take up with any sperm they happen to meet. A cat can have kittens sired by two or three or more toms, each one more squincheyed, bowlegged, lanky, and particolored than the last. The lineup of patchwork pirates courting Betsy in the backyard spoke poorly for the futures of their offspring until the black cat showed up. He was partly Persian, fluffy, and round of eye and ear, all black and clearly a gentleman, dismayed by the bad language and scuffling among the competition; he seemed to have brought candy and flowers instead of brass knuckles. I invited him in. I locked him in the laundry room with Betsy for the night. In the morning I gave him breakfast, thanked him, and sent him home.

There were four kittens, three of them with "alley" stamped all over them. The fourth was Sidney. His whiskers were a curving waterfall of whisker, his round gold eyes were outlined with mascara, his nose was a sculpture of a nose, and all about him was shaped with generous grace. (Unfortunately, he was black and white in irregular patches, with a crooked black moustache, and ignorant people laughed and called him the Hitler Kitten. It takes cat people to see through the fur to the quality of cat beneath.)

From the way the female in heat carries on, you'd think any tom at all would do, but there does seem to be a certain selectivity at work, incomprehensible as it looks to us. Friends of mine had two cats, mother and daughter, who obliged the neighborhood toms by going into heat simultaneously, and obliged each other by babysitting their simultaneous litters. I was there when they were in heat, and a tom came to call. To the ignorant human eye he was immensely handsome, a most desirable father, a mackerel tabby with a dapper white bib and an ardent, anxious expression in his whiskers. They loathed him, mother and daughter. They exhausted their vocabulary of virginal distaste, these veterans of many litters. He clung to the windowsill, whimpering fondly, and they laid back their ears and hissed. Why? What were they looking for; what was wrong with this big, handsome lover? It's going much too far to suppose they sensed some genetic flaw in his ancestry. They rejected him; given a choice, female cats do choose.

Even the male can say no.

I thought about mating Morgan. Morgan thought about it too. Carl van Vechten refers to the female's "little amorous coos like the tender sighs of the eighteenth-century lover," but van Vechten wasn't thinking Siamese. When a Siamese female is calling for love the world hears, and it isn't exactly tender, either. Morgan called pleadingly for the first day or so, but then she lost patience completely and snarled with rage. She raced from window to window screaming threats like a fishwife, hoarsely furious with the absent unknown for his absence.

Hoping for kittens at least mostly Siamese, I tried to arrange things with my sister's blue-eyed Zachary. I put them in the basement together and closed the door. Morgan's screams made all the plumbing vibrate. Zachary tried to tear down the basement door to escape, and had left great splintery gashes in it by the time I let him out. He was almost two years old, but perhaps he wasn't ready. Science writer David Zimmerman believes that male cats, even when physically capable, need to mature socially and emotionally before they think about breeding, and Zachary's traumatic childhood and subsequent position as baby of the family may have retarded him. Or maybe the noise gave him a headache. Or maybe he was just rejecting Morgan. As soon as she calmed down, I had her spayed.

The feline penis has barbs on it, facing backward like the metal teeth guarding the gateways of parking lots, that may or may not influence ovulation. At the climax the female gives a piercing shriek and pulls away and slaps the tom. Some say this is because the barbs are painful, and some that this is just her way of showing pleasure; it isn't a point very likely to be resolved.

Infertility is not a feline problem: sex leads to kittens. For the good old domestic shorthair, gestation is from sixty-two to sixty-four days, while the Siamese takes longer, sixty-five to sixty-nine days. It's a good idea to check with a breeder before panicking about the various purebreds; gestation varies. We get a vitamin supplement from the vet, feed generously, and, toward the end, make a suitable kittening bed. She appreciates our thoughtfulness and likes to know the place is ready; some cats have even gone so far as to have their kittens in it. Bottom bureau drawers are often acceptable.

Many cats, even veterans, like encouragement and company in labor, and will follow us around talking about it, or wake us up to tell us. Abyssinians tend to get a bit hysterical, being Abyssinians. Some, even novices, take care of things alone. Blueberry woke me in the morning to show me her first and only litter, all clean and dry, in the box made ready for them. Sidney and his siblings were born on my bed, with me in it. Occasionally a worrying sort of cat will have them in a secret place of her own devising, often wildly unsuitable, like the clothes dryer or the pile of broken plaster behind the furnace or under the porch in bitter weather. When you finally discover them and move them to better quarters, she may keep on trying to hide them. Chippy was like that. Chippy hid kittens in boots and galoshes and under the attic floorboards and in the sleeves of my father's shirts in the laundry hamper. Her cleverest place was almost their last, far inside a roll of abandoned carpet in the basement, half smothered when we dragged them out. Chippy was striped: is this an aspect of what they mean when they say stripers are closest to the wild, that they don't entirely trust us with their young? Probably not; Chippy was always unstable.

If the cat has called on us to oversee the birth, usually all we need to offer is encouragement, kind words, and as much calm as we can muster. Once in a while there's trouble. When the kitten starts to come forth, whether front-end first or back, it should keep on coming. If it seems to have gotten stuck, clip your fingernails off short, wash your hands and grease them with Vaseline or butter or whatever's handy, and ease it slowly and gently out, holding the shoulders, not the head, and moving it out and downward from the mother's tail.

Kittens are born enclosed in a membrane like plastic wrap, and the mother's supposed to bite and lick this off their faces so they can breathe. If she seems confused and doesn't, break it yourself with your fingernails, swab the mucus out of the mouth, and perhaps give it a bit of a rub with a clean, soft cloth, all without moving it away from the mother. Watching you, she'll get the idea, and the kitten will mew for her, and she'll take over to finish the job.

She will eat the afterbirth. Don't recoil; this is important for hygienic and probably physiological reasons. She'll clean up the kittens and gather them to nurse, and purr. Bring her a snack and a bowl of water and tell her what a fine, brave cat she is. Replace the stained papers or old dish towels with something soft and go to bed. Quite likely in the morning you'll find one or two more kittens than you thought you had. They often pause in delivery like this; it's been suggested that in case some predator kills the first group, she'll have time to escape to a safer place and deliver another. Or it may just be that the double-lobed feline uterus empties itself one lobe at a time. Don't count your kittens before morning.

Sometimes there's a kitten refused. It may be the smallest and feeblest, or it may look perfectly all right to us but for some reason not to her. If it seems obviously sickly, maybe the best thing is just to let it slip away in its first hours, probably not suffering much, still deaf and blind, a marginal organism at best. If it looks healthy, we can have a try at changing her mind. Warm it with a hair dryer and a heating pad. Pick up a couple of the wanted kittens and mix them in our hands together with the unwanted one and then put them all back to feed; perhaps she won't be able to sort out the one she didn't want. If she still won't have it, and if we're enormously patient and stubborn, we can raise it as an orphan.

Sometimes something happens to the mother and we have a whole litter of orphans on our hands. And sometimes, cats being a queer bunch, she simply doesn't want her kittens at all. My sister's Mehitabel had her name before she had her kittens, but it was well chosen; she didn't like kittens. Maybe she'd been hoping for boys; she had no use for females. She refused to nurse them, and when people held her down and tried to feed her to them forcibly she hissed and slapped them, and wriggled free and ran away. When they peeped lonesomely for her, she left the house. Judy raised them on an eyedropper, but Mehitabel can't stand them even now they're grown.

The original Mehitabel, Don Marquis's, observes cheerily that she has left her kittens in an abandoned garbage can where they will surely drown if it rains before she gets back.

Orphan kittens need the warmest place in the house, and a heating pad or a heat lamp. When their eyes start to open they need a dab of antibiotic ophthalmic ointment from the vet to take the place of maternal licking. They need help in defecating, a gentle massage with a warm, damp cotton swab or washcloth after each meal. They need our touching and handling. Most of all they need food, and they need it almost all the time. Pet stores carry a pet nurser, a specially designed plastic bottle more practical than the traditional eyedropper. Pet stores or the vet can sell us Borden's KMR (Kitten Milk Replacer), which isn't cheap but it's carefully formulated to mimic mother's own and a lot less trouble than making the formula ourselves. If we can't get it, a standard recipe is a can of evaporated milk mixed with an equal amount of boiling water, an egg yolk, and a tablespoon of corn syrup or honey. Keep it refrigerated, and heat each meal before serving, maybe adding a single drop of human-infant vitamins for each kitten. Some experts say to feed them every four hours, but smaller meals every two hours seems safer. It's not a job to undertake lightly, and it's a hard one to abandon if we change our minds in midstream.

As they get older, they'll eat more and need it less often, like human babies, and eventually we'll be allowed to sleep all night again.

Happily, almost all cats make legendary good mothers. It's a rare slow season for news that goes by without the paper printing a picture of a cat who has adopted and nursed a baby squirrel, puppy, rabbit, ferret, monkey, what have you. My grandmother had a cat named Keezo who adopted a small black chick, hatched in error to a Rhode Island Red; the hen disowned it because it was the wrong color, but the cat didn't mind that it wasn't even a mammal.

Many are the stories of cats that have sacrificed their lives for their kittens. The theater cat in London, for instance, who had five kittens under the stage, and when the building burned carried four of them, one by one, to safety, and died struggling out with the fifth. (There's a worm at the heart of this story, as in the story of Ophelia's drowning reported in such close detail by Queen Gertrude's henchmen: why are you standing there taking notes, telling us what kinds of flowers she's holding, counting the desperate trips with kittens; isn't anyone going to *help*?)

Méry believes, and it seems reasonable, that the euphoric tenderness of the mother cat depends on her own security. A cat with a solicitous male in attendance, as in jaguar and some lion families, makes a joyful mother with playful young, while the tigress, who hasn't seen the male since mating, and the feral domestic cat make anxious parents with fearful, precociously aggressive kittens. In human households kind people take the place of fathers, usually, though a resident father can be a careful parent too, and the mother, secure in room and board and safety, purrs so lavishly and takes such blatant pleasure in her young as to put the rest of us to shame. As they get older, she introduces them to the world and, sometimes with help from other cats around, educates them patiently.

With the usual exceptions, of course. There was a cat in my mother's childhood named Mrs. Johnson. Something was lacking in her chemical makeup, perhaps, since she was well past two before she produced her first litter, giving birth to four fine kittens on a pile of carrot-tops in the pantry. The kittens were particularly attractive, and she was a conscientious mother and housebroke them in a row of flowerpots on the porch. When they were at the peak of their charm, prancing around with their tails stuck up straight, she was seen leading them out of the backyard. They followed her in a neat line, like ducklings. She was heading for a patch of suburban woods between the house and the next street. About an hour later she came back alone. She ate, she washed, she hunkered down with her paws tucked in and closed her eyes, ignoring the family's shouted questions. Everyone fanned out and searched the neighborhood. They scoured the woods, they knocked on doors, they asked everyone. The kittens were old enough to scamper briskly and to squeal piercingly, but no one ever saw or heard them again, nor did their mother ever ask after them. She lived for many years after that and never had another litter.

Méry tells of a female who, when each successive litter was a week or so old, apparently tired of them and dropped them one by one through a balcony railing to their deaths on the tiles below.

Any instinctive passion as awesomely strong as the cat's for her kittens may sometimes, from the unwieldiness of its sheer power, tip itself over the edge in a few individuals, and turn inside out from love to murder. Even our own rational species isn't entirely above it, to judge from the tabloids.

In other times and places it was customary to drown the kittens at birth, so as not to become overburdened with cats, or, grudgingly, to "let her keep one." Softer-hearted modern Americans are more likely to keep them all for as long as they're young and cute, and then turn them out onto the streets at adolescence to fend for themselves. People like us, of course, bend every muscle to the task of having kind and responsible homes waiting for them when they're ready for homes. In the meantime, we have kittens, an occasion for rejoicing.

Until very recently the word was to leave young kittens strictly alone. Touching and handling them made them sickly and upset their mother, and the family children had to stand well back from the box and gaze from a distance. Now the powers that decide these things have decided otherwise, and the word is reversed: kittens should be handled. It speeds their development and promotes human friendship later in life. With the usual scientific precision, they tell us that each kitten should be handled for twenty minutes a day for the first thirty days, though it's unclear how they worked out this figure, and petting a blind, wriggling, screeching kitten for twenty minutes while its mother hovers anxiously could get tedious. With a litter of six it works out to a two-hour daily stint of kitten-touching, fourteen hours a week. It's well to remember that, through the decades when handling was forbidden, legions of cats developed normally and found human friendship; all revelations should be swallowed tentatively.

Anyway, even if we can't work the recommended schedule into our busy days, it's nice to know we're allowed to touch when we want to, though I've known mother cats who wouldn't have stood for it, not with newborns. If we'd tried it on Chippy's kittens she'd have hidden them for good and all. Discretion is advised.

Weaning is a cat's first major step into the wide world. As early as four weeks we can start offering them a saucer of evaporated milk and water mixed with some human baby meats and maybe a spoonful of baby rice flakes to give it body. They plunge their faces in it, sneeze and wade through it, dripping and bemused. Their mother may demonstrate by drinking it herself, and they may or may not bother to watch. Sometimes there's one leader kitten, brighter or more curious and vigorous than the rest, the first one to scramble out of the box, who gets the point right away, and one shy and tentative one who doesn't seem to care if he never learns. All go back to mother for dessert; it puts them to sleep, round-bellied and still making blissful sucking noises in their dreams.

The mother, seeing our willingness to fill saucers, encourages the process. Makes herself less available. Supervises. Leads them to the dish. (Sometimes a childless cat will take her toys in for supper and arrange them around the bowl, heads, if they have heads, pointing toward it.)

The help we offer is highly acceptable, but proper cats should learn to earn their living in a pinch, and a good mother will bring in mice if mice are available and show the kittens what to do with them. Some cats seem to have made the mental leap from hunting to husbandry that took humans so many millennia: they start mouse farms, to ensure a steady supply. A friend of mine had a cat who kept mice in the bathtub, readily available and trapped by the slippery sides. One writer claims that his Siamese stored mice in his grand piano, and when the kittens grew up and went away she lost interest in the mice, being a good mother but not a serious hunter, and the unused supplies flourished and multiplied and made merry in the workings of the piano for years.

There's a lot to the education of a kitten, and it's best to leave them with their mothers for as long as possible, nine weeks at least. Unfortunately, weaning time, six weeks or so, is often considered departure time, since the mother's owners are understandably anxious not to get stuck with kittens far advanced in gangly adolescence. But there's so much we can't teach them; who knows how much? A friend insists that his mother cat spoke to her kittens for fifteen minutes every morning. It wasn't scolding, he says; it sounded like an instructive lecture, and the kittens paid close attention. No one can guess what she told them, but their various later owners all swore they grew up to be the finest and smartest cats in the entire state of Georgia.

Aside from us primates, only cats have been tested and proven to learn from watching others, and tree climbing is definitely a case in point. Going up is instinctive; getting down is not, as many a cat-owner has learned. The kitten goes up gaily, gets to the first branch, or the fifth or sixth if it's brave and reckless, and sits on it and screams for help. Then its mother or another cat will climb up to it and demonstrate "down," backwards, to take advantage of the hooked claws, and looking over the shoulder like a rower until it's close enough to jump. Sometimes the kitten is too busy screaming to pay attention, and I've watched an unrelated adult male climb and unclimb a tree three times, infinitely patient, before the kitten understood.

If we insist on keeping the kittens until their education

is complete, we have that much more time to watch kittens. This is entertainment of a high order, witty, charming, and sophisticated; comic routines refined for thousands of years, dancing Geminis of stagecraft, masters and mistresses of the "Oops, where did I put it? Oh, there it is!" spin, vertical leap of pretended astonishment, king-of-the-mountain, mistaken identity, dance to inaudible pipers, and the quick over-the-shoulder glance; are you watching? are you laughing, am I charming enough, shall I have a home? Kittens play, of course; kittens play when no one is watching, but no regular audience can doubt that some of this is for us. We're being courted as well as entertained. Watch me, watch me hide and spring out on my sister, pretend to be frightened, dance onto my hind legs with my eyes wide and my paws outstretched: can you resist? If it's agreed, then we can put some of this aside. Sign here, and we will be free to become a cat. It's the way it's always been.

Step by step they learn the lessons in etiquette, communication, hunting, hygiene, competition, cooperation, and friendship necessary for their lives, and frolic to charm their way into homes, and begin to change from kittens into cats.

Kittens are not cats; kittens are hardly even similar to cats, any more than caterpillars are to moths. There's a change that takes place, if you're watching, toward the end of the first year, that has nothing to do with sexual maturity. The kitten deepens, and takes on the resonance and shadow of a cat. Cats go on playing, they play all their lives, but we're no longer being asked to laugh. We aren't being courted. The relationship has changed, and if we've taken the time to be a figure in its life, it will want something more from us, confident in its home and focusing on us now as complete and separate beings. It wants our friendship now, a friendship between very different equals, and even something more than friendship, for reasons neither we nor it will ever really understand.

Practical Cats

12

Allergies, human: Bulletin boards are laden with notices trying to give away cats because someone's allergic. In the Cat Hospital, a sad letter was posted by a young woman about to get married, looking for a home for a cat she clearly loved, a cat in middle age, a cat no one was going to want; her intended was allergic to it. People passing through the waiting room had added comments on its margins: "Don't marry him!!!" "You'll be sorry," and "Bad trade!"

My next-door neighbor loves cats, and always stops to converse with mine when they sit on the windowsill supervising the street. She had always had cats. Alas, her husband is allergic to them, and all she can do now is chat with Morgan through the screen.

My son brought home a kitten, and his girlfriend sneezed and sneezed and her eyes watered, and now the kitten lives with me instead.

In a book I found a recipe for allergy-proofing cats, involving a coat conditioner and a bath in a solution of Downy fabric softener, and asked Dr. McDonough about it; she thought the Downey solution was far too strong but that, suitably watered down, it was worth a try. She said sometimes she recommended wiping the cat down with the fabric-softener sheets designed to go in the dryer. Then I read about Dust Seal.

Dust Seal was developed initially for people whose rugs and curtains make them sneeze, but after investigation it was pronounced harmless for use on animals. I sent for some. It arrived promptly and proved to be an innocuous, odorless white gruel, the consistency of Spackle mixed on the wet side. Stir a tablespoonful into a pint of water and sponge cat with it. I tried it on Barney as being the most allergenic-*looking* of them all; I know it isn't the fur itself, it's the dander, and length of coat doesn't count, but the very sight of all that puffball fur makes some people sneeze. To his annoyance, I sponged him down thoroughly and sent him off to spend a week in a small apartment with my son's girlfriend.

He was homesick, but she was fine.

According to the accompanying literature, once a month is often enough to rinse the cat (or dog, or rabbit, or horse; a horse might run into money). Fifteen dollars plus postage buys what looks like enough for a year or two, at least, since the pint of the recipe makes more than enough for even a Persian, and it comes by mail from Willner Chemists, 330 Lexington Avenue, New York, NY 10157, or direct from the makers, L.S. Green Associates, 162 West 56th Street, New York, NY 10019.

Of course, there's the strong possibility that "allergic" is a euphemism, a polite way to tell a cat person that one hates cats, finds them sneaky, sinister, and untrustworthy, and has recurring nightmares about finding them in one's bed, briefcase, shoes, etc.

In these cases it's doubtful that Dust Seal will help, and you might have to consider finding a good home for the person in question.

Bathtubs: They make good playpens. Ping-Pong balls, for instance, are splendid cat toys but have a habit of finding their way under the furniture, out of reach. A nice thing to do for a housebound cat is to put a couple in the bathtub where they can't escape and make a satisfying billiards sort of noise against the sides.

Catnip: A member of the mint family, catnip is hardy and easy to grow and hard to synthesize; most "catnip" toys you buy contain only wood chips sprayed with a chemical substance supposed, by humans, to smell like catnip, though not very much like catnip.

The plant is easy to grow in any waste corner of the yard that gets some sun and isn't soggy; it will grow in a deep pot on a sunny fire escape or patio or balcony. The only problem is protecting it from its fans.

In 1774 Goldsmith's *Natural History* stated, "The cat . . . is excessively fond of some plants such as valerian, marum, and cat-mint; against these it rubs, and smells them at a distance, and at last wears them out." Cats have no agricultural restraint; carnivores live for the moment. Plant a nice stand of catnip, and as soon as it rears its little heads the nearest cat will bite them off at ground level and then roll in the remains to make a scented dust bowl.

Catnip seeds can be had from most seed catalogs, listed under herbs. Start them according to directions in a safe place: a sunny windowsill in a room you can close against cats, or a spot on the far side of a closed door or window. When started in or transplanted to the open world they need a cage. A strong cage. I tried chicken wire first, but the cats just leaned against it until it collapsed. Sturdy metal stakes or cages such as garden centers sell to support tomatoes would be fine. I was lucky to find part of a rusty roll of sheep fencing, and Sidney, cat of infinite patience, sat beside it all summer as if at a mousehole waiting for the sprigs to grow through to him.

In June and again before hard frost, harvest it by cutting it back halfway, and bring the results inside to a dry, airy place away from direct sun. Tie the stalks together in bunches and hang them head down, well out of cat reach, until the leaves are dry enough to crumble in your fingers. Lock the cats in another room and strip it onto newspapers, discarding the tough stems. The hard black specks that sink to the bottom are seeds, if you want to increase your holdings. The more catnip you grow the less the cats will bother it, being jaded with plenty and content all summer with an occasional nibble; by snowfall they'll be avid again.

Store the dried catnip in a plastic bag in refrigerator, freezer, or bank vault; don't suppose for a minute that the cat can't sniff it out through a plastic bag, or twenty plastic bags and a cupboard door. Dole it out sparingly. A pinch on the rug goes a long way and leaves the rug desirable for days.

When you have a surplus you use it as a Christmas present for other cat owners. For a while there I made it up into proper felt mice with yarn tails and whiskers, and then I degenerated into felt bags tied with ribbons, and now, being pressed for leisure, I hand it over in a sandwich bag; no cat cares about the container. It makes a more original party gift than the usual bottle of wine, and besides, it's free. Some few people object to it on moral grounds, especially those who reveled in recreational drugs in their youth and repented, but everyone knows cats have no morals.

No one seems to know exactly why catnip pleases cats. Chemists say the compound that does it is cis-transnepetatalactone, which doesn't clear things up much. Apparently circus trainers were the first to use it, dosing their lions, who dropped instantly into besotted docility. Lions must react differently; my cats chase each other in circles, knock over lamps, speak in tongues, and pile the rugs up in corners. I'd hate to be in a cage with a lion that felt that way.

The United States government, it grieves me to report, has been known to use catnip to lure bobcats and pumas to their deaths.

Most veterinarians approve of it as a tonic, antidepressant, and stress reducer, but some of the puritanical sources, bothered by the thought of cats having fun, refer to it sniffily as a "stimulant" and caution against offering it frequently, which is silly because its effects diminish quickly with overuse. If it's a drug, it's self-limiting; unlike the things humans play with, the more they have the less they want. For maximum effect, ration strictly.

You can steep yourself a tea of it and try it as a cure for colds, nervous headaches, and insomnia, but it won't make you feel the way the cats feel. Pity. We could use something like that, along about February.

So can the cats.

It's considerate little touches like a cushion on a sunny windowsill and a supply of home-grown catnip that make *Felis* glad to be *domesticus,* and satisfied to keep us company.

Diseases, human: There isn't much except fleas that people can catch from cats, but there is toxoplasmosis.

Although more human cases of toxoplasmosis come from eating undercooked meat or digging bare-handed in the garden, it's possible to get it from cats. It's caused by a parasite, and threatening mainly to unborn children as a cause of birth defects, so some cool-hearted doctors simply advise pregnant women to throw their cats away. This isn't necessary, and if your cat never gets raw meat and doesn't go outdoors or eat mice there's very little chance it could be infected. Still, there are some simple precautions to take. The parasite passes through the cat and into the litter box, where it has to ripen and mature for several days before it turns dangerous; obviously, if you take the feces out of the box every day you never get any ripe parasites. (I'm told that many doctors insist on having the husband or other nonpregnant family members clean the litter box, but this has resulted in blameless cats being taken to shelters or turned from their doors to starve.) Use a scoop to lift the feces out and flush it down the toilet. Wear gloves when gardening. Wash hands after dealing with raw meat. Don't eat raw meat or feed it to your cat.

The vet can test the cat to see whether it's been exposed and the doctor can test the woman to see if she has; like measles, it doesn't strike twice, and a pregnant woman previously exposed to toxoplasmosis has nothing to worry about.

I understand we expect a vaccine, to be given to the cat, not the person, but it isn't on the market yet. In the meantime, refrain from panic and keep the litter box clean.

Eye contact: A cat likes to look at you, and likes you to look at him. Simply patting him while trying to read the paper isn't good enough; you have to look. Looking is conversation for cats, and even the youngest kitten, as soon as it can focus, will look you straight in the eye from ankle level. Some cats, when feeling especially fond of you, slowly close their eyes, like blowing a kiss. It's polite to answer. Close your own eyes back at him, slowly. Because a cat feels pleasant to the hand, we rely too much on the crudities of physical contact, but, as the Egyptians knew, eyes matter in cats, eyes are their signature, and seeing is their deft and elegant touch on their friends. The hand without the eye is an empty message to send back.

Fur on clothes: A roll of Scotch tape, carried at all times, is useful for quick touch-ups before attending business meetings and dinner parties. Wrap a loop of it sticky-side-up around your fingers and dab.

Games: There are various games a human can play with a cat, such as trailing a piece of string or accidentally moving the toes under the blanket, and various games a cat can play with a human, such as making him throw things to be retrieved. I don't know if it's possible, or desirable, to teach this to a cat, but some seem to come by it naturally. Charlie retrieved crumpled cigarette packs, but only my brand, Pall Malls. He even retrieved them after they'd been put in the trash and covered with coffee grounds and eggshells. Guests thought it was cute, and encouraged him, and kept throwing his cigarette pack across the room all evening, and he kept on bringing it back, and the guests left with pitcher's elbow. It was a repetitious, unimaginative game more suited to dog than cat, but Charlie was an unimaginative cat.

Then my husband and I quit smoking. Charlie sulked, and languished, until one day my husband came to me and accused me of cheating; Charlie had just brought him a crumpled Pall Mall pack. Later, when I let him out into the courtyard between the apartment buildings, as was our custom, he vanished into the area where the trash cans were kept. Ten minutes later he bounded back triumphant with a crumpled Pall Mall pack in his jaws; somebody out there smoked our brand. I suppose it was the only kind appropriate for retrieving; I suppose they smell distinctive. The game went on. And on, and on.

Hot weather: When traveling with a cat on a hot day, put a plastic bag full of ice cubes in the carrier. Keep noticing how the sun slants in through the car windows as you drive and try to keep the case away from it. Black carriers are particularly lethal, soaking up heat. If you park in the shade when you stop for lunch, remember the sun moves; leafy shade at noon may be a red-hot broiler by one. Get a carrier with maximum air flow. If in spite of all your cat starts staggering from the heat, cool it off instantly with all the water available.

In China: A special breed of long-haired cat is raised for its meat, and forms one of the essential ingredients in the classic Dragon-Tiger-Phoenix dish, representing the tiger. The dragon is usually snake, they say, and in the absence of phoenixes their part is supplied by the humble chicken. I don't have the exact recipe.

Jumping: Just because none of our previous cats has ever been able to jump up onto something or down from some-

where doesn't mean that nobody can. Some are better ath-
letes than others, or braver, or sillier. Never assume that the
new kitten, when it gets a bit more growth on it, can't jump
from the balcony into the street below, or up from the deck
onto the neighbors' roof.

Some vets warn us to prevent pregnant cats from high
jumping. They don't say how.

Kittens, choosing: They tell us that if we have a litter to
choose from, to pick the number-two kitten. Not the first one
out of the box, the bravest and most curious, because, they
say, it's likely to make trouble. And not the independent one
who doesn't hang out with the others and goes off on its own,
because it may not want to socialize with us, either. And
while sympathy is a virtue, not the one that huddles sadly in
a corner with its coat rough and its eyes running.

Advice is useless; kittens get chosen for unscientific reasons like suddenly crawling into our lap and purring. When I
went to pick a Siamese kitten, one of them, bored with being
inspected, decided to leave the room and I tried to detain
him by his little spike of a tail, and he whirled around with
a preposterous great shout of outraged dignity; he's still
shouting, Corvo is, and when he asks for a lap the glassware
trembles.

Litter pans: There's an amazing variety of products available for deodorizing litter pans; things to spray on top of the
mess or stir in with it or spread out under it, and disinfectants
to wash the pan with and plastic houses to contain it and its
noxious smells. Changing the litter seems to be a kind of last
resort, to try only when all else fails.

If there's a dead horse in your back yard, you don't keep
spraying it with aerosol cans of Piney Woods or Strawberry
Fields, you have the horse removed.

Cat litter is a great nuisance. It's heavy, heavy to buy and
carry home and even heavier to drag out with the trash. People quite naturally strive to have each ten-pound bag last as
long as possible, and longer. After a while it smells.

Cats are sensitive about their toilet functions, and have sensitive noses. If the pan smells bad to us, it must be agony to a cat, and going into one of those plastic litter-houses something like walking into the jaws of hell. A cat outdoors covers up its droppings and then turns to sniff the area to make quite sure no other creature can tell what happened there. A litter pan that tells the world what happened must be a worry, and a cat will keep trying to erase the smell, scratching the floor around it, trying to pull the shower curtain down over it.

On the other hand, what the manufacturer says smells like Strawberry Fields smells to a cat of mysterious and probably threatening chemicals, the predators of outer space, Dobermans from Mars.

All in all, it's good of them to use a litter pan at all.

People who work professionally with problem cats say that nine out of ten cases of cats "breaking training," as they say (rather like a football player sneaking a cigarette), can be traced to pan conditions.

We must take up the burden of cat-keeping and carry it, home from the store, out for the trash. No chemicals. No roofs, no disinfectants, no scented sprays. Just fresh litter, and a little plain water to rinse the pan, or use a plastic liner. And instead of using twice as much as recommended, hoping to make it last four times as long, use half as much, to last half as long.

A handful of baking soda mixed with the litter does no harm, and some swear by a handful of 20 Mule Team Borax. But there's no substitute for a fresh start.

Moving: A lot of cats vanish during the chaos of moving. It's heavy stress for a cat, even more so than for us since the motives are inexplicable, and home is a deeply personal matter to a cat; to have great shouting strangers burst in and start manhandling his furniture must be a nightmare.

Put the cat in his carrier before the movers come, and put the carrier in the quietest place, the car if possible, parked in a cool spot, or the bathroom. Leave him in the carrier. Take him to the new quarters and put the carrier in the quietest place or leave it in the car. Don't let him out until the movers have been paid off and gone away and the door is firmly shut. Even then, it's sensible to turn him loose gradually; this is a profoundly shaken cat, and may be happier locked in a bedroom with a bowl of water and some used and personally scented clothing of your own thrown around. Even if it's a safe area for a cat to go outdoors, best to keep him in the house for a week or two to get his bearings and calm down. Get acquainted with the resident spirits and hallucinations before he has to deal with the territory problem. Spoil him a little. You can even butter his paws, if he likes butter.

Novelty: The more businesslike books on cat care feel that a cat's needs are entirely nutritional and medical, and once he's properly fed and vetted your responsibilities are over. Routine, they say, is soothing to a cat, and he resents change; feed him at the same hour every day and he will be content.

I don't know. I suppose some cats resent change, maybe an old and crotchety cat whose favorite sofa has been sold down the river, but a predator's natural life is pretty various. No two days are alike, and no two meals arrive in the same way, let alone at the same hour, and the scents of his surroundings change with every breeze. Grazing animals enjoy monotony, and in the unvaried routine of a zoo a zebra will stand broadside to the same sunlight in the same enclosure, his lower lip twitching with pleasure, every day for ten years, but the panther paces back and forth.

I think a cat in confinement needs as much novelty as we can arrange. Even in the city, a cat can be taken out in a safe figure-eight harness, can go to the park if he's not afraid of passing dogs. A view of a busy street and pigeons helps. An occasional dose of catnip, change of diet, new place to sit, new cat in the household, a visit to a neighbor's apartment, a canary in a cage to lust for, a wind-up toy, human guests. Something to think about. Cats are intelligent, however strangely their intelligence works, and how can an intelligent creature keep its mind awake contemplating the same walls and smelling the same smells for years without change?

Opening doors: Where cats go out, opening doors to let them out and back in again has been a source of irritation and marital discord ever since cats moved in with us. Cat doors can be made in human doors, through which the cat may come and go without having to wake up the whole household. Sometimes the cat will invite friends in. In the country, it's not unheard of for the householder to go downstairs in the night investigating strange sounds and trip over a skunk in the dark kitchen.

There are cat doors on the market that are opened by a magnet on the cat's collar, activating a solenoid that releases the catch on the door to admit your cat, and only your cat. I don't know why they don't extend the idea to people and people doors, eliminating the need for door keys.

Pussywillows: A long time ago in Poland, an unwanted litter of kittens was thrown in the river to drown. Their mother sat on the bank and wept so long and so bitterly for them that the willows growing along the river's edge took pity on her and held down their branches for the drowning kittens to cling to. After that, every spring the willow bushes have sprouted soft little velvet buds like kittens' paws.

Qualyway: In Cornwall, this will cure a sty:

Take the tail of a black cat and stroke your eye outward from the nose, giving one stroke to each phrase as you chant:

> *I poke thee,*
> *I don't poke thee,*
> *I toke the quell that's under the eye.*
> *Oh, qualyway.*
> *Oh, qualyway.*

Renting: In the United States, and only in the United States, land of the free, it's the rule rather than the exception for landlords and rental agents to make as much fuss over a house cat on the premises as if one were harboring a brothel, or a rock band. No one seems to know why we put up with this, or why it happens in the first place, unless Americans came so recently to a wild country that we distrust all animals as the opposite of civilization, as unpredictable, probably dangerous, certainly unclean.

In Soviet Russia, home of oppression and the trampling of human rights, everyone, no matter how cramped the apartment, has cats and dogs, though some of the newer buildings try to limit the number of dogs to three, and the government provides free veterinary care.

In America, cats make criminals of decent folk. Me, for instance. For my rented house I signed a lease swearing to have no pet of any kind, not even a caged bird, nor to let any sort of creature pass through or inhabit the premises no matter how briefly. I am careful to pay my rent promptly, to deal with and pay for all repairs myself, and to keep my fingers crossed. I can be thrown out onto the street without further ado if I'm discovered. There is no legal recourse. My landlord is under no obligation to prove damage or cite complaints. He holds a month's rent of mine as guarantee that I and mine will do no more than ordinary damage, but apparently the potential for feline destruction is more than that would cover.

Every rental agent makes his own rules, and I once had a most generous lease that allowed me to own as many as two cats or a dog that weighed no more than twenty pounds, but most stand firm against all creatures.

I read a letter from a woman who waited five years for a public housing unit, and when she finally got it was told she could have only one cat. She managed to find homes for the other two, and then was told she had to take out a twenty-thousand-dollar insurance policy against her remaining cat's killing or injuring anyone.

Countless once-loved cats are gassed in the shelters because of landlords. Countless lonely, law-abiding citizens live without companions because of them. Convalescents, the depressed, and the elderly, needing the medical benefits of pet therapy, go without it. It's a mystery impenetrable that pets are not subject to the logic of leases, that no one will wait till the damage is done and claim payment for it, no one will wait till the neighbors complain and then evict the cat, no one will wait till it does kill someone and then demand restitution; it's taken for granted ahead of time that pets will destroy the property, cause bodily injury, and enrage the neighborhood; they are guilty before the crime is committed by reason of being themselves.

Even more mysterious is why we, alone of the world's peoples, put up with it.

Stains & spots: A cat that wolfs its dinner often throws it up again almost immediately, unchanged. Rarely on the kitchen tiles, rarely on the bare floor, usually on rugs and upholstery. No matter how promptly it's cleaned up, it leaves a pinkish-brown stain. This is from the dyes added to the cat food to make it more appealing, more meat-like, to the human eye. Most of the scientific, non-supermarket cat foods are made without dyes, a good idea for vomiters. In the meantime, after wiping it up, wash the area with a dab of dish soap and douse it with club soda, which takes out the dye stains and odors. White vinegar works too.

A cat that has used the rug for toilet purposes may go back and use the same place again. After applying one of the above, cover the area with double-sided sticky tape, most disagreeable to the paws, until the matter has been forgotten.

Traps, household: Cats are always getting closed into things. It's the nature of the cat to get into closable places, private, secret places like cupboards and closets and clothes dryers, bureau drawers and garden sheds and furnace rooms. Being well down below eye level, they get locked in unseen.

Before combing the neighborhood and posting frantic signs offering a large reward, open everything closable.

Before turning on the washing machine, dryer, or even the oven, feel around inside.

Up or underneath: There's a basic psychological difference between the wary cat posted on high ground, on strategic vantage points like a bookshelf or a tree, and the cat squeezed underneath something and trembling in its farthest corner. Up is a good place to be; you can see farther, and you can leap down on the enemy, and you're safe from dogs. Up is sensible; under is stark terror, and the hope of being unseen by an enemy against whom you have no recourse. A cat checking out its territory goes up, a cat in a hostile new household goes under.

This observation does not apply to the cat under the bed, who knows full well how hard it is for humans to rout out and hopes to be left there until the people have gone to sleep so it can emerge and snuggle under the covers.

Variety: *See* Novelty, above.

Walking with cats: Country cats like to go for a walk with their people. Do not invite a cat to walk with you if you have a time limit, or even a purpose. Cats walk more slowly than people. Cats, except at dinnertime, do not think in terms of destination. And cats refuse to hurry when urged to and resent being scooped up and carried. If you've gone too far, they complain bitterly. A country walk with a cat should include various rocks, benches, or fallen trees where the human can sit and wait until the cat is ready to proceed.

People who want to sell us leashes and harnesses for walking city cats illustrate their ads with cats striding briskly along the sidewalk beside their owners. The truth is, a harnessed cat is no more goal-oriented than a loose cat, and the complex instructions for training your cat to walk down the street like a person are fairy tales; walking from point A merely to get to point B is not a catly concept. We can, however, harness and leash the cat and carry it to a quiet spot or vacant lot or park and let it poke around and smell the interesting smells. We follow it where it wants to go, unwinding the leash from obstacles. A cat outside on the common ground of a city is on very strange territory, territory not its own, land already claimed by total strangers, mostly dogs; it would be an insensitive cat indeed who could simply march through this alien wilderness like a man on his way to the bus stop.

When we get bored with standing around, we pick it up and carry it home again. "Walk" is the wrong word.

Extra cats: They go to the shelters to be gassed. Not out onto the streets to starve or be killed in traffic. Not out to the country to be pushed from the car in some wooded spot where, we tell ourselves, there must be plenty of mice. Not to be pressed on friends who genuinely don't want them. To the shelters. The shelters won't be surprised to see us; they kill millions every year.

Yowling: According to the surviving cartoons, it used to be the custom to throw shoes. I suppose shoes were the handiest heavy object in a dark bedroom, and perhaps they used to be cheaper than they are now. It's unlikely that a sleepy human pitching his footwear at a sound somewhere out in the darkness ever actually hit a cat, or stopped the yowling if he did.

We can stop our own from yowling by having them altered, but little can be done about those alone in the world.

Zero population growth: A goal to strive for. *See* Extra Cats, above.

When Chateaubriand was French ambassador in Rome, Pope Leo XII, near death, presented him with his own dear cat Micetto. Later Chateaubriand wrote to Mme. Recamier, "I have as companion a big greyish-red cat with black stripes across it. It was born in the Vatican, in the Raphael loggia. Leo XII brought it up in a fold of his robes where I had often looked at it enviously when the Pope gave me an audience . . . I am trying to make it forget exile, the Sistine Chapel, the sun on Michelangelo's cupola, where it used to walk, far above the earth."

The Team

Dawson Perkins

AGATE

Chicago

Printed in Canada.

Library of Congress Cataloging-in-Publication Data

Perkins, Dawson.
    The team / by Dawson Perkins.
        p.   cm.
    ISBN 0-9724562-7-9
    1. African American women—Fiction.   2. Basketball players—
Fiction.   3. Male friendship—Fiction.   4. Rape victims—
Fiction.   I. Title.
    PS3616.E745T43 2004
    813'.6—dc22

                                                    2004000856

10 9 8 7 6 5 4 3 2 1

Agate books are available in bulk at discount prices.
For more information about this or other books from Agate,
go to agatepublishing.com

To Everett and Jamie,
the loves of my life.

~

· Prologue ·

1998: One Year Later

IT TOOK LESS THAN FORTY-EIGHT HOURS. Less than forty-eight hours after Terry Stuart reinvaded Gwen's life like secondhand smoke, he was dead. His death came eleven years too late in Gwen's mind, but she wasn't going to complain. She only hoped his journey back to the hell where he came from was one blistering, fiery bitch.

Three days ago he had come to Atlanta for a basketball game; his team played the Hawks. Ironic. For many years throughout his pro basketball career, Gwen would sense when he was in town, yet their paths had never crossed again before now.

Terry's reemergence into her life two days ago had blazed across the television screen. Headline news. He barely played enough minutes anymore to generate sports news, and his team had lost to the Hawks the night before anyway. But it's what happened after the game that caused the media storm.

Gwen noticed it first. She drew her attention away from the boisterous conversation going on in the house and stared at the television set. Terry's chump-ass team photo stared back at her; his head shot loomed over the shoulder of the news anchor like a dark cloud. The rest of the house soon took notice, too; someone shushed the room silent and cued up the volume. Everyone wanted to hear everything; everyone had an interest in the story; they all knew Terry and therefore they all probably figured the news couldn't be good. And it wasn't.

Terry had been with a woman hours after the game. They'd had sex in his hotel room: Terry claimed consensual, the woman claimed sexual

assault. Terry had been picked up and questioned. No charges filed as of yet and an investigation was still pending. End of information.

The television volume had barely been turned down before the comments started:

"...that bitch is lying..."

"Not now, man..."

"I'm just speaking the truth. Hell, you know how them hoop-ho's can be..."

"Man, shut the hell *up*..."

A grunt followed, then a few seconds of silence, then more comments:

"Poor Terry, his life just seems to keep going downhill..."

"...that's cause some greedy-ass sister always tryin' to keep a brother down..."

"Will you shut the hell up..."

Gwen wanted them all to shut up; she hadn't spoken, hadn't moved, wasn't sure she had even breathed. She expected the comments she heard. Terry was an athlete. Snatching pussy wasn't something he needed to do, since it was normally as readily available as an ATM.

Poor Terry, those two words resonated in her head—*Poor Terry*. Fuck Terry. Why was this happening? Why did it have to happen here in Atlanta, where she lived, where she had just started a new beginning almost a year ago?

She had been kidding herself, that's why. She'd been playing with fire for the past year and now she was about to get burned in the ass.

Talk continued to buzz. She still hadn't spoken, too numb to talk right now. Her movements were slow. She grabbed her purse and walked out the door.

The next night Terry was dead.

· ONE ·

THE BED SHEETS COILED TIGHTLY around Gwen's leg, caught up in the battle she seemed to be losing—although that didn't keep her from fighting the good fight, giving her demon a good ass-kicking, and chalking one up for the home team. The home team needed points on the board; Gwen needed points for her battered psyche, even if the abuse was being doled out via nightmare.

The dream seemed so real, too real even for reality's sake. She was awake—at least she felt she was awake. The heavy bass of rap music thumped against the walls, keeping perfect time with each stab between her legs: sharp, painful stabs, like an anatomical, custom-made blade. And ice cream. Vanilla ice cream. She could see it so clearly, dripping, gooey, disgusting.

Even during the struggle, she wondered in a subliminal fog why her dreams couldn't start with once-upon-a-time pleasantries instead of this sadistic crap.

Gwen heaved a loud breath as her eyes jolted open and her body lunged upward like the living dead. *Shit,* she thought, *why now?* The laughter still squealed in her head like pigs in a slaughterhouse while she studied her hand, making sure the blood hadn't seeped from her nightmare and become reality. It hadn't, but damn if the subconscious didn't have a wicked sense of humor.

Gwen looked around, adjusted her eyes to the dark, and concentrated on the room. She wanted to make sure she was in her room, make sure curtains draped the windows instead of dulled-white bed sheets, make sure African American artwork hung on the wall instead of sports posters, and make sure her collection of porcelain and wooden elephant figurines stood watch from the glass display case

they called home, instead of those gaudy, action-figure-like trophies. She arranged her beloved elephants so they faced the bed, seemingly on guard as if they could magically come to life and stampede any unwanted intruders. They hadn't come to life but they still stood in her room. Thank God. She was in her room. *That wicked-ass dream,* she thought.

Gwen shuddered, ran her fingers through her hair, and blew hard. Now she was awake, really awake, and by the way her heart thumped against her chest and the mangled state of her bed, one thing was clear—no points were scored for the home team.

She leaned across her queen-sized bed and turned on the lamp. As always, she reached in the nightstand drawer and checked to make sure her Glock was still babysitting. She ran her fingers across the handle, stared at it a few seconds more, then slammed the drawer shut. The digital clock's wide numbers caught her attention. Three-fifteen in the a.m.: less than two hours before it was assigned to awaken her. She grumbled, pissed that she had been woken from her sleep, but then again, the sleep wasn't that good in the first place. Good sleep was the only sleep that mattered, anything else she considered a waste of time.

She stretched and yawned, feeling her T-shirt cling to her like cellophane. The room's temperature maintained its sixty-five-degree chill, yet sweat still bathed her body.

"Shit," she spat out loud. Nightmares pissed her off, and the thought that she hadn't had one in close to a year made her doubly uneasy.

Gwen jostled herself out of bed and into the bathroom. Might as well get up and get ready for work. She flipped the light switch, pulled her T-shirt over her head, threw it in the corner, and watched as it crumpled in defeat.

The image of herself in the mirror didn't please her. It hadn't pleased her in a long time. She pumped out a healthy dose of Olay facial cleanser and smoothed it across her face, working the creamy white lather over her brown skin—light brown, the color of chestnuts, sprinkled with a few freckles on each cheek. Once she rinsed her face, she looked at herself again.

She looked like her mother. Just like her mother—dark, reflective eyes, full lips, ripe cheeks easily pierced by dimples with the mere suggestion of a smile. Her father always told her she was growing into a strong, beautiful woman—as strong and beautiful as her mother, once she fully blossomed—but her mother often warned her about the responsibilities that came with being a woman, and to be careful in trying to rush the process. She ignored her warning for years—thought she was the finest thing since sliced bread. Now, she thought being pretty was so irrelevant in the grand scheme of things. And she wished she could have lived up to her mother's strength on the inside; maybe then she could have learned that outward beauty didn't mean jack. Her parents had been dead fourteen years. They never saw her blossom into much of anything.

Gwen usually listened to Stevie Wonder's *Songs in the Key of Life* while she got ready for work to get her going. Not this morning, though. She felt uneasy, still disturbed by that damn nightmare—not so much its contents, as it rarely changed, but just the fact that she'd had it. Not good.

Worry about it another time, she told herself. She had time to take an extra-long shower; she *took* an extra-long shower. When she finished, she wrapped a towel around her head, already feeling the wet strands begin to spindle into their naturally curly state. She would leave the towel in place for a while, let it dry her hair. She had hair like her mother, too. Curls she once hated. She spent a fortune on relaxers when she was younger, hell, just a few years ago even. Finally she gave up the battle; relaxers nearly ruined the grade of hair she had, handed down from her mother and her Nana. So now she wore it natural, cut close, tapered on the sides and back, with a bit more length on top; an option of less mess/no fuss that was becoming more and more popular for African American women. Short or weaved—those seemed to be the choices of the decade. Anything in-between vanished like the dinosaur.

Dressed in only her black bra and panties, Gwen began to make the bed, tugging on the yellow fitted sheet, and then noticed the soiled spot left by her night sweats. The nightmare again. She reached for the

cordless phone on the nightstand; she'd call Payton, tell her about it, ask for her thoughts on why she'd had it.

Payton was her best friend, a psychologist now living in Boston. They met in college at the University of South Carolina in Columbia. They bonded under strained circumstances, but had become best friends regardless. That was nine years ago. A year after the college thing. That's what Gwen called it. It made its true title sound less threatening, less vicious.

She dialed the number, then clicked the phone off. "What the hell," she mumbled out loud. It wasn't even five o'clock in the morning and she's trying to get a nightmare analysis.

Foolishness is what she thought of her irrational behavior. Payton would have called it "a spontaneous need to validate." Same thing—foolishness. Not that Payton would have cared if she called; in fact, she loved any opportunity to spew psychobabble, or even just babble-babble. That was Payton. Gwen called her a Southern white-bread valley girl trying to get initiated into flygirl sisterhood. Payton would agree, then laugh, then spew more babble. They kept in touch once a week, rotating turns, and still carried on like college kids. They spoke the same language, could even finish each other's sentences from time to time, and almost always allowed a little nonsense into their conversations. With Payton it seemed unavoidable.

No, Gwen thought, placing the phone back in the cradle. She would call Payton tonight at her usual scheduled time. The nightmare was nothing. She didn't need validation, at least not first thing in the morning, and by the end of the day it would be a blip on her memory. She caught a glimpse of herself in the full-length brass mirror and straightened her shoulders out, lifted her head high, slightly jutting her chin. Self-doubt had no place inside her; there was no room for guilt. She did a quick nod of her head, proudly.

Walking back into the bathroom, she retrieved the T-shirt from the corner. It still felt moist, and still smelled pungent from a night of angry sleep. She looked back at the clock: five-twelve a.m. Something inside her stirred; her hands felt clammy; the resurgence of perspiration twinged underneath her arms; her breathing heaved. She closed

her eyes and threw the T-shirt back down. She had time for another shower.

Gwen felt a little better as she cruised toward downtown Atlanta. She considered her morning commute one of the best, if not *the* best, moments in her day. It was rarely hectic; she regularly traveled to work while the sun, in all its blazing glory, rose right before her eyes.

This morning, *Maxwell's Urban Hang Suite* played softly on the car CD. A sweet breeze slipped through the partially opened sunroof and helped Gwen's need to shake her creeping malaise. The high-rises welcomed her in the distance; the sun's rays glistened down them like liquid energy, ready to be gulped down as if they were huge power shakes. Gwen inadvertently licked her lips as if savoring the last drop. Suddenly she felt empowered by them; she felt the urge to blast away her angst like the Incredible Hulk busting out of his shirt. *I am Gwendolyn Fagan, dammit. Get a grip...*

Gwen settled further into the gray leather seats, turned the CD volume up a notch, and smiled. Just the sight of the city, her city, her hometown the first fourteen years of her life, reinvigorated her.

After her parents died, she and her brother, Weldon, moved to Augusta, Georgia, and lived with their maternal grandmother, Nana. College came next. First, a one-year stint in North Carolina; then the college thing happened, and afterward she struggled four more years at the University of South Carolina, trying to get an education and maintain her sanity. Which she had.

She moved back to Atlanta almost five years ago and found her niche in the world. She was twenty-eight years old, independent and financially secure; occasionally she could claim to be content. In any case, these were three things she never imagined a hometown could provide.

It was only March and already 1997 was showing signs of being a year of good fortune. She had received a promotion at work three weeks ago and her yearlong relationship with Ellis had ended over a month ago. Things were definitely looking up.

The song *Suitelady* began, jazzy and soft, producing a pang of guilt inside Gwen's chest. Why did she have this CD playing in the

first place, she wondered? It was one of her favorites, but this song in particular had been cut from the best selection list. Ellis, knowing how much she liked Maxwell, had played this song on the night he proposed, maybe thinking the music would make up for the fact that she didn't love him and that she might accept his proposal anyway. Foolishness. She told him no.

Her car phone chirped excitedly, like a chorus of crickets on helium. Gwen looked at the clock—a few minutes before seven a.m.—and figured it had to be Payton. She was probably calling to babble off some *People* magazine gossip she forgot to relay last week. Maybe they could process the nightmare after all. With the phone on hands-free, Gwen pressed the send button and said, "Give me the dirt."

"Hi, Gwen, darling. It's me."

Oh shit...

"Ellis?"

"Yeah, I tried to catch you at home, but I forgot you leave at the crack of dawn."

"Wh—Where are you?" Gwen turned the CD volume down further. She definitely didn't want Ellis to hear it playing.

"I'm at the airport. My flight leaves in an hour."

"I thought you weren't leaving for Minneapolis until tomorrow."

"Change of plans. I wanted to go ahead and try to settle in. And since there's really nothing keeping me here..."

"Ellis..." Gwen felt another jab in her chest. She was the "nothing" he spoke of and she immediately resented it. It wasn't that she wasn't keeping him in Atlanta, but that she had refused to go with him; his transfer to Minnesota had given her the out she needed.

"Gwen, listen, I'm sorry. That was a cheap shot. I don't mean to sound like some kind of pathetic fool. You gave me your reasons for not coming with me and I'm trying to respect them."

Gwen remained silent. What could she say? Ellis wanted her to come with him, be his wife, but she had every valid excuse to turn him down—a job with promise, a mortgage, roots...

"Gwen, I just called to say goodbye."

"Ellis, I hope you have a safe trip and I'm sorry things didn't work

out." She really wanted to say, "See ya," but she didn't. They had hashed everything out days ago, over and over again. Ellis liked to push the issue in a passively annoying way. And now she was sure he would try again.

"You don't love me, do you?"

Shit!

"Ellis, why are you doing this?" Gwen asked in her stern, professional voice. At the office, she was known for her directness and rarely suffered bullshit.

Ellis sighed, as if her question disturbed him. "I guess that's a no."

"Ellis, it's a 'why are you asking this now' question. Huh?" She chastised him as if he were a child. He didn't answer. Neither one of them spoke. Gwen's resentment grew like kudzu. Why was he doing this? It was a classic case of boy-loves-girl-but-girl-doesn't-love-boy. And Ellis was a good man, a prime catch for most women.

He worked in computer software. She met him while her accounting firm conducted an audit of his company for a merger. Ellis always managed to manipulate his way into a seat beside her during meetings; he told corny jokes that made her laugh, sometimes, mainly because they seemed to tickle him to no end. She thought he was sweet, but dating wasn't something she wanted to do. When he asked her out the first time, she had the perfect excuse. Their working relationship precluded it and could cause a conflict of interest. He said he understood, but a week after the audit wrapped up she received a dozen yellow roses and a note requesting a dinner date. Sure, why not, she thought. One dinner wouldn't hurt, and Gwen still didn't think in terms of a relationship. Somehow it became one. She was still confused as to how.

Throughout the relationship, they conducted themselves more like business partners than dating mates; they mostly talked business, and only occasionally talked personal stuff, usually a one-sided conversation led by Ellis. He liked to talk about his childhood in upscale Connecticut—private-school upbringing, Ivy League education, Martha's Vineyard summers. Gwen revealed very little about herself and Ellis never seemed to notice. And when she insisted she meet him at functions instead of him picking her up, and insisted he not

stay overnight because she had bouts with insomnia, he didn't seem bothered by that, either. To Gwen, it seemed so obvious she didn't love him, but maybe to Ellis that's what love looked like. But they did become sexually involved, nonetheless. Gwen could tolerate the sex but she rarely enjoyed it, not like she had before the college thing. And with Ellis that was almost handled in a professional manner, too. Always in the missionary position with very little foreplay, a couple of kisses, a few gropes, and on to business, followed by separate showers. That suited Gwen just fine.

"Gwen, are you there?" Ellis asked.

"I'm here, Ellis. I just don't under—" Gwen slammed on the brakes. She saw the yellow light turn red as she approached it, but her reflexes didn't even bother to slow her car. The tires screeched; a shrill, piercing sound reverberated long after the car had stopped. Gwen froze, gripped the steering wheel, then looked up and wanted to cry.

What the hell is happening...

First the nightmare, then Ellis, and now she had nearly run down an old lady with a black knit cap pulled down over her ears. The woman stood in front of the car, one hand clutched to her chest and the other held out in front of her like one of the Supremes singing, "Stop! In the Name of Love." Her body jerked to a halt, literally bracing for the hit with one arm and one leg yanked up in defense. Gwen hated sports, but the first image conjured up in her mind was that the old lady looked like just the Heisman Trophy. Gwen threw up her hand, an apologetic peace offering of sorts, and received a nasty scowl. The old lady's body unfolded; she cursed Gwen for a few seconds, her dry lips moving about like mush, then she finally trudged away.

"I'm sorry I called you, Gwen. I didn't mean to upset you. But you know, I want to tell you something I think you really need to hear." Now Ellis sounded authoritative, almost pompous. "You're running from something, Gwen. I don't know what it is or why. But just don't run forever. You're too beautiful for that." Ellis paused, his words rising and falling above the ruckus of the Hartsfield International Airport.

Gwen slanted her eyes and exhaled sharply. "Goodbye, Ellis" she

said without giving credence to his last stupid statement; she cut his mumble short with a quick tap of the end button.

Gwen listened to the silence. Ellis could go to hell. She wished he hadn't even bothered to call and just left. His bullshit definitely wasn't even worth the minutes he'd just put on her cellular phone bill. Gwen took a deep breath. Typical man. Thought he knew so much, but really knew next to nothing.

She turned the CD player off and tuned into V103.3 FM. Chantay Savage crooned a soulful rendition of the classic disco hit *I Will Survive*. How appropriate. Gwen tapped her slender fingers against the steering wheel in perfect time with the beat. *Running*. Ellis wanted her to stop running. Further proof of how little he knew; she wasn't running, she was surviving.

By the time Gwen drove into the parking garage of the Wachovia Building, she had already purged Ellis's phone call from her memory. She left her black Infiniti with Ted, the parking attendant, and accessed the employee entrance with her security badge. She waved to the guard on duty and stepped onto the elevator with another woman to whom she issued a solid, "Good morning," yet received only a soft "Mornin'" in reply, as if the "good" had yet to be determined.

The woman was vice president of a large marketing firm; Gwen recognized her picture from a brochure left in the lobby after one of their orientations. Gwen smiled politely and pushed button number fourteen for herself, then looked at the woman for a request. "Number seventeen, please," came out as a haunting whisper, as the woman settled into the back of the oak-paneled elevator, nearly slouching two inches off her height.

The mirrored doors closed, giving Gwen a full snapshot of herself again. Now, as she did every morning, she took a visual inventory. This morning she had selected the coffee-colored Donna Karan pantsuit tailored to fit. Her jewelry consisted only of small diamond earrings, a diamond pendant necklace, and a watch. She wanted to look professional, assertive—take no prisoners and leave no evidence.

I am Gwendolyn Fagan, dammit. Get a grip...

She tugged on her jacket and took a deep breath. Whatever freaky

vibes had invaded the air and were causing all this foolishness would have to cease; she needed to get back into her tough-as-nails stance.

Gwen glanced at the woman still folded up like an accordion behind her. She hadn't looked away from her fingers, which she drummed against her briefcase. She wore an expensive red suit, a symbol of power to many, but the suit was a size too large, and her neutral hose and runover shoes screamed only one word—*defeat*. Bad move, Gwen thought. Don't ever give the appearance of defeat in public, only victory, confidence. Gwen glanced again. This woman looked as if she could be controlled by strings.

The elevator stopped on the tenth floor and three men moseyed in like cattle, as if the only time that mattered was their own. They were big men, wearing big suits, carrying coffee mugs and talking loudly, all at the same time. They acknowledged no one. Gwen moved to her left only slightly as one of the men reached for the button panel and pushed number eleven. Gwen frowned, *one floor up, no wonder they're so damn big.* They continued to chatter as Gwen looked in the mirror and tried to find the woman in red. She had moved further back, hidden behind a wall of houndstooth suit cloth, refusing to make her presence known.

Pick yourself up dammit, be a woman, stand tall, look proud...

Gwen wanted to jerk the woman in red to the front, pull her up by her lapels, and force her to look at herself in the mirror.

Don't ever let a man see you as weak. Ever.

Gwen felt pointless anger swell in her chest. She gripped the handle of her Coach briefcase and stewed momentarily. The elevator stopped and the men disappeared; floor number fourteen quickly arrived. She took a quick look at herself again and suddenly the nightmare flashed through her mind like a series of slides. Her eyes closed, the pictures flashed past, then she did a quick shake of her head to get rid of them. Again she looked at herself as the doors carefully opened. She looked in control, but didn't really feel it, not today. Not like she normally did. What was going on, she wondered? The woman in red smiled at her, her lipstick already chewed off and her hair stringy. Gwen realized

she looked like Gwen felt—beat down. The doors nearly shut before Gwen hopped off and marched into her office.

It wasn't quite midmorning and Gwen was caught up in the usual business of reviewing portfolios and meeting new clients. She loved it. She had worked for the Talbot and Talbot accounting firm for nearly five years and had carved out a reputation as one of the best certified public accountants in Atlanta. She was now consulting with an internal accountant for one of their major clients, trying to work out the details for a pending acquisition.

"Listen, I understand the anxiety you're ex—" Gwen stopped talking practically in midsentence. She watched as two men rounded the corner, getting a clear view of them from her open door. Gwen shook her head violently, thinking she couldn't be seeing the man she was seeing. Her eyes closed, she forced the lids shut, willing them to work some magic and make the image disappear. Make that person disappear. Hell, make her disappear. The client on the phone asked if she was still there. "Yes, yes, I'm sorry, where were we," she stammered, keeping her eyes closed. The client repeated Gwen's last sentence and she picked it up and continued. Her heart raced. She opened her eyes, slowly, one lid at a time.

This can't be happening...

The image remained. He stood with Vaughn Talbot, Jr., her boss and part owner of the firm. Vaughn was making introductions, hands were being shaken, and smiles went off like flashbulbs throughout the office. There were lingering looks from some of the females as they passed by, making their way toward her office. Hell, even some of the men took another gander. Gwen shook her head and frowned; her heart began to beat rapidly and her insides seemed to tremor on cue. This moment, right now, must have been the reason for the freaky vibes that were afflicting her. She looked again.

Xavier Dean, "Fessor X," as he had been known in college. It was slang for Professor, given the fact he was both an athletic and academic success, a rarity. But he had been one of *them*. One of the five

considered the elite, untouchable on the basketball court, thus making them omnipotent off of it. It was at the college in North Carolina, a Division I school that lived and breathed basketball. The 1987 team was considered one of the best there had ever been, led by Terry "The Man" Stuart, star center and Xavier Dean's best friend. All five starters had been dubbed "The Team" by the local media, who, like the entire campus, surmised that without those five young men there would be no team. All five were seniors and shared a three-bedroom townhouse off campus, and threw only the best parties, invited only the most popular females. One particular night, Terry Stuart chose one fresh-man girl to rape. Xavier Dean had been a member of The Team, and Gwen had been the chosen.

"Gwendolyn Fagan, I want you to meet our newest member, Xavier Dean." Vaughn was in her office making introductions before she had hung up the phone properly and before she could leap across her desk and slam the door in their face. It would have been an unprofessional move, but it would have bought her some time. Time to think. She stood, mechanically.

"Nice to meet you," Xavier extended his hand. Gwen just looked at him.

He hadn't changed too much—the basketball jersey had been traded in for a tailored suit, the sneakers for Cole Haans. He sported a silky black mustache, but there wasn't a hair on his head, which appeared to be shined to a high gloss, and he had maintained his athletic build, adding maybe ten pounds. He had been the quietest of the five, but they had never been thought of as individuals in the past and Gwen wasn't about to start now.

The anger swelled again; she could feel it telling her to spit in his face, telling her to shout, "Go to hell." But that hadn't worked for Terry, so it probably wouldn't do any good now. She forced her hand up like a wrecking ball, shook his, and said, "Welcome to the firm," not attempting to make it sound like she meant it.

He smiled pleasantly. His teeth were as straight and white as piano keys, and it was obvious he didn't recognize her. But why should he? They had been the stars, not her. His hand was warm and the grip re-

strained, yet it lasted a little too long; she jerked it back. His eyebrows rose, and he studied her. She studied back, defiantly. Xavier smiled again, not as wide, then put his hands in his pockets and looked to Vaughn. Gwen looked at Vaughn too as he steadily praised her talents, going on about how she seemed to be a magnet for new clients. Talbot clients wanted someone they could trust, someone who knew what she was doing, and more importantly someone who would give them the down and dirty without a lot of fluff. That was Gwen, and Talbot and Talbot was lucky to have her.

Gwen could feel Xavier's eyes on her again. Maybe she did look familiar to him. Of course, he had been there that night, the night of the college thing—the rape. Her rape.

It was 1987. The party had been thrown *by* The Team *for* The Team after their loss to Louisville in the NCAA Tournament Elite Eight. It was Terry's idea, and although the loss had been heartbreaking, he had vowed to party win or lose. And whatever Terry wanted Terry got. Like every day was Christmas.

That night, Gwen had gone to the party with one of her girlfriends who'd had a revolving crush on all of them at one time or another. Gwen tagged along without giving much thought to hooking up with a new guy. She already had a couple who wanted to be her exclusive, acting bold and possessive. But she just wanted to chill out, have some fun. A number-one brother wasn't on her agenda.

Until she saw Xavier. Instant crush, though she'd never noticed him before that night. Basketball wasn't her thing; she never followed it, regardless of how good The Team played. But that night, she thought Xavier looked so damn cute, standing against the wall, holding a beer and bobbing his head to the beat. She stared at him from a distance and took note of his humble features, particularly his warm smile and his lack of in-your-face bravado. Finally, her stare attracted his stare and he winked. For Gwen, that was a cue to go for it, not knowing whether he had a girlfriend or not. But back then, she didn't really care.

Except Terry intervened before any words could be exchanged. He

approached her, his long bulky body swaggering John Wayne style, and stood between her and Xavier.

Terry had hard features, eyes set deep in their sockets, and creases tightly sutured into his forehead like a Frankenstein creation. His bravado was so thick it smelled. He wasn't ugly, but definitely sinister.

His rap was lame: "Yo baby, why don't you and me see how many points we can score, with yo fine self." Gwen surveyed him up and down with a raised eyebrow like he had lost his mind, and replied, "Sorry, I don't feel much like playing..." Gwen blew him off in front of friends and fans. That made Xavier laugh, and he told Terry, "Guess she told you, my brother," then he left to talk to someone who had called his name. Terry grabbed her forearm and told her, "That shit wasn't funny," but Gwen snatched her arm back and said, "The shit sounded funny to me." He called her "bitch" as she pushed her way by him with a raised back hand, as if to say, *please, don't waste my time.* It was a signature move for her back then: a slight wave of the hand, a sassy flip of her long hair, and a swank in her walk.

The rest of the night went without incident until she was ready to leave. Gwen didn't see Xavier again until she went looking for her purse. The townhouse was large and the bedrooms were upstairs, separated from the party atmosphere, but the music still rocked through the house like thunder. She opened one of the bedroom doors and found Xavier on the phone. He gave her a double-dose angry look since her abrupt entrance allowed the party noise to filter into the room. She felt embarrassed and slipped out quickly, closing the door behind her.

She found her purse in the bedroom two doors down—the master bedroom, where Terry was waiting for her. He stood behind the door like black wallpaper and closed it once she walked in, then held her purse above her head and asked, "Feel like playing now, bitch?" Gwen smiled a little; she really was scared as shit, but she was sure she could charm her way out of the room. He was a man. A little stroking of the ego worked every time. She approached Terry, glided right up to him, but her smile quickly dissipated at the sight of his eyes—black as coal, showing no emotion, no compassion. He and Lucifer were good friends,

if Terry wasn't the devil himself. Gwen tried to put her smile back on, still figuring he had to be a guy who could be reasoned with—"Come on now, Terry, it's late and I really just want to go home. Come on now." Gwen's fingers trailed down his arm, hitting every bulge and pulsating vein along the way. He grabbed her hand so quickly she released a yell, but that didn't deter him from ramming her hand in his crotch, where she felt something that didn't feel quite natural.

"Bitch, you gonna ride my dick before you go anywhere," Terry said, throwing her purse to the side and jerking her like a rag doll into his abdomen. He gripped her wrist like shackles and held her other hand hard against his chest. The bulge in his pants grew twice the size it was before, her hand forced to massage him, make him harder, make him moan. He pushed her fingers against him, ran her hand down his balls, then up again. Still, this shit was just pissing her off; fear had not fully settled into her psyche. Terry was an asshole and she would treat him as such. She changed her tactic, thinking she was in a house full of people and this chump-ass brother thought he was going to *take* without an offer. Like hell.

"You stupid motherfucker, you can kiss my ass." Gwen drew up a mammoth glob and spat in his face. Terry ran his hand across her saliva, then stuck his fingers in his mouth, tasting her anger. He let go of her hands, but still stood in her way. She rubbed her wrists, pushed her hair out of her face, and thought she had won. Terry smiled, re-vealing a row of crowded teeth, and spoke, evenly: "I like my bitches with some fight. Makes my dick hard."

Gwen's eyelids drooped; every ounce of victory drained from her body. She made a quick run for the door, but he scooped her up like a toddler and threw her body, wrapped by his, onto the bed. She screamed *"NOOO,"* a long, desperate wail, but Terry was inside her before she finished it. He ripped her apart and ignored her pleas, which only served to strengthen his strokes.

Gwen closed her eyes at the thought, then opened them, in her office again, as Vaughn continued to talk. She glanced again at Xavier Dean. He had been two doors down that night. She often wondered what

role he had played in it. Maybe he was the one who walked in and immediately excused himself, as if he had interrupted two young lovers just trying to get busy away from the crowd. Gwen just remembered the door opening, the music swarming in momentarily, and someone saying, "Shit, sorry, Terry," before the door slammed shut. Gwen alternated between trying to fight and trying to just ride it out, thinking that if she just laid still he would come and be done with it. Then the rage she felt would take control of her again, and again she would squirm underneath him like she was tied to the tracks and the train was coming at her. Terry lay on top of her, holding her arms over her head as he rocked wildly back and forth. He was so strong, so painful; he pinned her body with his and chanted, "Say my name bitch, The Man, say it…" She never did. She just stared at the ceiling, at the poster plastered above, nauseated at the sight.

Maybe Xavier was the next one who walked in, laughing, a laughter so high pitched it squealed. He said he wanted next, told Terry, "Don't stop fucking that bitch, give it to her, give it to her…" each time Gwen begged Terry to stop. Terry had no intention of stopping, and the laughter persisted above the thumping rap music that blasted downstairs where people continued to party. Gwen could barely see who was in the room with them that night; she could only hear his whiny voice, laughing, taunting. She was being raped and someone thought it was funny. Through grunts, Terry told the cackling audience of one to leave: "Yo homey, step." Whoever it was—whether Xavier or not—had grumbled through slurred speech, telling Terry to get him when he finished so he could get a piece. Then he finally did as he had been ordered and stepped back out the door.

Terry's liquor-laced sweat dripped onto Gwen's face. Her body felt numb underneath his and she finally stopped fighting, closed her eyes, and wished she were dead. He finally finished and came all over her thighs, like lava from a volcano. Then he laughed, saying, "You think you all that and yo pussy wasn't about shit." Terry raised off her and dropped to the floor, doing push-ups, almost as if raping her had been part of some insane warm-up exercise.

Gwen rolled onto her stomach, pushing up by her elbows. She

clutched her head with both hands, smothering her cries in the sheets that smelled as if they had been doused in pickle juice. Robotically, she drew her blouse up around her shoulders, then pulled her skirt down from around her hips. Her hand brushed against something wet, thin like water. She ignored it as she managed to turn herself over, sitting on her bottom, which was so painful she yelled as if she had just felt the first strike of a thorny switch. Blood covered her palm like paint; her hand trembled as she wiped it against her black skirt, watched as it blended in, turning a dull brownish-black like a ketchup stain.

Terry counted out twenty quick push-ups, then hopped up, looked at her, and laughed again. He grabbed her purse and threw it to her, and told her, "Get your tired ass out of my bed," unless he wanted her to call his boy back, who had a thing for "secondhand pussy." Gwen rolled off the bed slowly, all her fight diminished. The room spun around like the view from the suspended swings at the state fair; her head hurt from being beaten against the headboard, and she didn't know what to do. Cursing him was out, right along with screaming. Terry was crazy and he'd kill her if she even thought about it; of that she felt certain.

She inched toward the door, snail-like, her legs held together tightly, so sore and bruised she feared that if she extended them her insides would fall out. And what if he rushed her? What if he only told her to leave just to grab her again and do it all over? But Terry had retreated to the bathroom and on to the business of relieving himself, clearly not too worried about her whereabouts.

She left, broken, bruised, and infuriated, a very different eighteen-year-old girl than when she had arrived. She never told anyone, at least anyone of authority, something she often regretted. But who was going to save her sanity? Who could put her back together, physically and emotionally, return her carefree spirit, her naiveté, her sexuality? Those were the things she thought of back then and still thought of from time to time now. A few weeks later, she just left: left North Carolina, left the campus. She never saw anyone from The Team again.

And now The Team had found her. She held her stomach with one hand and pressed her other hand against her mahogany desk. The

taste of bile filled her throat. She was going to throw up. She looked at Xavier and watched a smile spread across his face like first light across a desert. *What the hell is he smiling at...*

Gwen straightened up, refusing to give this asshole the satisfaction of seeing her disintegrate. Her look bore holes into him, sending a clear message: *keep smiling and I'm gonna fucking dropkick you.* She knew karate, now, and would gladly use it. Xavier drew his head back as if he had been struck and stopped smiling. Message received. Gwen reverted her glance again to Vaughn.

"Xavier's new to Atlanta, Gwen. Moved here from D.C., where he worked for the Barker firm. Of course you know their reputation, and they've recommended Xavier highly. Not that he needed it." Vaughn patted Xavier on the back. "Fessor X's academics received almost as much publicity as his game. I have painful memories of that team, I tell you. You guys beat up on my alma mater pretty good in the Sweet Sixteen, but I have to give it to you, y'all were awesome." Vaughn gave Xavier another attaboy chuckle while Xavier stood shaking his head, appearing almost shamefaced. Gwen's nausea bubbled.

"Come on now Vaughn, you're embarrassing me. I haven't heard 'Fessor X' in years. I'm sure Ms. Fagan doesn't want to hear about a decade-old basketball game." Xavier looked at her and smiled again, cautiously. Gwen didn't smile back.

You got that right, asshole. I don't really care to hear a damn thing about you or the past; where you came from, why you're here, and what you've done...

"I've never really followed basketball," is how she responded instead. Energy was finding its way back into her.

Never let a man—especially an asshole—see you as weak.

Gwen picked up a manila file she had opened on her desk and flipped through the pages, giving the indication that she had work to do and they were keeping her from it. There was an awkward silence. Vaughn's hazel eyes, shadowed underneath thick eyebrows, twitched. He issued a peculiar look, like what gives, what's the problem? She ignored it. He cleared his throat and turned to Xavier.

"Well, Xavier, why don't we go back upstairs. The Senior should

be back in and we'd like to take you to lunch." The Senior was Vaughn's father and founder of the firm. The elder Talbot was a man of few words, and even fewer appearances, while Vaughn Jr. was sometimes—like now—a man of too many of both. Xavier nodded as Vaughn led him to the door. Xavier stopped just short of walking out and turned to Gwen.

"I look forward to working with you, Ms. Fagan."

Asshole.

"Yeah." Gwen glanced up from the file and looked down at it again.

"Gwen, we'll talk later." Vaughn stressed the "later."

Gwen took her seat and picked up the phone; she had promised the client she would call him back, but really she just wanted to give Vaughn and Fessor X the impression that she had no time for them. At all. She mumbled, "That's fine," to Vaughn and watched him eye her as he closed her door and left.

She slammed the receiver down, picked it up, and slammed it down again, repeating the ritual of anger until she broke a nail. She wanted to cry but fought to compose herself. Xavier Dean and she would be coworkers. What were the chances of that? Out of all the accounting firms in the world, here he was at Talbot and Talbot. Gwen flexed her fingers, still numb from attacking the phone, then swung her chair around and stared out the window, wanting to leap out of it.

Just how fucking small was this world anyway?

Vaughn called her to his office around three o'clock. Gwen knew it was coming. She wanted to go home, should have gone home after they left her office, but she and Vaughn needed to discuss Cyntex—although she knew his call had nothing to do with work.

She left her office on the north end of the building and trekked down the hall, Cyntex file in hand, wire-rimmed glasses perched on her head like a headband. She still looked the part, still looked kept together, but inside she was unraveling.

Vaughn's office was a floor above, and Gwen decided to take the stairs. Normally when she walked through the office, she took time

to notice the beautiful, color-splashed abstract paintings hung everywhere. They definitely added flavor to the bland gray walls and standard office-issue speckled carpet. But now she paid them no attention. She reached the exit door to the stairwell and took note of the once-empty office in the corner. Xavier Dean stood poised, hands shoved in his pockets, smiling and yukking it up with some office fans he had already collected in less than a full day's time. She couldn't really tell who was in there with him, but could only see him. He spotted her and waved. She smirked, jerked the exit door open, and let the gust from her exit reply.

Vaughn's office was extraordinary, three times the size of hers with a breathtaking view of the city. Gwen walked in with the Cyntex file, fully prepared to brief him on the latest developments, but he said they could discuss that later. He told her he wanted to talk, off the record, more as friends than colleagues. He walked around from his desk and sat beside her in one of the Victorian style wingback chairs. She knew this was his way of approaching her behavior earlier in a "can't we all get along" manner instead of demanding an explanation.

Vaughn was the partner known for his "people" skills. He had boyish looks that always reminded her of the comedian Tim Allen, but with blond hair, which added to his air of merely playing executive, at forty, in his daddy's firm. He lived in the exclusive area of Alpharetta and had twin sons, both basketball players on their high school junior-varsity team. He had a wife Gwen had never seen. He mentioned her occasionally, and if she hadn't called once during their monthly staff meeting, Gwen would have thought she never really existed.

But Gwen and Vaughn had a good working relationship; he trusted her judgment and rarely pulled rank. Personally, Vaughn liked to think he was hip and well read on both black and white cultures. If the opportunity ever presented itself, Vaughn felt comfortable asking Gwen about black folks, exploring certain things he didn't understand and wanted to. For example, some of the hostility he experienced and received without warning or, to his knowledge, provocation. He once asked what he could do to not be viewed as a condescending white boy who didn't have a clue. Gwen laughed and told him, "Just don't act

like a condescending white boy who doesn't have a clue." Now Vaughn looked serious, worried about her behavior with Xavier.

"Is there going to be a problem having Xavier here, you two don't have some kind of..."

"Some kind of what?" Gwen asked, immediately on the defensive.

"I don't know, history, perhaps."

"History?"

Vaughn rubbed his chin, "Maybe I read too much into what happened when I introduced you today. You just seemed a bit..."

Hostile.

Gwen finished his sentence in her head and she knew she had to fix things, for the time being anyway. "I'm sorry about that. I had just gotten off the phone with Phil from Cyntex and I guess I was still caught up in the moment." An outright lie, but she didn't want Vaughn thinking there was any kind of "history" between her and Xavier. If Vaughn got that impression, what did Xavier think?

"Well, good. I think you and Xavier would be an exceptional team. I..."

"Team? What do you mean team?" Gwen stood up, flustered. "I've never needed a partner before, you know I prefer solo!"

"Wait a minute, just calm down." Vaughn stood too, holding his hands up. "I'm not talking about you two being joined at the hip, for God's sake. I just think once he gets himself acclimated he could be a big help on the acquisition for Cyntex. He's headed up major acquisition teams in the past, and..."

Gwen cocked her head. "So now he'll be heading up this acquisition? Is that what you're trying to tell me?"

"Of course not. Please, calm down and have a seat." Vaughn took a deep breath and held his hand out toward the chair.

Gwen sighed and felt her face grow hot. If tears spilled from her eyes while she stood in front of Vaughn, she would come off looking like a fool, all credibility lost. She tightened her face to stifle them and sat down, clasping her hands together on her lap to keep them from shaking.

Vaughn took a seat and his voice mellowed. "Gwen, you will still

be the lead auditor on this acquisition, you know I would never pull a stunt like that. I just know that you're going to need help, and most of the other accountants are working with a full caseload. With Xavier being new, he should have the flexibility to give you a great deal of support. But, listen, he hasn't even started his orientation yet. I was just thinking ahead; I had no idea it would cause a stir." Vaughn leaned forward, "Is that what this is all about, you see Xavier as some kind of threat?" Vaughn's voice rose with worry.

Not the kind of threat you're thinking about.

"No…" Gwen softened the creases in her face and tried to appear calm. "I didn't mean to overreact. Let's just see how he works out. I'm sure it will take him awhile to get into the Talbot way of thinking. And then after that, um, wherever you think he'd be best suited, I'm all for it." Gwen smiled, making it really wide, overdoing it a bit.

Vaughn still looked uneasy, but said, "Now that's the Gwen I'm used to." He told her to take the rest of the day off, in fact, maybe she should take a couple, it was fine with him whatever she decided. She had enough comp time and he could have someone cover any emergencies or keep the clients at bay, if necessary. She thanked him and said she could probably use a day off, but definitely didn't need two. Giving Vaughn the impression that she was unraveling would not be wise.

Shayla found her in the restroom right after she left Vaughn's office.

Shayla was part of the office clerical staff, a pretty girl in her early twenties with rich mahogany skin and a body worthy of an NC-17 rating all by itself. Gwen thought she had a little too much of everything—make-up, weave, nails, and attitude. But Shayla knew how to work it, and reaped the rewards she set out to achieve: men. She liked men and she liked to talk about how she liked men, what they could do for her, what she was willing to do for them. There was no shame in her game. But in the same breath she would complain about not having one long-term, and damn if she could figure out why. Gwen had a good idea why. Instead of asking, "I wonder what

books he likes to read, or I wonder what his favorite color is," Shayla usually said things like...

"Gwen, girlfriend, did you see that tall glass of iced tea that walked through the office today? Girl, I wonder what his fine ass is like in bed, it's got to be good."

Shayla joined Gwen at the sink. She pulled out her comb and began teasing her weave. She alternated between a straight, Naomi Campbell-prowling-the-runway motif and the one she wore now, a curly, slightly big-haired Janet Jackson replica, circa the *Rhythm Nation* years. One week she dazzled and amused the office with a blond creation, in homage to Mary J. Blige, Gwen guessed. But the next week the platinum horror had been abandoned with a reason she explained to Gwen as, "I don't know girlfriend, it just wasn't natural." *Duh*, was Gwen's only thought. Now Gwen said, "Hey Shay" and blatantly ignored Shay's sexual assessment of Xavier. She mindlessly started to wash her hands.

Suddenly, Miss Mabel stormed through the door like a drug raid, maneuvering her cleaning cart into the foyer. Her feet shuffled across the floor, past Gwen and Shayla, where she stopped and placed her hands on her hips.

"You know, there some nasty-ass bitches in this building. Seem like if folk got enough sense to work in this here fancy building, they'd have some home training. Bathrooms just be filthy." Miss Mabel spewed her caustic commentary as if talking to the wall; an audience was never a requirement. Sometimes Gwen found her in the hallway mumbling under her breath, occasionally raising her voice to utter a choice curse word. She had been cautioned to watch her language by the human resource stiff shirts, but Miss Mabel didn't pay a bit of attention to the warnings.

"Damn nasty bitches, these folks could fire me if they want to, but I bet they'd be offering me a whole hell of a lot of money to come back if they had to clean up this shit..."

Gwen and Shayla said, "Hi, Miss Mabel." She glanced at them; black circles surrounded her eyes, and her lips were thin, usually dry

as cotton. She flashed gold teeth and said, "Hi darlings," then went back to ranting, "This don't…"

"Darlings" was a good sign that they weren't considered members of the nasty bunch. Had they been, Miss Mabel would probably have just grunted or wouldn't have spoken at all, a big indication that she considered them one of the bitches. She tipped into one of the stalls and groaned. "Humph, nasty-ass folks, I tell ya…"

Shayla chuckled and leaned forward, pressing her thighs against the counter, which raised her skirt another inch. She slathered on more blood-red lip gloss and tapped Gwen's hand, still asking about Xavier.

"What was he, about six-five? Ooh he was fine, make my coochy wet just thinking about him." Shayla did a little jiggle. She always talked her slang trash around Gwen—not that they were great friends, but Shayla liked to think that since they were both African Princesses, any talk was acceptable.

Gwen walked behind her, jerked three paper towels from the holder, and began drying her hands. Sometimes she wanted to tell Shayla she was afraid for her. She feared she would some day get fucked by someone she didn't want to fuck, and she feared no one would believe it wasn't consensual. She'd tried to tell her one time. She said, "Shay, do you really think it's such a good idea to let a guy see everything you have to offer in the first five minutes?" Shayla took major offense, snapped her neck back and forth in true sister style, and put her hands on her hips. "Gwen girlfriend, you know I like you a lot, but don't even try and tell me about something you obviously know nothin' about." Gwen raised her hand and said, "Fine. I didn't mean to offend you." Shayla blew in a huff, then rolled her green eyes (courtesy of contact lenses, of course) and laughed. "We all right, girlfriend. You know we tight." Gwen said, "Uh-huh," thinking they weren't, but whatever. Shayla could take care of Shayla, but Gwen still feared for her sometimes.

Now Shayla looked at her in the mirror and bugged her eyes, saying, "Well girlfriend, did you see him?"

Gwen sighed, "Yes I saw him, and I'm sure he's probably marr—"

"Nope, not married. You know I already got the scoop on that."

Miss Mabel emerged from the stall shaking her head, which was covered by a wig that had long lost its sheen. For lack of a better word, it was just plain nappy. It came down on one side, almost covering her left eye like a patch. Gwen had never seen a wig that seemed to need a wig itself.

"Damn near all the toilet tissue I just put out on Friday is gone. That sho was a lot of toilet tissue. Damn bitches, it's like they got teeth up they ass." Miss Mabel disappeared into another stall, grumbling.

Gwen didn't bother to ask how Shayla knew about Xavier's marital status or what the scoop was. She told Shayla she would see her later and left the bathroom thinking it only figured—The Team never did seem like the marrying types.

The drive down Peachtree Street, through the Georgia 400 freeway and past the toll into Dunwoody, seemed to be completed on auto-pilot. Gwen pulled into her two-car garage, entered her house through the kitchen, and began stripping out of her clothes as she walked up the stairs. The light on the answering machine blinked repeatedly and she tapped it before she began fumbling through her dresser drawer. Payton's voice filled the room.

"Hey, long-distance sister girlfriend, this is your phone psychologist calling. I know it was your week to call, but I had to let you know that I'll be out of town until Sunday. Yeah, well, bad news is that Psycho Bob figured he knew all he needed to know about bipolar disorder, so he passed on the seminar and I became his last minute fill-in. Good news is that it's in Key West. Ooh wee, baby, got my suntan oil and bought three new bathing suits. This past winter in Boston was a bitch. I'll send you a postcard. But hey, I'll call next week, since it will technically be my week. But, if we need to talk, you know, *need to talk,* then just give me a call on my cell. Talk to you later. Love..." *BEEP*. The machine rewound itself after a few seconds.

Gwen felt relieved that she wouldn't be expected to call; she didn't really feel like talking anymore. She found her gray, loose-fitting sweat pants, replaced her lace bra with a sports bra, and threw on a white

tank top. Seal was her music of choice for the evening. She started the CD player in random selection order and cued the volume as "Kiss From a Rose" began to fill the house, which was wired in every room.

She flipped on the light to the basement, walked down the stairs, and found the tape for her fingers. Her biceps bulged slightly as she lifted her arms over her head and stretched. The stretching lasted about ten minutes before she began the fluid yet tight, disciplined moves with her hands and feet. She had learned karate years ago for protection. She refused to find herself in a position of helplessness again, and if karate didn't work, she was sure her nine-millimeter Glock would.

Gwen could see the bag in her peripheral view beckoning her. She put on her Spalding gloves with the fingers cut out and flexed her hands until the fit felt right. Then she began punching the bag, not really hard, more like taps. The punching bag, suspended from the ceiling, helped relieve her tension and lessen her anger. She hadn't fought with it in weeks, as she'd been feeling content, almost satisfied. But now she felt like she was about to explode. She felt like she had felt in the past—like everything was her fault.

Like the death of her parents.

Like the deterioration of her remaining family.

Like the rape.

Gwen's easy punches became forceful, rapid-fire jabs as tears streamed down her face.

Maybe the rape had been her punishment for basking in attention, for wanting to be the center of it while appearing coy. She'd liked the attention she received when she walked into a room, liked the way heads turned and men stared. That night in 1987, she felt the eyes on her from the time she walked in the door. She wore her sexuality like a badge, and felt entitled to tease as she pleased and deny anyone that didn't appeal to her. Terry didn't appeal to her; Xavier did. And that night, maybe he sat in a bedroom two doors down; maybe he heard his best friend raping her and got a kick out of it. Maybe they took turns reeling young girls in, throwing parties as bait, and then savagely attacking them for fun. What kind of person was Xavier Dean? And

why did he have to step back into her life, when she finally had it under control? Or did she?

Gwen stopped jabbing the bag and began beating it with her fist, throwing her hands against it as though she were banging on a door. Her sobs were loud, saturated with guilt and despair. She pushed the bag away forcefully, then felt it snap back an instant before it knocked her to the floor. Gwen lay there, curled herself into a fetal position, and listened to Seal while she cried like a baby.

· TWO ·

*D*AMN! *D*AMN! *D*AMN!

Gwen tapped her pencil against her bottom lip and inhaled with measured breaths, trying to control her rapid breathing. She sat in the monthly staff meeting, held in the executive conference room overlooking Centennial Park, and knew the Cyntex acquisition was on the agenda. That meant Xavier would be brought onto the project. Vaughn had re-emphasized his desire to have Xavier help her with the acquisition a few weeks ago—that is, after he finally stopped gushing about the athlete Xavier had once been. "Sure was a shame his knee injury ended his NBA career with the Bullets before it really got started, but I guess their loss is Talbot's gain..." Vaughn raved to her once. Gwen said, "Yeah, shame," really thinking, *NBA's loss, our gain, whoopee, who gives a damn.*

The entire office buzzed about him, though. Men wanted an autograph and basketball tips while women wanted whatever little attention he threw their way. *Pathetic,* Gwen thought.

But it looked as if he were here to stay, and Gwen thought long and hard about what she wanted to do. A month had come and gone since his arrival, and between Xavier's two-week orientation and Gwen's scheduled meetings outside the office, they'd had minimal contact. She actually considered finding another job and leaving Talbot and Talbot. But that was defeat, and she wasn't taking that route because of a man again. Her college years were over; she had moved on. She was a grown, successful woman and, as far as she was concerned, he was a nobody. Until today. Now he would be assisting her with the Cyntex acquisition and she would have to suck in her hate for him or find

herself looking for a job anyway. Talbot and Talbot was her turf; Xavier would have to play by her rules.

Gwen listened to Vaughn as he conducted the meeting. He talked with animated hands and kept the momentum flowing, allowing liberal input from the staff. Across from her, Xavier scribbled notes onto a pad; his class ring beamed at her almost maliciously. She glanced over at him out of the corner of her eye. He still had a humble face. The last ten years had been kind to him; his skin looked smooth, brown as a perfectly baked pound cake, and his mustache and eyebrows looked so richly black they appeared to have been penciled in with a marker. He looked up quickly, probably feeling someone's eyes on him. Gwen darted her eyes downward, then looked up as Vaughn called her name.

"Gwen, I'd like you to bring Xavier up to speed on the Cyntex Corporation. I have a feeling their acquisition goals will be a bigger challenge than most, and although we all know you're Superwoman, Xavier's assistance could prove invaluable."

Vaughn sat at the far end of the mahogany conference table, looking down at them with a glow of admiration. The other colleagues followed suit and turned their attention to Gwen and Xavier as if they sat encased in glass on display. The lump in her throat couldn't be dislodged with a full blast from a fire hose. She felt almost forced to look at him. He smiled at her. She gave him a half-smile, half-smirk and looked away.

"Excuse me, Gwendolyn, is now a good time for you?" Xavier stood at her door.

Nope, how about never...

"I guess now is as good a time as any." Gwen looked at him for a split second before shuffling papers on her desk. She hated being in this position, and still wasn't sure how she would handle containing her hostility—or if she even wanted to. She buzzed Mary, her secretary, and asked her to bring in the summary file for Cyntex, which Mary did almost immediately. Xavier stood tall in front of Gwen's desk. She

hadn't offered him a seat and fully expected their first meeting was going to be a quick one. He gave Mary a cordial "Good morning," and Mary, all of sixty if she was a day, blushed a bit and looked at Gwen like a fourteen-year-old schoolgirl. Gwen cringed in her seat.

Jeez, what's wrong with all these people, have they never seen a black man in a suit?

"That'll be all, Mary, unless there's something else?"

"Uh no, should I hold all your calls?" Mary looked at Gwen and then back at Xavier.

"Just send them to my voice mail, this meeting won't be long." Gwen spoke to Mary who continued to look at Xavier. "Mary, thank you," Gwen stressed.

Mary finally realized she had been dismissed and left saying, "Yes, of course. Have a good day, Mr. Dean. Um, let me know if you need anything else, Gwen." Xavier told her "Thank you," and sort of chuckled, clearly pleased with his effect on his admirers. Gwen rolled her eyes slyly, thinking this sort of behavior seemed almost cult-like.

She flipped through the file before holding it out to him, waiting for him to turn back around and notice it. When he did, he took the file and smiled.

"She's a pleasant woman. Everyone here has been very nice. Sort of feels like family already." Xavier's voice ranged somewhere between baritone and bass. He didn't open the file, but simply held it and attempted to elicit conversation instead.

Gwen ignored him. "Why don't you take a day or two to review the file, longer if you need it." *Please take years if you like.* "The file's pretty complete. This is Cyntex's first acquisition and their internal personnel are pretty green on acquisition experience. But I feel confident that we've assembled a good team, and I also feel confident that I've identified all the areas that will need to be audited in depth." Gwen paused and released her next statement practically through gritted teeth: "Of course if you have any questions or additional input, then we can sit down and discuss."

She slipped her glasses on her face and began rummaging through

another file, a completely different file that suddenly needed her complete attention. She could see Xavier hadn't moved, and his presence before her made her snap.

"Is there something else?" Her tone cut.

"Well, now that you mentioned it, there is. But I was hoping that you would let me in on it." Xavier pulled one of the decorated chairs perched against the wall up to Gwen's desk and made himself comfortable. He crossed his legs, placed the Cyntex file in his lap, and fiddled with his chin while concentrating on Gwen.

Gwen took her glasses off and played the dumbfounded role. "Let you in on what?"

"What it is about me you dislike so much?"

You son of a bitch...

"I have no idea what you're talking about." Gwen made an effort to look directly at him. His eyes met hers. They were light brown, like sun-brewed tea, and soft. She focused on his nose instead.

"Well, I thought at first it was my imagination. I mean, I couldn't think of anything that I may have done to offend you. But then…how can I say this? I guess you come across as someone who's known me all my life and hated me for most of it. And, I guess, now is as good a time as any to ask what the problem is."

"There is no problem, Mr. Dean. Listen, maybe we should set the record straight right now. This is a professional environment and we are colleagues, nothing else. If you've gotten the impression that I don't like you strictly because I'm about business, then I really don't know what to tell you. Talbot and Talbot isn't some kind fraternity or sorority, and I come here each day to do the best job possible, not to make new friends. Now, if you ever have a problem with my professional etiquette, please, by all means let me know and I will rectify things. Anything other than that is really not up for discussion."

Have I made myself clear?

Gwen relaxed back into her leather chair and raised an eyebrow, self-assured and powerful. Xavier barely flinched, motionless in his seat. He rubbed his chin once more, caught her eye again, and they stared at each other. Gwen had no intention of looking away; she was

the sheriff in this town, and she waited for his eyes to harden, turn dark and evil, but they didn't. The sincerity in them bothered her. She started to speak, started to ask if there was anything else he needed to know, but he finally made a move. With his hands raised in surrender, the Cyntex file held high, he stood up and spoke.

"Thank you for clarifying things for me, Ms. Fagan. I'll review this file and get back to you as soon as possible." He put the chair back against the wall and strode out the door, his demeanor rather stiff and his manner upgraded a professional notch. Gwen adjusted her glasses back on her face, which burned with anger laced with just a hint of satisfaction. *That's right, Fessor X, you're playing on my team now, and it's an entirely different ball game.*

"So, you really read him his rights, huh?" Payton asked, her southern drawl peppered with Boston influence.

"I guess. He asked. I answered," Gwen stated calmly. She was settled on the sofa in her den wearing a red, white, and blue oversized Atlanta Olympic Games T-shirt, one of many she had picked up the previous summer, although she hadn't attended any of the events. Payton had just called, and their conversation began as they all had begun in the past month—with the daily happenings at work with Xavier. Gwen muted the television yet kept her eyes on the set. Unfortunately, most of the programs lately were repeat episodes.

"Are you OK, you know, with all this crap going on?" Payton asked above the sound of her own TV, which Payton never muted.

"Uh-huh. Just fine."

"You sure? I know it's got to be rough having him around." Payton's voice drew serious.

Gwen shrugged, throwing her palm against her forehead and pushing back a handful of curls. "I admit I'm not thrilled about it. He's come in like he owns the joint and everyone seems to be falling at his feet. Talbot and Talbot has turned into fraternity row." Gwen sighed, then directed her gaze back to the television.

"Your office sounds pretty pathetic. And he played pro basketball for how long?" Payton again asked about Xavier.

"I think five years, something like that."

"Still got that jock mentality, huh?"

"I guess," Gwen said, unsure. She didn't hang around Xavier enough to know what mentality he had.

"And how are you handling the other part?"

"Other part?"

"College. What happened. Is he a constant reminder?"

"You know, Payton, you're off the clock," Gwen reminded, sarcastically.

"Well, consider this a freebie." Payton laughed, her perky voice radiating through the phone. Gwen imagined that Payton was probably flopped across her bed, belly down, her thick crystal-blond hair framed around her face, and her always French-manicured nails strumming through *People* magazine while keeping her sleepy gray-blue eyes on the television set between articles. "How are you holding up, Gwen, seriously?"

"I'm doing better. He has no clue who I am, that our paths have ever crossed before, so that's a good thing. Keeps the playing field slightly in my favor."

"And nightmares?"

"Slowing going away."

"I admire you, you know that?"

"For what, working like I'm supposed to?" Gwen smirked.

"For working with a man who takes you back to such a painful past, and you're showing him who's boss. You go, girl!" Payton cheered, still trying to score more slang points for her sisterhood initiation.

"Well, don't crown me yet. We start working together tomorrow and that will be the real test. Hell, Vaughn suggested we converge in one of the conference rooms, for space's sake. I just smile and agree. He's right, I know we're going to need to set up shop together eventually, at least for a few weeks. But damn, I don't know what it's going to be like—probably too close for comfort."

"He's an asshole, huh?" Payton's voice dropped, her question more of a statement.

"Who, Vaughn?"

"No, Xavier Dean."

"Probably," Gwen said, remembering the wounded expression plastered on Xavier's face when she flexed her professional muscles in answer to his question. He didn't seem like an asshole, what with the way his eyes had changed from soft to serious, seemingly confused at her hostility. It tugged a little on her guilt strings. Then she felt like a fool for feeling anything remotely close to compassion. He was Fessor X; he'd survive. "Let's get off this subject, OK?"

"Cool beans." Payton chimed.

"'Cool beans?' That sure ain't in the flygirl sisterhood codebook." Gwen sat up, crossed her legs on the couch, and intended to drudge up some silliness.

"Well, unfortunately I do digress occasionally. How about 'word up'?" Payton giggled.

"A bit outdated, but…hey, wait a minute. Why are we even on the phone in the first place? I thought you had a date tonight?"

"Oh yeah. That." Payton offered no more.

"Yeah, that, did you go or what?"

"Uh-huh."

"What the hell happened? Tell me." Gwen could hear the opening music to *ER* on Payton's television.

"Well, it sort of ended quickly. He was kind of weird."

"Like?"

Payton sighed, "Like he wanted to smell my underarm."

"Excuse me?"

"Yeah. Wild, huh? Gwen, I opened the door and there stood this somewhat normal-looking guy, with soft blond hair and baby-smooth skin, and before we even leave my apartment he asked to sniff my underarm. He definitely showed signs of compulsive behavior."

Gwen began to giggle, "Sounds obvious. But did he explain the underarm fetish?"

"Well, I did ask what purpose it served. He said it was a little habit of his; he could always tell if his date was excited about going out with him by the way her underarm smelled."

Gwen stretched out across the couch again, resting her head against the arm. "I assume this is when the date ended."

"Nope, I let him smell it, but only one."

"Excuse me?!"

"Look, I spent all evening getting ready for this date. I took off early from work, washed my hair twice, and wore my little black dress. *The* little black dress, you know, the one I picked out at Macy's when I visited you last year."

"Yeah, I remember. It *was* a nice dress."

"You better believe it. So if he wanted to smell my underarms I wasn't going to nix the date solely on those grounds."

"If you say so. Then what? Did your underarms not pass the test and *he* nixed the date?"

"No, I guess they passed. But the more I looked at him the more uncomfortable I got."

Gwen rose up slightly where she was sitting. "Why? What did he do?"

"Oh don't worry, he didn't really do anything." Payton paused, then said, "Gwen, his eyes were too far apart."

"Excuse me?"

"His eyes. He had too much space between his eyes. First I tried to ignore it, but the more I looked at him the farther apart his eyes seemed to get. After a while it was almost as if his ears could see. It just gave me the creeps. You know I've always said that I feel certain I would know Satan right off the bat because..."

"He would have too much space between his eyes," Gwen and Payton chimed in unison. Gwen relaxed again and laughed out loud.

Payton joined in. "So in the middle of dinner, I kind of did my little spastic moves as if I'm trying to keep myself from throwing up. Worked like a charm. He offered to take me home, but I insisted he stay and enjoy the dinner. Yep, sister girlfriend, hailed myself a cab and came on home. High five!"

"High five!" Gwen tapped the receiver. After a few more laughs, they both fell quiet for a few seconds.

"So, how goes dating with you?" Payton's voice once again switched from joking to serious.

Gwen shrugged and mumbled, "It goes nice and quiet."

"Hmm, well, that's good, I guess, but…" Payton cleared her throat, then dropped to an even more serious tone, "but does it look to be in your foreseeable future?"

Gwen squirmed a bit and felt herself getting annoyed. "Payton, if you search your memory you might recall that I just finished dating. Remember Ellis?"

"Oh, yeah. Ellis," Payton stated sarcastically, "is that what you two were calling it?"

Gwen smirked, "Uh-huh, be funny if you want to. I'm quite content with the fresh air he left me with."

"Yep, fresh air is nice. But after a while it can get kind of stale."

Gwen rolled her eyes, "Not by my tastes…and you can stop worrying about me. I'm good, my social life is just the way I like it, and I don't need a man to turn my good upside down."

"Who's talking about need?"

Gwen smiled slyly. "Payton…"

"OK, I'll back off. I just think there's someone out there for you, that's all. For me too, I hope."

"And if it's going to happen, he'll find me. But I'm not looking. My daddy used to tell me, 'One of the most attractive things boys find in girls is the way they look when they're not looking.'" Gwen smiled sadly, then closed her eyes. She could hear her daddy's heavy but gentle voice in her head; she could remember the way he joined her on the front steps while she moped after another standard argument with her mother, and the way he draped his long, dark arm around her shoulder and pulled her into him.

"Your daddy had a pretty profound play on words."

Gwen slowly opened her eyes, "Uh-huh. He always tried to use the adult approach with me once I hit puberty. You know, he tried to find subtle ways of slowing my fast butt down without belittling the situation. But there was no stopping me; not then. I was fourteen and I didn't want to be attractive—who cared about attractive? I wanted

to be hot, happening, the bomb..." It wasn't until Gwen snorted out a tortured-sounding laugh that she realized tears were spilling from her eyes.

"Gwen, you were young. You have to stop blaming yourself."

Gwen shook her head without speaking.

The night her parents died still tormented her. The brazen sound of her own hateful voice as she cursed her mother for treating her like an immature girl, because she said Gwen hadn't a clue what a real woman was—and what kind of responsibilities came with being one. The slap her mother delivered across Gwen's cheek could still be felt, sharp and deliberate. The whole fight that night was so stupid. So adolescent. Looking back on it now, Gwen could see her own recklessness, but at the time reckless didn't look or feel like reckless. It felt like freedom.

It was fourteen years ago, New Year's Eve. Gwen wanted to go to a party being thrown at the Omni, filled with Morehouse College fraternity men. She and her girlfriends had designed a scheme, the old sleepover scam, but her parents saw right through it. They told her they would rather she stay in; it was New Year's Eve and her fourteen-year-old, out-of-control hormones needed to be at home. But that rule didn't apply to her older brother, Weldon. He was eighteen and stepping out for the night, probably all night; her parents never did keep a tight rein on him. The fight escalated: screams, finger-in-the-face taunting, cursing. That night was awful.

Gwen sat up on the couch, still wiping away tears, half-listening to Payton's words of comfort. Gwen touched her left cheek. At times now, she'd force herself to feel her mother's slap, try and recapture its loving sting. It still wasn't adequate punishment for feeling like she caused their death, but sometimes, if she concentrated hard enough, it could still beat her up pretty good.

· THREE ·

GWEN AND XAVIER sat across from each other in the conference room located just outside her office. It was small, but adequate to accommodate all the paperwork and files and equipment they needed to get their work done.

They had been working together on Cyntex for six weeks, the last three literally spent in the conference room. Sometimes they worked without conversation; other times they discussed issues pertinent to the case. Gwen relaxed her guard just enough to appreciate Xavier's intelligence. He was smart—very smart. And Vaughn was right, Xavier was becoming a big help with the acquisition. But that was as far as she would allow herself to appreciate him as a person, still remembering where he came from and what company he had been known to keep.

As for Xavier, Gwen noticed he had relaxed with her. He was still much more professional in her presence than he was with others, yet it appeared that he sensed a working relationship with her was acceptable for both of them after all; he didn't treat her with malice, as she had expected he would after the tongue-lashing she gave him, and he began calling her Gwendolyn again. She could only bring herself to call him Dean, if she had to call him anything at all.

Gwen and Xavier looked up from their paperwork at the same time, summoned by a strong whiff of Estée Lauder Beautiful perfume.

"Well, well. Here you two are again in this stuffy little conference room." Shayla stood in front of them with one hand on her hip and the other clutching a clipboard to her bosom.

Gwen removed her glasses and rubbed her eyes. "Hey, Shay. What's up?"

"Hey, Gwen," Shayla said without looking Gwen's way. She was turned toward Xavier. Her voice rippled with a phony soprano pitch, like the last two keys on a piano. "Hi, Mr. Dean, how are you doing?" Shayla leaned forward, tapping her two-inch nails on the table, enticing Xavier's view.

Gwen glanced at Xavier, who blushed with embarrassment. Gwen shook her head in amusement and began working again. She was not even going to attempt to play these kinds of games.

"Shayla, I'm fine. And I thought we agreed you would call me Xavier."

"That's right. You're so sweet, EXavier." Shayla tossed her hand out in a flirtatious manner and drawled his name, emphasizing the "X."

Unable to control her amusement, Gwen released a small snort, then quickly looked up at Xavier, who smiled at her. She looked down again and continued to write.

"You two have sure been putting in the hours. Isn't this room too cramped for y'all?" Shayla looked around, fanning herself.

"The room's been just fine. Did you need something, Shay?" Gwen relaxed back in her chair and folded her hands across her stomach.

"Oh, yeah, I did come in here for something. This Friday is the junior Talbot's birthday. And as usual he would like us all to meet after work for appetizers and drinks. So I came to get an RSVP." Shayla held the clipboard in her hand and steadied her pen. "Gwen, will you be bringing that fine young brother you brought last year?" Shayla meant Ellis, and she stood poised to write his name.

Xavier leaned forward, obviously unable to hide his curiosity at Shayla's little announcement. They both waited on Gwen's response.

You bitch. You know damn well Ellis and I are no more. Shay, cut the crap. I am of no threat to your little scheme to screw Xavier, believe me.

"No, put me down for one. Thanks." As usual she would take the high road and keep the low road confined to her head. Gwen placed her glasses back on her face and started tapping the calculator. If Vaughn wasn't her boss, and if she hadn't gone to his office birthday

celebration every year, she would have declined. Gwen had a feeling there would be more of this same bullshit at the party, and she was in no mood.

"OK, Gwen is a show. How about you, EXavier?"

"Yeah, put me down. Is it OK if I bring someone?"

Shayla stammered a bit. "Of course. The more the merrier. Can I have his name?" Shayla didn't need a name, only a head count. The "his" was bait.

"Actually, he's a she. Her name is Carmen."

Gwen coughed to keep her smile at bay. So, Fessor X did have a woman in his life. Carmen. Pretty name. Gwen wanted so badly to see the look on Shayla's face, but she didn't want to seem too interested. However, her calculator tapping did slow down a little.

"Oh." That was Shayla's only response.

Gwen glanced up to see her jotting the name down. Shayla's face had practically dripped onto the paper like batter to the griddle. Gwen cut her eyes to Xavier, who looked at her and winked. She looked away and began beating the calculator keys, annoyed.

Don't wink at me, dammit, do not...

"OK, I've got Gwen. And Xavier and Carmen. An email will be coming out with the time and place. See y'all there." Shayla had suddenly become very official, abandoning the soprano shrill for a more low-key alto. She left the room in a huff.

"Sounds like this should be fun." Xavier offered.

"Uh-huh." Gwen didn't bother to look at him.

"Gwen, girlfriend, are you in here?"

Gwen could see Shayla's calico stiletto heels underneath the bathroom stall door.

Unbelievable...

Gwen rolled her eyes. People never ceased to amaze her. Shayla actually stood in front of the bathroom stall, hunting her down. And now she was 'Gwen-girlfriend,' when just a couple of hours ago she was Gwen-enemy.

"Yes, Shay. Can you give me a minute?"

"Sure, girlfriend. Hell, I got to go myself." Shayla clomped her way into one of the stalls just as Gwen emerged. Shayla yelled, "Don't go nowhere, girlfriend."

Gwen rolled her eyes again, said, "Uh-huh" and began to wash her hands. She could hear Shayla rustling to hurry up and she knew she was about to be pumped for information. Miss Mabel entered the restroom with another woman on her heels.

"Hey, Miss Mabel." The woman patted Miss Mabel on the shoulder before passing by her and entering a stall. Miss Mabel grunted. Must be one of the nasty bitches, Gwen thought. Miss Mabel began cleaning at the far end of the long row of marble sinks; she greeted Gwen with a "Hi darling," and Gwen responded in kind. Shayla wiggled to the sink beside Gwen. Gwen had already washed and dried and was really only waiting to get this little gossip session Shayla was about to start over with so she could get back to work.

"Ooh, Gwen. I thought I was going to pee a river. Hi, Miss Mabel." Shayla began washing her hands and leaned into Gwen, whispering "Who else is in here?"

Gwen didn't bother to answer. The toilet flushed and the woman walked past them, smiled, and walked out the door. The sink didn't appear to be an option.

"I tell ya. Just nasty asses." Miss Mabel summed it up. Gwen and Shayla gave a collective, "Uh-huh."

"OK, Gwen-girlfriend, give me the scoop. Who the hell is this Carmen?" Shayla grabbed a couple of paper towels and dried her hands. She then turned to face Gwen, pressing her very rotund butt against the counter. No time for messing with her hair and make-up—Shayla was on a mission.

"Shay, I don't know." Gwen put her hands out to the side and shrugged.

Shayla rolled her eyes, leaving them in the up position. "Come on girlfriend, all the time you spend with him and you trying to tell me he ain't never talked about her?"

"I'm not *trying* to tell you anything, it's the truth. Dean and I don't swap personal information. It's not part of our job description."

This was not completely true. No, they didn't talk on a personal level, but there were certain things about Xavier Gwen couldn't help but notice. Like his scent. Xavier wore Chanel's Pour Monsieur cologne, a cologne her father used to wear. It was very light, very unassuming, and it seduced her nose when he sat beside her, diligently pointing something out relative to the acquisition. And he liked to hum Marvin Gaye's "Inner City Blues (Make Me Wanna Holler)" on a whim, usually bringing it to an abrupt halt when Gwen would cut her eyes at him. He probably suspected it bothered her, but it didn't. She liked Marvin Gaye's earlier work, too. But these were things Gwen figured Shayla would find out for herself, in time.

Miss Mabel made her way down to their end and asked Shayla to excuse herself. Gwen turned to leave. Shayla followed.

"Listen, Shay. I've got to get back to work."

"Wait a minute, girlfriend. You trying to tell me all the time y'all been spending together, all y'all been talking about are assets and liabilities? Humph, I find that hard to believe." Shayla jerked her body. Gwen raised an eyebrow.

Believe what you want, bitch.

Gwen stood in the bathroom foyer with her hand wrapped around the door handle. Shayla stood beside her with her arms crossed tightly against her chest. This pushed her breasts upward—not that they needed further help spilling out of the attractive, low-cut, white crossover blouse she wore. A small rose tattoo peeked out, its petals colored a bright red and outlined in black. Shayla was definitely a woman of extremes.

"Shayla, let's clear the air now. I am not interested in him. If he's what you want and he's willing to accommodate, then go for it. But, please, leave me out of it."

"Oh, I know he's more than willing to accommodate. Girlfriend, he smiles at me like he could sop me up with a biscuit." Shayla ran her hands down her body and jiggled.

Gwen walked out of the bathroom, feeling more bothered by Shayla's statement than she should have been.

He smiles at everyone...

"So, Shayla's got some competition, huh?"

"Payton, if you could have seen her face. It was like someone kicked her in the teeth. But she'll rebound all right. Men can usually find a way to squeeze in a fuck if it's being offered, girlfriend or not." Gwen sat up in bed, knees raised to her chest and remote in hand.

"Gwen, you can be so crude."

"I like to think of it as graphic honesty." Gwen flipped the channels. She dropped the remote on the bed and left the TV on the Turner Network. A commercial was on.

"Well, what did *you* think when you found out he had a girlfriend?"

"Excuse me? What do you mean, 'what did I think?'" Gwen oozed across the bed onto her stomach, pulling her oversized Tweety Bird T-shirt down over her panties. Her legs, crossed at the ankle, bumped against the headboard.

"Just, what did you think?" Payton asked again, in her formal psychiatric voice.

"I didn't think anything...I...Where is this line of questioning coming from and where exactly is it going?" Gwen drew her attention to the TV. It was an NBA playoff game. She started to turn it, but left it there instead.

Payton's call waiting clicked. "Gwen, hold on a second."

Gwen looked at the TV. Chicago and New York were playing, or really brawling—Rodman looked crazy, Jordan looked in charge, and New York looked like they knew they were going to lose. Gwen secretly watched basketball sometimes. Really, she just watched the pregame stuff. And she only watched to make sure Terry Stuart was where he was supposed to be, which was nowhere near her.

He had made it to the NBA, but his career did not fare as well as people had hoped. In the past ten years he had been traded to three

different teams and now pretty much kept the bench warm for one of the new expansion teams.

No surprise to Gwen. Terry had remained more than rough around the edges throughout the years. He had a problem with drinking and drugs, which landed him on league probation early on in his career and was widely publicized by the media, who went from mourning the wasted talent of this troubled man in need of redemption to labeling him an on-court hoodlum destined to self-destruct.

Satan's best friend, what'd you expect?

Gwen saw it as small vindication, but still not enough to satisfy her hatred for him. She intended to follow his career as long as he had one, and she would continue to wish him failure every step of the way. The Chicago game was just in the first quarter. Gwen flipped the channel to Showtime and left it on *A League of Their Own.*

Payton clicked back, "Sorry Gwen. That was Dylan. His band's in town for a concert tomorrow. They're trying to nail down a record deal, so they've got some gigs along the east coast. We're going to get together afterward. Should be interesting. You remember him from college, don't you?"

"Uh, sort of. Wasn't he kind of Adonis-looking?"

"Yeah, that would be him."

"So what's happening with you two—a late-blooming relationship?" Gwen poked fun.

Payton sighed. "Hardly. Just between you and me, he's gay, and carrying on a torrid secret relationship with his new drummer. Very hush-hush. So needless to say I'll be his beard for the evening. Having a gay brother makes me an expert on how to handle these situations."

"Hmmm, I'll bet. Keep me posted on that one."

"Absolutely. So back to the original question?"

"About Dean and Carmen? Why *would* I have any thoughts about them?"

"Now don't get hostile. I've just sensed in our last few conversations that he's not as bad as you originally thought. Kinda got a feeling you've warmed up to him a bit."

Gwen felt her face flush with embarrassment. "I have not. Don't

say shit like that." Her hostility simmered; the curt tone of her denial immediately struck her as adolescent.

"Whoa, sorry. I didn't mean to suggest that there was an attraction or anything. I mean, there isn't, is there?" Payton asked as cautiously as a creeping cat.

Gwen twisted her lips and breathed heavy. "Look, I will concede that he is intelligent, and I will also concede that he has been putting out some great work on this acquisition, but don't start reading shit into this." Gwen winced, pissed at herself for getting so bent out of shape.

"All right, just take a breath, will ya?"

"I'm breathing, thank you very much."

There was silence. Gwen tried to relax. She knew her brutal objection only served as confirmation. It was true. Xavier still had that same appealing charm Gwen had first reacted to ten years ago. He opened doors, pulled out chairs, offered to share lunch or get lunch—one day, she more than expected him to say that he'd make lunch. His courtesy extended to everyone and his popularity in the office was soaring. Gwen declined every offer, caught her own doors, and sat down before he had a chance to assist. But his qualities were admirable if they were genuine, which Gwen liked to believe they weren't. He was still Fessor X, best friend to Terry Stuart, and that alone shredded his credibility.

"I'm sorry, Gwen." Payton broke the silence.

"It's fine. Let's drop it." Gwen's voice remained terse.

"Just don't forget you're still a woman..."

"Thanks for the update."

"...Your emotions are very natural..."

"Shit, Payton. You are pushing the damn envelope."

"Well, yeah. I have an envelope-pushing habit."

"Well, knock this shit off. I'm not going to stay on the phone if this is where the conversation is going." Gwen pulled herself to the edge of the bed, ready to hang up.

"Why are you so pissed?"

Gwen breathed in exasperation, "Excuse me?"

"I'm assuming I'm supposed to know why you're upset, but to be honest with you, I don't."

Gwen rolled her eyes, "Oh please, Payton."

Payton remained quiet, allowing her bewilderment to linger. Gwen rustled her curls and bit her bottom lip. What could she say? She did find Xavier attractive; she found herself thinking about him at odd moments, like when she brushed her teeth, which would make her think of his teeth, his smile, his laugh, his voice. They were all so...receptive, she thought. His smile released a kind of warm energy, practically drawing people in like a shelter from the cold; his laugh was deep, hearty, not piercing or taunting; and when he spoke, when he called her name, insisting on saying Gwendolyn, it rolled out of his mouth like bubbles being blown in the breeze. Gwen touched her cheek and smiled. It was true. Xavier Dean was definitely attractive.

"Gwen?" Payton jolted the dream.

"What?" Gwen's voice strained with confusion, disturbed by her romantic thoughts.

"Wanna talk?"

Gwen rubbed her forehead. *This is some wacked shit.* She shouldn't find him attractive; she shouldn't be thinking about him; and she didn't want to talk about it. "No, Payton. Let's call it a night OK?"

"Uh, OK. You all right?"

"Yeah."

"We all right?"

"We're fine...I'm fine, I think. I didn't mean to snap at you."

"OK, I'll take that as an apology. Just remember what I said."

"Yeah."

They said their good-byes and Gwen hung up the phone and sat. A tear pumped its way into the corner of her eye and trickled down her face. Gwen wiped it away, stroking it across her cheek.

By Friday, Gwen's body felt tight and her emotions confused. She felt as knotted up as if she were in a straitjacket, which is what she was beginning to think she needed. She keyed the same figures into the

calculator that she had keyed ten minutes ago. She pushed it away and stood up, stretching her arms and sauntering over to the window.

"Gwendolyn, you OK?" Xavier asked, bringing his own diligent calculator pecking to a halt.

"Uh-huh. Just a break." She didn't look back at him, but heard his pecking resume as she crossed her arms and viewed the bustle of activity down on Peachtree Street. It was still early in the day. Vaughn's birthday bash was just a few hours away and Gwen wanted to go home, skip the whole party, and crawl into bed, throwing the covers over her head.

Something was wrong with her, that was for sure. She still had warm thoughts about Xavier, and the more she cursed herself for having them, the more intense they became.

His hand grazed her hand the other day—not intentionally, they both just happened to reach for the same file without paying attention. His fingers touched her fingers. They were soft—not feminine-soft, more like stimulatingly soft. Gwen imagined what it would be like to hold his hand, press it against her face, run it down her body. She went in the bathroom and washed her hands, nearly scraping the skin off as if she were shucking them like ears of corn. Confusion settled deeper into her constitution, and the pit of her stomach ached.

She needed therapy, that's the conclusion she came to. She had been in therapy before, after she and Payton met: after her suicide attempt. Judith Emory, Payton's mother and a well-known psychiatrist in Charleston, had been a lifeline for Gwen, and Payton's family became her surrogate. But now she figured maybe what she really needed was an extended stay in a mental institution.

She was attracted to a member of The Team. She hadn't been attracted to a man like this in ten years—not, she realized bitterly, since her original attraction to Xavier at the party.

The party.

The rape.

Gwen did a brisk shake of her head, trying to jar loose some common sense. Not only were her thoughts unhealthy, they were damn near unnatural. Foolishness, she surmised. Foolishness.

Gwen hung around the office well after five o'clock, still reviewing the statement of cash flow for the acquisition candidate. Xavier had left earlier, telling Gwen, "I need to take care of some things; you don't mind, do you?" Gwen gave him a chilly, "Don't mind," without making eye contact. Then he asked, "You're still coming tonight, aren't you?" Gwen looked at him this time; his pinstriped blue jacket draped over his arm, his sleeves rolled up just below his elbow, the soft dark hair that lay smoothly on his arm. Thoughts of his arms around her filtered through her mind, which pissed her off, which made her answer with a blunt, "Yeah." He said, "Good, I'll see you then," and left wearing that damn smile. Gwen watched him leave, then mumbled another pathetic, "Yeah."

A few minutes after seven, she left the conference room and went back to her office, where she sat in her leather chair and basked in the solitude. She closed her eyes. No ringing phones or squealing fax machines or the thick noise of simultaneous talking made for one beautiful sound of silence.

"Best time of the day, isn't it?"

Gwen opened her eyes at the sound of Vaughn's voice and smiled up at him. "Right now, I can't argue with that. What are you doing here? Did you skip out on your own celebration already?"

Vaughn chuckled and walked into Gwen's office. He had loosened his silk tie and removed his jacket, revealing a stiffly starched dress shirt that bore few wrinkles. He had gotten his brownish-blond hair a new cut, more tapered on the sides and back. But his face looked worried and worn.

"Not quite. I told Edith to let everyone know that I might be a few minutes late. What about yourself, did you plan on being a no-show?"

"Of course not. As a matter of fact, I was just on my way down." Gwen stood up. The party was being held in a private club located in the building.

Vaughn pointed to her desk, "How's everything going? You and Xavier got everything under control?"

"Everything is going fine, Vaughn. I know you don't want to spoil your birthday by talking business, do you?"

"I'm forty-one, Gwen. Birthdays don't seem that important anymore. Hell, some people can hardly remember them. Just ask my wife." Vaughn tried to keep his tone light, but the latter part came out bitter. He had been out of sorts lately, Gwen had noticed. Often, he trudged into the office looking less like a top dog and more like a whipped dog.

"Listen, I'll see you downstairs." Vaughn left her office with his hands shoved deep into his pockets.

Gwen hung around a few minutes longer, until she was sure Vaughn had gone. Maybe she should have stuck with her first instinct and declined the party invitation. Vaughn didn't seem to be in any mood to celebrate, and Gwen was really only going for his benefit.

A pit stop in the restroom was in order before Gwen took the elevator to the fifth floor. She could at least freshen up a bit, make an attempt to look as if she hadn't worked a twelve-hour day. She patted her face with a damp paper towel and ruffled her curls with a rakelike comb. After unzipping her olive green pants, she readjusted her caviar-beaded sleeveless blouse, put herself back together, and slipped into the matching olive green jacket.

The ride from the fourteenth floor to the fifth went swiftly. As she approached the restaurant, she spied the elder Talbot making his exit. Like Vaughn, he too resembled Tim Allen, but with gray hair and an extended gut. He nodded to Gwen as they passed and Gwen figured he had probably done what he did every year—patted his son on the back, gave him a blustering, "Happy birthday, Vaughn Jr.," and shook his hand as if they had just closed a major merger. For his part, his son normally maintained the formalities with, "Thanks, Vaughn Sr.," not father or dad or daddy-o—just Vaughn Sr. Warm and fuzzy they weren't, but who was Gwen to judge family bonds?

As soon as she walked in, Gwen could see the office gang laughing and drinking before the hostess even had a chance to inquire about her seating preference. She pointed toward the crowd, said she was with them, and followed the crescendo of chatter. The turnout was good-sized, a little less than last year but definitely enough to constitute a party.

Vaughn waltzed from table to table, holding a martini in one hand

while his other remained stuffed in his pocket. Gwen approached him, wished him another happy birthday (she had emailed him one earlier), and acted as if she hadn't just seen him upstairs. He removed his hand from his pocket and squeezed hers, telling her thank you. There was a round of "Hi, Gwen," from her coworkers, and Gwen responded with "Hello," or a wave of wiggled fingers. Someone in the crowd asked Vaughn if his wife would be joining them; Vaughn answered with a flat, "No."

Vaughn handed Gwen a glass of champagne, which Gwen only took out of courtesy, knowing full well she had no intention of drinking it. Champagne had a tendency to go straight to her head. And Gwen had always vowed to leave a place in as close a proximity to the sober state in which she had arrived. Once she found a table at which to plant herself, she intended to order a glass of Kendall-Jackson chardonnay, engage in some idle chitchat, and be home in time enough to catch Tavis Smiley on BET. That is, if Shayla didn't foil it.

Shayla sashayed up to Gwen and Vaughn in a slinky silk sheath dress with spaghetti straps and an extremely low back. Her weave was pulled away from her face, and she had replaced her usual heavy "office" make-up with heavy "evening" make-up. It was obvious she must have ditched work early to create this diva masterpiece. Gwen had to admit she looked good, and had no doubt Xavier would think the same.

"Happy birthday, Vaughn." Shayla planted her hand on Vaughn's back and rubbed it lightly.

"Shayla, thank you." Vaughn wrapped an arm around Shayla's waist and pulled her into an embrace. Shayla kissed him on the cheek. Gwen pursed her lips, astounded; Shayla had nerves of steel. Vaughn gulped down the last of his martini, put it on the table, then chased it with champagne.

Gwen smiled nervously and wanted to caution Vaughn to slow his roll; whatever problems he was having could only get worse following gin with champagne. But then again, Vaughn was a big boy. Gwen kept her mouth shut.

A group of people at another table called Vaughn's name and he

excused himself, but not before downing the glass of champagne and grabbing another.

"So, Gwen-girlfriend, where's our man?" Shayla held her champagne glass up to her mouth and looked around the room.

Our man? Please...

"If you're talking about Dean, I haven't seen him. Sorry." Gwen walked away from Shayla and found a table for four, with two seats apparently taken. There were near-empty drinks on napkins, but no actual occupants. Shayla followed her.

"He and Carmen are probably doing the nasty deed right now. Girl, I bet his dick is made out of gold."

"Shay, I thought I told you to spare me."

"Aw damn, girl, loosen up. Hell... well, will you look at this?" Shayla sipped her drink and motioned toward the entrance to the room.

Xavier and Carmen had just walked in. Correction—Xavier walked and Carmen rolled. She was in a wheelchair.

Xavier wore khaki dress pants and a white Ralph Lauren button-down shirt, upgraded from casual to semidressy with a patterned tie and a sport coat, required by the club. It was all put together rather well and Gwen thought he looked nice. Shayla was steadily talking, but all Gwen caught was "What the hell, blah, blah, blah..." and "I'll be damned, blah, blah, blah..." Shayla's actual words were irrelevant.

Gwen watched as Xavier stood behind Carmen's wheelchair and made introductions to Vaughn and the others. Carmen looked to be in her middle or late thirties and had a traditional aura about her. Her looks suggested sophistication without pretense. She wore her hair pulled back tightly in one large bun, and her skin, the color of cinnamon, was flawlessly beautiful. For some odd reason, Gwen liked her already. Shayla jabbed Gwen in her ribs as they approached. Gwen suppressed the urge to rip Shayla's fingers out of their joints.

"Hi Gwendolyn, Shayla." Xavier smiled pleasantly.

Shayla said, "Hi yourself," and Gwen threw another one of her wiggle waves.

"I'd like you two to meet my sister, Carmen."

Sister? Hmmm. Dean, you sly dog, you milked the Carmen theme all week. Good one...

"Nice to meet you." Gwen extended her hand and shook Carmen's.

Shayla exclaimed, "Your sister!?" She seized her chest as if she had just been given a one-way ticket into Heaven. "Um, Carmen-girlfriend, please, y'all join us. Xavier, have a seat."

Xavier looked at Gwen. "Y'all sure you don't mind? Was someone sitting here?"

Before Gwen could tell him that she wasn't sure, Shayla had said, "No, have a seat." Xavier pulled one of the chairs out and moved it to another table, allowing Carmen to roll into its place. He then took a seat beside Shayla, who somehow squirmed in her chair, strategically scooting it closer to his.

So damn obvious...

Gwen shook her head and muffled a snicker. A waiter approached and laid down two large platters filled with seared crab cakes with warm bacon dressing and grilled chicken quesadillas. More champagne was also provided, and he requested orders from the bar. Gwen put in her chardonnay order; Xavier asked for a Heineken; Carmen said chardonnay sounded good and ordered the same; and Shayla put her empty champagne glass on the waiter's tray and picked up two more, one for now and one for later. She then leaned over seductively and whispered something in Xavier's ear. Gwen turned her attention to Carmen.

"My baby brother here has told me a lot about you, Ms. Fagan...is it OK if I call you Gwendolyn?" Carmen's light brown eyes sparkled.

Gwen smiled. "Of course. Call me Gwen. And don't believe everything you hear." Gwen said this jokingly, assuming Xavier couldn't have given her a good review.

"He has nothing but high praise for you. And I see why."

Gwen smiled, surprised and slightly embarrassed. She glanced at Xavier. Apparently he had managed to divide his attention between Shayla's sultry advances and Gwen and Carmen's conversation. He looked at Gwen and winked. Gwen looked down, feeling he could see

her emotions right through her clothes. God, she hoped not. Shayla straightened herself up and decided to drum up some conversation of her own.

"So Carmen, are you new to Atlanta, too?" Shayla leaned back in her chair and caressed the champagne glass against her lips.

The waiter arrived with their drinks. Carmen raised the chardonnay to her mouth and shook her head.

"Oh, no. I've lived here for years, since college. I'm an English professor at Spelman College. Once baby brother here decided he needed a change of scenery, Atlanta became his first choice. Really, I think he just wanted to make sure I was getting along OK. He and our parents are very protective of me, regardless of the fact that I take care of a husband and two kids; they think this chair has turned me into breakaway glass." Carmen patted the chair's arm and looked lovingly at Xavier. He grabbed her hand and held it.

"Don't believe a word she says. She's right about me wanting to be closer to her, but really it's for a home-cooked meal whenever I want one and to have someone look after *me*. Carmen is the protective one. Don't let her fool you."

Gwen soaked in their banter and felt the warmth from it. She and her brother, Weldon, had once been close like that, before their parent's death.

Her older brother's full name was Weldon Jefferson Fagan II, a name Weldon hated—the Weldon part anyway, just as Gwen was never too fond of Gwendolyn. Old-fashioned names—too old for two happening teens. The family always called Weldon Weld, which sounder much hipper than what they called Gwen—Gwenny. That just sounded country.

But before the death of their parents and Weldon's subsequent spiral into the world of drugs, Gwen and Weldon were close. She idolized him and would tag along behind him whenever she could or whenever he would allow it. Being four years older, Weldon upheld his older-brother responsibilities to the fullest. He taught her how to drive when she was twelve and took up for her when some of the older, rougher neighborhood girls felt she needed bullying just

because—just because she thought she was cute, just because she acted stuck-up, those petty just becauses.

One breezy fall day, Weldon gave her a crash-course in self-defense. The course was conducted in their family carport; Gwen stood like a stick figure with her hair in two curly pigtails, still wearing her plaid, pleated, private-school uniform. Her fists were raised in a spastic position while Weldon stood in front of her, his mega Afro blowing in the breeze, a stern look on his boyish face, palms up and out, telling her to punch. Gwen's punches were rather wimpy her first few tries, which only angered Weldon. "Punch, Gwenny. Punch with some damn confidence," he'd shout. He told her she already had an advantage over her opponent with her height. (Gwen stood her full and final five-feet-eight by the time she was ten.) "If you just look like you won't take no shit, then you probably won't have to touch 'em," Weldon advised that day, then shouted, "Now stop being a punk-ass and punch." With that said, Gwen faked a jab to his face, and when Weldon went to cover she slammed her fist in his gut. He doubled over in pain and Gwen began to cry. She didn't mean to hurt him. She told him she was sorry as she helped him up; he laughed and said, "Now *that's* what I'm talkin' 'bout, Gwenny."

As Gwen got older and puberty hit, she and her mother clashed often. This created a rift between her and Weldon. Weldon was a mama's boy and although he back-talked plenty himself, he couldn't stand the fact that Gwen seemed more consumed with being "uppity-ass cute," as he'd say, than listening to their mother. Their parents' death in essence became the death of Weld and Gwenny. He hated her after that, and soon she felt very little for him in return. Only God knew where Weldon was right now, where his addiction had taken him. And Gwen, after remembering the last time she saw him, didn't really care.

But this bond between Xavier and Carmen obviously was special; he continued to hold her hand, resting it on the arm of her wheelchair.

"Carmen, how long have you been in the cha..."

"Shay! For God's sake." Gwen wanted to punch some manners right through Shayla's nose.

Carmen touched Gwen's hand, "It's OK, really." She looked at Xavier, inquisitively, "It's been what...ten years now? Yeah, this past March was ten years."

Xavier dropped his head. "Yeah, ten years."

Carmen squeezed his hand and smiled. It was obviously painful for him, seemingly more so than for Carmen.

"Car accident?" Shayla asked, just starting the back-up glass of champagne.

Gwen glared at her.

"Technically, it was a motorcycle accident. But I'm sure you don't want to hear the gory details." Carmen looked at Xavier as she spoke. She was undoubtedly considering his feelings, something Shayla was not.

Before Shayla could stick her big foot in her mouth again, Gwen spoke up. "No, that's really none of our business. We're sorry if we brought up painful memories."

Carmen said that was all right and Xavier looked up and directed his gaze at Gwen in an appreciative look. Gwen didn't look away like she normally did; instead she gave him a slight smile.

The champagne must have finally kicked in; Shayla stood up, staggering a bit, and said she had to go to the restroom. She looked at Gwen and suggested Gwen had to go as well. "Shay, I'm fine. We'll keep your seat warm," Gwen replied.

Shayla stood there for a moment, as if Gwen was going to change her mind, then finally swaggered off, her dress swishing back and forth like a pendulum.

"Is she going to be all right?" Carmen asked, still looking back at Shayla. Gwen grabbed a crab cake and said Shayla would be fine, really wanting to say, *if the bitch falls in the toilet, we should all be grateful.*

"Gwendolyn, let me guess. You worked up until party time, right?" Xavier took a swig of his beer and leaned forward.

"Something like that."

"Carmen, I don't think I've ever seen a person so dedicated to work as Gwendolyn."

"So you've said, baby brother." Carmen smiled at her brother, fully

59

aware that her words and its tone would make him blush with embarrassment, which it did.

Gwen fiddled with the large cloth napkin in her lap and felt uncomfortable; she got the feeling her name had come up more than once between brother and sister.

"Gwen, are you originally from Atlanta?" Carmen began to get personal.

"Yes, originally."

"Is your family still here?"

"Um, no. Um, my parents are deceased."

Gwen looked at Carmen and smiled, weakly. Xavier held his beer bottle to his lips, seemingly immobilized by her words. Carmen suddenly became apologetic.

"I'm so sorry...I..."

"It's OK." Gwen didn't want her to feel she had overstepped her bounds like Shayla. "They've been dead for about fourteen years now. They were killed in a car accident when I was fourteen." Gwen paused, trying to keep her voice even, feeling it was on the verge of cracking. "Um, anyway, after their death I lived with my Nana in Augusta." She issued a fractured smile and fiddled some more with her napkin.

"Gwendolyn, we're very sorry." Xavier's voice exuded genuine sentiment. Carmen nodded in agreement and they all sat around in silence.

That New Year's Eve night, the night Gwen's mother slapped her across her face, Gwen stomped out of the house. She hopped in her brother's Datsun, not knowing her parents would soon try to follow. She never imagined they'd come after her; not as angry as her mother was, and as disappointed as her daddy looked. She figured they'd just let her act out, be the spoiled brat, without lending any sympathy to her behavior by looking for her. But they had. Gwen had only driven a few blocks to a burger joint and sat in the parking lot for two hours feeling like a fool. They were struck by another car in a nearby intersection, killed instantly by a drunk driver who walked away from the accident. A police car was in the driveway when she returned home.

Gwen cleared her throat. The silence began to feel uncomfort-

able. Xavier and Carmen still looked a bit remorseful, and Gwen was surprised she had confessed anything about her life to Carmen and Xavier, of all people. Maybe it was because Carmen had shared information about herself, so Gwen felt she should reciprocate. Maybe it was because Xavier seemed so thoughtful. Gwen gave him a soft look; he returned her look and added a humble smile. Gwen again looked down at her napkin.

Soon Shayla returned. The swagger was gone and a mischievous grin rested on her freshly touched-up ruby lips.

"Y'all check out who Vaughn's sweet-talking over at the bar?" Shayla stood behind Gwen, resting her hands on Gwen's shoulders and pointing toward the bar. Shayla was giggling, practically falling all over Gwen and no doubt smearing make-up all over Gwen's jacket.

Gwen leaned back, not only to improve her view but also to try to shake off Shayla, who was draped over her shoulders like a cape. Shayla finally took her seat, picked up another glass of champagne, and began leaning all over Xavier, still giggling.

Gwen spotted Vaughn, another martini in his hand, chatting with a rather statuesque black woman. He wore a cheesy grin, rested his hand on hers occasionally, yet barely looked at her face, especially since her ample bosom was in perfect line with his mouth. From what Gwen could see, she wore false eyelashes and a close-coiffed wig. Gwen couldn't quite understand what Shayla was laughing about—except for the hair, the two women could have passed for sisters.

"OK, Shayla, what gives? You apparently know something about this woman that the rest of us don't. Want to give us a hint?" Xavier asked the question for everyone.

"I'll give you two—testosterone and a dick."

"Shay!" Gwen chastised Shayla, appalled.

Shayla ignored her. "Vaughn may not be getting enough at home, but if he keeps fooling around with our fair drag lady, then he might end up getting more than he bargained for." Shayla's giggles gurgled into her glass.

Carmen said, "Oh my God," and looked back again at Vaughn. Xavier nearly gagged on his beer. Gwen strained to get a better look.

The woman was very attractive. Her make-up appeared flawless and her body, toned and nicely outfitted in business attire, could stop traffic. If she was a man, then Gwen was Johnny Cochran.

"Shay, cut the nonsense. You're trying to tell us that *that woman* is a man? Please..." Gwen dismissed the idea.

"Uh-huh. Miss Thang over there works with my cousin in customer accounts at the Ritz-Carlton and he truly believes he's a she. And if he didn't have that inconvenient tool between his legs, he'd have everyone else fooled, too." A rush of giggles began again. "Looks like he's got Vaughn already."

Gwen looked at Vaughn, who was clearly oblivious to what type of woman, or man if Shayla spoke the truth, he was talking to. Gwen glared again at Shayla, threw her napkin on the table, and stood up.

"Gwendolyn, where are you going?" Xavier stood too.

"Where do you think I'm going? I'm not going to sit here and just let my boss make an ass of himself." Gwen moved to take control of the situation. She respected Vaughn, and no one deserved to be humiliated on his birthday.

Xavier stopped her. "Gwendolyn, sit down, please. I'll take care of Vaughn."

Gwen thought for a moment before sitting down. Xavier touched Carmen on her shoulder, asking if she was doing OK. She nodded and said she was fine. Shayla saw her chance to get Xavier to herself and volunteered to help. He told her that wasn't necessary, but she grabbed hold of his arm and held on anyway.

Gwen watched Xavier walk up to Vaughn and pat him on the back. Vaughn began making introductions, while Shayla held onto Xavier's arm, occasionally burying her head into Xavier's shoulder, stifling laughter and acting cute. Gwen felt a rush of frustration that felt a lot like jealousy. She sighed heavily. *Get a grip.*

"Gwen, leave it to Xavier. He has a knack for rescuing people out of odd situations. He'll take care of Vaughn, don't worry." Carmen looked back at her brother and then again to Gwen.

Gwen smiled and watched to make sure. Vaughn did seem to be moving away from the bar, under the tutelage of Xavier. They seemed

to be heading in the direction of another table surrounded by Talbot and Talbot employees. Vaughn remained standing, Xavier by his side and Shayla by Xavier's.

"You and Dea...I mean, Xavier seem very close." It was the first time Gwen had actually uttered his first name, pronouncing it "Zavier," as Carmen had.

"Yeah we are. Always have been. Listen, I didn't mean to be abrupt about my accident. It's hard for Xavier to talk about or listen to any discussion about it. This chair seems to say all there is to say. In some bizarre way, Xavier feels responsible, ludicrous as it sounds." Carmen savored another swallow of her wine and stared into the glass.

Gwen looked at Xavier, who had pulled up a chair at the distant table and had coaxed Vaughn to do the same. "Why would he feel responsible...if I'm not being to nosy?" Gwen knew she was, but wanted to talk to Carmen without a crowd.

"Oh of course not, you're fine. Responsible may be the wrong word, but I know he's beat himself up over the past ten years. My fiancé and I were on our way to a party Xavier and his team members were throwing after the Elite Eight...I'm sorry—I don't even know if you're aware Xavier played college basketball—or if you are familiar with the dramatic names the NCAA gives the rounds in its basketball tournament?" Carmen added, looking pleasantly at Gwen and waiting on an answer.

Party...Elite Eight...Ten years ago... Gwen rubbed her forehead, stunned.

"Gwen, are you all right?"

"Wha...Yes, Carmen. I'm sorry." Gwen tried to calm her rapid breathing. "I'm vaguely familiar with it."

"Well, my fiancé and I decided to travel by motorcycle. It was his new toy and we didn't think much about the ride from Georgia Tech; we were both doing our graduate work there at the time. We left early and had enough time to stop and visit my folks in Charlotte, then left for the party. In hindsight, we were really too tired to be traveling." Carmen's voice dropped, "The accident to this day is a blur. We only had one helmet, which Cyrus insisted I wear. Funny, I wasn't going to

worry about wearing one at all. Strange how things work." Carmen seemed caught up in recollecting.

"Was Cyrus your fiancé?" Gwen asked as cautiously as she could.

"He was." Carmen's lips trembled; she grabbed her glass and finished off the last of her wine, then forced a shattered-looking smile, "He didn't make it."

Gwen touched her arm. "I'm so sorry."

Carmen nodded. Gwen wondered how an evening of celebration had turned into such a relentless discussion of death and doom.

"Listen, I've seemed to put a damper on the night, I didn't mean to." Carmen wiped underneath her eyes with her napkin. She tried to make her voice light and hearty.

"It's OK. Uh, what does Xavier beat himself up about? I mean, it wasn't his fault." Gwen felt she was pushing the subject, but she couldn't help it. The door to 1987 had been opened.

Carmen didn't seem to mind. "Believe me, I have told him so many times that none of it was his fault. I guess it's one of those cases of 'if I hadn't…' I think Xavier feels that if he hadn't insisted we come to the party, the accident never would have happened. But believe me, Gwen, don't let this chair fool you as to the type of person I was and still am." She leaned in. "I love a party." Carmen chuckled, and Gwen smiled in return. "But I always try to assure Xavier that I'm fine. I let him know my legs may be paralyzed but the rest of me is alive and kicking. Sometimes I tease him by saying that I feel guilty for spoiling his party. Apparently the party was still jamming hard when he got the call. Xavier must have bolted in a skinny minute, because he was at the hospital in record time from what our Pops said." Carmen chuckled dryly, "Pops said Xavier had hung up the phone before he could tell him to take his time and be careful; shoot, he was scared Xavier would have a wreck himself trying to get there, especially since he had been partying and drinking. But damn if that brother of mine didn't get there."

Xavier on the phone in the bedroom…

Gwen's head spun: was this a joke, a setup? Were these people for real? She looked at Carmen, with her natural, pleasant manner.

Gwen rubbed her temples; her paranoia swirled, and for an instant she feared an elaborate scheme had been plotted. But for what motive—ten years after the fact, Xavier wanted her to know he wasn't involved? Even to Gwen that was foolishness. Xavier didn't remember her from Adam.

He wasn't there while Terry raped me, plain and simple. He wasn't there.

Gwen wanted to believe this; she needed to believe this, to add up with all the wonderful qualities she had seen in Xavier over the past few months. She shifted in her seat, her smile trembled; when asked again, she reassured Carmen she was fine.

Carmen began to change the subject, saying something about the extraordinary revenue the 1996 Olympics had generated in Atlanta. Soon, a few other party attendees approached and the idle chitchat began again. Gwen nodded every now and then, threw in a few words to prove she was listening, but couldn't direct her eyes away from Xavier.

He was laughing and being sociable, occasionally looking over at Carmen to make sure she was doing OK. This time he caught Gwen's stare and his smile blazed across his face like wildfire; it was his usual smile, not unlike all the other smiles he had bestowed on her in the past. She looked away, feeling that her emotions were again flamingly visible. She believed he wasn't there that night ten years ago. But she had to ask herself the next question—*now what?*

· FOUR ·

XAVIER ANSWERED THE JANGLING PHONE in the conference room with his usual professional coolness, then smiled, spun his chair around away from Gwen's view, and lowered his voice. He still sounded professional, but the call was clearly personal.

Shay, Gwen concluded, annoyed. She thumped the keys of her IBM laptop so hard that Xavier took a second to look back at her. She raised her eyes over the top of her glasses that slumped down her nose, saw him looking, then looked back at her screen, unfazed. She suspected she could thump with a little less energy, but instead she decided to pound with added enthusiasm.

I'm here to work, not play. So take it outside if you have a problem.

She told herself, often, to *get a grip, get a grip, get a fucking grip.* But she couldn't, or she didn't want to, she still hadn't figured out which. In the three weeks since Vaughn's party and Carmen's revelations, her relief at learning that Xavier wasn't a part of the rape ten years ago—or not directly, it seemed—had the effect of increasing her anxiety about the attraction she felt toward him. It didn't feel so unnatural anymore, just out of character. For her anyway, if not Shayla.

Shayla still found any mundane excuse to come into the conference room where Gwen and Xavier continued to work. Her snare tactics were so damn obvious she would practically offer the likes of coffee, tea, or herself on a platter as if surrounded by gravy and biscuits. Gwen tired easily of Shay's little show and spent a great part of her day away from the office. Now, as she shut down her computer, she decided it was time to leave again.

"That Shayla is something else," Xavier chuckled as he hung up the phone.

Yeah, and when you figure out what, keep it to yourself.

Gwen said "Uh-huh" and collected all the files she needed to put in her briefcase. Xavier stood beside her and began thumbing through one of the files he had been working on.

"Heading back out to Norcross?" Xavier asked as he closed the file and turned to face her.

"Yeah, Phil's gonna meet me out there. And remember we have a meeting with the acquisition team at Cyntex, three-thirty sharp." Gwen paused to look at him, then finished packing up her briefcase.

"Yeah, got it scheduled. You've been spending a lot of time out there, I feel kind of guilty. Maybe we should break it up—say, I go one week and you go the next, something like that?" Xavier walked over to the credenza to pour himself a cup of water. As he leaned back against the credenza, the window framed his muscular body, the clear blue sky serving as a picturesque backdrop.

"Dean, that's not necessary. I think we've got a good thing going..." Bad choice of words, Gwen thought; she looked up at him and felt her face flush. "I mean, I think it works well with me gathering a lot of the data and meeting with key people while you continue to keep the productivity flowing here. Don't you think?" She issued a quick, polite smile.

He issued back one of his wonderful ones. "Yeah, Gwendolyn. I think we've got a good thing going."

That was a flirt. I think.

Gwen blushed. She couldn't help it. She turned to leave, hoping he hadn't noticed.

"Oh Gwendolyn, what are your lunch plans today?" Xavier rushed to open the door for her. They stood, her face to his broad chest, and Gwen startled into brainlessness by the question.

"I haven't given it much thought, why?"

"Well, Shayla invited me to join her and some of the folks in her department over at Planet Hollywood, I just wondered if you'd like to join us?"

How much you want to bet those other "folks" never materialize?

Gwen wanted to roll her eyes, but she didn't. "No thanks, Dean. I'll probably just grab a bite in my travels."

"Are you ever 'not working,' Gwendolyn?"

"What can I say—I like my job." Gwen's voice softened and her eyes traveled up to his face, where his square-jawed, masculine features looked so inviting she wondered suddenly what his kisses felt like. She held his stare; something inside her said, *hold his stare...*

Xavier's grin slowly vanished from sight; his lips looked smooth, supple, and his usual happy-go-lucky demeanor was replaced by an expression Gwen could only describe as romantic. He looked as if he were wondering the same thing about her kisses. Then the computer chimed, indicating Xavier had new email. They both looked away, embarrassed; she was sure he must have sensed, too, that something between them had just ignited.

"Um, Gwendolyn, I, uh...you have a productive trip, now," Xavier said, sounding flustered. He shifted his weight and looked away from her, then back at her again, "And try not to give Phil such a hard time."

Gwen walked out saying she wouldn't. She and Xavier had connected, and Gwen couldn't help but smile.

Cyntex Corporation, located on Buford Highway in Doraville, was fast becoming the little software company that could. Although this was their first acquisition and they were anxious to have it wrapped up, they kept their anxiety in check and allowed Gwen and the rest of the team to conduct the audit in as much time as was needed. The president of Cyntex, as well as other key associates, didn't want to own a company that could prove detrimental to Cyntex's productivity and credibility. They trusted Gwen to take care of everything, and that's exactly what she planned to do.

She and Phil, Cyntex's internal accountant (who Gwen had initially viewed as an arrogant, twenty-three-year-old executive-wannabe, and now saw as a little-less-arrogant, twenty-four-year-old, executive-wannabe), spent most of the morning and part of the afternoon

evaluating financial documents and meeting with personnel at the candidate's office on Technology Parkway in Norcross. They were starting to dig into the tax aspects and Gwen could already see that the upcoming Memorial Day holiday weekend would be spent in the office. But that didn't bother her much. Cyntex was one of their largest clients and in the end, once the acquisition was signed, their appreciation for her efforts would most likely be quite rewarding.

She and Phil went their separate ways about an hour before their three-thirty meeting. Gwen had a bite to eat at a Hardee's down the street from Cyntex and sat at a relatively clean table by herself. She nibbled on her burger and wondered how the Planet Hollywood lunch had gone. She wondered if Xavier found Shayla's attractiveness to his taste, if he'd be interested in her in any other way besides the obvious. And if he did take the obvious route (i.e., screwing Shayla's weave loose), would it be so good he would want to keep going back for more?

Stop wondering about him, Gwen; he's not your man...

Gwen dumped her burger and her untouched fries back into the bag and slammed them into the waste receptacle on her way out.

The meeting lasted less than an hour and Gwen and Xavier walked out together. Dark clouds had replaced sunshine, making Gwen feel like going straight home and curling up in bed with a good book.

"Are you headed back to the office?" Xavier pressed the remote to his champagne-colored Acura Legend, unlocking the door. He had parked next to Gwen's car. Gwen looked at her watch.

"I had planned on it, just for a couple of hours."

"Of course, that was a stupid question," Xavier chuckled. Gwen smiled and placed her briefcase on the passenger side of her car.

"Here, let me get your door." Xavier walked around the front of her car and opened the door. Gwen followed, thinking he had a patent on chivalry.

"Gwendolyn, did you get yourself some lunch?"

"Yes, I got a bite." A bite was the absolute truth; her stomach growled right then. "How was your lunch?" Since lunch had been brought up.

"Good. Um, there were some scheduling problems with Shayla's coworkers. They couldn't make it, so it was just her and me. It was enlightening, to say the least."

Bingo. I should market my psychic abilities.

Gwen faked a cough to disguise her smirk. She stepped inside her car just as thunder sounded in the distance.

"Looks like it's gonna pour." Xavier looked up, scrunching his face. Then he looked at Gwen and smiled. "I'll see you back at the office, Gwendolyn."

"See ya." Gwen slammed her door and started the car; her stomach grumbled and her thoughts gnawed away at her.

Enlightening, eh, Dean? Is that a new way of saying Shay's campaign is working?

Gwen arrived back at the office to find Shayla perched on the conference room table like a cat in heat, her legs crossed and her hand playfully fiddling with her necklace. She and Xavier were talking, laughing, and clearly doing little work. It was the end of the day with a long weekend ahead, and most of the staff had either already left or were socializing, bullshitting, doing anything to pass the time, ready for the Memorial weekend to begin. And if that's what Shayla wanted to do, then fine—but Gwen would really appreciate it if she would do it elsewhere and with someone other than Xavier. He had plenty of work to do, she fumed: or couldn't he see past Shayla's ripe breasts and plush thighs to find it?

Stop the fucking madness...

Gwen marched in with a grimace painted on her face and noticed how quickly the two cut short the fun and games.

"Gwen girlfriend, we thought maybe you went home. What you doing back here?"

"Work."

Gwen hoisted a box of files, full of tax documentation, onto the table. Xavier stood to help her, apologizing, but sat back down once he saw she had handled it fine without him. Plus, the look she gave him carried enough force not only to sit him down, but to thrust him right

through the wall into the next office. Shayla hopped off the table and slowly ran her hands down her too-tight fuchsia skirt, giving Xavier an eyeful.

"Well, I better be going, let you two get back to work." Shayla leaned forward and lowered her voice, but still loud enough for Gwen to hear whispered, "EXavier, I can't wait for us to get together tonight. Save your energy," she giggled, "I mean, we might be out late."

Gwen looked at her, then Xavier, whose smile had the pensive cast of the guilty as charged. Shayla flowed out of the room like syrup, her hips swishing from left to right, as if preparing themselves for all the bumping and grinding they would be doing later.

The room was silent once she left. Gwen began writing out an agenda for the next week, her anger so apparent that she snapped the lead of her pencil. Water, she needed water. Anything to cool down. She pushed her chair back and walked to the credenza.

"You don't think it's a good idea, do you?" Xavier finally spoke.

"Don't know what you're talking about." Gwen looked out the window, seeing his reflection as he remained sitting in his seat, looking at her.

"I don't know why Shayla said what she just said, letting you know of our plans. She likes to play games, I guess."

You asshole. You like to play games right along with her.

"I hadn't paid Shay much attention." A lie.

"Well, we're going out tonight..." Gwen could see Xavier swivel a bit in his chair, seemingly uncomfortable with the idea. "...and that's probably not a good move on my part, being that I'm an associate and she's a coworker."

It's not a good move for lots more reasons than that.

"It's not my place to give advice on matters like that." Gwen took a sip of her water and felt completely drained. She wanted to go home and forget the entire week.

Xavier stood behind her before she even realized it. "I'd like it if you shared some of your wisdom, anyway." His voice was deep, set on a low volume that she found instantly arousing.

Gwen turned around, seeing Xavier was suddenly closer than she realized. He stepped back, a respectful gesture, and leaned against the conference table.

"Dean, I'm not about to get involved with anything you and Shay have going. Sure, dating coworkers can be hazardous, but the two of you are adults and should know how to conduct yourselves." Gwen walked away from him and began clearing documents off the table.

She had already packed the necessary files in her briefcase and decided she would work in her cozy study at home, instead of seeing this office, this conference room, over the weekend. Let Shayla and Xavier get it on all weekend if they liked. She didn't care.

I care like hell.

Xavier sounded somewhat disappointed, "Thanks, Gwendolyn. I appreciate your honesty."

Gwen looked at him, but didn't respond. He smiled a little, raising only one corner of his mouth. She started to speak up, to give him some real honesty, to tell him—*ask him*—not to go out with Shayla. Gwen yanked her briefcase down by her side and gave him a pathetic, phony smile. To hell with it. Her own feelings were too confused right now, and to tell him something like that would not only be inappropriate, it would be downright outrageous.

As usual, he opened the door for her.

"What are your plans this long weekend?" Xavier said, attempting to drum up some light conversation at the end of a very heavy day.

Gwen wasn't in the mood—in fact, she was pissed. Pissed at Shayla, pissed at Xavier, and pissed at herself for being so pissed. "No big plans. See ya later." She walked out of the conference room without looking back.

"...then the psychiatrist on call had the nerve to tell me, 'Step aside little lady, I'll take over from here.' And that was *after* he had been paged over an hour ago and *after* I had already evaluated the patient and made the necessary recommendations. Oooh, that infuriated the hell out of me..." Payton rambled on.

"Uh-huh." Gwen was watching Robin Givens put a sexual hurting

on Eddie Murphy in *Boomerang,* and all she could think about was Shayla and Xavier. They'd been on her mind ever since she left the office on Friday. Now she sat stiffly in her plush recliner, thinking she truly needed to get a life.

"Gwen?"

"Uh-huh."

"Are you listening to me?"

"Yeah, sure. You were infuriated."

"Yeah, infuriated. So, then after they wheeled me down to the morgue, Elvis the medical examiner began to saw my head open and found the words, 'Gwen is not listening' inscribed on my medulla oblongata. Then they pretty much wrapped my toe up with a pink bow and slid me into the freezer."

"Uh-huh."

"OK, what the hell is wrong with you?"

Gwen turned the television off. No more tonight. It didn't matter if she were watching *Gilligan's Island,* the sight of Ginger and the Professor would still make her think of Shayla and Xavier.

"Hello, anyone home. Hello..." Payton tapped the receiver to wake Gwen up.

"I'm here, Payton. I'm here."

"Well, isn't that a relief. You want to let me into your world? It's got to be better than the one I'm trapped in at the moment. Can you believe Mother had the gall to invite Bobby, the high school geek who is now a dentist geek, over to the house yesterday? I know they want grandchildren one day, but their tactics have got to stop..."

Gwen still barely listened. Payton was calling from Charleston, where she was visiting her parents for the long weekend, and was already thinking about heading back home to Boston. Suddenly a wave of laughter echoed through the receiver.

"What is all that noise there anyway?" Gwen asked.

"Hello, it's only been going on the entire time we've been on the phone. David and Tony are here and you'll never believe what they're playing."

"Don't make me guess."

"OK, Twister. Yes, you heard me right. The game of Twister. Gwen, visualize my two fifty-seven-year-old parents and two gay men playing Twister. It ain't a pretty sight."

Gwen laughed, remembering quite well how funny Payton's family could be. As the old saying goes, the apple doesn't fall far from the tree...

"Gwen, I should have come to visit you, but no, I hadn't seen my parents and David for almost a year, so I decided to be the dutiful daughter and sister. And look how they treat me. So far, I've been to a gay club with David and Tony—yeah, as if I'm going to meet a future husband there—although I did meet a woman who told me she could rock my world better than it had ever been rocked before. Gwen, she looked *just* like Shaun Cassidy, and all I could think about is that she would probably be rocking my world to the tune of "Da Doo Ron Ron." I told her pass. Then Mother took me to her Saturday bridge club meeting, and after two bottles of cheap-ass wine, they nearly killed each other when they found out Mrs. Benson was cheating. Mother took some of the women to the side and tried to administer some therapy and asked me to do the same, when all I wanted to do was tell them they were all crazy and to get the hell over it. And now, on a Sunday evening, they're playing Twister." Payton took a breath. "Hey, there's still time. Why don't we meet each other in Augusta, go visit your Nana."

"No can do. Nana is in Japan visiting Uncle Earvin and his wife. She'll be there the rest of the summer. I talked to her the other day and she's having a nice time, except they treat as if she has one foot in the grave and the other..."

"On a banana peel."

Payton and Gwen laughed.

"So what's bugging you, anyway?" Payton asked again.

"I never said anything was bugging me," Gwen replied, attempting to avoid the issue. She and Payton rarely talked about Xavier, not since she'd jumped all over her for making such painfully correct assumptions about her feelings. She had told her about meeting Carmen and that bit of news, But even then Payton hadn't pushed for more information, and Gwen hadn't offered.

"So, do you ever talk to Ellis?" Payton asked, fishing for dirt.

"Nope."

"Just asking. Thought maybe y'all keep in touch."

Gwen rolled her eyes. "Um, I do have some good gossip, if you're interested." Gwen decided she would ease into this conversation, that way maybe she could bail out quickly if it got too deep.

"Hell yeah, sister girlfriend. What's the four-one-one?" Payton asked eagerly.

"What's the four-one-one?" Gwen repeated with a laugh.

"Good, ain't it? I'm getting there, sister. I'm getting there. So, what's the news?"

Gwen took a deep breath. "Dean and Shayla went on a date Friday night."

"You lie!"

"I lie not."

"Hmmm." Payton didn't speak for about ten seconds. "Shayla tell you this?"

"In an indirect, direct way."

"Nothing will probably come of it. She can't be his type, not by the way he seems to be," Payton assured her.

"All men like to fuck," Gwen stated as fact.

Payton faked an alarming gasp, "You and that damn graphic honesty." Laughter erupted again from Payton's end, "Gwen, let me switch phones, these grown people don't have a lick of sense."

While Payton changed phones, Gwen eased out of the recliner. Her joints were starting to stiffen from her intense workout earlier. Heading toward the kitchen, she stretched her arms in the air and rotated her neck. Her bright red kitchen, trimmed in white, sparkled from the massive cleaning she gave it Friday night while she'd been imagining Xavier and Shayla doing some massive business of their own.

Stop thinking about them, stop it.

Gwen grabbed a soda from the fridge and pressed it against her forehead, trying to freeze her thoughts. She reached the upstairs phone in her bedroom just as Payton came back on the line.

"OK...Gwen, are you there?"

"Oh yeah, I'm here."

"Well it's so quiet on your end."

"It's always quiet."

"Yeah, now that you mention it, it is. Anyway, let's see. I guess I'd be pushing that envelope if I asked what you thought about them going out?"

Gwen took a swig, put the can on the nightstand, and fell back onto her bed. "I don't like it, there's your answer," Gwen retorted quickly. Payton was her best friend and it was foolishness not to share her feelings, as confusing as they were.

"You like him, don't you?"

"Yep."

"Well, that's great...or no?"

"You're the psychologist, you tell me."

"You mean about college?"

Gwen closed her eyes, "They were best friends, Payton. Probably still are." Gwen never said Terry Stuart's name out loud and never planned to.

"Maybe not. And he's not him." Payton knew the rules, too.

"But with who he is, does that really matter?" Gwen opened her eyes and stared at the ceiling fan, watched it spin, felt its breeze. Her insides churned with mixed emotions.

Xavier Dean had walked back into her life and she still wanted him like she had wanted him before. But she was no longer a carefree, reckless teenager; now she was a woman who, over the past ten years, had fought hard to put herself in a position of never wanting a man again. She never gave much thought to being passionate. Now she feared she was incapable of it.

"Gwen?"

"Yeah?"

"You're still a woman."

"I believe you once updated me on that." Gwen tried to laugh, but really felt like crap.

"Don't be ashamed to tap into that sensual side."

"Oh, I have one?" Gwen joked as tears filled her eyes.

"Duh. Of course you do."

Gwen rose up and grabbed a tissue from the nightstand, "You know, let's squash this conversation. It's all a moot point, anyway. I'm sure he screwed Shayla the other night and he's probably screwing her right now as we speak. I don't do sloppy seconds."

"What if he didn't?"

"Doubtful."

"But what if he didn't?" Payton stressed.

"Then he didn't." Gwen sniffled.

"Are you crying?"

"It's just my period." She lay back down, sideways, and drew her knees up to her stomach. "Don't read a whole lot into it, I always get weepy before the visit from Aunt Flow."

"Yeah, the Red Baron takes no prisoners," Payton quipped, then her voice swiftly softened. "I think it's time you loosened that emotional suit of armor you've created. Even if it's not with Xavier Dean. Let yourself go, just a little."

She shoved the tissue hard against her mouth, her voice crackled from tears, "It's real hard..."

"I know it is, Gwen. I know." Payton comforted, sounding misty herself.

Gwen wrapped her arms around her aching waist and pulled herself up, wiping her eyes, before grabbing more tissue to contain the flood. "Um, look Payton, I better go." She sucked in harsh breaths, trying to compose herself.

"You sure?"

Gwen exhaled slowly, "Yeah. Anyway, your family's probably wondering what happened to you." She raked back a hand full of curls and laughed pitifully.

"Yeah, sounds like they've started a round of Broadway show tunes. Now that's one of my favorites." Payton laughed, then covertly dropped her voice, "Don't tell the flygirl sisterhood committee I said that."

Now Gwen really laughed, "Your secret's safe with me, sister girlfriend."

"I love ya, Gwen."

"I love ya too, Payton. Thanks."

Gwen told Payton she would call her next week and hung up the phone. She blew her nose and swallowed a deep breath. Tomorrow she was going to do something, go somewhere, redeem her stagnant being and get a life; or at least she'd try to find a little of it.

Gwen held her stomach, nearly doubling over in pain. She headed to the bathroom. First she had to take care of Aunt Flow's arrival.

· FIVE ·

SHAYLA ENTERED THE RESTROOM with another woman, yakking away in her hip-hop voice—the voice she used when she wasn't playing professional, and which she normally reserved for those girlfriends who spoke the same language, or at least understood it without needing a translator. Gwen understood them fine; she just wasn't in the mood.

Damn. She crossed her arms and reconsidered her decision to leave the stall. She frowned in disgust, wishing she could click her heels three times, close her eyes, and propel her body over the stall and out the door like an Olympic gymnast. It beat the alternative—listening to Shayla go on in graphic detail about how good Xavier was in bed.

Gwen moved further back in the stall, wedging herself between the toilet and the wall like a child relegated to time-out. Shayla and her coworker/girlfriend kept talking. At least now Gwen knew why she hadn't seen Shayla in a couple of weeks. She had been on vacation to some place that was "fun, but too damn hot," from what Shayla said.

Gwen was thankful for the reprieve; she and Xavier seemed to get more work done with Shayla away. Gwen was rather cold to Xavier, though, the first few days after his and Shayla's date, about which he wisely kept to himself.

He hadn't seemed very different the Tuesday after the date; at least, he didn't come into the office whistling a Jodeci bump-and-grind tune or wearing a sleazy "Shayla and I did the nasty all weekend long" grin on his face. He simply asked Gwen how her weekend was, to which she replied, "Fine," and she started to ask the same of him but decided his answer, however generic he made it, would fill her with jealousy. So she didn't ask.

But after a few days passed and Gwen's hostility decreased (plus the fact that there had been no more visits from Shayla), things were beginning to happen between Gwen and Xavier. They were becoming friends, or at least that's what it felt like to Gwen.

Xavier started it. He just started talking to her about other topics besides the acquisition. Nothing real personal, just small talk about Atlanta and how he liked it better than D.C.—transportation was better, there was less crime, and the political types were tame in comparison. At first Gwen would only issue a slight smile and reply, "Uh-huh," still really pissed about Shayla. But then it became so obvious he was making an effort, a real effort to be something more than just a colleague, that she started to give a little, smile a little, laugh a little, almost everything but flirt a little or make herself seem aggressive. She really did want to take Payton's advice and loosen her emotional armor, but not at the expense of her dignity. So she still handled herself in a reserved manner where Xavier was concerned.

Yet, she couldn't deny that she liked the way it felt—the way Xavier made her feel. In the past two weeks they had bonded a bit. But now Shayla was back and she seemed to have an extreme case of verbal diarrhea.

"Girlfriend, have you seen that fine brother on the twelfth floor?" Shayla asked the unknown girlfriend.

"Mean the real dark-skinned brother with the bowed legs?

"Girlfriend, that's him. He must be new, cause I ain't never seen him before. His ass is fine as *hell*," Shayla stressed.

"Yeah, Shay, the brother got a little somethin'-somethin' goin' on," the unknown girlfriend agreed.

Gwen heard a whispered, "I know that's right," followed by giggles. She rolled her eyes, frustrated and annoyed that Shayla would rather gab than piss and that she stood squeezed in the back of a stall like a coward. She picked invisible lint from her burgundy pantsuit and told herself to stop acting stupid. Just as she decided to make a move and expose herself to whatever sex details Shayla had to give, she heard Shayla and the girlfriend clomp their way into stalls, where latches clinked and yakking resumed.

Gwen lifted her eyes to the ceiling, placed her hands prayer-like to her chin, and thanked God for perfect timing. She tiptoed out of the stall, washed her hands quickly, and headed for the door.

Shayla's conversation shifted from the bow-legged brother to Xavier. The girlfriend asked why she was scoping out fresh meat when just a few weeks ago Xavier was the only meat she was interested in. Shayla ignored the question with a "Child, please..."

But their little exchange stopped Gwen in the foyer. She let the door, which she had already opened, close, and decided she wanted hear what was said. Hearing the details this way, indirectly, seemed less of a threat than hearing them from Shay up close. This way, if it got too explicit she could leave without giving Shayla the satisfaction of seeing her jealous blood boil. Gwen moved away from the door and stood, waiting on the toilets to flush as her cue to bolt. But Shayla and her friend seemed to have made themselves comfortable and kept talking.

"...uh-uh, Miss Shay, don't be trying to avoid the question. I thought Mr. Fine Basketball Brother was the one for you. What happened with that?"

"Who? EXavier?"

"Girl, you know I'm talking 'bout him."

"I don't know, girlfriend. We went out a couple of times before I went on vacation. But he ain't all that."

"Oh really? Looks 'all that' to me," the girlfriend retorted.

"Child, please. Don't get me wrong, he's nice and all but...are we by ourselves?"

"I think so. Someone just left out."

"Anyway, EXavier is real sweet, but, I don't know...I think he might be gay."

Gwen's mouth dropped open so fast she had to slam her hand against it to keep it from hitting the floor. *Was Shayla out of her damn mind?*

"Gay?!" the girlfriend repeated, equally incredulous.

"Shush. Damn, girl, don't talk so loud."

"Shay, he don't look gay to me."

"Well, maybe not," Shayla mumbled.

"Hell, Shay, I thought he used to be married."

"He was, *and* he's got a little girl. But..."

Oh, really? A little girl, Gwen thought as she heard Shayla and her friend rustling; her time was limited. But Shayla talked on.

"...but he don't really like to go out to clubs, and he be listening to old music, like Luther Vandross and Teddy Pendergrass..."

"Whaaat? Girl, he ain't got no Tupac or Lil' Kim?"

"*Hell* no. And he likes to talk. I mean talk about all kinds of shit that I ain't interested in. Girl, I want to do more than talk, shit..."

Toilets began to flush and Gwen made her exit, smiling from ear to ear.

Shay didn't get fucked, bottom line.

Gwen giggled to herself. Shayla made it so obvious what the real deal was with all her commentary about Xavier being gay and listening to "old" music. Xavier didn't sop Shayla up with a biscuit after all. Gwen felt immensely happy.

When she returned to the conference room, still grinning, Xavier greeted her at the door.

"Gwendolyn...whoa, what is that all about?"

"What?" Gwen walked past him.

"That smile. I don't think I have ever seen your smile, um, quite so big." Xavier looked down at her and gave a sly grin of his own. "Want to tell me what's got you so happy?"

Gwen tried to squash her grand smile, but it wouldn't budge. She turned to face him, seeing him at last as a handsome, available man. Her reply was coy: "Oh, I just heard some interesting news that's got me tickled, that's all." She wanted to giggle again, but didn't.

"Must have been good." He walked towards her with his hands in his pockets and his smile shining.

Gwen gave an upbeat, "Uh-huh," and accidentally flexed her eyebrows at him. A definite flirt.

Embarrassment clouded her face and she immediately tried to backpedal. "The news wasn't that good, just, um...never mind." Gwen

waved her hand dramatically and sat down, wanting to crawl under the table.

She fumbled with her computer, waiting for Xavier to take his seat. He didn't. Not immediately. She could feel his eyes on her, and she knew they were dancing the way they did when he looked at her, which often made her wonder if he liked what he saw, or if his eyes just did that with everyone. The silence was starting to feel uncomfortable.

"Dean, did you have something to tell me?" Gwen looked up at him, presenting her question in a business-like fashion and trying desperately to flip the awkward atmosphere.

Xavier cleared his throat, still a bit charmed. "Uh, oh yeah. Vaughn just called. He wants to see us both in his office at two o'clock." Xavier took his seat across from her just as she said, "Oh, OK," and nodded with a smile, not quite as radiant as before. Xavier's smile broadened. "Uh, you wouldn't happen to know what that's about, would you?" he asked.

Gwen pushed her laptop forward and folded her arms on the table. "Uh-uh, and what exactly are *you* smiling so big about?" She leaned forward, her question asked in a flirtatious manner, something that was making her feel less and less uncomfortable.

"Oh, I guess you could say I just saw something that's got me tickled." He winked. Gwen blushed and looked at her computer. Flirting was starting to be a whole lot of fun.

"Gwen, Xavier, please come in and have a seat," Vaughn implored, standing to greet them.

Gwen and Xavier, both with legal pads and pens in hand, sat down as directed and listened attentively. Gwen couldn't help but notice how tired Vaughn looked. He looked like he had lost some weight, which made his suit hang on his once broad frame. Gwen didn't get to see much of him these days, since the acquisition consumed all of her time. But now she wondered just how bad things really were at home. Rumor had it that he and his wife were having problems. Vaughn was probably sniffing elsewhere, screwing someone on the side while his

wife took care of the homefront, Gwen figured. He didn't seem like the type, but then again he was a man. Enough said.

Vaughn sat down and started the meeting. "Listen, I've got something of a dilemma and I need to solicit the assistance of you both, particularly you, Xavier."

"Sure, Vaughn. What can I help with?" Xavier replied.

"Well, as you both know, Janice had her baby last week, two months early. I spoke to her the other day and the baby has to stay in the hospital several weeks, but they're both doing fine. And I was thinking that Simon and his team could manage the upcoming due diligences without her. But this morning Todd had a family emergency that will possibly keep him away for two weeks, three at the most. With the due diligence team being two short, that really puts us in a bind. Xavier, I need you to change gears and join Simon and the team for the due diligence in Colorado and possibly another one in Chicago." Vaughn raised his hands before Xavier could comment. "Now, I know you're immersed in this acquisition, but I was hoping Gwen could spare you. You guys tell me where you stand."

Gwen looked at Xavier, who was already looking at her. Xavier spoke first.

"Vaughn, I don't have a problem with going. I've been on due diligence teams in the past and if Gwendolyn doesn't have a problem with it, just let me know who I need to contact and when we head out." Xavier looked at Vaughn and smiled, then looked at Gwen, at which time his smile evaporated.

What was that look for? Gwen wondered, getting the distinct impression Xavier was upset. She blew the notion off with a quick shake of her head. "Vaughn, it's not a problem on my end. The acquisition is going smoothly and Dean and I have a pretty good idea what each of us has been working on, so it shouldn't be too hard for me to pick up wherever he leaves off." Gwen smiled and looked at Xavier. He kept his attention on Vaughn, clearly ignoring her.

What is wrong with him? Gwen continued to look at Xavier, a bit perplexed. Vaughn started talking again, and Gwen removed the smile and turned to Vaughn.

"Well, that's good to hear. You don't know how important this is. And Xavier, I appreciate your flexibility, I know I've been pulling you in all directions, and I can assure you that it won't become a habit."

Xavier said, "No problem," and he and Gwen received all the necessary information. Vaughn apologized again for the abrupt nature of the assignment, but unfortunately the Colorado trip was coming up fast and was expected to last for ten days, almost up until the Fourth of July holiday. He knew that didn't give Xavier much time, but the circumstances couldn't be avoided. Xavier was to meet with Simon, who would brief him on everything he needed to know.

They talked for a few minutes more before Gwen and Xavier headed back to the conference room. Xavier strolled down the hall a few feet ahead of Gwen. He didn't talk, and Gwen waited until they were back in the conference room before she spoke.

"Dean, it's getting late. Do you want to get together first thing in the morning and you can brief me on where you stand with the acquisition before you meet with Simon, or do you want to brief me afterwards?" Gwen stood with her palms pressed down on the conference table. Xavier sat across from her, concentrating on his work papers.

"Uh-huh," was his response.

Gwen leaned in, making her voice stern. "Is that 'uh-huh' to before or 'uh-huh' to after?"

Xavier shuffled his papers to the side and looked up. "Whatever works for you." They stared at each other, Gwen in confusion, Xavier apparently upset.

"Dean, is there a problem? I mean if it's too much for you to go on this trip on such short notice, let Vaughn know." Gwen didn't get it. If he didn't want to go, or *couldn't* go, then he should have spoken up, instead of sitting here taking it out on her.

"There's not a problem with me going." Xavier paused, stared down at his papers again, then looked at Gwen, as if debating his next statement. "I take it by that big smile you were sporting earlier that you knew about this beforehand."

Excuse me?

Gwen remained standing, yet pushed away from the table and crossed her arms, and said, "No, I didn't." That was about as convincing as Don King with a Jheri Curl, but she took major offense at his assumption.

Xavier raised an eyebrow in disbelief, then relaxed his face and nodded. "Of course. That sounded petty, didn't it? Listen, let's say we get together early, before I meet with Simon." He smiled, a little smile that seemed to indicate he wanted to believe her, but didn't.

Gwen tried to smile too, but felt like crap. She released her defiant stance and sat down, telling Xavier that early was good for her too. They both went back to work. It bugged her that Xavier thought she was happy about him leaving. She wasn't, and she wanted to tell him that she wasn't. But how could she say anything without it sounding unprofessional and, at the very least, trifling? She glanced at him and decided to forget it. Letting herself go, even just a little, was already getting her into trouble. To elaborate would only make her look like a fool. They worked the rest of the day in silence.

Gwen walked around Perimeter Mall on a shopping mission that had so far come up nil. Perimeter Mall wasn't very far from the acquisition candidate's office in Norcross, where she had been spending so much time, and since she hadn't been to Perimeter in ages, she figured a new suit and maybe a silk scarf would pull her out of the funky mood she had been in since Xavier left a few days ago.

Except for their early morning meeting the day before he hopped the plane for Colorado, they hadn't talked much. And since he had been gone, Gwen had divided her time between her office and Norcross. The conference room just wasn't quite the same without him. She missed Xavier. She missed his smile, his scent, his voice—him. All of him.

Gwen gazed through the glass window of a boutique that specialized in business suits—expensive yet conservative, just the place to shell out big bucks and drown her self-pity woes in debt. She started to waltz right in when someone called her name, in a familiar voice that turned out to be attached to a friendly face. Carmen.

She looked a little different, with her hair pulled back into a pony-tail and very little make-up, but her smile was radiant as she rolled up, flanked by two young girls: one the height of a young adult but with the face of an innocent, and the other about four or five, petite and angelic. Gwen immediately smiled, happy to see her.

"Well, isn't this a surprise. What brings you out to our neck of the woods?" Carmen held out her hand and squeezed Gwen's.

"I guess you could call it shopping. I just hadn't decided if it was going to be on a 'look' level or a 'spend' level." Gwen laughed.

Carmen said, "I know that feeling," before the older of the two girls tugged on her arm and pointed to the toy store straight ahead.

"In a minute, Cec...I'm sorry, Gwen. This is my daughter, Cecelia, and this little one is my niece, Kendra. This is Miss Gwen, she works with your daddy." Carmen stroked Kendra's hair with her thin fingers, and the girl blushed sweetly and buried her head into Carmen's shoulder.

Gwen gave them both a pleasant, "Hello," accompanied by a wiggle wave, and received a soft, "Hi," from Cecelia and a timid grin from Kendra. Gwen could see Kendra's resemblance to Xavier—she had his soft brown eyes. And both little girls were adorable.

"So Gwen, I see you got my brother out of your hair." Carmen joked, almost evoking a protest from Gwen. Once she realized Carmen was only kidding, Gwen told herself to settle down and get a grip.

"Well, Vaughn knew he'd be a great help to Simon's team, but he was such a big help to me that it's sort of hard to manage without him."

"Oh, that's so nice of you to say. But I'm sure you have it all under control. Listen, this is so bizarre seeing you here. I was planning on giving you a call tomorrow..."

A flood of teenage boys, all with their hair out of control and their jeans dropped below their underwear, looking like MTV rejects, nearly knocked Carmen and the girls over without so much as an "excuse me." Cecelia helped push Carmen further into the entrance way of the boutique, while Gwen wanted to run behind the group of

delinquents and drop-kick all of them into the middle of next week. There was absolutely no excuse for such bad manners.

"Whoa, we seem to be in the line of fire." Carmen twisted to look over her shoulder, trying to make sure there were no more stampedes. "I guess I could move faster if I had my motorized wheelchair, but I hate that damn thing, the gears stick all the time and...oh my, I'm rambling. Thank you, Cec, baby." Carmen patted her daughter's hand and Cecelia kissed her cheek.

Gwen smiled and felt a light tickle against her hand. Kendra stood next to her, swaying back and forth as one of her braided pigtails brushed against Gwen's fingers. Gwen instinctively stroked the child's hair. She stopped herself quickly, feeling it was not her place and wondering what in the world possessed her to do it.

"Anyway, Gwen, I was wondering what you were doing next weekend for the Fourth?"

"The Fourth?"

"Of July." Carmen chuckled, knowing she was being sarcastic.

Gwen shook her head, embarrassed. "Of course. Um, I usually go to Augusta, but not this year. I guess I haven't given it much thought."

Since Nana was out of the country, their usual Fourth of July get-together, which entailed cooking out early in the morning and spending the rest of the day eating, socializing, and eating some more, all in that order, would have to resume next summer.

"Well, I would like you to join us." Carmen held her hand out to the two youngsters. "My husband and I...who is around here somewhere with our son," Carmen looked around, then abandoned the search with a flip of her hand. "They're probably still looking at more overpriced tennis shoes, as if they need more pairs. But, we usually get together with family and friends and cook every meat imaginable, steam some crabs, fry some fish, basically party and gorge until the fifth of July." Carmen laughed again. "Please Gwen, join us. I'm sure Xavier would love for you to come."

Don't bet on it.

"Uh, it sounds like it's a family affair and I would hate to intrude,"

Gwen stated, almost certain that Xavier had no desire to be in her company.

Carmen leaned forward, "Gwen, it's family *and friends*. Please give it some thought. We'd love to have you. Here, let me give you my number." Carmen retrieved a pen and pad from her Liz Claiborne satchel and jotted down her number. "Think about it and give me a call, or I can call you sometime next week with directions, especially since I'm sure by then you will have decided to come." Carmen's eyes and smile twinkled with that same sly quality as Xavier's. This woman was definitely not short on persuasiveness.

Gwen took the number, knowing already that she wanted to go, wanted to be around nice people like Carmen and her family, and wanted to be around Xavier. But making a fool of herself was never high on her agenda, and after she and Xavier's last meeting she felt certain he wasn't interested in seeing her at all.

Before they parted ways, Gwen said she would consider it and Cecelia began tugging on Carmen's arm again while Kendra played the bashful role. Carmen soon caved in to their toy demands, and the two girls squealed with delight. Carmen rolled her eyes playfully and they headed to the toy store. Gwen decided she didn't need a new suit and headed home with Xavier on her mind.

"Hello." Gwen cradled the phone, a pencil stuck in her mouth, still keying figures into her laptop without skipping a beat.

"Gwendolyn? Hi, it's Xavier."

Gwen stopped typing and dropped the pencil from her teeth, listening as it struck the desk before it plopped onto the carpet. "Dean? Um, hi."

"I tried reaching you at the office but I caught Mary before she left. She told me about the electricity in the building. I hope you don't mind me calling you at home, but Mary seemed to think it would be OK. I was really just calling for a status check on Cyntex."

"No, it's fine. I..." Gwen stammered, losing all train of thought.

It had been almost two weeks since Xavier left. He was due back

in Atlanta the day after tomorrow, but not back in the office until the Monday following the Fourth of July holiday. He had called once before, asking about the acquisition, but she wasn't in the office and he'd left a message that simply said, "I'm just checking in. Call me if there's a problem." He left his number at the Sheraton, but Gwen figured he didn't really want her to call him back, and since there wasn't really a problem, she shouldn't bother. So she hadn't.

Now, he had caught her at home. There was some kind of electrical shutdown at the office, so everyone had been advised to call it a day and check back tomorrow, at which time the electrician said all power should be up and running.

"Gwendolyn?"

"Yeah, Dean. I'm here. Everything with, um..."

Cyntex, you fool...

"...Cyntex is fine. We're very close to sealing this deal, and let me tell you, I'll be glad when we do." Gwen finally gained control of her tongue and senses again.

"Good. That's good. Um..."

Don't let him get off the phone just yet!

"So how is everything with you? How's the due diligence?" Gwen leaned back in her chair and propped her feet up on the table.

"Things are going well. I think we're all a bit homesick. I know I am."

"Yeah, I bet." They were losing momentum. An awkward silence loomed for a few seconds.

"Listen Gwendolyn, I better let you go."

"Yeah...oh, I saw your sister last week," Gwen threw in as a conversation piece, not mentioning she had seen his little girl too.

"Yeah, Carmen told me. I talked to her yesterday and she said she faxed you the directions for the cookout this weekend."

Gwen nodded, "She did. I'm pretty familiar with that area, but that was considerate of her to go the extra mile. I, um..."

"We hope you can make it."

You do?

Gwen smiled. "It was very nice of her to ask me."

"Carmen really likes you and she'd love to have you come." Another silent moment. Gwen's smile faded. Xavier didn't say *he'd* love to have her come.

"Well, Dean, I forget you're in a different time zone. I'm sure Simon is keeping you hopping. I better let you go."

"Yeah. I guess I'll see you in a few days. Unless you decide to join us on the Fourth—then I guess I'll see you sooner than that." The smile in his voice resonated through the phone.

"Well. You just might." Gwen held the phone close to her mouth, her voice dropping to near a whisper.

"Good. I'd like that. I'd like that a lot." Now Xavier's voice sounded sexy—very sexy, as if he were talking to his woman instead of his coworker. Gwen stroked the phone, imagining Xavier's face, touching it, tracing his lips with her fingertips, kissing him softly. She closed her eyes at the thought.

Then Xavier spoke, sounding a bit embarrassed, "Um, listen, I better go."

Gwen opened her eyes, "Uh yeah, OK. Thanks for calling."

"Sure. Bye."

"Bye."

Gwen listened to the phone click, then silence, then the dial tone. She held the receiver against her chin and smiled, enjoying the warmth she felt inside.

What the hell is happening to me?

· SIX ·

O N THE FOURTH OF JULY, Gwen drove into the Spalding Bluff subdivision worrying, feeling her anxiety swell inside her chest like Jiffy Pop popcorn. It was bad enough she was about to see Xavier, who consumed her thoughts so thoroughly that last night she couldn't sleep. But now her worries were compounded with thoughts of Payton.

Last night when they'd talked, Gwen had started off by asking Payton what her plans were for the Fourth; she was so caught up in her own angst that she needed a diversion. Payton provided a diversion, all right.

First she told Gwen she was on call at the hospital for most of the weekend, the best parts of it, anyway. Then, after much hemming and hawing, she accidentally, (probably on purpose) made the mistake (probably intended) of telling Gwen, "Um, Collin called me..." Gwen cut her short by screeching, "Collin?!" Payton said, "Uh-huh," like a pitiful child. "*Why?*" Gwen asked. Payton said, "Well, he called me the other day and said he'd be in town for a few hours, an extended layover on his way to Vancouver, and he wondered if he could stop by. That's all." Payton's voice collapsed into child-like innocence, then she added, "You don't think it's a good idea, huh?" Gwen said, "It's Collin, right?" Payton said, "Um, yeah," which led Gwen to clarify that they were indeed talking about the same person. She broke it down into terms Payton could understand. "The same Collin you dated in college, the one who drove the red Miata—you know, girl car?" This made Payton giggle nervously, "Yeah..." Gwen continued, "The same asshole Collin who used to call you stupid all the time in front of your friends—hell, in front of your family even—and the same one who said you'd look

just a little bit better if your hips weren't so big, and the same Collin you caught in *your* bed screwing the waitress from Hooters who *was* actually stupid and had hips bigger than yours and mine combined? That same Collin?"

They were quiet for a few seconds, before Payton gave an "OK, Gwen, you've made your point," through sniffles. Gwen sighed, "Payton, I'm not trying to hurt your feelings, but he's so unworthy of even a moment of your time. Do you really want to see him?"

Payton said, "I'll be honest, I'm feeling lonely, and yeah, I was willing to settle for the old booty call. No strings, no morning-after excuses, just some lovin'. Some familiar lovin'. My life in Boston has been nothing but work—sex life uneventful, and relationships non-existent. So yeah, I figured Collin and I could get into a couple of hours of trouble. No harm, no foul." Payton laughed dryly.

Gwen wanted to scream, *Don't do it! Collin's ass is not worth it.* But instead she said, "Payton, you're a grown woman, I'm not going to tell you what to do. Just be careful and have fun, I guess." Gwen couldn't think of anything else to say. Payton believed in love and romance and enjoyed all the sexual excitement that came with both. Maybe she figured she could just think of her and Collin's good times, and shove all the bad times into the back of her mind, at least for a few hours. Payton mumbled, "Yeah, well, we'll see," and their conversation ended with Payton literally begging Gwen to have a good time at the cookout and not waste her time worrying about her. Gwen simply said, "Uh-huh, yeah right. I'm calling you tomorrow."

And she meant it. Gwen decided she would call Payton bright and early tomorrow morning just to make sure her friend's spirits were good with whatever decision she came to concerning Collin. She hoped she wouldn't find her best friend wallowing in one-night-stand guilt. But now, as she drove through landscaped, upscale Norcross, she had her own personal worries to consider.

Like the two bottles of Kendall-Jackson chardonnay she'd bought just minutes before; maybe it was inappropriate for a cookout. She didn't want to arrive empty-handed—that was just tacky. But maybe she should have brought a watermelon or potato salad—deli-prepared,

of course, because her homemade was so bad it may have killed them.

Then there was her outfit. She'd gone with the lavender print skort set, one of two she'd purchased just for the occasion, but now it felt too short. Her legs, seldom revealed, felt naked without the protection of pants. And what if she came off looking loose, like a woman who wanted the attention of someone other than Xavier?

Then there was Xavier. What was she thinking? Was she crazy? They worked together, that was all, and maybe that was all it should be, she kept telling herself. But she was feeling like a woman who wanted more. But did she really want more? And did it really matter what she wanted anyway? Xavier may not be giving her a second thought; hell, he might be at the cookout with his girlfriend, or using it as an opportunity to find the woman of his dreams. That probably meant somebody sexy and curvaceous, with hair down her back and a personality so lively it would just be icing on the cake. This might be the perfect setting for them to get things rolling. Gwen didn't consider herself as possessing dream-girl qualifications.

"Shit," Gwen cursed out loud, wanting to turn around and go back home. But before she realized it she had parked alongside the curb in front of Carmen's beautiful home. Carmen, already greeting other guests at the front door, waved to her. Gwen waved back and took a deep breath. Worrying wasn't going to do her a damn bit of good; the moment had arrived.

"Gwen, I'm so glad you decided to come. And this..." Carmen held up one of the bottles of wine, "...this is perfect. I have to remember to invite you every year. Do you see this, Avery?" Carmen held the bottle up toward a man nearby, whom Gwen took to be her husband. He was a big man, heavy in size, but his height seemed to distribute his weight nicely. He stood just outside the kitchen door and shook his head. Carmen said, "Avery, come meet Gwen. You know, she works at Talbot with Xavier."

"Oh lord. Gwen, it's wonderful to meet you. But see what you done already? Makin' me look bad. Now I'll never hear the end of it." He shook his head and laughed.

"That's right, baby." Carmen placed the bottle on the kitchen counter, still teasing her husband. "Gwen, Avery gets so worked up about this shindig that he usually overdoes it on the soda, juice, and beer, but wine—*good* wine—ends up being an afterthought. Usually when everyone's too drunk to go out and get some." Carmen smirked, still looking at Avery.

He shooed her with his hand and said he was going to check on the grill and the guests, who at the moment were still few in number. But before he left, he walked up to her and leaned down, asking if she needed anything, anything for him to do or get?

Carmen sat in her motorized wheelchair and looked as she had looked at the mall: fresh-faced, free of makeup except a touch of lipstick, her hair pulled back in a ponytail. She wore a denim dress with buttons down the front that revealed her thin, immobile legs. She stroked Avery's face and spoke softly, saying something that broadened Avery's smile, which Gwen had noticed was now so wide that it seemed to reduce his eyes to thin slices of merriment. He kissed her lips with a soft peck and said, "Woman, you are so bad. Gwen, keep an eye on her for me, hear?" Gwen said she would and Avery left the kitchen trailing a hearty laugh that echoed throughout the house. Gwen had no idea what was said between them, but it was obvious how much they cared for each other.

"Carmen, your house is beautiful. Did you decorate it yours—" Gwen dropped the question, fearing it sounded insensitive.

"It's OK. I *directed* most of the decorating and yes, I had a hand in some of it. I'm glad you like it. Let me show you around. I think I can sneak out on my hostess duties for a moment."

They left the kitchen and toured the rest of the house, which had to be at least three thousand square feet. Gwen wondered where Xavier was; she hadn't seen him, and so far Carmen hadn't mentioned him. Most of the guests she met were neighbors, and there were a few relatives in from out of town, but they mingled amongst themselves outside around the beer cooler.

Gwen marveled at the exquisite detail in every room; the color scheme of burgundy, blue, and forest green created a unified theme

for the entire house. The artwork ranged from bright colors of children playing, to huddled jazz musicians, to a baptism outside a small country church. All African-American art, something Gwen had an interest in as well. Then there was the room of pictures.

Carmen called it the music room, and it did contain a piano, which she played, and an acoustic guitar she claimed Avery fiddled with from time to time, but it also had built-in shelves filled with pictures. There was one large portrait of a woman in a white dress walking on the beach with the sun setting in the background. Gwen waltzed in to get a closer look.

"This portrait is lovely. Is this someone in your family?" Gwen studied it. The face of the woman in the portrait was tilted just slightly with raised eyes, as if suddenly discovering she was being photographed.

"Yeah, that's me." Carmen rolled up beside Gwen, studying the portrait herself.

"You're beautiful." Gwen couldn't think of anything else to say, and it was the truth.

"Well, thank you. That's so nice of you to say. That's a picture Cyrus painted from a photograph he took while we were in Jamaica in 1982. We went after we graduated from college. Painting was another one of his hobbies." Gwen nodded. She knew Cyrus was Carmen's fiancé, the one who died in the motorcycle accident.

"He did a wonderful job. I guess it's nice to have something special to remind you of him." Gwen looked down at her.

"It is. But he left me with more than just this portrait. I have Cyrus Jr.; we call him C.J."

Gwen opened her mouth, but nothing came out.

"I forgot, you didn't meet my son at the mall. He's thirteen and looks just like Cy. The Lord works in mysterious ways, I tell ya. You know, when I got pregnant, I was just about to start graduate school and a baby was not one of my goals. Not then, anyway. Cy and I weren't married and I didn't want him to think he had to marry me because of it. I debated long and hard about getting rid of it. But Cy and I talked about it and I talked with my Moms, and she and my

Pops said they would take care of the baby for me, at least until I finished school. Then I had the guilt of burdening my folks, who had just unloaded Xavier into college, and here I was with C.J." Carmen shook her head as if transported back in time. "But things worked out better than I could have imagined. C. J. is a wonderful son, a little hardheaded sometimes, but he and Avery get along as if Avery and I had conceived him together. And then I was blessed with the ability to give birth to Cecelia despite this chair." Carmen paused again, looking reflective, before continuing.

"And C.J. and Cy got to spend three good years together before Cy died. Of course, C. J. doesn't remember it, but I do. And I know Cy is still watching over him." Carmen raised her eyes, probably seeing more in that portrait than Gwen could ever envision.

"Carmen, you are truly blessed. I can't wait to meet your son." Gwen liked Carmen more and more.

Carmen wiped underneath her eyes. "Well, C. J. and his sister and cousin are with Xavier for some last-minute grocery store items. I told him he didn't have to take all of them with him, but he said 'No problem.' They've been gone almost an hour. Probably running him crazy."

Gwen walked around looking at the other pictures. A group photo of several men and women, all sitting at a large round table at what looked like a wedding, gave a toast to the camera. Gwen leaned in. There was Xavier, a bit thinner and with hair on his head, smiling and holding onto a woman wearing a cobalt blue bridesmaid dress. She was very petite and beyond pretty. Hell, she was beyond beautiful. The photo looked as if someone had cut and pasted a model's picture out of a fashion magazine and latched her onto Xavier, with her head resting on his shoulder.

"That was taken at my wedding, in 1989." Carmen offered.

"They all look so happy." Gwen hadn't taken her eyes off Xavier and the woman to notice anyone else in the picture. They could have all been asleep for all she knew.

"Yeah, that was in happier times. At least for Xavier and Tracey."

"Tracey?" Gwen knew she was being nosy, but what the hell. Carmen liked to talk.

"Xavier's ex-wife. They were married a few months after me and Avery. But things..." Carmen let her voice trail.

Gwen barely heard her anyway; she finally took notice of the other people in the photo. Terry Stuart sat on the other side of Xavier, holding the glass of champagne (with which he was supposed to be toasting) to his lips. She leaned closer, her nostrils flared; it was almost as if he was staring back at her with his black eyes. The sight of him made her blood boil.

"Gwen, that picture really fascinates you, doesn't it?"

Gwen stepped back, but didn't stop looking at it. "It's just this guy in the photo looks familiar." OK, she was going set bait.

"Which one?" Carmen rolled next to Gwen. "Oh, you must be talking about Terry." Carmen leaned forward and nodded her head as Gwen pointed to Terry in the picture.

"He's an NBA player now, so you've probably seen him on TV. Although a few years ago you probably saw him more on the sports news than on the court. He and Xavier were friends for years. They played college ball together and went into the NBA at the same time."

Gwen pretended she was looking at other pictures. "They're not close anymore?" She turned and looked at Carmen, trying to seem as if she were simply making small talk. She would try to read Carmen's facial expression to pick up if she was being too damn obvious.

Carmen sort of shrugged her shoulders. "I don't know what happened with those two. I think they just grew apart, you know, with Terry still being in the pros and Xavier having moved on, pretty much leaving that lifestyle behind. But if you knew Terry, it wouldn't surprise you that much. He can be a pretty wild young man, and I know he's been going through a lot in the past few years. Keeping in touch with old friends probably isn't a priority." Carmen chuckled.

Gwen forced a smile, trying to unclench her locked jaws. She glanced at the picture again, haunted by Terry's stare, practically hearing his laughter.

I'm such a fool. I shouldn't be here.

Had she lost her mind? She was about to spend time with Fessor X and his family. For weeks she had all but forgotten that Xavier had

been a member of The Team, forgotten that he and Terry were once best friends. This was crazy. She rubbed her forehead. An illness was about to come on, that would be her excuse. She needed to get out of here.

Carmen touched her arm, "Gwen, are you OK?"

"Uh, no. Carmen listen, I..."

"Xa, man, didn't I tell ya they were probably in here?" Avery laughed.

Gwen turned to see Avery and Xavier standing in the doorway. Gwen hardly recognized him without his suit and tie, but damn he looked good. His attire was simple—a white T-shirt with a blue swoosh logo on the left side of his chest and a pair of blue jean shorts that revealed solid thighs and sculpted calves. She noted a jagged scar right below one of his kneecaps and figured it was an NBA battle wound, but even that seemed to add a touch of rugged character to his appeal. Sunglasses dangled around his neck and an Atlanta Braves cap covered his head. Ankle socks and what looked like a brand-new pair of Air Jordans finished the ensemble. If "fine" were a new drug, Xavier should be bottled and FDA approved.

Carmen said, "Finally, you made it back," and rolled over to greet them. Gwen didn't move. Xavier smiled at her, nodding as Carmen talked, but not really taking his eyes off of Gwen. Gwen threw a wiggle wave and now wasn't quite sure what she felt like doing. Xavier walked up to her and took her hand.

"Gwendolyn, it's good to see you." Xavier squeezed her hand, then released it.

"It's good to see you, too." Gwen knew her smile was weak, but Xavier didn't seem to notice. He just kept smiling at her, his eyes dancing.

"Look here, folks, ain't no party going on in here. Let's hit it." Avery clapped his hands once and laughed.

Carmen rolled her eyes in that playful way of hers and left the room with Avery at her side. Xavier walked to the door, then looked back when he noticed Gwen wasn't walking along with him.

Gwen looked one more time at the photo. Maybe Carmen was

right; maybe Xavier had moved on from that part of his life—Fessor X, The Team, Terry Stuart. Maybe she should try to do the same. If she could.

"Well, Gwendolyn, let's say we go have some fun." Xavier held his hand out to the door, beckoning her to lead the way.

Give it a try, Gwen. Give it a try...

Gwen took a deep breath and smiled. They walked outside together.

"Cookout" was an understatement: this was a party, complete with plenty of food and drink, smooth R&B music, and enough people to populate a small city. Carmen and Avery's huge backyard was more than accommodating. Besides the tri-level deck with ramps as well as steps, there was still enough room for a volleyball net and an above-ground pool.

Gwen and Xavier barely had enough time to discuss his trip to Colorado; friends and relatives made appearances constantly, saying hello and catching up on old news, gossip, and anything deemed a conversation topic. Gwen met people left and right, knowing she would never remember their names if they approached her again.

She met Carmen's son, C. J., a cute teenager with the typical look—oversized clothes, a small, neat afro, and a stud in his left ear. He seemed well mannered and kind of shy. After Carmen paraded him around to some other folks, she finally released him to a group of his own peers. There were several groups at the cookout. All the kids under the age of ten were divided between boys and girls. This included Carmen's daughter, Cecelia, and Xavier's daughter, Kendra, who Gwen noticed was much more animated than she had been in the mall; they were all off playing with their respective toys—either dolls or action figures—except for one little boy who stuck close to the girls and insisted that he be able to load up Barbie's custom van with dolls and chauffeur them around the deck. Gwen took a closer look and noticed that the van was full of Ken dolls, about four of them, and Barbie was nowhere in sight. She shook her head, thinking she was not even going to go there.

The teenagers all hung out together, boys and girls combined, of

course. The boys stood around trying to act cool and unconcerned with life in general, while the girls, with their crop-tops and piled-high hair, giggled and flirted. Some were quite bold, unafraid of being viewed as aggressive. The sight of *them* scared Gwen to death.

After about an hour she'd seen numerous women, quite a few of them with dream-girl qualities, swarm toward Xavier like bees to honey. Gwen didn't want to disrupt his game. She didn't want it to appear as if she were competing for his attention, or claiming him as her own. But standing around while other females eagerly and shamelessly made their intentions known only served to piss her off. Being jealous was a new emotion for Gwen and lately she found herself wearing it out. During one conversation, a woman wearing an itty-bitty halter top, with her nipples poking through the thin fabric like little rocks, stood in front of Xavier wiggling and jiggling as if she had to pee. She ignored Gwen and smiled up at Xavier with big teeth and flared, double-barreled nostrils that revealed long, grass-like nose hair. At that point Gwen thought she had better leave before she broke down in laughter or grabbed a lawnmower to shove up the woman's nose. Xavier said, "Gwendolyn, you don't have to go," but Gwen raised an eyebrow, accompanying it with a tickled smile, and said, "Oh, I think so." Her next stop was at the picnic table lined with food.

Gwen filled her plate with a hot dog, blackened to perfection, and slaw, baked beans, and pasta salad, then made her way to one of the many rows of steps and sat. She balanced her plate on her knees and placed her soda beside her ankle. She was having fun, but there were few events like this that weren't the better for a few moments of stolen solitude.

"Gwen, are you having a good time?" Carmen rolled down the ramp beside the steps.

Gwen wiped her mouth, "Yes, I am. This is a monster party. You all do this every year?"

"Yeah, for the past four..." Someone called her name and Carmen looked over her shoulder. A young man approached, methodically placing one foot in front of the other, giving his stride a certain swish.

Gwen assumed he was trying to be suave, when if truth be told, he came off looking feminine.

"Hey, cuz." His voice was whiny. He kissed Carmen on her cheek before he turned, stroked his chin, and beamed at Gwen. "Say, cuz, how about introducing me to this lovely lady?"

"Oh I'm sorry. Gwen, this is my cousin, Jackson. Jackson, this is Gwendolyn."

Gwen nodded and held out her hand. He took it, only holding onto her fingers, and bent down, kissing her knuckles. Gwen raised her eyebrows, annoyed.

Oh damn, not today...

"*Gwendolyn*, now that's a beautiful name. Fits you nicely, I must say." He held onto her hand and laughed, whinny-like, his tongue protruding.

Gwen slipped her hand from his and suddenly lost her appetite. Jackson was nice looking—in fact, he was damn pretty. It was obvious he spent a great deal of time and money on his high-priced hip-hop clothes, his freshly styled hair, and his body, which was well packaged and well built, ready to conquer. He was definitely not a stranger to vanity. He eased by Carmen and picked up Gwen's soda, so as not to knock it over as he sat beside her on the steps.

Now ain't this some shit.

Gwen tilted her head in his direction, then immediately leaned back. He was too close for comfort.

"So, *Gwendolyn*, tell me about yourself." He kept sounding out her name as if he were the Big Bad Wolf and she was little Red Riding Hood.

Before Gwen realized it, Carmen had rolled away, trying to pull a couple of the young girls off the boy with the Barbie van, whose ass they were about to kick in order to get their van back.

"Listen, Jackson. I've got to go inside. Will you please excuse me for a minute?" Gwen held her plate high in the palm of her hand and stood up. He stood with her.

"You know, it is hot out here. How 'bout I come inside with you?"

Oh, hell no...

"Well, I..."

"Hey Gwendolyn, I'm head—Jacks my man, what you been up to?" Xavier said, appearing from out of nowhere. He threw his hand out to Jackson; the two of them exchanged the "we are real men" hug, with a forearm in between.

"Xa man, I'm good. I was just sittin' here, talking to fine Miss *Gwendolyn.*" Jackson stroked his chin again, like some pimp daddy from the seventies.

"Oh, I'm sorry, I didn't mean to interrupt." Xavier directed his comment to Gwen.

She quickly spoke up, "You didn't interrupt, really. Um, did you need me for something?"

God, please say yes...

"Uh, no not really. I was just about to head to the store again and I was wondering if you needed anything?" Xavier smiled, and his smile was like a life preserver.

Gwen ditched her plate in the large rubber trash bin beside her, since a platoon of flies had basically stormed it. "Well, actually...is it OK if I ride with you? I do need to get something." Gwen stretched her eyes, trying to give a signal.

"Aw *Gwendolyn,* I'm sure if you tell Xa man here, he'll be glad to get whatever you need. Ain't that right, Xa?"

"Uh, sure..."

"No." Gwen chimed loudly. "I mean, Xavier wouldn't know where to look, and besides it's not really something a man goes to the store for, if you know what I mean." Gwen smiled bashfully.

Please Dean, play along...

Xavier coughed, trying to disguise a laugh. "Yeah, Jacks man, you understand. But, hey, you're not about to go, are you? There's plenty of food left, and I think some of those ladies over there would love to hear about some of those new rap artists you've recently signed." Xavier pointed in the direction of some of the dream girls, smiling in that devilish way of his.

"Yeah man. True dat. True dat." Jackson and Xavier bumped fists before Jackson slithered away.

"I take it you don't really need anything at the store?" Xavier retrieved his keys from his pocket as they walked to his car.

"Not really. Was I that obvious?" Gwen stepped aside as Xavier opened her door.

"I don't think Jackson noticed. But when you called me Xavier, I knew something had to be up." Xavier shut the door once she had settled in, and poked his head through the passenger window. "It sounded good, though. Please feel free to use it often." He winked, then walked to the driver's side. Gwen blushed in reply.

Xavier cruised up the street and stopped at a mini-mart located on the corner of Spalding Drive and Holcombe Bridge Road. He picked up three bags of ice and two cases of beer. During the trip, he and Gwen's conversation never veered much from the normal business tête-à-tête—Cyntex, acquisitions, due diligences, blah, blah, blah. On the way back, though, Xavier decided to break from the norm.

"Looks like I caught cousin Jackson on one of his major mack-daddy moves." Xavier glanced over at Gwen.

She sat on the passenger side, feeling safe and comfortable listening to Al Green on Magic 107.5 FM. "I don't think he had started the 'major' part yet," Gwen replied, as she tapped her fingers against her leg while Al pleaded, "Let's Stay Together."

"He usually doesn't have to work too hard. Women have a tendency to flock to him."

"Is that a fact?" Gwen kept her face forward.

"Uh-huh."

Finally she turned to Xavier, "No offense, Dean. Your cousin seems like a nice guy..."

"But...?" Xavier stopped at a red light. He looked at Gwen.

Gwen shrugged and looked away, "But nothing, really. I guess I'm just not real comfortable in a social setting with strangers."

"I find that hard to believe. The Gwendolyn I've always seen handles herself quite well." Xavier pulled off slowly as the light turned green.

"I didn't say I couldn't handle myself. And besides, the office envi-

ronment is an entirely different arena. One, I will admit, I feel much more at ease in."

Parties weren't her thing anymore, and she realized that if she'd known that Carmen's cookout would be as large as it was, she probably would have reconsidered coming, Xavier or no Xavier.

"Well, you've got a point, but I like getting a glimpse of the 'social' Gwendolyn. She's very attractive."

Xavier and Gwen looked at each other quickly, then both looked away. Gwen felt that same warmth as before, but she also felt embarrassed at the same time.

"Uh, thanks. Uh...looks as if you were having some 'major moves' thrown your way yourself." Gwen wanted to get the attention off herself.

"Hmmm, is that what you would call it? I was hoping having you beside me would serve as protection, but then you left and..."

Gwen widened her eyes, "Oh. I didn't think you wanted any protection." This was getting interesting.

They pulled into Carmen's driveway and Xavier put the car in park, but didn't turn the engine off. He leaned against the center armrest, looking Gwen directly in her eyes.

"I tell you what. Why don't we make a deal to stick close to each other the rest of the night? That way, maybe we can enjoy the remainder of the evening without having to fend off any 'major moves.' How's that sound?"

Why couldn't we have made that deal ten years ago?

Gwen inhaled a healthy dose of his cologne, which was still captivating. "Sounds good to me." Her voice, soft and sexy, didn't sound familiar to her.

Xavier leaned closer; his smile reduced to slightly parted lips. Gwen's heart raced and she cast down her eyes, a panicked reaction. She said they better get back to the party before the ice melted. Xavier cleared his throat and agreed.

They stuck to their deal and managed to park themselves at a round table located on the top-level deck, overlooking all the happenings.

The table lay covered in newspaper, and a load of steamed crabs sat on top of one another. Gwen and Xavier sat facing each other, elbows on table, cracking and breaking and digging for crabmeat. Avery and Carmen joined them, and Gwen was actually having fun.

The younger groups had somehow evaporated; the small kids were in the house playing in the huge playroom, while the teenagers settled in the great room, watching a slasher movie on video. C.J. tried to talk Carmen into allowing them to go to the bowling alley with one of the licensed-driver teens, but it was the Fourth of July, roads were dangerous, and Carmen gave him a firm, "No." He grumbled, but once Avery threw him one of those, "Boy, don't make me have to get up" looks, C.J. didn't push the issue. It was almost ten o'clock and the adults were just getting their second wind.

"Xa man, ain't that the president of your fan club down there?" Avery sat next to Xavier and elbowed him slightly.

Xavier didn't even look up, "Yeah, man. You talking about Uncle Retro? I already spent my mandatory two hours with him yesterday when he rolled into town. I tell you, I love my uncle, but he can talk you to death. And I distinctly remember telling Carmen here to call Moms and tell her to drop some big hints about him staying in North Carolina."

Carmen chuckled, "Y'all leave Uncle Purvis alone. And for your information, I did call Moms, and she told me she did more than just hint, she flat-out told him to keep his ass at home because he didn't need to be hanging out with us young folk. But you know Uncle Purvis, he thinks he's the youngest man on the planet." Carmen laughed again, then leaned closer to Gwen. "Uncle Purvis absolutely idolizes Xavier, talks about him all the time. He sometimes even tries to dress like him."

Gwen nodded and caught Xavier's eye. He shook his head as Avery began to tease him.

"Uh-huh, check him out right now. Hell, Xa, he looks just like ya."

Xavier began to laugh himself as he looked up, searching for Uncle Purvis. "Man, look at him. Uncle Retro is a trip."

"Why do y'all call him Uncle Retro?" Gwen asked, trying to remember if she had met him earlier.

Avery and Xavier looked at each other.

"Xa man, naw, she didn't just ask that? Should I tell her or do you want to do the honors?" Avery cracked another crab and wiped the resulting splatter from his face with the side of a brawny arm.

Xavier looked at Gwen and smiled. "Since you got your back to him, let me describe him to you. Then maybe you can figure it out."

"All right." Gwen put her crab cracker down and listened.

"Well first of all, he's bald-headed..."

"Uh-huh, he did that after Xavier went with the clean look," Avery offered.

"Man, hush. Anyway, his head is unusually large. I mean, a mega-head." Xavier held his hands out on each side of his head, trying to reinforce the description.

"Gwen, he look like Elmer Fudd," Avery added. Avery and Xavier broke into laughter. Gwen began to giggle herself.

"Avery and Xavier, y'all need to stop," Carmen chastised through the laughter.

"Let me finish the description for Gwendolyn. Let's start from the bottom up. Right now, he has on sandals with black dress socks..."

Gwen began to shake her head. "Oh no, he doesn't."

Xavier nodded, "Oh *yeah*. People just don't know—Uncle Purvis is one of the original gangsters. Then there's the white starched shorts, with the large pockets, except now it looks like they're decorated with barbecue sauce, and with a few watermelon seeds dangling too." Xavier covered his mouth, laughing. Gwen, Avery, and Carmen didn't bother to disguise their amusement. They were practically falling all over each other. "Let me finish. He's got on a muscle shirt—minus the muscle—and a bandanna wrapped around his forehead. Hmmm, looks like he had to tie two together so there would be enough material to stretch across his head." Xavier strained to look, adding some feigned seriousness for effect. He looked again at Gwen. "Now can you figure out the 'Retro?'"

Gwen could barely speak. She could tell Xavier was just being funny, but she never would have guessed he had such comedic talent. She turned around slowly and spotted Uncle Retro, a.k.a Purvis, a.k.a. Elmer Fudd, just as Xavier had described him. Gwen covered her mouth and laughed uncontrollably. He looked like a serious throwback from the Seventies.

Uncle Purvis noticed his audience of kinfolk, plus Gwen, and raised his fist, giving a shout out. "Nephew! You the one, Xavier, my number-one nephew! You the one!"

Gwen turned back around, still trying to control her laughter and beginning to crank out some tears. Xavier didn't help matters, either. He beat his chest twice and raised his own fist in response, "Uncle Purvis, it's all you my man, it's all you!"

"Dean, I don't think this is a good idea. I haven't danced in years, plus there's no one else out here." Gwen hesitated as Xavier pulled her out onto the mid-level deck. The S.O.S. Band's "Just Be Good to Me" brought back memories of her youth.

"Well, then maybe we'll set the tone. Come on, Gwendolyn. Trust me." He smiled and tightened his hand around hers. Gwen acquiesced, happily.

They moved with mid-tempo rhythm. Gwen sort of swayed back and forth, popping her fingers to the beat, while Xavier bobbed his head and moved around smoothly. Gwen was quite impressed. She upgraded her own moves accordingly, and soon she and Xavier were jamming in perfect sync. Others joined them, and in no time the deck was full.

"Told you we could set the tone." Xavier wrapped his arm around her waist and pulled her close. The music changed, a slower groove: Whitney Houston's "You Give Good Love."

"Uh, I think we better sit this one out." Gwen looked up at him.

Xavier released her just slightly. "Of course, I don't want to make you uncomfortable."

"That's not it. It's just that, I've been perspiring, and eating crabs, and..."

"None of that bothers me. If it doesn't bother you." Xavier pulled her close again.

Gwen told him it didn't bother her, and they began to dance. Xavier kept what Gwen thought was an appropriate distance. They held hands out to the side and Gwen rested her left hand on his chest while his right arm held her around her waist.

"Gwendolyn, I hope you've been having a good time," Xavier said into her hair; she could feel his breath through her curls. Through perspiration and crabs, he still smelled wonderful.

Gwen looked up. "It's been nice. Real nice." Being so close to him, at last, began to arouse her. She shuffled a few steps apart, hoping he didn't notice she was trying to put a little distance between them. "Um, do you live near here?" Gwen looked down and closed her eyes for a split second.

Why in the hell did I just ask that?

"Not far. Of course I spend more time here than at my place. And with this trip I just had to take, Kendra's been like a second daughter for Carmen. But she loves spending time here, too."

"Do you have her for the whole summer?"

"Just about. She'll be going back home in a few weeks."

"She's very pretty. Your wife is very pretty, too." Gwen looked up at him.

"You mean my ex-wife. Thank you, but, uh..." He stammered, then fell silent. When he spoke again, the subject had changed. "Most people become fascinated with Carmen's music room. As you could see, she loves music *and pictures.*"

"I could tell. She and Avery are good people. They seem to have a pretty solid relationship."

Crap! She was batting a thousand. Now Xavier probably thought she was trying to imply that his relationship with Tracey could have taken some lessons.

He didn't seem fazed by her statement. "They do. They've known each other for years, even before the accident. He's good for her, and she's wonderful for him. It all balances out nicely. They're my inspiration."

Xavier took a second to let his statement linger. "So Gwendolyn, what about you?"

"What about me?" Gwen didn't mean to sound defensive, but she knew even as it left her mouth that it came out hostile.

"I was just wonderi—Look, never mind."

Gwen felt bad. "Dean, I didn't mean to..."

"Hey, it's OK. And I thought we had gotten beyond you calling me Dean."

Gwen raised an eyebrow. "Well, I don't hear you calling me Gwen."

"*Touché*. But I have reasons for calling you Gwendolyn."

"Oh really?"

"Really."

"Such as?"

"It represents you well. It sounds sophisticated, just like you. And intelligent, just like you," Xavier pressed his forehead to hers, "...and very, very prett—"

Gwen stopped dancing. "Um, you don't...I mean...," she stammered, not quite knowing how to handle herself with a man she was so attracted to, who seemed to be attracted to her as well. She shuffled back some more, adding more distance.

"I've embarrassed you?" Xavier pulled her back gently.

"A little, yeah."

"I didn't mean to," he whispered. Gwen mumbled, "It's OK," and moved slowly into him, pressing her hand against his chest again. The dancing resumed and neither of them spoke for a while. Gwen kept her focus on his chest, knowing that if she looked into his eyes he would be able to read every emotion she felt. And she felt vulnerable, and warm, and totally sexy. And that bothered the hell out of her.

"Can I ask you something, Gwendolyn?" Xavier again whispered.

"Sure," she quietly responded, still looking at his chest.

He hesitated a bit, then said, "It's been bothering me, and I keep telling myself to drop it, but...anyway. Listen, did you suggest me as the candidate for the due diligence assignment?" He stopped grooving for a second, then continued.

Now was her chance to make things right. She drew her face

upward to ensure she made direct eye contact with his incredible brown eyes, and in her most sincere voice she softly said, "No, Xavier. I found out when you found out, and I wasn't thrilled about your going. Really."

Damn if she didn't make things right. The relief in his eyes sparkled and he only nodded as he pulled her closer.

Xavier walked Gwen to her car after Gwen said thank you and good-bye to Carmen and Avery. The streets were relatively empty, but not exactly quiet. Fireworks sounded loudly every few minutes, igniting from the backyards of neighbors. Gwen and Xavier looked to the sky as they stood beside her car, watching a shower of sparkles and glitter. A pause in the light show gave Gwen the opportunity to say her goodnight.

"Dea—I mean Xavier, thanks again for such a nice time."

"You're welcome. I'm just glad you had some fun." Xavier leaned down, playfully trying to get her to look in his eyes.

Gwen looked at him and smiled, thinking what an awkward position she was in, but that she couldn't think of any she'd rather be in at the moment. "I did. Thanks for sticking close, you didn't really have to do that."

Xavier slowly took her hand. "I wanted to."

Gwen could hear his deep reply above the sound of another firecracker. She lowered her gaze and studied his hand as he toyed with her fingers, then she gracefully lifted her head and looked into his eyes. "Xavier, I better go." Her voice was soft and sexy again, a tone that felt more and more natural for her when she addressed him.

"Yeah, I guess so." His was equally sexy, and if anything even deeper than before.

A chill rippled up her spine; her head dropped slightly, and she found herself staring at his chest again. He lifted her chin toward his face, gently. Gwen gulped, hard.

"I guess it would be very inappropriate for me to kiss you goodnight—you know, with us being colleagues and all." Xavier stared down at her with a look so serious she nearly lost her breath.

"You want to kiss me?" she managed to ask, not knowing why she asked such a stupid question.

"Yes." He responded without wavering as he pulled her close, slowly, perhaps making sure it was all right. Gwen didn't resist; his arms around her felt good and strong and gentle and safe. *Safe.* What a concept. She nodded, telling him, *Yes, kiss me please,* with a tender smile. He tilted his head just as she lifted hers to meet him and he gently kissed her forehead, then the tip of her nose, then her lips. It was a sweet kiss, not real dramatic. Gwen accepted his kiss but didn't completely open up, wondering just how much either one of them really wanted to at this moment. His lips left her mouth and softly kissed her chin, at which time Gwen felt compelled to nuzzle her nose against his cheek. She did want more; apparently, he wanted more too, because his lips found her lips again, and this time she felt his tongue brushing her lips and she opened up to welcome it.

Oh damn, this is good...

Gwen reached up and held his face in her hands; they kissed deeply, filling each other's mouth with their tongues: plush, soft kisses Gwen wanted to continue, but instead she found enough restraint to stop. "Xavier, I better go." A bit of breathiness added to her whisper.

Xavier leaned down again and muffled his words in her hair, "I could follow you home. You know, see that you get there OK."

"You don't have to, really. I'll be fine. But thanks for the offer." She stroked his face, letting him know the gesture was sweet. But part of her wasn't sure if she wanted him to know where she lived. Or if he'd be this sweet once he got there.

Xavier nodded, but neither one of them made any moves to let go of each other, or stop looking into each other's eyes, or refuse the urge to go at it some more. He kissed her forehead again and she closed her eyes, waiting for him to travel back down to her lips. He didn't disappoint her. This time Gwen added her own flavor to the kiss, gently touching his tongue with her tongue, tasting the sweetness of his lips as he eagerly tasted hers.

Back in the day, Gwen loved kissing. She thought it was the most expressive form of intimacy a person could experience. Kissing told

so much without giving away any secrets. And it could be so creative, so emotional, so intensely satisfying, especially if the other person kissed with the same energy, evoked the same passion, and just plain knew how to work it. Xavier knew how to work it. Damn, did he know how to work it.

Their simple goodnight kiss had turned into something serious: the way their lips and tongues touched and pulled played like a well-choreographed dance; the way Xavier caressed the small of her back as his mouth explored hers like a man who wanted the experience of his journey to last long after it had ended; the way Gwen stroked the side of his face and pressed her body deeper into his, feeling his warmth, breathing his scent, and kissing him with more emotion than she had ever dared think she possessed. This was no longer a goodnight kiss, rather more like a *hello!* The soft moan that suddenly escaped her lips made her stop and pull away.

"Xavier, I really should be, uh..."

Going, you fool, going...

Gwen blushed, knowing she needed to go, but...

Xavier spoke, "I guess, um, I should probably let you go."

Gwen nodded, then traced his lips, something she had dreamed of doing. His lips, those incredible lips made her want to grab his face and drink up every ounce of his being. Instead, she kissed the tip of his chin and asked, "Xavier, what are we doing?"

Xavier leaned his body against her car, slumping down a bit and pulling her into his embrace. "You mean..." he kissed her lips lightly.

"Yeah, I mean...this. What are we doing?" Gwen asked this quietly, her voice laced with sexiness. She knew what they were doing; she just wanted to know if he knew the same thing. Reading a man's thoughts was not one of her strengths. Xavier kissed her forehead again and Gwen fiddled with the swoosh on his shirt.

"I hope we're getting close. Is that a problem?" Xavier asked.

"I'm not sure, considering our professional relationship." Gwen really thought *damn the professional relationship,* but she needed to hear what he had to say.

"Gwendolyn, I know how to separate the two. I wouldn't walk in

the office making a play for you, or anything like that. And you don't seem like the type—"

"I'm not." Gwen stated, letting him know "fatal attraction" wasn't part of her genetic makeup.

"So there's no problem," Xavier kissed her forehead, "and I have to admit, I like what we're doing. I like being close to you, and I've been wanting to get close to you for a long time, I just didn't think you'd ever...I don't know, I didn't think you'd be interested."

Gwen looked at him and smiled. *And what was Shay, a little detour?* Gwen wanted to say, but she didn't feel like ruining the mood. "Oh really?" came out in its place.

"Uh-huh, really. That surprise you?"

"A little."

"Bother you?"

Hell no.

Gwen averted her gaze. "Uh, no, not really."

He touched her chin and drew her face back to his. "You sure? I mean, you're not going to have Monday morning regrets when we get back in the office, are you?"

She shook her head and whispered, "uh-uh," as she traced his lips again before kissing him, teasing his tongue with her tongue, and listening to the deep-breathed moans he made as she took control of the action. Finally, when they pulled apart from each other she asked, "Is that convincing enough?"

"*Oh* yeah." His eyes danced, then grew serious as he cupped her face. "You're so beautiful."

Instant turnoff. Gwen pulled back. "Let's not go there, OK? I don't need my vanity inflated." Her voice lost its sexiness and her posture stiffened. She moved further away from him.

"Hey, I'm sorry." Xavier straightened and grabbed her hand, "Gwendolyn, I wasn't using some line to score points. I wasn't try—"

"Let's drop it, OK?" Gwen hadn't softened much.

"Hey, come here," he tugged on her hand. Gwen hesitated, cautiously took note of his sincerity, and moved back into him, slowly. "I was just making an honest observation, that's all. I had no idea it

would set you off." He spoke soothingly while leaning down and attempting to elicit a look from her. "We OK?" he asked. Gwen looked at him and nodded, slightly flustered and embarrassed at her overreaction. They watched more fireworks without speaking.

"I need to be going," Gwen said, a little softer, a little less hostile.

Xavier nodded. "Uh yeah, OK." He scratched his head. "I didn't mean to spoil the evening."

"You didn't."

"No?" He toyed with her fingers, obviously a habit of his.

Gwen raised herself on the balls of her feet and kissed him, then ended it with a gentle peck on his chin; "No," she told him. He smiled and held her hand as they walked around to the driver's side. Keeping to his normal standard of chivalry, he opened her door and she stood just inside of it as he leaned against the outside of it, facing her.

"So you're off to Chicago next week?" Gwen asked, reaching to caress his cheek, unable to keep her hands off him.

He grabbed her hand and kissed it. "Uh-huh, Wednesday."

"How long this time?"

"Another two weeks." Xavier paused. Gwen said, "Oh," practically missing him already. He began again, "I, um, would like to see you again, you know, like this." Xavier looked around and chuckled, "Well, not in the middle of the street, but on a more personal level. You know, talk, get to know each other, and..." His kiss started off slow, but quickly found the rhythm that was becoming very comfortable for them both. "...Hmmm, and maybe see where things go."

Gwen touched his face, smiling as he smiled, and wondering what in the hell she was doing. Just what in the hell *was* she doing? Laughing, dancing, and exchanging some pretty heavy intimacies with Xavier Dean, best friend or once best friend of Terry Stuart—monster, rapist, asshole, the list was endless. Maybe Xavier was the same way; maybe his almost shy, humble manner was just a game and once Gwen released her guard the true menace would reveal itself. Kissing him felt good; being in his arms felt heavenly; but he was still Xavier Dean and she was still Gwen Fagan and they had history. Just because she was the only one who knew about it didn't change that.

She couldn't keep seeing him, not like this, regardless of how good it felt, regardless of the fact that it was the first time in years being with a man felt this right. It was out of the question. Completely outrageous. The answer would be no, she kept repeating in her head, *the answer will be no.*

So why she kissed him one last time and climbed into her car as he leaned down beside it, and why she touched his face and told him, "I'd like to see you again too, Xavier," was anyone's guess.

· SEVEN ·

IT WAS EIGHT-THIRTY P.M. when the phone rang. Same time every night for the past nine nights. Gwen sat up in bed, already in her Victoria's Secret cotton two-piece sleep set, with only the lamp on near the bed and the stereo down low, over which Chanté Moore's *Sexy Thing* whispered at a pitch only she could hear. The book she was reading, *Black Ice*, was good, but she could barely concentrate on it, as she was happily awaiting the call. She knew who it was; she knew it wasn't Payton, having already talked to her for the week.

Payton was doing well and had recovered nicely after the Collin catastrophe. Surprisingly enough, Payton had beat Gwen to the punch and called Gwen late that next morning, after the Fourth, as Gwen still lay in bed barely awake.

Payton needed details about what had occurred between Gwen and Xavier. Before Gwen was willing to tell her anything about her own romancing, though, she asked about Collin. "Oh that," Payton had stated, unfazed.

"Yeah, that. Give me the dirt." Gwen sat up in bed, her hair frantically tousled, still a bit amazed at the way she and Xavier had carried on the night before in the middle of the street. And still amazed at the way she had dreamt of him while she slept that night and the way she wondered, even as she spoke with Payton, what he was doing at that very moment.

"Let's just say I didn't get my groove on," Payton had answered about Collin, finding any opportunity to use what slang she'd been able to pick up. "Change of heart, huh?" Gwen asked. "Hell, no. I was more than ready to get a little," said Payton. "So," asked Gwen. Payton breathed a deep breath and began, "So. He was awful. Just awful. What

on earth happens to a person in four years? Gwen, he wasn't just losing his hair; his hair had divorced him and run off with his comb to some remote island. But the worst part was his teeth. I don't care how cute you are or how nice you may dress, if you've got bad, mucked-up teeth, all appeal is lost." Gwen had to agree, and Payton finished the details. "So that was it. Collin came in and five minutes into our conversation, like magic my pager went off. I couldn't have planned that rescue in a million years. Damn, I might as well just donate my deprived libido to Goodwill. Maybe someone could put a lampshade on it and sit it in the den."

Gwen was sure Payton's libido would survive, but she couldn't resist telling her best friend that she was happy things had turned out badly. Collin's ass wasn't worth the drama.

Now, Gwen answered her phone on the third ring as usual.

"Hey there," he murmured.

"Hey you." Gwen purred, feeling *very* comfortable with the soft and sexy voice now issuing through her vocal cords.

"What ya doing?" Xavier asked.

"Just reading a bit. What are you doing?"

"Uh, I was finishing up a report, but I couldn't quite concentrate."

They both laughed. After-hours they could only concentrate on each other, only wanted to concentrate on each other, something they both now knew. Xavier wasn't afraid to express himself about this, either, Gwen quickly found out.

The first night he had called her, an evening before he even left for Chicago, he told her how nice it had been to kiss her and how much he wanted to kiss her again. Gwen blushed, glad for the fact that they were on the phone and not face to face, where he'd be able to see her squirm and fidget like a schoolgirl. She quietly said, "Oh really?" keeping her tone cool, to which he replied, "Oh yeah, really," which only served to make her blush more.

She kept trying to tell herself that Xavier was a man, a man most likely thinking of sex, and when and if they ever got to that point, afterwards there would be no more compliments, or three-hour phone calls, or gentlemanly behavior. She kept telling herself not to

fall for him—he would hurt her, ultimately, she knew; but then when he'd patiently listen to her talk and seemed genuinely interested in what she had to say, (which she normally edited before speaking out loud, not wanting to reveal too much of herself too soon); or when he'd engage her in long conversations that covered a variety of topics, without dominating them, she fell for him more and more.

Gwen decided her mind needed to stop telling her what to do, because her heart wasn't listening to any of it. She liked Xavier, a lot; it was a simple fact that wasn't going to change any time soon. And one of his best qualities was that he hadn't mentioned Terry Stuart's name once. Nada. Zippo.

Now, as with every call, their first topic of conversation was work. Gwen gave him some updated acquisition news. The audit package was complete; she had compiled the last audit findings Xavier had left with her before leaving for Chicago. Now it was just waiting for Xavier's return to the office so he could review and sign off on it before it would go to Vaughn for his approval.

Xavier had lived up to his word about business and pleasure; he could separate the two without difficulty. The Monday after the Fourth, Gwen stepped off the elevator and spotted Xavier first thing, crossing the hall on his way to see Simon. She immediately felt as jittery as if she was walking onto the fourteenth floor in the nude. Xavier stopped just as he saw her and waited as she walked up to him. She said, "Good morning"; he said, "Good morning," followed by a wink; they laughed nervously as the tension lifted during their brief conversation about nothing in particular before they went their separate ways. When they saw each other again later that same day, they carried on, business as usual, playing professional. But it was probably a good thing he was working on the due diligence and the Cyntex acquisition was wrapping up, because now that she had tasted his kisses and felt the warmth of his touch, sitting across a small table from him in a closed conference room on a daily basis would no doubt require a ton of willpower.

Their talk about work lasted only ten minutes and dwindled to less and less time with each call.

"I'm looking forward to our date Saturday night," Xavier said.

"Me too. I'm all ready." Gwen replied, thinking of the elegant black Calvin Klein dress she'd bought the other day. The first dress she had bought in a decade. It was understatedly fashionable, appropriate for the Rachelle Ferrell concert at the Fox Theater and dinner after at a swank Italian restaurant in Alpharetta.

"I just hope Kendra doesn't get mad at me for stealing her daddy away so soon after you get back." Gwen fluffed her pillow and got in position for some good talk.

"Oh, don't worry about Kendra. I've got her covered. Not only is my suitcase loaded down with toys, but we're going to spend most of Saturday together. There's some kind of children's exhibit going on at the Underground. I'm sure by the end of the day she'll probably be asleep before I even leave the house."

"She'll be with Carmen?"

"Yeah. Thank God for Carmen. I can't wait to see them all. And you, too."

Gwen smiled, though she still struggled to accept his compliments without suspecting his motives. "How much longer will Kendra be here in Atlanta?"

"Hmm. I've got a week's vacation scheduled in August and I plan on taking her to see my folks in Charlotte before I drive her back to D.C."

"I'm sure Tracey must miss her."

There was silence.

"Gwendolyn, um. I need to tell you…Tracey isn't Kendra's mom."

Excuse me?

Gwen rose up in bed, confused, and said, "Oh." She quickly did the math in her head with what information she knew. Xavier and Tracey divorced in 1993, Kendra was born in 1992.

Well, I'll be damned…

"So…" Gwen didn't know what to say.

"Uh, yeah. Kendra was conceived during my marriage."

Ain't this some shit.

"Oh," she said again, really thinking, *So, you were fucking around,*

and ended up actually saying, "So, you were screwing around?" She still spoke low, but her voice was definitely not as sexy.

"Uh, well...you put that in pretty blunt terms, but yeah, I guess so."

"You guess so?" Gwen challenged.

"Yeah, I was screwing around. But there were a lot of other things going on."

Gwen felt herself grow angry. Typical man. He would try to justify his actions: "there were a lot of other things going on." Bullshit. Complete and utter bullshit. She breathed deep and held the phone.

"Gwendolyn, can we talk?"

"So is that why you two broke up? Or was it a combination of you creeping and 'a lot of things going on?'" Now she was being a smart-ass.

"You're pissed off."

Damn straight.

Gwen didn't answer. Why was she so upset? She didn't know Xavier then. She wasn't married to him. But it was just the thought: he had cheated on his wife, conceived a child with another woman. Plus, they had talked about Kendra quite a bit the last couple of weeks and he'd had plenty of opportunities to tell her this little news. But he hadn't. Yeah, she was pissed.

"Gwendolyn, are you going to talk to me?"

"And say what?"

"Say what you're thinking."

Gwen shook her head. "No. Why don't *you* talk, Xavier?"

"OK. That's fair. " Xavier breathed deeply into the phone. "Listen, at one point in my life I used to live an entirely different lifestyle. I liked to think I was the same person I am now, inside anyway. But living in the limelight of the NBA can give you an altered sense of being. Things tend to be offered to you without question. Money, women, respect, more women..."

"So, what? You just couldn't resist? Had to have all you could have, marriage set aside?" Gwen's hostility increased.

"Yeah, I guess so, in a way. Resisting wasn't really an option in my mind. I didn't give it much consideration. I was young, and like a lot

of guys, you get caught up in all the hype. It can be overwhelming and I admit, I got caught up."

Gwen didn't speak. Xavier wasn't so different after all. She wanted to cry.

"Gwendolyn, baby, listen, Tracey and I were different people looking for different things. We probably should never have gotten married in the first place. Neither one of us really took our vows seriously."

Gwen wasn't going to let the way he called her "baby" influence her anger, although it sounded so damn good. "So what are you trying to say, Tracey cheated too?"

Xavier sighed, "Look, I'm not here to dog out my ex-wife. Let's just say, she liked the idea that I was who I was and I had the profession that I had. And I liked the idea that I had a beautiful woman who could stroke my ego. Like I said, we got married for all the wrong reasons. When the going got tough, things began to fall apart. And we were both at fault, me more so, I admit."

Damn, he was being up-front. But still...

"And what kind of relationship did you have with Kendra's mom?" Gwen asked.

Xavier breathed deep again, "Um, a sexual one. That was about it."

Shit...

"Is that still it?" Gwen really felt like crying now.

"Now? Gwendolyn, baby, no. Not at all. Kendra's mom is married now, and we've all moved on, put the past behind us. We only have Kendra's best interest at heart. That's it."

That "baby" thing was really working on her. But she still felt uneasy about everything. Neither one of them spoke for a few seconds.

"Are we going to talk?" Xavier asked softly.

Gwen wanted to just hang up the phone; she hated talking when she was angry, it usually landed her in trouble, "Xavier, maybe we shouldn't."

"Shouldn't talk, or...?"

Gwen fell back onto the bed, staring at the ceiling. "I don't know. I..."

"Just come with it, baby. Let me know how you really feel."

"Really?"

"Absolutely."

Gwen took a deep breath, "OK, I'm not sure I want to get involved with a man who has a history of fucking around." She exhaled.

"Whoa, you really do come with it, huh?"

"You asked."

"Yeah, I did." Xavier paused. "Hey, I'm sorry I didn't tell you about Kendra sooner. I wanted to. At the cookout, I started to, but being with you felt good and I guess I thought that would have ruined it. Gwendolyn, I like what we've got going, the talking, the chemistry... at least that's what it feels like for me."

Gwen warmed in response, her anger melting, at least a little. "Yeah, me too." She curled onto her side. "But..."

"But you think we should quit before things get too serious?" He finished her sentence.

"Yeah, maybe."

"Is that what you want?" His disappointment sounded heavy.

Gwen ran her fingers through her hair, "Xavier, I don't know. I...It's just..." Gwen lifted up onto her elbow. "I guess there are a lot of things we don't know about each other," she finally got out. She realized with a rush that what Xavier didn't know about her past dwarfed the issue of how Kendra was conceived.

"OK, so let's find out."

"Excuse me?"

"Let's do a little revelation test, right now. You know, tell each other what we like; what we don't like. Our strengths, our weaknesses. How 'bout it, you game?"

Gwen smiled, but didn't speak. A revelation test: now that was a spooky concept. There were a few things they already knew about each other, little basic personal tidbits. She knew Xavier had celebrated his thirty-second birthday last month in June; he'd been born and raised in Charlotte in an upper-middle-class household—his father owned an auto parts store while his mom worked as a homemaker.

He always knew he wanted to play basketball. He played one-on-

one with his Pops every night after supper and homework. He was dunking by the time he was twelve and working on his autograph by the time he made the varsity squad in middle school. Gwen had never been a sports fan, but she enjoyed listening to Xavier talk about basketball and how it had affected his life, given him confidence at an early age. Xavier said he felt awkward growing up, really never fitting into the cool crowd with other brothers who seemed to have an innate ability for talking the soul-brother talk and walking the soul-brother walk. But with his basketball talent, it was hardly noticed; he had game, and that pretty much catapulted him into the top echelon of popularity. But he jokingly said that he still knew deep down he was basically Clark Kent disguised in a basketball uniform. Gwen whispered, "I always liked Clark Kent," and Xavier whispered back, "Is that a fact"? When his NBA career ended, it was heartbreaking, but he tried not to dwell on it. Throughout all his confessions he still had never mentioned Terry Stuart's name.

For Gwen's part, she'd shared some personal history too, although in tightly rationed doses. Xavier knew a little bit about her parents and the relationship she'd had with them before their death—her father had worked as an accountant for a school supply store, and her mother taught elementary school. She revealed that she and her mother were not as close as she now wished they could have been. Her mother could be a stickler for discipline and ladylike behavior, and Gwen rebuked her at every turn. Her father was less strict, but sadly caught in the middle between a wife he loved and a daughter he cherished. So far, that was the extent of her discussions with Xavier about her parents; he didn't know the circumstances surrounding their death, and she didn't tell him how she wished she could tell them to their faces that she was sorry, and how much she loved them. She mentioned she had a brother named Weldon, but that they weren't close.

Xavier also knew she had a best friend in Boston, but she confessed that she didn't really have any close friends in Atlanta, and was too busy with work to concern herself with making any. He knew she graduated from the University of South Carolina, but had no idea she ever attended college elsewhere.

"Gwendolyn?"

"I'm here." Gwen sat up in bed again, "Uh, I guess I'm not sure what you want to know. Why don't you start."

"OK, well I just told you about Kendra. I love my daughter, but I admit if I had it to do over again, I would do it differently. I'd do a lot of things differently, but you know what they say about hindsight."

"Yeah." Gwen had softened again. "Uh, well I don't have any kids. How's that?"

Xavier laughed, "That's a start." He stammered a bit before he asked, "What about someone special?"

"Someone special?" Gwen lay flat on her back.

"You know, has there been a special man in your life..."

"I date occasionally, but nothing serious." The only man she'd really dated for more than six months had been Ellis, and she didn't see any point to elaborating on that.

"Too busy with work?" Xavier asked, still on the dating issue.

"I guess."

"You're not big on revelations, huh?" There was a hint of frustration in Xavier's voice.

"Sorry, I guess that's a weakness." Gwen knew she wasn't playing the game right. But their relationship was still so new, and Gwen had spent years keeping her painful past locked up.

"What's your weakness?" she asked, putting the ball back in his court.

"Hmmm, how many do you want to hear?" He laughed; Gwen giggled a little. "OK, let's see. Um, I can be a jealous person sometimes."

"Oh really, how so?" Gwen wondered if he meant natural jealousies or scary jealousies.

"I don't know. I just like to know I'm the only one, I guess."

A pinch of anger jabbed at her. "But that doesn't work both ways, huh?"

"You mean...?"

"Uh, yeah, I mean you screwed around, Xavier. You want to be the only one, but you want as many as you can get? Come on." Gwen

125

shook her head, feeling she wasn't going to get past the knowledge of his philandering.

Xavier sighed. "That was then, not now," he said. Gwen groaned loudly, but Xavier continued, "Gwen, I don't claim to be a saint, but I do claim to have gotten wiser with age. Having every beautiful woman in the world isn't what I'm after. Just one beautiful woman, with substance and chemistry, that's what I'm looking for."

A wave of arousal engulfed her, but that merely increased her confusion. "Is that what you were looking for in Shay?" Gwen asked, wanting to get this out in the open at last.

Xavier paused. "Shayla? I didn't think you cared too much about me going out with Shayla." A smidgen of delight was definitely detectable in his voice.

Gwen didn't want to give him the satisfaction; she gave him a stern, "Xavier, you're avoiding the question."

"Oh. What was the question again, baby?" He made it obvious that Gwen's attempts to act nonchalant were unconvincing.

"Xavier, if you're going to play with me, let's just drop it."

"Gwendolyn, are you really wondering if I slept with her?" Xavier asked, still delighted.

"Did you?" Gwen asked, quietly. She had a good idea he hadn't, but she'd rather hear it from him.

"No, baby, I didn't." His voice mellowed, all joking aside.

"Oh. OK." She said sweetly, feeling a fire igniting between her legs. "You believe me?"

"Uh-huh. I just know how Shay can be when she really wants a man, and you fit the category."

"Yeah, she's a bit…aggressive. But I was willing to see if there was more to her than what she presented, so when she asked me out the first time, I accepted. The date didn't go very well; I was a bit preoccupied, and Shayla didn't seem to be interested in the same things I am. Then, afterward, I felt I hadn't been very fair to her, so I asked her out on a second date. And that one went worse than the first. I have to admit, I wasn't very good company."

"What was the problem?" Gwen hopped out of bed and stood up, stretching, trying to shake loose her erotic desire.

"Want the truth?"

"Uh-huh."

"I had you on my mind."

Gwen wanted to say, *Stop the fucking madness,* but she didn't. She said nothing, but felt everything—like what was now an incredible wet, simmering warmth between her legs.

"Gwendolyn, I'm not playing games with you. I mean everything I say. I like the way you carry yourself, you're very grounded, kind of guarded, but honest at the same time. And I have no shame in admitting that everything about you turns me on."

Gwen sat at the edge of her bed; her nipples tightened, and the wetness between her legs teased her. "Xavier, I..."

"I've embarrassed you again?"

A smile crept across her face. "Yeah, a little. I, um, I don't have sex on the first date, just so you know." She stated this emphatically, then immediately regretted the tone, thinking it made her sound like a snobby prima donna.

"Do you think I was hoping you would?" Xavier asked, seemingly unoffended.

"You tell me," Gwen said, not sure what he expected. Now that she knew he had run around on his wife, she didn't know what to think. He was an athlete, so she should have figured he was sexually addicted. It came with the territory.

"Gwendolyn, I didn't ask you out on a date thinking we'd make it to the bedroom at the end of it." Xavier paused, "But I will admit I think of making love to you, especially now that we've gotten closer. Gwendolyn, you're incredibly attractive, as much as you hate to hear it, which I haven't quite figured out. There's something about you, baby; something I like a whole lot." His deep voice dropped deeper. Sexy, sexy, sexy.

Gwen felt her face grow hot, along with a couple of other places on her body, too. She was so wet it was a wonder her panties didn't

just slide right off. At the end of this phone call she planned to run a warm bath, fill the tub with her favorite SunRipened Raspberry Bath & Body Works scent, light some candles, and take matters into her own hands. Xavier did things to her; he did it with every phone call, and this one had been the most intimate to date. But tonight, her own fingers would have to provide satisfaction.

But she still played it cool, or at least tried to: "Can we take things slow?" A soft whimper stumbled from her lips. Gwen yanked the phone away from her mouth, but she knew he had heard it.

Xavier sounded equally aroused when he said, quietly, "You set the pace, baby, and I'm there."

· EIGHT ·

B Y LATE AUGUST, nearly five or so weeks after their first official date, Gwen was more than willing to take Xavier into her
bedroom or his bedroom or whatever bedroom they could find. Her
apprehension about his past infidelity had faded with each romantic
moment they'd spent together. She and Xavier seemed right for each
other; she felt it, and she had a good feeling that he felt it, too.

Now she sat in her office trying to concentrate on work, but
couldn't help but look at her watch, waiting for the day to end so she
and Xavier could celebrate her birthday the way they had planned.
The plan didn't include party hats—or any other clothes, for that
matter. She tapped her new crystal Cartier watch as if it were broken,
though she knew it wasn't. She'd received the watch express mail a
couple of days ago from Nana as a birthday gift. And her new gift was
telling her it was only 11:34 in the morning.

Last night she'd spent some time with Xavier in the company of
Kendra and Carmen's family, which had often been the case in the
past weeks, and when he took her home he'd presented her with a
birthday gift of his own. He said, "I hope you like it, I'm no expert on
these kinds of things, but..." Gwen took the small box, jokingly told
him "Shut up," and opened it to find a crystal elephant figurine to add
to her collection; she'd nearly been brought to tears.

Gwen had a thing for elephants—stuffed, wooden, porcelain, crystal, any way she could get them. Where her elephant passion came
from was a mystery; she loved Dumbo when she was a child and
absolutely despised circuses, feeling more sympathy for the elephants
than she did the monkeys.

She thanked Xavier, gave him a sweet kiss that quickly became

eager, and they nearly ended up in the bedroom a night earlier than they had planned. But restraint kicked in, along with the fact that Xavier needed to get back to Kendra. She would be spending tonight with her Aunt Carmen, while Xavier and Gwen spent the night celebrating. Gwen looked at her watch again, tapped it again, then laughed out loud at her absurdity.

Accessing the master spreadsheet in her computer, she decided it was time to earn her wages. Before she could even get started, the familiar chime of a new email tickled her ears. She smiled, knowing it was Xavier before she had even backed out of one system and into the other. His name, **Xavier Dean**, stared at her in bold letters and the subject read: **tonight**. *Tonight indeed,* Gwen thought as she answered her ringing phone before opening the email. It was a client needing information, and forcing her to do some work. She did, unable to read the email at the moment, but that beaming **tonight** was beginning to make her ache.

Gwen couldn't wait to make love with Xavier. She had never felt this kind of strong, passionate desire for a man. Sex in the past had always seemed like a chore, a dreaded chore at that. But she cared for Xavier so much, and making love would completely define her feelings, of that she felt certain. Although she already had a pretty good read on her emotions, as scary as they were. It was a simple case of falling in love. Gwen Fagan was falling in love with Xavier Dean. Go figure.

She pretty much knew this was happening well into their first date five weeks ago (OK, she probably knew it sooner than that). And as first dates go, Gwen scored that one for the record books, rating the dinner as excellent; Rachelle Ferrell, better than excellent; and the atmosphere and company, well, Gwen rated them two notches above that. At evening's end he walked her to her door and opened it for her, and then they stood in the foyer kissing and carrying on as they had in the middle of the street on the Fourth of July.

Gwen liked the way he kissed: the way he tilted his body downward so she wouldn't have to reach so far; the way he hugged her, holding her tightly without using the hug as a diversion to reach around and

fondle her breasts or run his hands down her butt. And when he did touch her in more intimate places, it felt magical and special and right. Xavier still called her "baby," still told her she was beautiful, and still didn't rush the pace.

But she really wasn't the reason they hadn't progressed to the bedroom. In the past five weeks there had been so much going on that lovemaking hadn't been the highest priority. First on the priority list for Xavier was Kendra. Xavier needed to spend time with his daughter and he *wanted* to spend time with her, a quality Gwen found extremely attractive. Weekends were reserved for Kendra, leaving Gwen and Xavier to spend time together during the week when they could.

As was the case last night, Gwen would normally visit with Xavier and Kendra at Carmen's house, which didn't bother Gwen at all. They were such a close-knit bunch; they loved to laugh and talk and reminisce about their surprisingly normal childhood, when Xavier and Carmen had looked out for each other—that is, when they weren't trying to kill each other over normal sibling crap. Inevitably, she always thought of her brother Weldon, something she'd grown accustomed to trying *not* to do. She wondered where he was, how he was, even if he was alive. Happy as she was getting close to Xavier, she felt a new pain regarding her own family. Sometimes she cried for Weldon at night, and for her parents, and wished they were all back in her life.

But most times while Xavier was with Kendra, Gwen made herself scarce, not wanting to intrude. Some weekends, she would take the two-hour drive to Augusta to check on things at Nana's, where Gwen had spent the rest of her teenage years after her parents' death. She wanted to make sure everything was all right while Nana was still out of the country.

And at night, she and Xavier continued to log in countless hours on the phone, still learning more about each other. Gwen opened up to Xavier about her family, especially about her parents' death and the enormous guilt she felt because of it. She divulged more about Weldon and the sad hole of a life he had dug himself into. Xavier listened and didn't judge. His own family bond was incredible, but he

didn't seem to view it as privileged, or better—they were just one of the lucky ones.

But the rape was still unmentionable. She let it remain her own secret. Whatever it cost her to keep that secret, Gwen was not sure when or if she would ever be prepared to make it anything more than that. She couldn't even contemplate bearing the cost of revealing it.

There were some pretty dramatic changes going on in the office as well. Now that the acquisition was finished (though it was still being reviewed by Vaughn before it could be delivered to the lawyers), Gwen had begun working on a new project. For Xavier's part, he had an attractive offer from Simon, the senior executive in charge of due diligence, to join their team on a permanent basis.

After considering it for a few days, Xavier accepted, and he'd told Gwen about it as they had dined at Brookwood Grill two weeks before. He enjoyed traveling and all the fieldwork involved with going into different companies and areas. Gwen agreed it was a wonderful opportunity: due diligence work was never her favorite—all the plane flights, rental cars, and hotels—but Xavier would have great opportunity for growth in that area, and she told him she was pleased for him without telling him that she worried their relationship might suffer as a result. He broached the subject himself once they arrived back at her place after dinner that night.

"Gwendolyn, this new position isn't going to have a negative impact on us, is it?" Xavier had made himself comfortable sitting on the floor, with his back pressed against the sofa. Gwen, who'd changed into an oversized T-shirt and loose cotton shorts, sat on the sofa with her legs draped over his shoulders. He caressed her calves. "Negative, meaning..." she asked, thinking that if he kept touching her that way she would melt to the floor. She raised her legs off his shoulders as Xavier turned around and rested on his knees, coming face to face with her. "I don't know. While I'm away, some smooth brother isn't going to just waltz in with champagne and roses and sweep you off your feet?" Xavier said this jokingly, but no so jokingly.

Gwen stroked his face, "Hmmm, I don't know, Mr. Dean. I guess it depends on whether you're going to have a different woman in every

town." This time it was Gwen's turn to speak jokingly, but not so jokingly. Xavier took his hands and placed them under her shirt, rubbing her stomach. "I thought we got this straight a few weeks ago. I don't want every woman. Just the one I'm with right now." Xavier kissed her chin. Gwen purred, "Then I think we'll be OK. I'll let all those smooth brothers with the roses know that I'm not available. How's that?" Gwen smiled seductively and leaned forward to kiss him. He murmured, "Baby, I like your style," just as he leaned into the kiss that quickly turned passionate.

It was that night, two weeks ago, that they almost made love. Gwen wanted to so badly, not resisting as Xavier lifted her shirt, unclasped her bra, and gently tickled her nipples with his tongue. And when he held her face and said, "Gwendolyn, baby, I want you," Gwen kissed him and told him she wanted him too, but her smile was a bit strained, and he noticed it. "Something on your mind, baby?" he had asked. Gwen nodded and he joined her on the couch as she lowered her shirt. Her speech began, "Xavier, you know how much I want to be with you, don't doubt that...," before she took a deep breath and got down to the matter at hand, "...but I worry about protection." This wasn't exactly the truth, but she was getting close. "You mean condoms?" he had asked, fiddling with her curls. "Uh, sort of..." Gwen had stammered, then blurted out, "Xavier, have you ever been tested?" There, she had asked it. Xavier looked at her, then said, "HIV?" Gwen nodded and he scratched his head. "I guess this isn't a conversation we've had, huh?" They hadn't, and they needed to.

After the rape, she'd contracted chlamydia. She could have caught it from Terry Stuart, but she wasn't sure because she'd ignored the symptoms for months, still traumatized from the rape. Once treated, she got tested for everything, including HIV, and continued to get tested every six months for several years afterward. All she shared with Xavier was that she had been tested, but not in a couple of years. Xavier had been tested too, but Gwen was shocked to find that he didn't start using condoms on a regular basis until after Kendra's birth in 1993. This prompted Gwen to ask, "So, Magic Johnson's little announcement didn't faze you?"

Xavier squirmed a little in his seat that night and said, "Yeah it did. I mean, I think the entire league headed to the clinic before Magic had even finished his press conference. But I admit, after I got a negative result, I still didn't give much thought to a condom, unless of course the woman asked, which she rarely did." Gwen said, "Oh," and they sat in silence. Gwen really thought Xavier would have been more responsible. This disturbed her and it must have shown, because he took her hand and said, "Baby, let's talk." And they did.

That night, two weeks ago, they talked about the women in his life, who he admitted were abundant, specifically during his NBA years. Xavier opened up hesitantly; Gwen would smile a little, just enough to let him know that he could say more without fear of repercussion. It was no secret that she and Xavier both had had sex lives in the past, though his apparently was much livelier than hers. And yeah, his having been with a lot of women didn't make her happy, but that was just because she had come to see Xavier as all hers. He finished by saying he hadn't been with a woman sexually since he had moved to Atlanta six months ago. Gwen didn't bother to ask who he had slept with before then; she didn't really want to know.

When it was her turn to talk, she told him that the men in her life were few in number, maybe seven total. Besides Ellis and the boyfriend she'd had when she was sixteen, the others were insignificant. This didn't include Terry Stuart—as far as she was concerned he wasn't a man. She didn't elaborate on any of them to Xavier; she could tell by the way his eyes glossed as she spoke that he wasn't real happy to hear about the lovers in her past, either. But just as she had done, he tried to indicate with a gentle touch or a slight smile that he wouldn't hold it against her. She hated talking about it, men in her past; she wouldn't really categorize them as lovers—not the ones after the rape, anyway. The term "lover" would seem to suggest excitement or mutual respect, which hadn't been the case with any of them. But she had brought it up and it was necessary. She gave Xavier enough information without much detail, just as she was sure he had done with her; no names were mentioned nor were any circumstances elaborated.

Unfortunately, and much to her shame, most of the men in her

past were guys she had just screwed, just to be screwing; guys she used to try to forget about the rape—thinking that heavy drinking and sex, with men who could not care less about her, would be a good anesthetic. Of course, she was the one being used, but back then she really didn't care. Maybe, she thought, it would prove her normal, prove her recovered; this is why she wasn't sure who she contracted chlamydia from. But one thing was certain—each humiliating sexual encounter drove her deeper into depression, and in her mind, only further proved her worthlessness. It was only after her suicide attempt, less than a year after the rape, and the intense therapy sessions that followed, that she stopped traveling down the road of destruction and began to try to find her true self-worth. An easy fuck wasn't it.

By the end of that night, Xavier suggested they get tested together, put each other's mind at ease, so they could make love, make serious love, without being fearful or foolish. Gwen stroked his face and kissed him, thinking he knew just how to make things right.

Their results were negative. Gwen and Xavier had sat in separate little meeting rooms while counselors explained the importance to them of safe sex, and that if they felt they were still at risk they should test again in four months for added assurances, and that they should not feel intimidated about opening up with their partner. Communication was key. Gwen and Xavier totally agreed.

Now, tonight after work, they were going to make love. Some serious love. It was Friday, Gwen's twenty-ninth birthday, and she and Xavier planned on celebrating together, just the two of them, in bed.

When they had talked the night before, Xavier asked if she wanted to do something special for her birthday, maybe dine at that new French restaurant in Buckhead, or take in a concert at the park, something like that. He wanted to get an early start on the evening, especially since he would be going to Charlotte the next day, taking Kendra to visit his folks before he drove her back to D.C. He would be on vacation the entire next week to get all this done. And tonight, Gwen's birthday, would be the only time they could spend serious time together for the next seven days. Seven days. That was too long. It was time for them to connect, really connect, and they both knew

it. In response to his question she looked at him and said, "Xavier, I don't want to go out; I don't want to talk a whole lot either; I just want to be with you." His smile, his vibrant, beautiful smile, gave her his answer.

Gwen finally hung up the phone with the client—the call had taken far longer than it should have—and opened the email that read: **"Happy Birthday, beautiful. Just thinking about you—just thinking about us—and just making sure you're not having second thoughts about tonight. X"**

Is he crazy? Gwen thought, with a giggle. Normally they didn't exchange such personal memos, but this was just further testimony of how anxious they both were. Gwen typed, **"Uh-uh, baby. I'm there,"** but before she hit "send," something red drew her attention from the corner of her eye.

And when she looked up from her desk she saw Ellis standing in her doorway holding a mammoth bouquet of roses.

This can't be happening...

"Gwen, darling, happy birthday!" Ellis strolled in and placed the rose-filled vase on her desk.

Gwen stood up and hustled around to the front of her desk. "Ellis, what are you doing here?" She hadn't even said hello.

He kissed her cold cheek. "I'm here on business. Quick trip, my flight leaves tomorrow morning. How have you been? I've been wanting to call, but after our last conversation I thought maybe it was best I didn't."

"...Uh, Ellis, uh, I've been fine. Uh, Uh..." *Uh shit!* Gwen walked away from him and closed her door. She noticed her secretary, Mary, wasn't at her desk. Probably out to lunch. Good. Now she wasn't too worried that Ellis had been seen by too many of the office busybodies.

She walked back toward him and stammered some more. "Uh, Ellis, this is a surprise." She began wringing her hands.

"Did I catch you at a bad time?" He stood, left hand in pocket, smiling.

"Yeah…sort of." She tried to smile back, tried to tell herself to be polite. Ellis still looked official and conservative and stiff, yet handsome nonetheless. Tall and wiry, he was prematurely grayed with a matching mustache and beard, all nicely trimmed.

"You work too hard, Gwen, darling." He moved closer.

Stop calling me darling.

Gwen put on a phony grin, wondering what had possessed Ellis to walk into her office acting as if they were still together. He had to go. Fast.

"I've missed you." He moved even closer, and everything after that happened quicker than quick. Gwen began to say, "Ellis, I don't have time…" just as he reached for her face and kissed her on the lips, which made her cut the kiss short by stepping back and looking at him like he was crazy, which prompted a look of surprise from him, before his eyes traveled past her to the door, at which time he cleared his throat, seemingly embarrassed, and that made her turn around and see…oh yeah, Xavier.

Oh shit.

How long had he been there? Hell, she didn't even hear the door open, and she definitely didn't hear him knock. Expletives and questions and statements scurried through her mind, followed by more expletives.

Damn, Damn, Damn.

"Um, excuse me. Mary said she thought you were alone. I guess she was mistaken." Xavier said. He didn't move in or out of the door, but just stood there, looking noticeably pissed off.

Gwen walked towards him, sort of stopped midway, and stood in between the two men. "No that's fine…," she said to Xavier, thinking Mary's ass was at lunch.

"Xavier, this is Ellis." She had no intention of giving Ellis a title, not old friend, not old lover, nothing. Just Ellis.

Ellis walked over to Xavier, who still hadn't budged. They shook hands, then Ellis sank one hand in his pant's pocket and sauntered

over to Gwen. He pressed his other hand on her back, "So, you work with my Gwen here, huh?"

What the hell is that?

Gwen tilted her head and again looked at him like he had lost his mind. She moved away from him, too damn mad and confused to speak. She hated when Ellis displayed this pathetic, passive-aggressive bullshit. If he thought time and distance could somehow bring them closer together, he was sadly mistaken. She didn't want him, and now she only wanted him to go.

Xavier grunted. "Yeah. I guess I work with 'your Gwen'." He looked at her and smirked.

Gwen shook her head slightly, as if to say, *Xavier, it's not what it looks like...*

But Xavier was already maneuvering himself out the door. "I'll leave you two alone. By the way, that's a serious bouquet of roses ya got there. All that's missing now is the champagne." He smirked again, then closed the door behind him.

Gwen wanted to scream. Ellis of course was clueless to the champagne reference and asked if he and Gwen could have dinner, maybe catch up. The only catching up Gwen wanted to do was catch up with Xavier and explain. She just told him no, suddenly too drained to even pick a fight with him. Ellis finally left her after saying a few other things that just gurgled in Gwen's ears.

Not much time had passed before she was able to start looking for Xavier. He and Simon had just left for lunch, and after that lunch Xavier hadn't returned to the office. "Getting an early start on his vacation," his secretary stated.

Gwen struggled the rest of the workday, dazed. She called his house and left a simple message. "Please, call. Let's talk." His cell phone was turned off and Gwen debated calling Carmen, but then just dropped the idea. Xavier was angry, but she was sure that by the end of the workday he would be ready to talk, or really just listen. She was definitely ready to explain.

As usual, whenever Gwen felt like shit, she could always find Shayla. They rode down on the elevator together after work.

"Gwen, girlfriend, how you been?"

"Fine."

"Girlfriend, I saw them roses you got. I sure wish a man would send my ass some roses. What's your secret?" Shayla leaned into her, jabbing her in the side.

"No secrets." Gwen didn't feel like chatting.

"Humph, that's all right. Keep 'em to yourself. What is taking this elevator so long? I got things to do and people to see."

The elevator stopped on the twelfth floor and the dark-skinned, bow-legged brother Shayla had been talking about a few months ago stepped in. Gwen looked at him.

He was cute: a little rough around the edges, sort of an alley-cat-come-uptown design about him, but definitely appealing. Gwen took a glimpse of his left hand, which was jiggling his keys, and noticed another interesting design: he was wearing a wedding ring.

Gwen could see Shayla's eyes light up as the mirrored doors closed. She and the man both moved to the back of the elevator, Shayla abandoning her conversation with Gwen, which wasn't necessarily a bad thing. But then, to Gwen's horror, they started getting it on; Shayla stood slightly in front of him and he, in a not-so-discreet fashion, began holding her hips and rubbing her ass up against his crotch. It was outrageous. Gwen closed her eyes until she heard the elevator door ding, then open. When they all walked off, Gwen grabbed Shayla's arm and began walking to a remote corner.

"Uh, Gwen girlfriend, I got plans. Let's talk later, hear?"

"Shay, what kind of little display was that? *That* is the reason your ass doesn't get any roses. You are better than a five-minute fuck. When will you realize that? Huh? When?!"

"Girlfriend, if you don't get up out my face, you gonna get a beat down. How 'bout you realize *that*?" Shayla spat out between gritted teeth. Gwen released her. Shayla walked away a few steps, glaring at Gwen, then walked back to her. "No, let me tell *you* something. Your

ass don't know shit about shit. Look at you. You may be getting roses, but I bet you ain't gettin' much else. Hell, Gwen, do you even know what to do with a man, when and if you ever get one?"

Gwen didn't answer.

"Humph, figures. So you need to check *yourself.* A five-minute fuck is better than no fuck at all. And for your information, Tariq lasts *way* longer than that." Shayla walked away, laughing.

Gwen breathed deeply, fighting hard to force back tears, and walked away alone.

Nine-thirty p.m. and Gwen still hadn't heard from Xavier. She didn't make any more phone calls to his place and finally decided to get some dinner alone.

When she arrived back home around ten-thirty, she spotted Xavier walking away from her front door, heading to his car parked at the curb. He stopped in the driveway, twirling his keys around his index finger before slipping them into the deep pockets of his smoke-gray Duck Head slacks. As Gwen pulled up to the garage, she watched him pull the keys back out, twirl them again, then slip them back in as if he debated leaving or not. She lowered her window.

"Hey." Gwen spoke quietly.

"I see you've been out," he said.

Yeah, after waiting on you for almost four hours.

Gwen jerked her head, disturbed. "Uh-huh. How long have you been here?"

"Not long."

"Want to come in, or no?" She wasn't going to beg.

Xavier hesitated. He looked as if he wanted to, but didn't want to say he wanted to. Finally he said, "Sure, yeah, for a minute."

Gwen rolled into her driveway, entered her house anxiously, then paused before she opened the door. *Get a grip,* she told herself. Xavier had left her hanging for hours without a call, so she didn't want to fling the door open like a death row inmate waiting on a pardon from the governor. Although that was what she felt like. She breathed deep, straightened the bottom of her burgundy V-neck shell against her

black pants, and breathed deep again. When she opened the door, he stood sideways, looking as if he had second thoughts about sticking around. She opened the door wider and he walked inside. Gwen skipped formalities and cut right to the chase.

"I called you a couple of times. Why didn't you call me back?"

"Uh-huh. Thought maybe you'd be busy." His tone was as bitter as cough medicine.

"If I was busy, I wouldn't have called." Gwen crossed her arms harshly, prepared to get ignorant if she had to.

Xavier raised an eyebrow, clearly not intimidated, and repeated, "Uh-huh." Silence swept the room like an angry mob. Gwen unfolded her arms and calmed her stance. Technically, she was in the wrong and she wanted to rectify things. She kept her distance and spoke.

"Xavier, today wasn't anything like you're thinking or like it looked."

"Uh-huh." His only comment.

"Look, you and I talked about people we used to see, and Ellis was someone I used to see. He just—"

"Used to." Xavier cut her off with more of an unbelieving statement than a question.

Gwen felt a spark of anger, almost acted on it, then thought about that technically in the wrong thing, at least for now. "Xavier, Ellis and I dated. Past tense. He didn't know I was seeing anyone—"

"And I see you were real quick to tell him." He pushed the bill of his Nike cap up.

More sparks ignited, "I was going to—thank you very much! Why are you being like this?" Gwen held her hands out, her face bewildered.

"You got some brother all up in your face and you're asking me why *I'm* being like this?" He stepped toward her.

Gwen took a grand step back. "Yeah I'm asking. Last time I checked it was still the twentieth century, and you come in here huffing and puffing like you have damn papers on me!" Her voice shot up like an arrow. This wasn't how things were supposed to be going, and her mouth wasn't making things any better.

"Oh, huffing and puffing, huh?" He jerked his head forward, sarcasm in his tone.

"Did I stutter?" Smart-ass had always been her specialty, and her curse.

Xavier removed his cap and scratched his head. A smile, as condescending as a lawyer's, graced his lips. "Maybe you're right. Maybe I am acting 'like this.' But funny thing, I thought we, you know, I thought we had something going. I thought tonight was supposed to be, you know, us making it right. I didn't think there'd be a line for admittance."

Gwen's entire face trembled. "Get the fuck out," she spat, stepping aside. She no longer felt in the wrong.

"You're asking me to leave?" he asked, almost surprised.

Gwen shook her head, "No, I'm telling you to get the fuck out!"

He raised his hands, drawing his keys from his pockets. He walked up to her and stood close. It was then she smelled alcohol. Alcohol and anger were never a good mix. That instant, her own anger turned to fear.

"I thought you were different, Gwendolyn." He forced the words out, blowing alcohol fumes in her face.

"I thought the same about you."

So there. Gwen stood her ground, scared to death, but ready to hightail it to her bedroom, grab her gun, and use it if she had to. She looked at him; he looked upset, pissed off even, but not malicious. But she couldn't convince her terrified soul of that. "Xavier, why don't you just leave, OK? I...I don't like you like this." She moved further away, a stumble in her walk.

Xavier grunted. "What do you think, I'm gonna hurt you or something?" He asked, same tone, same demeanor.

"N-n-not if I can help it." The waver in her voice jumped out by accident. She put her fingers to her lips and noticed her hands trembled uncontrollably.

Xavier began to notice it too. He slanted his gaze and walked toward her slowly. "Gwendolyn, are you scared of me?" he asked cautiously, a little less upset.

"Should I be?" Gwen took two more steps back, moving away from

him. She wrapped her arms around her shoulders, an attempt to keep her quaking body still. The pit of her stomach felt taut; suddenly, her bladder felt heavy and ready to explode. She squeezed her butt cheeks together and pressed her thighs tight to keep from pissing out a stream of pure fear.

Gwen watched as Xavier studied her, his eyes darting from her shaking hands to her spasmodic posture to her face; judging by the concerned look on his face, these must have revealed a wealth of clues. She was so scared; she thought by now, ten years later, she would be far beyond such drama.

"Gwendolyn, I'd never hurt you." Xavier's entire mood had reversed.

"That's good to know. Can you leave now?" Gwen spoke convulsively. She shivered as if she had just swum naked across the Atlantic. She wanted to go upstairs, but not before he left. Suddenly a quick spurt of urine trickled in her panties. Going anywhere, at the moment, was out of the question. She squeezed herself tighter to stop the leak.

"Did someone hurt you, baby?" Xavier's voice was all concern now. He didn't approach her, but he didn't move to leave either. Gwen covered her mouth and shook her head—not really a denial, just a desperate request to dismiss the question. Xavier asked more, "That brother today, did he..."

"Go away! What is so hard for you to understand?" Gwen yelled.

"OK, baby, OK." Xavier sighed; he looked at her with such intensity, such understanding rested in his eyes. He knew, finally. He knew something had happened to her; she was making it so painfully, uncontrollably obvious. He walked to the door, looked back at her, and his mouth opened with maybe more questions or more words, but he chose not to express them. The door silently closed behind him.

Gwen stood still, wanting to cry, wanting to rip her weak, frail emotions out of her body and beat them to a pulp for embarrassing her this way. Finally she pushed her legs to the door. While setting the alarm system and latching all the locks, the tears began to cascade,

allowing her battered soul to vent. Her emotions weren't at fault to-night, she concluded, as she dragged towards the guest bathroom to relieve herself. She just didn't know when not to be afraid, that's all.

A couple of hours later, Gwen stepped outside again onto her deck, where the muggy air immediately enveloped her. She lounged over the railing; her only view was of similar backyards, similar decks, all vacated. Neighbors were either in for the night or out for the night.

And to think, she thought, by this time of night she and Xavier should have been stripped down, in each other's arms, making love so hard their two bodies would look like one. Gwen laughed, too drained for more tears, too empty for self-pity—just laughing at the wacked events of the night.

The phone bleated inside. Gwen ignored it, then thought of Nana. She was probably calling to wish her a happy birthday. Japan time kept Nana confused; last time they talked she told Gwen she would call when the feeling hit her, that she was too old to try and figure out time differences and too ornery to ask. Gwen rushed to the phone and answered with a brisk, "Hello."

"Hey baby. Um, I know it's late..." It was Xavier.

"Uh, hey."

"I've been riding around for a while. I'm kind of close, can I stop by?"

"Why?"

"I want to see you. Make sure you..."

"I'm fine, Xavier." Gwen didn't intend to be hostile, but at the same time she didn't want pity.

"Baby, let's call a truce. OK?"

Gwen bit her bottom lip. "OK," she said softly.

"Can I please come by? I won't stay long."

Gwen thought for a moment. She wasn't afraid, that wasn't it. And she really wasn't mad at him anymore, either. What she was was in love, and that currently led her by the heart like a puppy on a leash. She told him, "Sure."

Xavier arrived in less than ten minutes. He wore the same clothes,

but she had showered earlier and changed into a ribbed cotton top and pleated shorts. They walked to the kitchen, hadn't touched, hadn't kissed, just greeted each other with a couple of weak "Heys." He seemed sober and looked tired. She tried to put on a face that evidenced recovery, the face she'd really needed a few hours ago.

"I'm sorry," Xavier started.

Gwen handed him a glass of tea and hopped on the counter, parallel from where he stood. "Don't apologize. You believed what you felt." Gwen gulped her Evian water and shrugged.

"And I was wrong," he stated, clearly humbled by what he'd seen in Gwen.

"Were you?" Gwen played nonchalant.

He stepped to her slowly. With a hesitant reach, he touched her face. "Wasn't I?" he asked, the huskiness in his voice warming.

Gwen closed her eyes, then opened them. "Yeah," she said, almost silently.

He placed his glass beside her, reached with his other hand, and cradled her face. "Can I kiss you?"

Gwen looked into his eyes; she could see herself so clearly, vulnerable, as though she were floating in a sea of honey. Quietly, she said, "Yes." It was a soft kiss, sweet with remorse and forgiveness.

"If Ellis is the one who hurt you, tell me where I can find him," Xavier began.

Gwen touched his lips, "He didn't, OK. It was a long time ago."

"Here in Atlanta?"

Gwen shook her head. "No. Back in college, years ago. Things got out of control and I became the sacrificial lamb. End of story. Let's not talk about this, please?" Gwen fought to keep her tone even. It was obvious he knew the hurt was more than just a broken heart. But she didn't want to *have* to discuss it. Not now. But some sort of an elaboration, however limited, would be inevitable.

Xavier nodded, then kissed her again. She kissed back, harder this time. He caressed her shoulders; she wrapped her legs around his waist and attempted to change the subject. "What happened tonight, Xavier? You were so pissed off."

145

Xavier's face dropped with embarrassment. "I'm sorry about that."

"You don't have to apologize, just explain. I mean, I know Ellis showing up at the office the way he did looked all wrong, but I thought we had this communication thing going..."

"Yeah, baby, we do." Xavier played with her hair. "I guess I'm so used to being with women who like to play games, I've forgotten any other type exists. The concept of trusting and being trusted is still new."

"Is that your way of saying your old life of screwing around was a joint effort?" Gwen asked.

Xavier grunted. "Something like that."

"Tracey?"

"Tracey and my best friend. How classic is that?" Xavier grunted again.

Best friend...

Gwen's head reared back, knocking into the cupboard. "Wha— what best friend?"

"Old friend of mine from college. Terry Stuart."

Gwen could feel herself begin to shake again. She pressed her palm against her stomach. Hearing the name out loud felt like a punch in the gut.

Xavier didn't notice. "Gwendolyn, it was some messed up shit. We all used to spend a lot of time together during the off-season and I guess you could say Terry was taking care of business at home while I wasn't."

"But... but how do you know it was the truth?" she asked nervously. *Maybe Terry raped her,* she thought.

"Oh, Tracey let me know, loud and clear, how true it was." Xavier blew out, hard. "When she found out about Kendra, she went ballistic. Told me she had a good idea I was screwing around, but she couldn't believe I would get someone pregnant. She started screaming and throwing stuff, until finally she threw Terry up in my face. Said she fucked him, often, and it was good. But even she wasn't stupid enough to get pregnant. Like I was supposed to be proud of that."

Anger flickered in his eyes, then faded as he stroked Gwen's cheek. "Messed up, huh?"

"Yeah." Gwen dropped her legs from around his waist. "What happened with him?" She had to know.

"Who, Terry? I confronted him. He told me Tracey was tripping. He finally admitted to sleeping with her, after I kept pressing him. Especially since I was about to slam my fist into his head…"

You should have. You should have killed him. Gwen almost said this out loud.

"…but he said she came on to him. He was buzzing, a little high, and he said she started…she started doing things to him." Xavier shifted. "Shit, it was a mess. After a while the circumstances didn't change the truth. My best friend and my wife were fucking around; who made the first move didn't really matter. You know?"

Gwen nodded, "Some best friend," she snorted, still wondering how they came to be friends in the first place.

"Humph, yeah. Terry and I were different in a lot of ways. He's a pretty flamboyant brother, real big and likes to talk a lot of shit. But his upbringing was rough, father was pretty abusive until he finally left the family for good, and my family kind of became his family. I think he liked that, liked hanging out with my Moms and Pops and Carmen. And when he wasn't trying to act big-time and when he'd let up on the drinking and all the rest of the crap he was into, he could be a real person. That's the person I had as a friend, but after a while the stardom, the liquor, all of it kind of took over. It's sad," Xavier said, almost compassionately.

"He fucked your wife," Gwen snarled, without an ounce of pity. *And raped me.* She felt no compassion for Terry's sad life story. To hell with him.

He nodded, and his voice, when he spoke again, was flat. "Uh-huh. He did. Don't get me wrong, we *were* best friends, but now we're nothing. I haven't talked to him since."

Gwen pulled him close, flooded with relief from his statement. They hugged, tight and special, and it seemed to make up for the entire evening.

Xavier pulled away and cradled her face again, "Gwendolyn baby, I know I scared you tonight; I could see it in your eyes. Baby, I'd never hurt you. You believe me, don't you?" he pleaded.

"Uh-huh. I believe you." Gwen spoke quietly; she did believe he wouldn't hurt her, not physically. But she still hated that her emotions had forced her to reveal so much.

"Back in college...it was bad, huh?"

Gwen looked down. They had circled back around to her subject: the rape. She looked up at him with a thin, weak smile. "Let's just say it wasn't good."

"Wanna talk?"

"Nope. It's over; I'm over it. It's not worth verbalizing." She tried to make this big fat lie sound as strong as she could make it. But the truth was that Terry Stuart had emerged into their relationship from Xavier's past. Recounting the rape—even without using his name— still seemed unthinkable. And it was her birthday, dammit. She'd hold on a little longer—hold out was more like it, she knew. A little time was probably all she had.

Xavier paused, gave her a skeptical look, then said, "All right baby." He sighed, then looked past her at the microwave clock. "It's late. Think we can turn back time, you know, pre-Ellis and the rest of my shitty behavior?" Xavier joked, uncertainty in his tone.

Gwen looked at the clock as well; it was a few minutes past one a.m. "You've got a trip to take. I don't think turning back the clock would do either of us much good," Gwen replied quietly. Disappointment veiled his face, then she wrapped her legs around his waist again. "How about we move forward—you know, get together when you return from your vacation?"

Xavier smiled. "You still want to?"

"Absolutely." Gwen pulled her legs inward, drawing him closer. She kissed him, a gentle kiss turned hungry with the intention of letting him know how very much she still wanted him. And also an effort to give her emotions a lesson in not being afraid; Xavier was on her side, and Terry Stuart was out of their life.

They kissed some more in the kitchen. He apologized again; she

accepted again; and they both agreed it was going to take some time to understand each other, but that they both wanted to.

Once he left, Gwen reached the top of the stairs just as the phone began to ring. She answered it and smiled as Nana wished her a happy birthday two hours and twelve minutes after the fact.

· NINE ·

GWEN ARRIVED AT XAVIER'S CONDO an hour before he was to have picked her up at her place. He had asked, during one of their late-night conversations while he was on vacation, if she would spend the weekend with him: just them, together, all weekend. She agreed, thinking, *hoping*, that by the time he came back to town the nightmares she had been having would have stopped.

They began again the night after her birthday, the same nightmares she had battled in the past: Terry Stuart ripping inside her, his sweat dripping onto her face, the laughing, the pain. She woke up screaming, fighting, cursing. Afterward she tried to rock herself back to sleep, tried to will the nightmares out of her system. She hoped that by tonight, the first she and Xavier were to spend together, the nightmares would have lessened in severity if not disappeared all together. They hadn't. She had one last night.

"Gwendolyn?" Xavier answered the door with an expected look of surprise. Damn he looked good. Loose fitting black cotton pants, a nondescript gray T-shirt, and no shoes. How he could turn simple into sexy was truly a talent.

Gwen said, "Hi," accompanied by a nervous smile.

"Uh, hi. I thought I was going to pick you up."

"Yeah. Is it OK if I come in?" Gwen asked, trying to figure out how she was going to explain herself, something she didn't think about on the way over.

He said, "Of course," and she walked inside. He closed the door and they stood. Gwen looked around, as if trying to refamiliarize herself with the place again.

Gwen had only been there once before, after a shopping spree with Xavier and Kendra, when she helped the little girl put all her things away upon their return. It was a nice place, definitely decorated with a male theme—solid, masculine colors; French blinds as opposed to curtains; clean, not real structured, yet cozy. Very cozy. The only feminine aspect could be found in Kendra's room, which had been put together by Carmen, complete with a canopy bed, matching curtains and bed dressing, plus loads of stuffed animals. But now Kendra wasn't there; it was just Gwen and Xavier, still standing at the door.

"Has there been a change in plans?" Xavier asked. They still hadn't touched, still maintained space between them.

"Sort of. I mean...I just thought it would be best if I drove my own car. I should have called, I'm sor—"

"No. No problem. You want me to get your bag out of the car?" He motioned to the door.

Oh hell...

"I didn't bring any." Gwen tightened her purse strap on her shoulder and shuffled her feet.

"Oh." He didn't seem upset or disappointed, just confused. Gwen wanted to explain.

"Xavier, I, uh. Listen, I know we discussed this, but I..."

"You don't want to, right?" Xavier began to walk towards her.

"That's not it. I... it has nothing to do with you, really... it's just..."

OK, just say it.

"...I've never spent the night with a man before." Gwen's voice dropped.

"You haven't?" he asked, again surprised.

Gwen frowned, a bit embarrassed. "Uh-uh." She shuffled again, feeling stupid, like a twenty-nine-year old dating trainee.

She had no intention of telling him about the nightmares, but she wasn't lying about never having spent the night with a man. She hadn't. Not an entire night, and definitely not a romantic night. Ellis had often asked, and Gwen declined every time. She never felt comfortable with the idea of falling asleep in a man's arms and waking up

to engage in small talk or pillow talk, or, heaven forbid, more sex. But with Xavier she wanted to—except that now that the nightmares had started up again, she was afraid it wouldn't be safe.

Xavier stood in front of her. He touched her lips, then trailed his fingertips down her chin, where he lifted her face to meet his. Finally he had touched her, and it felt so good.

"I guess this is one of those 'it's going to take time' things we talked about, huh?" He smiled.

Gwen smiled back, comforted by his touch, and whispered, "Yeah." She moved closer, breathing in his scent. "I missed you," she said as she rose up to gently brush her lips against his lips. It was important that he knew how much she wanted to be with him.

His arms wrapped around her waist and his eyes lit up. "Baby, I missed you too." They kissed, long and soft.

Gwen and Xavier spent a good part of the evening talking, eating, and laughing—sometimes simultaneously. Xavier grilled T-bone steaks while Gwen tossed a salad. They boiled up some corn on the cob and finished with cheesecake topped with strawberries—store bought, but still pretty good. Gwen nursed a glass of chardonnay throughout while Xavier stuck to Heineken.

Afterwards, they moved from the dining room to the den. Gwen flipped her shoes off and sat on the couch, while Xavier went to the entertainment center, preparing to put a video in the VCR.

"So Xavier, you didn't tell me how Kendra felt about going back home after being away so long."

Xavier looked back at her. "Well, Kendra did...all right. She cried a little. I think she's still too young to understand everything. You know, why I can't stay, stuff like that. I have to admit it was pretty emotional for me, too." He smiled, but his voice was sad.

Gwen walked up to him and stood slightly behind him, stroking his arm, "I'll bet. You OK?"

Xavier leaned his head back and kissed her forehead, "Yeah, baby. Um, it was a little tough. But Kendra's mom and stepdad are pretty good at providing positive support. I'm sure she's bounced back by now." He took her hand and led her back to the couch where they sat.

"Do you two get along? You and Kendra's mom?" Gwen asked, suddenly remembering the sexual history they once shared. She couldn't help but worry if maybe they still had the urge to get it on.

Xavier shrugged. "We get along so-so, under the circumstances. The trip was pretty brief. I really just dropped her off and talked for few minutes, then I left. They all seem happy. She's expecting next month. Twins."

Gwen's eyes widened. "Kendra's mom?"

"Uh-huh. I just hope Kendra doesn't feel slighted when they arrive. I don't think she will, but it is something I worry about sometimes."

Gwen leaned forward and kissed him, feeling reassured and a little guilty for thinking Xavier wanted another woman. "You're a pretty all-right guy, you know that?"

Xavier's eyes began to dance. "Hmmm, you think so, huh?" Gwen nodded and they kissed again, but Xavier cut it off before it got too deep. "All right baby, are you ready for the movie? I'm telling you now, it's one of the best I've ever seen."

Gwen almost said, *let's skip the movie and hit the sheets,* but of course she didn't. Xavier seemed to be stalling, though. *Maybe...*Gwen began to field doubts, but quickly dismissed any negative thoughts before they fully developed.

She studied the video box while Xavier left to turn the lights off. "*The Last of the Mohicans,* huh?"

"Yeah. You sure violence doesn't bother you? Some of this can be pretty bad." He sat beside her again on the couch.

"I think I can handle the violence. It's war stuff, right?" She asked. Xavier nodded. "I think I'll be OK, but if it gets too bad, can I run to you for cover?" The sexiness in her voice returned for the first time this evening.

Xavier wrapped his arms around her, pulling her into him. "Absolutely."

The movie was excellent. Gwen became mesmerized by it—the love story, the music, the dialogue, scenery, even the costumes. All of it. And yeah, there was some violence too. But it seemed so secondary. At movie's end, Gwen found herself wiping away tears.

"Hey baby, you OK?"

Gwen laughed, and choked a little, before saying, "Yeah, yeah, I'm fine. Whoa, that was a good movie. I guess I got a bit caught up in it." Gwen wiped her eyes again and faced him, crossing her legs Indian-style on the couch.

He just nodded, staring at her with a loving smile. He grabbed her hand and the finger play began. Neither one of them said anything for a while. Gwen watched him play with her fingers.

She wondered if he was thinking about what she was thinking about: being together, making love. They had somehow managed to maintain a level of award-winning restraint the entire evening—for the past few months, it seemed. Xavier appeared to be directing the night's activities in baby steps—the dinner, the movie, a gentle kiss here, a light touch there. It felt special and romantic, but now Gwen wondered if maybe...

"Xavier?" She looked at him.

His eyes met hers. "Yeah, baby."

They both whispered.

Gwen hesitated, not knowing how to word her question: *Don't you want to make love to me anymore?* "Is something wrong?" she asked, taking a less obvious route.

"Wrong?" He played with her curls, lightly stroking her forehead.

"Never mind." Gwen shrugged it off, feeling frustrated.

This wasn't working; this felt awkward. Maybe things had changed. Maybe while he was on vacation he had had time to think about what he had learned about her past: what happened in college. Maybe he saw her as too much work. Especially now that she had confessed about never having spent the night with a man. Maybe he saw her as fragile, someone who might crumble when undressed, someone who might freak out once he entered her, someone who couldn't be pleased and couldn't please back. And maybe she couldn't.

Gwen went back to looking at his fingers play with her fingers.

"Baby."

"Yeah." She didn't look up.

"What is it about you?"

His question forced her attention; she looked up and rested her head against the couch. "What?"

He smiled. "What is it about you that makes me—I don't know, you seem to take me back about fifteen years. Like I've never..." he chuckled, "like I've never done things before you came along?" Xavier shook his head, "That sounded corny as hell, didn't it?"

Gwen smiled back. "I like it. I feel the same thing." She took her hand from under his and rested it on his thigh. "I feel a lot of things when I'm with you." She moved forward, snuggling her cheek against his shoulder and rubbing his thigh slowly, inching upward. Initiative. She decided to show a little initiative.

"Care to get more specific?" Xavier touched her chin, trailed his fingers down her neck, and toyed with the buttons of her tapered denim blouse.

Gwen smiled coyly. "I'll get more specific if you get more specific." She touched his earlobe with her tongue, nibbled it gently between her teeth, then let her lips linger down his neck, where she kissed him sweetly.

Xavier's body tightened; he whispered her name while he brushed her hardened nipple through her blouse. Gwen moaned, a very telling moan, and ran her own hand across his crotch, feeling every incredible inch of his hard-on through the fabric of his trousers. They began to kiss, strong and energetic. Gwen could feel his hand in her blouse, pulling her breast out of the bra cup, squeezing it, removing his lips from her lips and kissing between her breasts, over her nipple, up her neck before finding his way back to her lips. Xavier could work a kiss like nobody's business.

"Baby, how about we take this upstairs?" he suggested, pulling away from the kiss and admiring the parts of her body he could see through her partially opened blouse.

Gwen nodded, feeling nervous and excited and ready to get it on and on and on. He held her hand and led her up the stairs, into his bedroom. There she saw a balcony, a television and CD player, a desk and chair that served as a study, and a bed—a king-sized bed, waiting on them.

They stood by the desk. Xavier turned on a small lamp, very dim but just right for the occasion. He hit the stereo remote and soft music surrounded them. Will Downing. *Moods.* Absolutely perfect.

Gwen moved forward to kiss his neck in the little dip right below his throat. It was a tender kiss, not hungry or anxious as it had been downstairs. Time to slow the pace, pull back on the initiative, reinvent the romance. Xavier wanted her; he really, really wanted her. No more doubts; no more maybes.

She kept touching his neck with her lips and tongue while he gently held her head, running his fingers through her curls. Her lips finally maneuvered their way to his lips and the energy kissing began. Gwen could feel him hard against her; his tip tickled her navel.

With Xavier's doing, Gwen felt her khakis loosen, then drop around her ankles. His fingers caressed the back of her thighs, up to her panties, where he glided one finger of each hand just underneath them and began slipping them down. The eagerness of Gwen's kisses lessened; she was too aroused by his touch to keep up the momentum. The wetness that filled the crotch of her panties could be felt against her ankle once they fell to the floor. She stopped kissing and stepped back: just a couple of steps, out of her pants and underwear that lay in a puddle around her feet. She began to undo the buttons of her blouse that were still buttoned. Xavier stepped toward her and made a simple request: a beautiful, simple request. He kissed her lips and whispered, "Please, let me."

Gwen nodded slowly. Xavier unbuttoned each button of her denim blouse. She held her arms straight down by her side and felt the shirt slide right off. Xavier had unclasped her bra, which hooked in the front, before the shirt hit the ground. The bra quickly followed. Now she was completely naked, and completely comfortable with it. This time Xavier took a step back. He studied all of her; Gwen gave him a devilish smile.

I'm naked. You're not. Please, the suspense is killing me.

Xavier returned her smile with his own and shed his shirt and pants quickly. He stood. The patches of hair on his chest resembled

his mustache, silky and black. He wore boxer-briefs. He was big. Muscular. Fine.

My, my, my, my, my...

Gwen began to move further back, away from Xavier, in the direction of the bed. Xavier followed. Once she felt the bed against the back of her knees, she stopped and stood. Xavier reached her and stood, too. Neither one of them touched.

"Baby, you OK?" Xavier spoke softly.

Gwen nodded, no longer smiling, just aching for him. He caressed her cheek; his eyes never left her face. She smiled a smile that said she was OK; better than OK; *way* better than OK. He kissed her forehead, much like he had on the night of their first kiss, then kissed her nose, then her lips. Next was her chin, then the length of her neck with his tongue. Gwen held his head between her hands, consumed. His tongue traveled down her chest, soft and wet, working its way to each of her breasts.

"Ooooh, yes," Gwen heard herself say, or rather proclaim. The way his mouth toyed with her nipples was energetic—pulling, licking, saturating. If Gwen didn't know better, she would swear her nipples were kissing him back. Soon he was on his knees, his hands holding her hips, kissing her stomach, her navel, until finally burrowing his lips and tongue between her legs and tasting her clit.

He had found it. He was there. All the way there. No one had been there in years; not since she was a sixteen-year-old girl, screwing around with her very first lover. After that, it had just been her own fingers, warm baths, scented candles. But now Xavier was staking claim to the domain. And he wasn't playing.

Gwen held his head, rubbing it with her hands as if making a wish. So far, it was being granted. Xavier stopped, just long enough to pull her hips down onto the bed. She sat, showering his head with kisses. He eagerly kissed her stomach, then gently fondled her nipples again with his tongue. Then he pushed on her shoulders, a light nudge; requesting she lay back; requesting she let him please her.

Whatever you want, baby. Whatever you want.

§

She lay back on the bed and, without hesitation, spread her legs like wings. Xavier went back to his mission. His tongue was wet and warm. Gwen could feel his fingers part her lips, making sure he didn't miss it, making sure he got all of it. And he did. The brother had skills.

OOOOH WEEEEE!!!!

Her moans were a series of soft variations on, "Oooh, yes baby..." And Xavier was making some deep, breathy sounds himself.

Go ahead on, Xavier. Go ahead on...

Gwen began to feel the sensation creeping up and down her legs. The strokes of his tongue began to linger, steady and rhythmic. And Gwen's moans changed. Now she repeated, "Ahhh, that's it, that's it." The sensation, that slow, creeping sensation, increased in speed and spread in territory. It felt electrical, magical, powerful. Once it seized her entire body, Gwen lunged upward, pulling from the small of her back. Her hands left Xavier's head and clutched the sheets; if she didn't hold, she was sure her climax would hurl her into the ceiling. There was no sound. Her mouth was open wide, no doubt rejoicing. But Gwen couldn't hear a thing. She could only feel. Feel everything. Every incredible charge, every sensation, on every part of her body. *Every part.*

Slowly she began to hear sound again. It filtered in quietly—the music; the sound of her own labored breathing; the thumping of her heart. Her body lay flat on the bed. Her hands released the sheets and reached out to wrap around Xavier's waist. He loomed over her, on all fours, with her in between. He kissed her chin, sweetly. They held each other's gaze.

"Baby, you OK?" Again he asked, softly. It sounded so special.

Baby, I'm more than OK. I AM ALIVE.

Gwen just nodded, like before. Then she smiled, blushing. He smiled too. Gwen raised herself forward, resting on her elbows. He leaned down to meet her and they kissed. Gwen took control, very much aroused and wanting more. More of Xavier. And she wanted to give him more of her. Much more.

She raised up further, wrapping her arms around his waist, then slipping her hands below. His butt felt strong and muscular. She

slipped her hands inside his boxer-briefs and slid them down. Xavier stopped kissing, moved to the edge of the bed, and pulled his underwear off completely.

He retrieved a condom from the drawer, a decision they had both agreed on. Gwen wasn't on birth control pills, not yet. And she had long ago abandoned the temperamental diaphragm. So they had agreed on a condom for protection, for now anyway.

Gwen sat on her knees behind him, kissing the back of his neck, down his spine, then back up again. Her kisses were greedy, but controlled. Xavier climbed the bed again and they both rested on their knees, facing each other. Gwen touched his face, then lightly raked her fingers down his chest. Xavier closed his eyes. Gwen continued the journey down and felt his tip, then closed her hand around him entirely. He moaned, a deep, heavy moan. Gwen looked down at him and studied the hardness in her hand.

Oh Xavier. You are truly gifted.

He was hard and chiseled, and growing longer in her grasp. Gwen leaned into him, kissing his chest, playfully teasing his nipples with her tongue.

"Oh yeah, Gwendolyn." Xavier chanted.

They lay down together, his hands on her, her hands on him. She had never been so wet, so aroused. Serious foreplay ensued: Gwen only grew wetter as Xavier grew harder.

"Now, baby..."

They sat up at the same time, Gwen kissing his shoulder, Xavier grabbing the back of her head gently and kissing her forehead, her cheeks, her lips. Gwen pushed on Xavier's chest until he lay flat, then she smiled.

"Please. Let me."

Gwen climbed on top of him. She leaned down and kissed him some more—anxious, hard. She felt him rub against her. Then she felt his tip between her lips; she rocked forward slightly, then back, feeling him slide inside. They both breathed out, "Oh yeah." Gwen kissed him again before she sat up straight and felt him slide deeper inside her, all the way in. She lifted up, just a bit, up a bit more, then back down,

feeling him go deeper inside with each rise and descent of her hips. She stroked him with a steady pace, tightening herself around him each time he filled her. He fondled her nipples with the palms of his hands, back and forth, until Gwen took his hands, holding them with hers, putting his fingers to her mouth and kissing his fingertips. "Oh Gwendolyn...yes baby, you feel so good," Xavier said; his excitement was melodic. Gwen moaned, "Uh-huh." That was one compliment, finally, that she would take without argument. He grabbed her hips, rocking her pelvis, helping her stroke him; he told her how beautiful she was and how wonderful she felt and a few other things that only served to increase her arousal. Gwen loved it all, every moment, every inch, every sensation. She loved his voice, its rich, aphrodisiac cadence; she loved the way he made her feel—sexy but not tainted, uninhibited but not vulgar; good *and* bad without guilt. Good bad. There was such a thing.

Gwen could feel it, that sensation again. It was creeping, gaining speed, gaining intensity. The sounds in the room were beginning to dull. Xavier's repeated moans of "Oh yeah, baby," began to growl, then fade from earshot. The sensation took over just as Xavier dug his fingers firmly into her hips; his eyes closed and his face glowed with that sudden rush of intense pleasure. He peaked just as she peaked, totally in sync. Damn, they were good.

He rose up; Gwen wrapped her legs around his waist, and they kissed each other. He caressed her back, then held her tightly, pressing her body with his. She was exhausted, fulfilled, completed.

Xavier cradled her face and looked into her eyes. "Baby, you are so beautiful; stay with me tonight."

"Oh, baby," Gwen crooned, kissing his lips softly. She wanted to stay: stay in his house, his bed, his arms. Right now, at this very moment, it seemed impossible that anything sinister could corrupt her dreams. But then again...

"I probably shouldn't..."

"Stay." He kissed her lips and smiled, a mischievous sparkle in his eyes.

"Hmmm, Xav—"

"Stay..." another kiss, "...stay," another kiss, "...stay..."

Gwen smiled, feeling his lips between her breasts. She teasingly rolled her eyes, "Well, if you're *really* sure it's what you wa—" Gwen screeched in laughter as Xavier rolled her off his lap onto the bed. They were kissing again; she was staying, and sleep looked to be light-years away.

· TEN ·

CHRISTINA'S RESTAURANT in Stone Mountain had become their favorite dining spot, a small cottage-style eatery, very quiet and relaxing, with a fireplace and candles lit at every table. They had happened upon it a couple of months before while driving around on one of their weekend jaunts to nowhere in particular. Now it had become the place they'd dine, usually before Xavier left for an out-of-town trip the following week, as sort of a prelude to a romantic night beginning with dinner and ending with divine sex and soppy sentiments of how much they missed each other when apart.

Except tonight they were dining off schedule, since Xavier would be in the office the coming week, a slight reprieve from his travels. Unfortunately, his travel schedule for the rest of the year was relentless. After this week, Gwen would be lucky if she saw him much before Thanksgiving, and she probably wouldn't see him then since she was supposed to be spending the holiday with Nana in Augusta. But Nana's phone call a few days ago had made her not want to go anymore.

Gwen kept stirring her soup, preoccupied with thought.

"You didn't seem too interested in working out today. Feeling OK?" Xavier asked, reaching across the table and stroking Gwen's fingers.

"Yeah, fine," Gwen gave him a small inflection of her mouth, nothing real warm and fuzzy. She went back to stirring her soup, trying to tell herself to snap out of it. Xavier removed his hand.

Normally, they worked out three times a week in Gwen's basement. Xavier had added more equipment, things he'd had in storage. Gwen already had an exercise bike, a treadmill, and the punching bag. Xavier had provided some free weights and a few top-of-the-line Nautilus machines, and her basement had been transformed into a formidable

gym. Xavier divided his own workout time between her basement and the Gold's Gym at which he had a membership, and had gladly offered to get Gwen one as well since she seemed to really enjoy working out. But she told him she'd rather exercise at home; she didn't need to spend money on a gym she knew she would barely see. Gyms were usually coed, which meant men, which could mean unwanted attention, which could possibly mean trouble. Pass.

"How's Payton been?" Xavier asked.

Gwen didn't look up. "Fine."

"She'll be in town on Friday?"

"Uh-huh."

"Well, at least I get to meet her before I go to New York."

"Uh-huh."

Xavier sighed. Gwen looked up and did that small inflection thing again with her mouth. Xavier did the same.

"If you stay in this mood, you're not going to be very good company with Vaughn," Xavier offered, taking a swallow of his iced tea. Vaughn was insisting that he take them out to dinner on Thursday in appreciation for all their hard work on the Cyntex acquisition.

"I'm not in a mood." Gwen stopped stirring and sat back.

"No?"

"No." She knew damn well she was in a mood, and now it was fast becoming a bitchy one.

"OK, fine." Xavier surrendered patiently. He nibbled at his salad while Gwen attempted a taste of her soup. It was cold.

She felt a sudden cramp, a tussle in her gut. Aunt Flow had returned this morning and that always added more drama to her mindset. She stood up. "Baby, excuse me for a minute, OK?" She gave him a smile and he said, "Sure," and stood as she left the table.

On the way to the restroom Gwen kept telling herself to get a grip, stop being a bitch, and stop treating Xavier like crap. He wasn't supposed to be able to read her mind, yet she treated him as if he should know better than to make small talk while she festered.

It wasn't his fault her Nana had called with the news that Weldon was back with Nana, back in Augusta, which undoubtedly meant he

was back to cause trouble. Nana refused to believe it, but Gwen knew better.

Gwen freshened herself up and made her way back to the table with a new attitude. She would apologize to Xavier, explain what was going on, and talk to him about it. They always talked, although Xavier was better at it than she. He liked to talk things out; Gwen liked to let them fester. That was just one of their differences.

Nothing real major—Gwen called them little "idios," stuff like Xavier's leaving the toilet seat up, or his tendency to procrastinate, putting things off and then rushing to squeeze them in at a later, much more pressure-filled date. Xavier claimed he liked handling things that way; working under pressure kept his adrenaline pumping. Gwen would roll her eyes and mutter, "Yeah, right."

But she had her idios too, she would admit, like trying to get the last word in on a discussion or an argument, and then being bratty when it looked like Xavier wasn't going to let her have it. Or like being a bitch now and taking it out on Xavier when he wasn't to blame. Their idios balanced out their personalities; their good together outweighed any bad, and Gwen thought his admitted imperfection was one of Xavier's most attractive features.

Now as she walked towards the table she smiled, until she saw that some big-haired, broad-shouldered woman wearing a neon green jumpsuit had taken her seat across from Xavier, arching her back and holding her auburn-colored hair back behind her ear as if it hindered her hearing. Gwen breathed deep. Another idio, the way Xavier attracted attention in public.

"Oh, I'm sorry, I'll bet you want your seat back, huh?" the woman asked as Gwen stood before her. Xavier stood and rubbed the small of her back, giving her a wink.

Gwen tightened herself into a knot. "Something like that," she mustered in response to the woman's stupid-ass question. Suddenly that new attitude resembled the old bitchy one, with an added punch.

The woman feigned embarrassment and moved out of the seat, standing on the other side of the table as if she still had a need to be there. Gwen had news for her—she didn't.

Xavier began, "Um, I'm sorry, what was your name again?"

"Tasha."

"Tasha, this is my lady, Gwendolyn."

Nice save, Xavier, but no cigar. Gwen stood, stone-faced. Tasha, Sasha, or whatever, reached across the table in her tacky-ass jumpsuit and said, "Nice to meet you"—the nerve, knowing damn well she had just been cold-busted trying to move on Gwen's man. Gwen stared at her hand, pursed her lips, and shook the woman's sweaty paw, when she really wanted to crush her fingers.

"I, uh, was just telling Xavier here that I work for the McMillan sports agency downtown and he looked so familiar. Thought maybe I could luck up on a new client during my off time. Perhaps the Hawks had signed a new forward without telling anyone." She laughed, phony as a three-dollar bill. "At least I was right about the athlete part; once an athlete always an athlete, right Xavier?" She cackled again. Xavier nodded and chuckled himself.

Gwen thought, *Please. What was your first clue on the athlete part, you unoriginal bitch,* and mumbled, "Funny," with a transparent look of disbelief.

Xavier cleared his throat. "Uh, Tasha, if you'll excuse us, we were just about to order dinner." Attention always seemed to be hurled his way like a giant in-your-face whipped cream pie. He couldn't help his too-handsome self—six-foot-five, two hundred thirty pounds of muscle; smooth caramel-colored skin; high-voltage smile. Usually Gwen ignored it; sometimes she found it flattering; but tonight she was in no mood for some big-haired, lying, trifling-ass female interrupting their dinner.

Tasha feigned another round of embarrassment, said "Of course," apologized for the disruption, to which Xavier replied, "No problem," and left.

Xavier scratched his head and chuckled again. Gwen looked at him like *what the hell is so funny,* and felt herself about to get ignorant—that level of neck-jerking, eye-bulging, street-talking ignorance that anyone, regardless of social status, was capable of reaching. Payton liked to call it "trailer park," and after a while she and Payton settled

on one very appropriate universal name for it all—"Jerry Springer folk."

"Why don't we just go?" Gwen suggested, knowing better than to make a scene in public, although she was tempted.

"You don't want to order dinner?" Xavier asked, as if that would pacify her anger, which at the moment would be like feeding a scrap of bacon to a rabid dog.

She adjusted her purse strap and walked past him without answering. *Let him figure it out.*

The ride back home started out silent. Then the car yielded to the demands of traffic. Something had happened up ahead; it was too late for construction, so it was probably an accident being gawked at by a bunch of nosy-ass rubberneckers. It was at this point that their argument began.

"Why are you so pissed off, baby?"

"Didn't say I was pissed." Gwen stared out the passenger window.

"You don't have to say it. Your attitude is screaming in my damn ear."

"Whatever." Gwen's flipped her hand up without giving him a look. Like a true bitch.

Xavier kept quiet for a while. Gwen knew he had reached his tolerance level with her petty behavior; she could tell by the way he breathed deep, exhaling loudly through his mouth. Traffic kept inching.

"She was out of line," Gwen mumbled, hardly audible.

"Who?"

Gwen jerked her head to look at him, "Don't 'who' me, Xavier. That damn Sasha in the Granny Smith apple suit, that's who." She huffed and rolled her eyes.

Xavier smiled, "Baby, I think her name was Tasha."

The mere sight of his smile brought on a higher level of rage. "I am so glad you think this shit is funny," she hissed.

Xavier kept smiling. "I didn't say it was funny. I just think your jealousy is kind of...um, flattering." He chuckled.

Gwen rolled her eyes. "Jealous? Please."

"Oh, so you weren't jealous?" His smile radiated.

Hell yeah I was jealous... But Gwen didn't like being called on it, and she wanted to wring his neck for smiling so damn much. She added, "Look, if having the Green Hornet sit across from you boosted your ego, more power to you. But don't try and instigate a cat fight, cause I'm not with it."

"I'm not trying to instigate a thing. You're the one blowing this whole thing overboard. The woman was a sports agent, I know how they are, they're an aggressive bunch. She thought I was someone worth talking to. That's all. You're the one who thinks a hidden agenda was involved, Miss Anti-Cat Fight." He rubbed her hand and laughed. Gwen moved it away and folded her arms across her chest.

She squinted, ready to unload. "You love all this, don't you? The old idolized athlete syndrome, is that it, Xavier? You know as well as I do what that woman wanted, and it wasn't a shoe endorsement. And if it *was* on the up-and-up, then why did she wait till I left the table to drum up some business? That's bullshit, Xavier. She was hoping you think like all jocks think—maybe you could break her off a little something-something, you know, maybe you two could drum up some business between the sheets. 'Once an athlete always an athlete,'" Gwen mimicked with a whine. "So damn obvious." Gwen watched his smile collapse like dominoes before she jerked her head back and looked out the window. She had unloaded both barrels and still felt tight as a tick.

Traffic picked up more speed and again they were silent.

"Gwendolyn, not all jocks think with their dicks," Xavier stated bluntly, using a term he normally didn't in her presence.

"Uh-huh." She didn't feel like talking in complete sentences anymore.

"But that's what you believe, huh?" His voice grew stern.

"Let's drop it."

"You have a problem with jocks?" Xavier wasn't going to drop it. Gwen didn't answer.

"Back in college, what happened? Was he a jock?" Xavier asked, a bit softer.

Gwen still didn't answer. They didn't talk about the rape. She hated

that he knew what little he did, what little she had revealed the night of her birthday.

He had only brought it up once before, shortly after her birthday; he had asked if she had ever told anyone about it, maybe told her Nana. Gwen told him that Nana had her hands full with Weldon and telling her about the rape would only add to her burden. She said she dealt with it the best she could, that she'd had some help from Payton and moved on; it was history, history not up for discussion, and then as usual she requested they drop the issue. He asked if she was sure, and said he'd be willing to listen if she wanted to talk. Her "no" trumpeted a bit too loudly, even by her own admission, for an incident she claimed to be a blip on her memory. "I don't deny there are subtle reminders from time to time, but the emotional scars are hardly visible," she told him. She could tell by the look on his face back then that he hadn't believed her, and now it had been brought to the forefront again.

"Was he on the USC football team? Basketball...?" Xavier ignored her silence; he knew she graduated from the University of South Carolina, so naturally he figured that's where it happened.

Gwen turned to face him and flailed her hands. "He was nobody, dammit. Can we please drop this?"

"No, Gwendolyn. You got this theory on jocks, I'm assuming by the way you're acting you're lumping me in with them, and I'd like to know where all this hostile bullshit is coming from."

"I'm not lumping you in with anything. I don't think you're a typical athlete. Really, baby." Gwen softened her voice, finally, and reached over to caress the side of his face.

She had to stop this madness—madness she had started. She had decided not to give him details about the rape. Whatsoever. Sometimes she felt deceptive, but most of the time she felt justified. It wasn't any of his business. It was her drama, her pain, her anger. Xavier had no need to know. He wouldn't understand. No man could.

Xavier heaved another breath. Her caress wasn't working. Gwen removed her hand and folded them together in her lap, trying to

figure out what to say to flip the atmosphere, and how to say it nicely. More silence.

"You're not going to tell me about him?" Xavier asked, not giving the issue a rest.

Gwen's heart pounded. *"Nope."* So much for nice.

"You don't like opening up to me, huh?" Now he sounded hurt.

"I open up all the time, Xavier. How can you say that?" She looked at him; now she was hurt.

"I think you pick and choose your topics."

Gwen clenched her jaws, "Oh, like you don't."

"I don't. Anything you want to know, I'll tell you."

Gwen huffed, jerked her arms across her chest again, and stared out the window again. She had no counterargument to present, knowing Xavier spoke the truth. Over the past four months he'd been more than open about his past.

One night she asked him about Tracey—not really knowing why, because it could ultimately lead to Terry Stuart, though luckily it didn't. Gwen wondered if maybe Xavier still had feelings for her; maybe as he talked she could detect a hint of desire in his voice or a touch of sadness about their divorce.

Xavier willingly opened up about Tracey and their marriage, or lack thereof. He said he met her during his rookie year with the Bullets and that she pursued him relentlessly, and that, almost single-handedly, had turned him on. Gwen joked with an incredulous tone, "Xavier, I've seen a picture of Tracey, and I'm sure her hot pursuit wasn't the only deciding factor." Xavier laughed. Tracey was a pretty girl, there was no denying that. But Xavier said her beauty couldn't make them compatible or save their marriage. They traveled entirely different roads once the honeymoon dust had cleared. Gwen didn't pick up any vibes that night, nothing to indicate he still wanted his ex-wife; then, as usual, she silently chastised herself for thinking he would.

Personally, Gwen thought Tracey was stupid. Any woman who willingly and repeatedly chose to sleep with Terry Stuart must be a fool.

Terry Stuart never made it into their conversations, nor did Xavier talk much about his college glory days, probably because they involved Terry. And of course, Gwen never asked and she never planned on asking.

Traffic rolled along steadily and they were almost to her house.

"So are we going to talk about this?" Xavier asked again.

Gwen looked at him. "There's nothing to talk about. You're assuming all this bullshit, that everything tonight has to do with what happened in college..."

"And it doesn't?" He looked at her just as traffic jolted to an abrupt stop, with cars bottlenecked at the exit.

She felt like crying. "No, it doesn't." A tear formed in the corner of her eye. She looked out the window again.

"Then what's the problem? I know it's more than that woman tonight." Xavier wanted to talk and Gwen did too, or at least she had about an hour ago. Now she felt drained, felt her emotions shutting down, felt her desire to talk turned off.

She didn't look at him when she said, "Nothing," but she startled a bit when she heard him reply, "Fine. Just fuck it."

It wasn't often they found themselves pissed at each other. Throughout their four-month romance, they'd rarely argued; then again, she rarely found herself so bitchy. They still made incredible love, first thing in the morning, late at night, in the shower. She still daydreamed about him, still anticipated his phone calls when he was out of town, still talked with him well into the night; she was still very much in love with him. One day she planned to tell him so. *Maybe tonight...* if she could ever find a way to make up from this fight.

Xavier parked his Acura along the curb instead of pulling into the garage. He wasn't going to stay. *Maybe not tonight.*

Xavier turned the engine off and blew another deep breath. Gwen looked at him, tightened her face to keep from crying, and asked in her softest voice, "You're not coming in?"

Xavier shook his head, frustrated, "You've had an attitude all damn week; you spend all day gruntin', and most of the night fighting in your damn sleep. If you'd rather be left alone, tell me and I'll

oblige. But don't keep me around just to watch you pout." Now Xavier grunted. He eyed her for a second. Gwen looked away, telling herself not to cry.

Her mind raced. She hadn't had any nightmares lately, at least none that she knew of. Did she have fitful sleep without waking up? Is that why Xavier had been grilling her tonight on the college thing? Gwen remained silent; her insides coiled in the pit of her stomach.

"Why don't we just scrap this whole evening? I think we've battled enough for tonight, don't you?" Xavier reduced his level of anger, just a notch.

Gwen wanted to say, *we don't have to battle,* but instead said, "Whatever," figuring romance couldn't be recaptured if she had a net. She pulled her keys from her jacket pocket, remembering she had slipped them in there earlier to keep them from drowning in the abyss she called a purse. Xavier opened his door as she opened hers and they walked to her front stoop. They mumbled good night, he pecked her on the cheek, and then he left. Gwen didn't stop him.

When she made it upstairs, it took her less than two minutes to peel herself out of the clingy knit, black, maxi-length dress that hugged every curve she could claim. Dresses were becoming her thing since she'd been with Xavier, and the first time she wore this particular one a few weeks ago, he nearly peeled it off her himself before their date got started. It turned him on something fierce.

Most things about her turned him on, or so he always said. Like when she washed her hair, and her curls glistened on her head like twinkling stars; or right after a bath, when the smell of the bath gels and fragrances that silkened her skin aroused his senses and his hormones, making him want to taste every inch of her. Or the touch of her hand, which felt so slender and so unbelievably soft he couldn't stop playing with her fingers, couldn't stop pressing them against his face, and when she wrapped her hand around his hardness it took all the stamina he could conjure up to keep from erupting. Xavier said these things to her all the time, and now as she sank into a lonely Saturday night bath, she missed him, ached for him, and wanted so badly to make up.

Dionne Farris's *Wild Seed—Wild Flower* mellowed and rocked on the CD. Gwen needed Dionne's wisdom tonight. The bath's intense heat relaxed her body but couldn't quite ease her mind. Even through all of the conflict with Xavier, Nana's call still tormented her.

Weldon was back. And Gwen was sure their volatile relationship would resume right where it had left off.

The last time she saw him was four years ago, a suffocatingly hot summer day in Augusta. Gwen had been visiting with Nana for a few days, having taken a week's vacation from work to pamper her grandmother and be pampered in return. Nana had been particularly agitated that summer. She had, against Gwen's urging, taken Weldon back into her home for another chance at redemption. He had shown up at her doorstep a few months prior, looking like a chewed-up piece of gum and saying he was clean with no place to go. Weldon was her grandbaby; she unhesitatingly opened up her heart and home. But soon afterwards his old patterns started up again. Money missing; borrowing the car to go to the store and not returning for hours; sleeping all day; self-destructing all night. Gwen hadn't seen him the entire time she was visiting until she and Nana returned one evening from shopping.

They had walked in on him trying to steal every electronic gadget Nana owned, right down to the blender. That day, things got ugly. Weldon and Gwen got into a shouting match, the same old shit, him blaming her for the pathetic man he had become. She had killed their parents and destroyed the promising life he should have had. Gwen told him to get the hell out before she called the police; she went for the phone; he came after her; Nana tried to intervene. Weldon pushed Nana down and this sent Gwen into psycho-bitch orbit. She shoved Weldon, whereupon he reared back and punched her in the nose. She felt it crack across the bridge while he glared at her with that crazed look. He hated her; his hollow eyes hadn't changed at all since the day their parents died, and all she could see was hate. Nana kept screaming, saying, "Weld, that demon's taken your soul, my baby. Them demons you keep shoving up your nose, they just want your soul, baby..." Wel-

don left Gwen and walked to Nana, helped her up, and wept while she held him. Gwen grabbed her gun from her purse; she never traveled without her Glock. Weldon watched, virtually unafraid, as she held it in front of him. Nana screamed for her to put it away. "Get the hell out, Weldon, now. Before I send your soul to hell…" Gwen had told him. Weldon wiped his bucked eyes and grunted. He walked past Gwen, the barrel of the gun followed his every move. He opened the door and stood, his back to Gwen, almost as if he were hoping she'd pull the trigger. Minutes passed. Nana kept crying, praying to Jesus to save her babies. Gwen stood, still holding the gun up, still trembling, still listening to Nana beg for their souls, long after Weldon had walked out the door and closed it behind him.

The bathtub water began to cool. Gwen reached for the hot water knob just as a series of cramps ganged up on her and cut her bath short. As she dripped out of the tub, she opened the bathroom drawer in search of a fresh tampon. There was only one left. She pulled it out and rummaged through the drawer, almost sure she had more than this. Gwen dried off, inserted the only surviving tampon, and then remembered she had shoved a bunch in her purse. She'd need them, especially since the first day of her cycle always resembled the Red Sea.

After donning cotton panties and wrapping her paisley robe around herself, Gwen brushed back her wet hair and searched for her purse. It wasn't in her room or downstairs. Gwen began to panic. Her purse was missing. Her purse had everything in it—her credit cards, her driver's license, her tampons. Her address. "Oh shit," she muttered, a tremble in her lips. The last thing she needed was her purse in the hands of strangers, her credentials in the hands of strangers, her address in the hands of strangers.

Gwen walked back up the stairs slowly, trying to think of the last place she had it. At the restaurant; she did have it at the restaurant. That's good, she was starting to think. Let's see, she pulled her keys out and placed them in her jacket before she and Xavier left for dinner. Did she have it when she left the restaurant? Gwen sat down on the top stair and beat her head.

She had it when she went to the restroom, and had it on her arm when she returned to find the Green Hornet in her seat. Gwen visualized herself in the restaurant, visualized her purse on her shoulder as she grabbed her jacket on the way out, visualized climbing in Xavier's car and dropping her purse down by her foot. Xavier's car. She had left it in Xavier's car.

She went to call him just as the doorbell rang, and she changed direction to the door, wrapping her bathrobe tight around her. The peephole revealed Xavier's fine self, holding her purse.

"Hi." Gwen greeted.

He looked at her and smiled a little smile. "Hi." He held up her purse, "Missing something?"

Gwen took it, blushing. "Yeah, I just realized it was gone. I was freaking out there for a second. Thanks."

"You're welcome."

"Why don't you come in? It's kind of cold out there." Gwen offered, not wanting to foil her second chance to make things right.

"Uh, I probably should go, you look like you were into something." He gave her a once-over and couldn't help but smile.

"I was into a bath, and now I'm out of it. Come in, please."

Xavier relented and walked inside. Gwen had no intention of letting him go, now that she had him.

"You and Dionne jammin', huh?" Xavier joked, as "I Know" blasted from her stereo.

"Yeah. Let me turn it down a little. Have a seat, take your jacket off." Gwen knew she could run upstairs and change her clothes, but decided her present attire was more conducive to making up.

When she returned Xavier was still standing in the foyer, still had his jacket on, and didn't look as if he planned to stay.

"Look I'm going to, um, go."

Gwen crossed her arms, not so much in defiance, but to keep her robe together. If she said "OK," then he would leave. She didn't want him to leave and tonight was the night she planned on opening up more, or at least enough to make up.

She walked up to him. "Xavier, I'm sorry," she whispered sweetly.

"You were right, I was jealous." She ducked her head. "I don't mind women looking, but when they start sniffing around...well, I get a little ignorant." She lifted her eyes up to him, sort of innocent, sort of sexy, anything but ignorant.

Xavier hoisted his eyebrows, "'Ignorant,' huh?" The effort he put into concealing his smile was a poor show.

Gwen crept a little closer, "Something like that. When it comes to you I can get a little possessive, you know...you my man, me your woman...that kind of thing." She flexed her eyebrows and slipped her arms around his waist, loving his strength and gentleness.

Xavier laughed out loud. "Baby, you're a trip," he said, but he still hadn't taken his hands out of his pockets; he didn't seem completely ready to make up, although his face did appear to be warming. "Gwendolyn, that woman at the restaurant wasn't the whole story." He looked down at her; no more smiles, no more laughs.

"No, she wasn't," Gwen conceded quietly.

Before she could explain, another heavy duty round of kick-ass cramps attacked. Gwen winced in pain, thinking the three Advil she had popped earlier were losing their power.

"Gwendolyn, you OK?" Xavier finally removed his hands from his pockets and reached out to her.

Gwen moved away, holding her stomach, "Uh-huh." She managed a smile, "Cramps. Period. Part of the problem," she explained.

"Oh."

Gwen again smiled weakly, "Uh, yeah."

Xavier had a sister, he knew about these things, and he's the one who wanted her to open up more. OK, now she had opened. The cramps subsided and Gwen straightened back up as Xavier approached.

He stroked her cheek. "Better?"

She held his hand to her face. "Better."

"Carmen says there should be some kind of support group for PMS," Xavier said, laughing a little.

Gwen moved a little closer. "She's got my vote, except my PMS is usually pre, during, *and* post. I normally only average about one good

week a month." She giggled, then wrapped his arms around her waist and purred.

"Hmmm, I hadn't ever noticed before."

"That's 'cause when I'm with you most of my days are good days. To be honest, since I've been with you, all my days have been pretty amazing." She lifted to kiss his chin.

"You're doing things to me, you know that?"

Gwen nodded. "All good, I hope."

She knew it was. The look in his eyes said it all; her hair was still pretty damp, her body scent permeated the air between them with irresistible fragrances, and Xavier's eyes were doing their dance again.

His hands slipped below her waist and fondled her butt. "It's better than good. But tonight you confused the hell out of me," he whispered.

"I confuse the hell out of myself all the time," she whispered back. When he leaned down and kissed her softly, she knew they were on the way to recapturing the romance.

He pulled away and stroked her hair. "So we can blame everything on the evil apple?"

Gwen looked down. "Uh, not entirely."

"Oh." Xavier said, frustration sneaking into his voice again.

"Weldon's back," Gwen stated quickly, her eyes filling with tears.

"Back? Back where?" His frustration turned to concern. He knew about her stormy relationship with Weldon.

Gwen gave him what she knew about Weldon's return, which wasn't much. She told him about Nana's call, and that she didn't know where Weldon had been for the past four years, why he was back, or what his state of mind was like. She did know that her Nana wanted her to come home to Augusta and see her brother; Nana wanted to see her two grandchildren make peace. And as much as Gwen struggled with her own emotions, she didn't want to disappoint Nana—not the one woman who had seen her through so much, and loved her so unconditionally. It was at this point in the conversation that Gwen broke down into tears, wrapped in Xavier's arms, still standing in the foyer.

"I'm sorry," Gwen said through sobs.

"Shush, baby. It's OK."

Gwen couldn't stop crying. She had never cried in front of Xavier. For that matter, not only had she never shared the real depth of her pain with a man, she had never thought she would ever have the desire to do so in life.

Usually when Gwen talked about Weldon or her parents, she did it when they talked on the phone, while Xavier was out of town, and she could usually keep her tears at bay until after they hung up. Hiding them now seemed not only impossible, but ridiculous; the comfort she felt in Xavier's arms as he wiped her tears and kissed her forehead and shushed her apologies made opening up to him the most natural, most comfortable thing in the world.

"We should probably move out of the foyer, huh?" Gwen managed, wiping her eyes.

"You OK?" Xavier asked, his voice all compassion and sincerity.

"I'm fine." Gwen forced a smile, then added, "I'll *be* fine. Really." She laughed. Xavier laughed too. "Will you stay?" she requested.

"You want?" he asked, as if he wasn't sure.

Gwen held his hand to her lips and kissed his fingertips. "I want."

His smile broadened and he nodded. They finally moved from the foyer and went upstairs.

Xavier loved her bedroom, said it looked just like her style, delicate and soft with subtle pastel colors and large fluffy pillows, feminine and sexy with the scent of a woman, his woman, Gwendolyn. She excused herself to the bathroom to get herself together. She threw cold water on her face and stared at herself in the mirror. The face that stared back still didn't please her that much; she still found it difficult at times to see the woman Xavier seemed to see; but she wasn't going to worry about that tonight.

When she walked out of the bathroom, Xavier had been at the CD player. The sound of Kenny Lattimore's smooth vocals made her smile, and the sight of Xavier, wearing only his boxer-briefs and a T-shirt, made her bite her quivering bottom lip.

"Wanna dance?" He held out his hand.

Gwen nodded and moved into him, wrapping one arm around

his neck while her other hand rested on his solid chest. They slow-grooved right there in her bedroom without speaking for a while.

"Gwendolyn, are you sure you're going to be OK going to Augusta by yourself?"

"Uh-huh. I'm not too worried about my physical state, if that's what you mean."

"I mean all of it." Xavier lifted her chin.

Gwen flashed a brave face. "I'll work it out."

"Yeah." Xavier's voice dropped. "You know, baby, you don't have to be the tough little soldier all by yourself."

Tears filled her eyes again. "Is that your way of telling me you'll fight my battles?"

"Without question." Xavier lifted her off her feet and hugged her. Gwen hugged back, feeling the tears stream down her face and soak his T-shirt. Xavier whispered in her ear, "But I can't fight what I don't know."

Gwen sniffled, "I know, baby. I'm sorry about tonight." She stood on her tiptoes and kissed him before saying, "It's never been real easy for me to open up, but it doesn't mean that I don't want to. It doesn't mean I don't love you as much as I do. It's just hard." Gwen continued to kiss him, but Xavier stopped and said, "What?"

"What? What's wrong," Gwen asked, wiping her eyes and trying to figure out what exactly he was questioning.

Xavier raised an eyebrow, "Uh, did you just hear what you said, or did I just imagine I heard something I've been wanting to hear?"

"What?" Gwen pulled away and tried to retrace her words. *...open up, but it doesn't mean that I don't want to. It doesn't mean I don't love you as much as I do...*Gwen looked at him shyly. "...Oops."

He stepped to her and scooped her up by the waist, "*Oops,* huh? Is that a retraction?" He kissed her before she answered. Gwen could taste his joy at hearing her words.

She held his face. "No retraction. I meant it."

"Yeah?" he whispered, seriously.

More tears flowed. "Yeah."

"That's good to know." He wiped away her tears, then gently kissed her lips.

"Is it?" she asked. He hadn't said it back and now she worried if maybe she spoke too quickly. Not that it really mattered. She loved him; it was a fact that wasn't going to change anytime soon.

Xavier nodded. "Come here," he said, taking her hand and leading her to the full-length mirror she had in her room. He turned her around toward the mirror and there they were reflected, a portrait of two young people in their underwear. Xavier wrapped his arms around her waist, leaned down, and said, "I believe I've loved this, you, the us I see right now since the first time I saw you." He smiled and kissed the back of her head. Gwen turned away from the mirror, buried herself in his arms and cried some more.

That night they continued to dance, sometimes without music or laughter or discussion; occasionally one of them would utter "I love you," as if breaking it in, and the other would smile and reciprocate; each time they held each other tightly, as if sealing the commitment with the strength of their embrace.

That night Gwen lay in Xavier's arms, feeling the steady beat of his heart, the patient rise and fall of his chest against her cheek, his rhythmic breathing dance against her curls.

That night Gwen fought to keep her eyes open, not wanting to fall asleep, not wanting her perfect moment, this moment, as she lay in the arms of the man she loved, poisoned by any demons that might prey on her fragile slumber.

That night Gwen quietly wept, wiping her eyes and muffling her whimpers in the sheets. She felt happy, and she felt scared. She wanted Xavier; she loved Xavier, but things were moving too fast. She wanted them to slow down, needed them to slow down.

She began to drift and felt sleep kiss her goodnight without making any promises.

· ELEVEN ·

"Good thing I brought an evening outfit along. Who knew?" Payton held her hands out to the side and shrugged.

"*Uh-huh,*" Gwen said, her voice thick with disbelief.

Payton stood in Gwen's bedroom, the full-length mirror before her. She pulled an aubergine sarong dress over her hips, slipped her hands in the sleeves, and swung her blond hair forward, catching it around the front of her shoulder, out of the zipper's path. Gwen, already dressed in a basic black suit dress, zipped her up, then stepped back, folding her arms across her chest. Payton said, "Thank you," twinkling those baby blues and flashing her near-perfect teeth. Gwen couldn't help but smile back, although her best friend never failed to amaze her.

Payton had rocked into town in true Payton fashion. She showed up in Atlanta a day earlier than expected, arriving at Gwen's office door with Vaughn at her side. He said he had found her wandering the halls and thought he'd give her a personal escort just to make sure she didn't get lost. Payton greeted a surprised Gwen with a hug, a kiss, and a typically cryptic, original Paytonist explanation: "I didn't want to travel on Friday, spooky vibes." She wiggled her fingers with ghost-like drama and laughed. Gwen laughed too, giving her another hug, thinking her best friend was like an earthquake on a sunny day—always unexpected and destined to shake things up, yet still warm and bright, oblivious to the effect she was having on people in her path.

Namely Vaughn. He stood at the door, his hands shoved deep in his pockets, smiling. Gwen hadn't seen him smile in months, not like he was smiling at Payton. But who could blame him? The sight of Payton made most men smile. Tall, a couple of inches taller than

Gwen's own five-eight, Payton had bouncy, healthy, and very blond hair that fell just above her shoulder blades, and was usually worn down to cover her ears, which she described as "Dumbo comes south" or "Dumbo goes East" depending on her current geographical setting. She was slightly pigeon-toed, which made her stride rather clunky, but Payton made sure she measured her steps, not moving too fast unless absolutely necessary—that way she looked like she walked with purpose, instead of trying to keep herself from falling flat on her face. Her figure was full and shapely—she refused to starve herself in an attempt to fit into a single-digit size. She'd been that route before and knew that a size six on her body turned out to be very unflattering. She happily accepted her size-ten shape, knowing that it looked better and felt better, and said it suited her just fine. And her personality radiated, illuminated, damn near blinded anyone who came close.

Payton didn't seem to be paying much attention, but Gwen couldn't help but notice that Vaughn, who remained standing at the door awaiting a formal introduction, looked as if he should have been standing on a street corner wearing dark sunglasses and holding a tin cup.

"Well, how do I look?" Payton took a few steps backward, standing beside Gwen, still looking in the mirror.

"You look good. I expect Vaughn will be drooling in his soup." Gwen laughed.

"Oh stop it. It was very nice of him to invite me, but really I think he just did it because he didn't want you to feel guilty about going out while I was in town. You know, poor me, all by my lonesome." Payton poked out her bottom lip in a feigned pout.

Gwen rolled her eyes. "Uh-huh."

"Gwen, you should have told me you had plans tonight, I would never have showed up at your office, making the whole situation so awkward."

"It slipped my mind. But it's no big deal. I'm glad you're here. It'll be fun." Gwen walked up to the mirror and checked her make-up again. She looked at Payton and smiled.

"You sure?" Payton asked seriously.

"Of course. When have we not had fun?"

Payton relaxed. "You've got a point there. Good, as long as you want me there, I feel better. And the Sun Dial restaurant—now that's what I call a first-rate appreciation dinner. Your boss has extremely good taste." Payton swung her hair as she headed out the bedroom door. Gwen laughed while following close behind, leaving another "uh-huh" in the air. They hustled downstairs and into the car, still talking.

"But you know Gwen, you never told me your boss was so cute." Payton slanted her gaze, seductively, as Gwen pulled out of the garage.

"Hmm, I thought I did. You know, somewhere between he's got two kids and a wife," Gwen teased, trying to drive a point home for clarification's sake.

"Oh yeah, kids...wife. Hmmm." Payton mulled for a minute. "I guess he just forgot to put his wedding band on this morning. I hear that happens."

"Payton..."

"Hey, I'm not asking for any personal gain. Look, I am very proud of the fact that I have an impressive track record of never, I repeat *never,* having been involved with a married man." Payton flailed her hands out to the side. "Although the down side is that my track record has consisted of a long list of *losers.*" This time she L-shaped her fingers in front of Gwen's face.

Gwen nodded in agreement, then laughed. "Well, I wouldn't categorize Vaughn as a loser. More like a man who seems to be going through change."

"Hmmm. Tough. Nice guy?"

"Yeah. I can honestly say that Vaughn's a very good person to work for. Oh, he does have a tendency to get on my nerves sometimes, but for the most part he's a pretty decent guy." Gwen swung onto Vermack and headed south toward the Perimeter, I-285.

"So what's going on with him?" Payton flipped down the passenger-side mirror and began doing facial exercises.

"Oh, I don't know. I mean I've heard some of the office gossip,

but that's usually so liquored up, it reeks by the time it's completely circulated. All I know is that whatever the hell is going on, he ain't happy. Today was the happiest I have seen him in a long time. Girl, you've got skills."

"Me? I think not. You probably just caught him on a good day. But I will admit that my showing up at your office wasn't completely without motive. I did kind of want to see some of the Talbot characters I've heard so much about over the years—you know, Shayla, Miss Mabel. Hell, I only saw Miss Mabel, and I don't think it was long enough for me to get the full effect, but one out of two ain't bad. Xavier and Vaughn were an added bonus."

"Yeah, Shayla and I aren't exactly bathroom buddies anymore. She barely says two words to me. But life does go on."

"Indeed it does. You know, it's OK if you and Xavier want to spend some time together, alone, before he heads out of town. I am not one to stand in the way of a progressing love affair...oh, and good sex." She giggled. "But really, I mean it."

Gwen mumbled, "Uh-huh," caught up in deep thought about her time with Xavier last night—actually, in the wee hours of the morning. She could still hear him telling her he loved her, still hear them both alternately chanting and whispering, "I love you" through their moans. It seemed to add an extra zing to their already skyrocketing sex life. Their relationship seemed to be getting better all the time. So why was she so worried the walls could cave in at any moment?

"Earth to Gwen...come in, please." Payton snapped her fingers in Gwen's face. Gwen blushed. Payton smiled grandly. "Looks to me like someone's good has been turned upside down, or is it right side up?"

They arrived at the Peachtree Plaza. The car slowed to a stop and was greeted by a valet, and Gwen looked at Payton and bashfully responded, "Um, it's pretty damn upright."

They high-fived and laughed.

Xavier stood at the bar looking like he'd walked out of the pages of *Black Enterprise* in his coal black suit with a gold tie. Gwen and Payton

approached, still chuckling from more girl talk. Xavier greeted Gwen with a soft peck on the cheek—not exactly professional, but not suspect either.

"Hey you." Gwen beamed.

"Hey *you*. You look nice." He took a quick head-to-toe of her, then winked. "Real nice." Xavier stood, his grin an almost mirror image of Gwen's. They both had only slept about three hours last night, but they glowed like two new pennies.

He turned his attention to Payton, who stood beside them, majestically crinkling her smile, obviously thrilled her best friend had found love. "Payton, it's good to see you again, since what...four hours ago?" Xavier held his hand out and squeezed Payton's.

Payton laughed, telling him, "It's good to see you, too," then glanced at Gwen with a quick flex of the eyebrows, a sign Gwen knew as Payton's "you go girl" look of approval.

Xavier spoke again. "Vaughn's upstairs in the private dining hall, making sure everything is set. I told him I'd be on the lookout for you two. So baby, you ready to go play professional?" He reached out to touch her, a hesitant caress of her cheek, before quickly realizing he had better play it safe. He blushed a bit; Gwen blushed too and said, "Let's do it," while Payton soaked it all up with a cheesy grin.

Thirty minutes into the dinner and everyone seemed to be getting along swimmingly. Too swimmingly. Gwen took a moment to survey the party. Xavier as usual was charismatic, ingratiating, and full of ready dialogue. Gwen rather enjoyed watching him in action while they played the professional role, the way he handled himself, the way he walked the walk and talked the talk. It turned her on.

Occasionally, they would glance at each other and let the look linger; she would smile, methodically reducing it to a closed-mouth, full-lip pout, which in essence emaciated Xavier's broad grin into the ever-tantalizing look of romance.

It was doubtful Vaughn even noticed. He could hardly take his eyes off Payton, who was simply Payton—witty, engaging, and on. All the way on. Full blast. But one thing was definite: a party initially designed for business had somehow, without question, become a double date.

"So Payton, you're a psychiatrist. That's a pretty complicated field. What made you choose it? If that's not too personal," Vaughn asked, lifting a glass of Villa Antinori chianti to his lips; the entire bottle was resting off on the side, and everyone was reaping the benefits. Even Xavier had abandoned his standard Heineken for the night.

Payton nibbled off a piece of shrimp and smiled cunningly. "Actually, I'm a psychologist; and you're not trying to imply that the field might be too complicated for a woman, are you?" Classic Payton, answering a question with a question.

Gwen glanced at Xavier, who raised an eyebrow while tasting a spoonful of French onion soup.

Vaughn turned to face Payton, intrigued and apologetic. "Of course not, I wouldn't think of implying such a thing. It was really an innocent question; I guess I didn't preface it in a politically correct manner. I didn't mean to offend you. I'm sorry."

Payton released her serious face and smiled brightly. "Aw, I was just pulling your chain. Well, let's see..."

Gwen and Xavier snickered; Vaughn looked taken off-guard, possibly thinking he had truly done some offensive damage, and then smiled as if someone had just thrown a warm blanket over him after a very cold rain.

Payton rambled a bit about her history: her mother, herself a highly reputable psychiatrist in Charleston, and Payton's own early childhood declaration to never venture close to the mental health field, having been subjected to it for so many years. But then she found herself always on the listening end of her friends' woes: some, serious issues; others, normal teenage traumas that felt critical at the time just because no one knew any different. Yet, she never felt satisfied just listening, or giving some condescending statement equivalent to "get over it." No, she wanted to help, really help.

"So, I guess, you could say the profession chose me." Payton polished off her first glass and shrugged.

"Very interesting. And you practice in Boston?" Vaughn asked, still smiling, still intrigued.

"Just outside of Boston in Belmont. I'm on the staff at McLean Hospital,"

"I've heard of it. Quite impressive. They're affiliated with Mass General, aren't they?" Vaughn asked.

Payton jutted the corners of her mouth downward in amazement, "Why yes. Now *I'm* quite impressed. Are you just naturally familiar with hospitals and their affiliates, or are habitats for psychosis a little hobby of yours?" Payton teased, obviously becoming taken with Vaughn. Gwen knew her too well, and she and Xavier watched the bantering back and forth like it was tennis match.

Vaughn chuckled, "Not really. Um, my wife is originally from Massachusetts and her father is a retired neurosurgeon. I know of McLean's reputation. I guess you could say more by association than by trade." He raised his glass to Payton. She nodded with a smile.

"Hmmm, your wife wasn't able to join us tonight?" Payton nibbled another shrimp and caught Gwen's stare. She slanted her gaze and smiled. Gwen shook her head and smiled back, a sly grin; she knew the fishing expedition was about to begin.

Vaughn squirmed a bit before issuing, "Uh, no." He offered no more.

"Oh." Payton swallowed, then went to nibble again, but stopped. "Do you have children...if I'm not being too personal?" She knew the answer to this, but in order to fish effectively she pretended she didn't. Gwen fiddled with her napkin, still slightly grinning. *Payton, girl, you are a trip...*

"Oh no, you're fine. Yes, I have twin sons—Jeffrey and Jason. They're great boys. Really great. Um, I'll have them this weekend and, um...," Vaughn paused, obviously realizing his statement carried a bit of mystery. "My wife and I are going through a divorce." He squirmed again, then gulped some more chianti.

"Oh, I'm sorry to hear that," Payton said, bait taken, fish on the hook. But Vaughn looked pained. Payton studied him for a second, then looked at Gwen, at which time she curled one side of her mouth inward and widened her eyes in remorse. A classic Payton-oops, knowing she had carried it too far. But that was Payton. Silence took over for a few minutes.

"Well, it's a little too quiet for my blood," Vaughn finally announced. He called for the waiter to fill everyone's glass, then he held his high. "I'd like to make a toast to Gwen and Xavier. I must say I am truly honored to have you two with the firm. I knew you'd be an exceptional team."

Gwen and Xavier both said "Thank you" while Payton said "Hear, hear" as if she were a member of the firm, too. They all drank to a job well done and more years of prosperity. Gwen and Xavier looked at each other: exceptional team indeed.

The conversation continued to flow without interruption except for a somber moment of silence when Payton brought up the death of Princess Di; Payton idolized her, and Gwen would have to admit she admired the princess herself. After that, most of the chatter was lively, led mainly by Payton and Gwen, the old friends in the group, but with the two men participating plenty as well.

No issue was left untouched. Everything from critical entertainment opinions: "If Jenny McCarthy can have her own show, then I should definitely have enough material for at least a miniseries, if just on armpit noises alone," Payton contributed.

To movie picks: "I hope I don't offend anyone when I say *Sling Blade* was one of the best white trash movies I have ever seen," Gwen offered, receiving a round of "hear, hear" from the group.

To deep medical issues: "Bipolar disorders, related to manic episodes, are much more common than the average person would like to imagine. I think when the public comes in contact with episodic people they naturally assume that the person is simply being overly dramatic, or eccentric, or just plain moody, when there could very well be a larger mental issue at stake." With that said, Payton turned the trivial conversation more serious. The girl had skills. Once again the table was silent. It didn't last long.

Soon the men began to dominate the conversation. First a bit on politics, then a little on business, before finally settling on the topic Gwen hated most: sports. She had to admit, sports was the one pitfall to her and Xavier's relationship. He loved sports, every type, regardless of the season. And Gwen secretly liked the fact that his business

travels and his devotion to spending time with her diluted his desire to catch live events. That would eventually change, as time wore on, but she tried not to worry about the future. She probably needed to; sometimes she feared she probably really, *really* needed to.

"Xavier, do you ever see any of your old college basketball team-mates? You know, The Team," Vaughn asked. Xavier smiled. Gwen cringed.

"Well, not really. We used to keep in touch quite a bit, right after college. But you know how that goes..." Xavier finished the sentence with a wave of his hand. He relaxed back, smoothing out his tie. "The last time all of us were together was at Squeak's wedding back in '91."

Squeak...

Gwen frowned, thinking what a peculiar nickname, but not quite remembering a Squeak being one of The Team. Payton smiled at her a little, trying to gauge Gwen's reaction. Vaughn laughed out loud.

"Squeak? Who on earth is that? I don't remember a Squeak," Vaughn bellowed.

"I don't expect you do. His real name is Eric Summers and he was second string, really more like third. He was a junior our senior year. And if you ever heard him laugh, you'd know why we called him Squeak. It was a real high-pitched...well, squeak."

Gwen dropped her fork hard onto her plate.

Squeak...a high-pitched laugh. Oh God...

"Sorry, it slipped." Gwen smiled weakly, her heart beating so loud she could hardly hear her own voice. Payton issued a look of concern, completely in line with Gwen's realization. This Eric Summers had been the one cheering Terry on during the rape.

Xavier smiled at her, unaware, then continued, "Yeah, Eric was one wild guy. Terry sort of adopted him as the honorary sixth member of The Team. He idolized us—well, really he idolized Terry, who took all of The Team business much more seriously than the rest of us. What started as a media compliment sort of turned into an ego circus. Of course we all kind of bought into it, but Terry...well anyway, that was Terry." Xavier chuckled dryly.

"You know, it's a shame about Terry. *The Man,*" Vaughn gruffed

the nickname from his lips, making Terry sound larger than life. Gwen began gritting her teeth. Vaughn finished, "He had so much talent. I guess I shouldn't talk about him in the past tense—he still has talent. Seems it's gotten a bit sidelined in the past few years, though. Surely the two of you still keep in touch?"

Gwen looked at Xavier, who glanced her way as well. "Not really. You know how those things go..." Xavier again left the explanation without an explanation. Gwen looked at him intently. He looked at her and winked. She softened a little and smiled.

"Yeah, I guess," Vaughn replied, sounding as if the news was heartbreaking. He looked to Gwen and then to Payton. "Do you ladies follow sports much?"

"No," Gwen stated without elaboration, sipping some more chianti.

Payton began to talk. "You know, basketball's never been my thing. No offense, Xavier, I'm sure you were quite good. But it's too fast. All that back and forth, up the court, down the court, between the legs, in your face, a fight squeezed in for added drama. Whoa, it makes me dizzy." The table laughed. She continued, "I'm more of a baseball fan, you know, slower pace, tighter uniforms, less sweat, greener scenery. It even seems as if they're spitting less these days..." again Payton mulled. "...OK, maybe not. But anyway, baseball is my sport of choice. *Salute!*" Payton crinkled her smile and held a spoonful of tiramisu up high before slipping it in her mouth. As everyone else laughed some more, Gwen smiled, thankful to Payton for deflecting the topic.

"Baby, Payton seems to be the belle of the ball," Xavier murmured, as he inched his chair closer to Gwen.

"That's just vintage Payton. I knew she'd turn the dinner into a festival. I'm glad she's here." Gwen smiled, taking her hand and slipping it under the table, resting it on Xavier's thigh. "I'm glad you're here, too."

They still sat at the table, while Vaughn and Payton took a tour of the Sun Dial's spectacular view of the city. It was Vaughn's idea, and he asked if Gwen and Xavier wanted to join them. They declined, saying

they had seen it, but insisted he give Payton the grand tour, which he did without hesitation.

"Hmmm, this was nice. But I'm glad I kinda got you to myself, for a while at least." Xavier stroked her hand, rubbing it lightly with his fingers. "You got a little quiet on us there for a while. Still worried about seeing your brother?"

"I guess." Gwen looked down. He touched her cheek, a bold move, but a move Gwen needed. She looked at him and smiled. "Xavier, think you can stand some late-night company on Sunday, you know, before you leave on Monday morning? I got one free pass from Payton. She'd never want to stand in the way of a 'progressing love affair,'" Gwen whispered with a giggle.

Xavier nodded; his eyes danced. "Oh, I think I can stand it." He winked, then moved his face a little closer to hers. "I love you, Gwendolyn."

"I love you."

She wanted to touch him, to kiss him, but feared they had probably already gone too far. Not that Vaughn would have a problem with their relationship, but tonight was not the night to announce it. They pulled apart from each other, noticing Vaughn and Payton in the distance, talking, laughing, and obviously doing some progressing of their own.

Gwen could see the television on in the den as she slowly walked down the stairs. Conan O'Brien being goofy, as usual. Gwen tightened the belt of her paisley robe and walked around the front of the couch. Payton lay across it, her hair sprawled like a scarf blowing in the breeze. She stared at the television without blinking, looking as if she were consumed in deep thought, until she finally noticed Gwen.

"Oh, hey. Is the TV too loud?" Payton sat up, hitting the volume of the TV lower. It was already barely audible.

Gwen sat on the couch beside her. Payton curled her feet up further; Gwen crossed hers Indian style. "The TV's fine. What time did you get in?" Gwen asked of Payton's evening out.

"'Bout an hour ago."

"Hmmm. Have fun?"

Payton looked at her and smiled unevenly. "Uh, yeah. I did."

Gwen nodded. They sat in silence. Pamela Anderson, Conan's guest, cooed and jiggled in playful fashion.

Finally Payton rose up and stretched. She took the brush she had set on the coffee table and began stroking her hair. Gwen held her hand out, requesting she do the honors, and Payton relinquished with glee. With Payton sitting on the floor in front of her, Gwen began to brush. It was like playing with Barbie.

"Boy, this visit went fast. Can you believe it's already time for me to go?"

"It sure as hell snuck up on us," Gwen agreed, already missing Payton.

Tomorrow was Thursday and Payton would be boarding a plane to South Carolina, finishing the rest of the week with family. Gwen wasn't due back at work until Monday, and the time off she had spent dining, laughing, and having a great time with Payton had felt like liberation. It felt like their time in college, except better. Gwen, for one, could now claim to be much more fun to be around.

Payton dropped her head back, "And thanks for my one free pass."

"My pleasure. Just returning the favor for Sunday." Gwen continued to brush. "So, how *was* your date with Vaughn?"

"Hmmm, fine. Yeah, it was nice." Payton spoke softly. Gwen wasn't going to ask more than she needed to know. Payton stayed silent for a few minutes.

"He cares for his wife, you know?" Payton offered.

"Does he?"

"Yeah."

"So what did he do, give you the standard, 'my wife doesn't understand me' statement?"

"No. More like, he would keep his family together if he could. But his wife has other plans. Plans he doesn't understand and hasn't been made a part of. She doesn't love him anymore and pretty much said so in a four-page 'Dear John, see ya later' letter."

"You're kidding."

"Nope."

"Oh, damn." *Poor Vaughn,* Gwen thought. "Did you two spend all night talking about his wife?"

"No," Payton laughed. "But if we didn't, we probably would have ended up in bed." She laughed again.

"Oh. Hmmm." Gwen mused. "So what does he want to do?"

"Hell, I don't think he knows. He thinks there's another man in his wife's life, but he doesn't have any proof and he's not sure if he really wants to know. She's back in the house with the boys and he's moved out and they're trying to be civil for the boys' sake. That's where all the emotion comes in. Sometimes the boys seem to be holding up fine, then other times they alternate between blaming Vaughn or their mother. They're all confused." Payton paused. "Hell, he made me all confused."

"You're really into him, huh?"

"Yeah. He's like you said. Real decent. And damn if he ain't a good kisser." Payton chuckled.

"Oh really?" Gwen asked, amused.

"Hey, we didn't spend *all* night talking. There was some serious face-sucking going on." She turned around and flexed her eyebrows, "Some damn good face-sucking." Payton laughed and held her hand high, which Gwen high-fived with an "I heard that," and they laughed like schoolgirls. Payton assumed her original position and Gwen resumed brushing.

"But..." Gwen asked.

Payton sighed. "But I'd be wise to let it run its course. Plus, I've outgrown my one-night stand days, you know, kinda decided I need to effectively go through the pomp and circumstance of courtship before I vote a man valedictorian. Although Vaughn was definitely *up* for the challenge, and I was pretty hot to get my groove on too. But then what? Yeah, that 'then what' is what made me stop swallowing his tongue." Payton tried to laugh, but the mood didn't call for it. "And besides, he's still, technically, a married man, and I've got to uphold my stellar losers-only track record." Payton attempted another unconvincing laugh. She sighed again. "Vaughn's not ready for

a new relationship. He thinks he is. But...but he's too bogged down with...stuff. His own stuff. And I don't want to influence any decisions he may come up with."

"Hmmm, I think by the way he responded to you the other night, the damage may already be done." Gwen stopped brushing.

Payton joined her on the couch. "Well, let's just say I'm not going to further complicate things by being the aggressor. But there is something about him. Real something. The stuff that counts." Payton grabbed a handful of her hair, pulling it away from her forehead.

"Anyhoo, we'll see how it goes. He asked if he could call me sometime, maybe shoot me an email, and I said sure. Another phone partner. Go figure. Speaking of phone partners—talk to Xavier tonight?"

"Of course. In fact, I had just gotten off the phone with him before I came downstairs." Gwen wrapped her arms around her shoulders.

Payton leaned over and hugged her. "Hmmm, that man *loooooves* you, sister girlfriend. It practically oozes out of his pores."

"Yeah, he does," Gwen acknowledged quietly. "And I love him."

"Duh, I think I knew that a long time ago." Payton threw her head off to one side, valley-girlish.

Gwen blushed, then tightened her face.

"So why do you look like that's bad news?" Payton stared at her.

Gwen sighed loudly. "'Cause it's getting harder to justify my silence."

"About..."

"Yeah, about the rape." Gwen raked her hair. "I've kind of backed myself into a corner and now I'm in that damned if I do, damned if I don't position." Gwen tried to smile; the attempt brought tears.

"It's still such a struggle, isn't it?" Payton's eyes puddled too.

"Um. I guess...a little."

"Well, you two are together, in love...he *loves* you, Gwen. That in itself carries a lot of weight. Say you told him. How do you think he'd react?"

Gwen wiped her face. "I don't know." She looked at Payton. "And that scares the shit out of me."

· TWELVE ·

Thanksgiving Day, Gwen sat across from Weldon as he gra-
ciously volunteered to bless the food. Nana, seated at the head
of the formal dining table (big enough to sit eight), smiled in that
fat-cheeked, perky way of hers and nodded. Her grandbabies, Weld
and Gwenny, were home; that's all this seventy-eight-year-old woman
could have asked for.

Gwen had promised herself before she left Atlanta that she would
not think negatively; she would not spoil her Nana's joy, and she
would not, no matter how much Weldon tried to push her buttons,
she would absolutely *not* pick a fight and have to kick his ass. Or
vice versa.

Weldon began the grace, "Dear Lord, thank you..."

Gwen raised her head and opened her eyes to get a good look at
him while no one else was watching. She squinted her eyes and studied
him like an ink blot, trying to figure out if he seemed truly reformed.
Like she'd know.

He looked healthier, at least in the weight department; last time
she saw him, she guessed he weighed under one hundred and fifty
pounds, which for Weldon—who stood six-two—made him look in
dire need of meat and potatoes, in mass quantities. He still appeared
thin, but not sickly thin. His dark hair, slightly grayed at the temples,
lay on his head in soft waves, cut low with a two-inch rat tail in the
back. Gwen thought tails went out years ago, but whatever. It used to
be a mangled afro mop, at a time when afros weren't quite back in style
yet, but back then regular haircuts and hygiene weren't at the top of
Weldon's to-do list. That was another thing; he smelled better. Thank

194

God. His brown skin looked muddied in spots, something Nana would blame on too little vegetables and not enough water intake. He didn't look jittery or bug-eyed, so maybe he had recovered, or maybe he was just recovered for the day.

So much for negative thoughts. Gwen bowed her head quickly, then raised it and murmured "Amen" as the grace came to an end.

Weldon looked up, directly at her, and stared for a few moments, much as he had when she arrived last night. When she got to Nana's house, Weldon had opened the door and just stood, staring at her. She mumbled, "Hey," he mumbled, "Um, hey Gwen," and she walked past him to greet Nana. Weldon asked "How ya been?"; she said, "Good," and then he retreated to his room for the rest of the night. Nana hugged her again and whispered, "Give him time," to which Gwen replied, "He can have all he needs, I'm in no hurry." Bob Marley's reggae rhythm preached softly through the walls of Weldon's room for the rest of the night. Gwen locked her bedroom door and slept with her Glock where she could reach it; she would be foolish to take Weldon at face value after all the past drama.

Now he sat still at the table, staring at her. Gwen stretched her eyes and gave a *knock that shit off* smirk, and Weldon grunted and they both began to dig into the grub.

Nana's Thanksgiving feast—a twelve-pound turkey, gravy, glazed ham, macaroni and cheese, collards, shrimp salad, homemade yeast rolls, corn on the cob, and sweetened iced tea—spread across the entire length of the table like the Last Supper. She still cooked as if preparing to feed the whole family, like years ago, when there was her only daughter, Maxine, Gwen and Weldon's mother; their father, Weldon Sr.; Gwen and Weldon; and Nana's only son, Uncle Earvin, and his wife, who had never had children. Also there had been Nana's husband, Gwen's granddaddy, who passed away eighteen years ago from the combined poisons of a toxic disposition and an alcohol-eroded liver. If it hadn't been for Nana, all the money they'd made from selling acres of family-owned land to developers would have drowned in a bottle right with Grandaddy. But Nana had never been a fool; she just claimed

to have married one. She invested well and lived a quiet, secure life, content with traveling and spoiling her only grandchildren.

"Gwenny's got someone special in her life," Nana stated proudly, directing this comment to Weldon in her soft, church-lady voice. Nana didn't look seventy-eight; there was nary a wrinkle on her chubby, round face. Her hair, pulled behind her ears with a bobby pin on each side, looked like waves of hand-spun silver, and she was almost as wide as she was tall, which was just above five feet.

Weldon grunted again at Nana's announcement, nodding his head while he sopped up turkey and gravy with a roll. Gwen smirked again.

"When am I gonna meet him, sweetie?" Now Nana looked at Gwen.

Gwen rushed a swallow of mac and cheese before replying, "Soon, I hope. He travels a lot and he just got back from New York last night. He was thinking of maybe driving up tomorrow, but some kind of emergency has come up and he's going to Philadelphia later on tonight." Gwen issued a small look of disappointment and stacked some collards on her fork.

She had talked to Xavier last night; he called her on her cell phone as soon as he arrived back in Atlanta, en route to his condo from the airport. He asked how things were going with Weldon and said he couldn't stop worrying about her, or thinking about her, or wanting to see her. Gwen felt that now-familiar and welcome rush of warmth talking to him as she lay curled up in her old childhood bed; she told him she was fine, not to worry, and that she missed him something awful, too. They hadn't seen each other in almost three weeks, so when he offered to drive to Augusta later Thanksgiving day, Gwen said, "Now, that sounds like a plan..." But plans quickly changed.

Xavier had called her back early this morning sounding distraught. One of his NBA assistant coaches, apparently one who meant a lot to Xavier, had passed away suddenly. Xavier had gotten the message when he'd returned home late last night; the funeral would be in the coach's hometown of Philadelphia on Saturday. Xavier apologized for the abrupt change in plans. Gwen told him, "Baby, I understand. You

gonna be OK? Do you want me to come with you?" Xavier said he'd be all right; he appreciated the offer, but he'd be leaving Philadelphia after the funeral and heading directly to his next due diligence in Portland. Luckily the assignment would only last a week. He said he'd call to let her know where he'd be staying in Philly and Portland. Gwen had hoped to see him before he left for that assignment, but now it looked as if she and Xavier wouldn't be making any connections until the first part of December. A long time. Gwen could tell by the thick sighs of grief he released that his coach's death hit Xavier hard.

"You say he works with you, Gwenny?" Nana asked, still trying to engage her in conversation.

Gwen nodded, with a mouthful of food, before getting out a "Yes ma'am."

"What's he, the boss?" Weldon said a devilish smile, knowing his comment was smart-ass.

Gwen rolled her eyes. "No...stupid," the insult thrown in simply because she felt like it.

Weldon looked up, Gwen jerked her head out in a challenge, but Nana nipped it short.

"All right now, you two." Nana looked at both of them, an authoritative charge in her voice. Then it softened again. "What's his name again, sweetie?" She looked at Gwen.

"Xavier, Nana."

"Ooh, that's a strong name." Nana widened her eyes and glowed.

Weldon grunted. "A masculine name, huh, Nana? Told you I didn't think she was a dyke."

"Wha—?" Gwen bristled, her eyes widening.

"Weld, don't you start and don't be using that language in my house, boy," Nana reprimanded, her face tinted with embarrassment.

"What the—what are you talking about, Weldon?" Gwen knew cursing wasn't allowed either, but she was tired of his shit already. Another promise busted.

Weldon smiled, revealing his chipped and broken front teeth—ruined from years of smoking crack through aluminum cans. "Nana been wondering if maybe you was sniffing up someone's dress."

Gwen's mouth fell open. Nana raised her voice. "Weld, stop talkin' nonsense."

Weldon turned to Nana, "Nana, it's all right, you can stop frontin'. You know you used to be scared Gwen ain't like men. Go ahead and tell her. We all family."

Nana shooed him with her hand, "Boy, I ain't foolin' with your nonsense." She went back to eating, clearly nervous.

Gwen wanted to reach across the table and slap the taste out of Weldon's mouth, until she looked at him. He looked back at her with a devilish grin, and Gwen began to recognize that person. He resembled the Weldon of old, the one whose cutting sense of humor spared no one. At one time it had seemed like Weldon could have been a comic, along with the great ones he'd always idolized: Richard Pryor, Redd Fox, Richard Pryor, Franklin Ajaye, Richard Pryor, Eddie Murphy, Richard Pryor, Richard Pryor. Now, although the joke was being fueled at her expense, she decided to play along.

"Nana, is that really what you thought?" Gwen asked, pretending to be hurt.

Nana looked at her. "Don't you pay your brother no mind. Just because you wear your hair so short and you never talked about bringing any nice fellows around and you was always talking about your good friend Paysley, that don't mean I thought you was one of them kind of girls. Naw, sweetie, don't you worry." Nana reached across the table and patted her hand, then went back to nibbling.

Gwen looked at Weldon and thought she would burst into laughter. They held it together a bit longer.

Gwen reached for Nana's hand again and looked her dear grandmother in the eye. "Nana, those girls are called lesbians, and no, believe me, I'm not part of the club." She patted her hand and they all sat quietly.

Nana began to mumble through nibbles, "I know that, sweetie..."

More nibbles, "Your brother always trying to start somethin'..."

More nibbles, "I know my grandbabies better than anyone..."

More nibbles, then Nana stopped, looked up at Gwen, her face

looking a bit bewildered, and asked in all sincerity, "Sweetie…they got a club?"

Gwen and Weldon both lost it at the same time.

After dinner, Weldon volunteered to help Gwen with the dishes.

He sure is doing a whole lot of volunteering, Gwen thought, but she didn't discourage him. She did feel, however, with Nana in her room for an afternoon nap, that the time was due for the bitter fireworks to start between her and Weldon.

They stood at the sink. Gwen washed; Weldon rinsed and dried. Silence reigned through two china plates and a saucer. Finally Weldon cleared his throat.

"You like being back in Atlanta?"

Gwen nodded, "Uh-huh."

"Nana said you doing good in your job and all." Weldon grabbed a heavy drinking glass from her hand.

"Uh-huh." Gwen paused, drowning another glass in suds. "You're not here to put her through more shit, are you Weldon?" She handed him the glass and looked at him. Might as well fire the first shot.

He grunted. "I ain't plan on. I been clean for 'bout eight months." He didn't get combative, as Gwen would have expected. At first she said nothing, then she said, "That's good."

He muttered, "Uh-huh."

They washed more dishes in silence.

"So where you been?" Gwen asked.

"Around."

"Around? Doing what?" Gwen held another glass out to him. He didn't take it. This prompted her to look at him.

"Doin'?"

Gwen placed the glass in the adjacent sink, "Yeah…doing. You've been gone four years."

"Four years." He said this as if it was news to him, "Umph. Seemed to me just like one long-ass day." He grabbed the glass out of the sink and rinsed it.

Gwen shook her head and looked away. He wasn't going to answer her question; hell, he probably didn't even know all of the where, when, and what of the past four years, or of his survival. And Gwen probably didn't want to know it, even if he did.

"You ever go see them?" Weldon asked quietly.

Gwen knew he meant their parents. "Uh-huh." She braced herself for the war.

They were both quiet.

Their parents were buried in LaGrange, Georgia, their father's small hometown fifty miles west of Atlanta. Gwen visited every few months, placed flowers on their grave, talked to them, apologized to them, cried for them and for herself.

"I guess if I asked how they were doing, the answer would still be dead, huh?" Weldon rinsed some more and grunted again.

Gwen closed her eyes, silently counted to five, and breathed out, slow and methodical, before letting loose. "Don't start, Weldon. I know it all—I killed them; I'm the uppity-ass bitch who only thought of herself, had to have my way, either my way or no way, and Mama and Daddy are dead because of it. Did I cover everything?" Gwen threw the dishcloth in the sink; suds flew up. She crossed her arms and turned to face him, leaning against the counter. Weldon shook his head and stared at her without speaking.

"And what the hell you keeping looking at?" Gwen leaned into him; she pushed the sleeves of her gray silk turtleneck up further, ready for him to bring it on.

Weldon looked undaunted. "You look just like her, that's all. Just like Mama. The shit is scary." He smiled, crooked and pathetic. "You gonna hand me another plate or what?" He held his hand out and grunted.

Gwen relaxed in stages, drawing her hands down, then loosening her posture before sinking her hands back in the basin and retrieving another bowl. More silence followed.

Weldon chuckled before saying, "Gwen, remember that time Mama straight up busted us watching Richard Pryor in concert on cable?"

Gwen laughed a little. "Man, we thought we were slick. Sneaking

back in the den, leaving the lights off. Hell, it took you ten minutes just to pull the TV knob, so it wouldn't be so loud. And we still got busted."

"Yep. Damn, how old were we?" Weldon gave her a sideways glance.

"Oh hell, it was in '77, or was it '78? I don't know, I guess I was about ten or so. As usual I was following *your* lead. Should have known we'd get caught. Mama always did sleep like a cat."

"Gwenny, remember she came stumbling in the den like a damn zombie. Her head all tied up, lookin' sleepy and shit. Walked in right when Pryor was talkin' about shootin' his damn car. How'd it go—'I told my wife if she was gonna be leavin' me, she'd be riding them damn Hush Puppies she had on'—or somethin' like that. That was funny as hell. And here come Mama. Looked at us and just shook her head, then walked up to the TV, turned that bad boy off and walked right on out. I was tempted to turn that mug right back on."

"Uh-huh. But we knew we were in for it. So what'd we do—we followed her ass right on out."

Gwen and Weldon nodded and laughed. Silence befell them again.

"I was supposed to be with Daddy that night, not Mama." He rinsed the same glass over again.

Gwen looked up at him. "Huh?"

"That night. Mama told me to go with Daddy to look for your ass. I told her 'Hell naw,' I had things to do. She told me to just go on with my selfish self, and she went with Daddy. Daddy said he could go by himself, told her to stay home. But you know Mama..." Weldon's voice trailed.

Gwen stopped washing. Weldon kept rinsing the same glass. Only the running water, the gurgle it made going down the drain, produced any sound in the room.

Weldon felt guilty, too.

Gwen exhaled hard, trying not to cry, trying to understand.

That night, after Weldon had retired to his room early in the evening, Gwen lay on the couch in the family room, wrapped in the quilt Nana

had made for her years ago. She and Weldon hadn't said much more after finishing the dishes. He went back to his room, and Bob Marley cued up again.

She lay with her head in Nana's lap as Nana stroked her hair in her slow, soothing way, babying her granddaughter with her familiar loving care.

After Gwen's parents died, Nana would comfort her many nights. She had lost her only daughter and a son-in-law she adored, yet still she found the strength to be there for her grandbabies. She would tell Gwen that all things happened for a reason; life had many lessons to teach and no one said they'd be learned the easy way. The ones most worth learning always came at a price—which was sometimes steep, and almost always painful. Nana's most familiar line had always been, "Life has no obligation to be fair; just to be life."

"You and your brother talked?" Nana asked.

Gwen nodded, "Yes, ma'am. A little."

She stared in the direction of the television set without paying it much attention. Some sort of Thanksgiving special was on—everyone looked festive and bright, singing and smiling. She tuned out again with a quick blink. Weldon *had* changed, it seemed, after fifteen-plus years of drug abuse and his own haunting memories. Demons lived in both of them; maybe he was finally winning the battle he was fighting against them. The old Weldon never could have said anything like what he'd told Gwen tonight.

Nana stroked Gwen's hair and said, "Weld starts a job on Monday, in carpentry, working with this old man who's willing to take a chance on him. His shop's down on Hawthorne Street. Your brother was always good with his hands, and thank the good Lord for some folk willing to see good in others."

"Yes, ma'am." Gwen's eyes closed; her Nana's hands felt blessed.

"He tell you about the group he's in, the drug reform group?"

"Uh, no ma'am. We didn't get around to that."

"Well, I don't know a whole lot about it, myself. I been with him a couple of times. The people seem real nice, hard to believe that some of them used to be all messed up with drugs and things. Got some real

young girls in there; old folks; white folks; black folks; I even saw an Asian fellow." Nana's voice pierced the quiet in awe. "There's another meeting tomorrow. Why don't you go with us?"

Gwen turned over, looking straight up at Nana. "If he asks me one day, then maybe I'll go. But I think Weldon and I need to take things one day at a time." Gwen held Nana's hand to her face and smiled. Nana nodded. Gwen turned back onto her side. Nana resumed stroking her hair.

"This Xavier good to you, Gwenny?"

"Yes ma'am, very."

"You love him?"

"Yes, ma'am, I do."

"You been going through things, sweetie. I may be old, but I know my grandbabies. You been going through things for a while."

Gwen closed her eyes again; they burned. "Yes, ma'am."

"I 'spect if you haven't told me about it in all these years, ain't no sense in me asking now. But you know me and my mouth, I'm going to say something anyhow."

"Yes, ma'am."

Nana tugged on Gwen's shoulder, and again Gwen turned to look up at her.

Nana stroked her face. The room was dark, illuminated slightly by the streetlights and the television. "Gwenny, it don't matter how much he loves you or how good he is to you; if you're not right with yourself, with who you are, then all his love and goodness can't make things all right. Love is powerful, but there are some miracles it just can't work."

Gwen closed her eyes as Nana leaned down and kissed her forehead.

"Yes, ma'am," she whispered.

· THIRTEEN ·

XAVIER WALKED INTO HIS CONDO, briefcase in hand and jacket over arm, looking weary from the flight. "Gwendolyn, baby, you upstairs?" he called without looking up. He flipped the light switch without even noticing the candles she'd lit around the place. Gwen had made sure she parked in the driveway so he would know she was there; she wanted to surprise him, not scare him to death.

She stood at the top of the stairs watching him. He was so handsome; his pinstriped dress shirt still looked fresh, though his tie was loosened at the neck.

He grabbed a handful of the mail Gwen had placed on the console and called her name again, "Gwendol—" He didn't finish it, finally noticing the hordes of candles blazing at every angle, lit for seduction and lightly scented for romance.

He smiled just as she hit the CD remote: Chanté Moore, her melodic voice flowing quietly like smooth water from a stream.

Gwen still didn't speak; she would wait for him to find her standing at the top of the stairs, barely dressed in a canary yellow butterfly print chemise. Her body glowed from silk bath oil; her feet were bare, delicately pampered from an early morning pedicure, and her curls were carefully strewn with white rose petals. This had taken her a couple of hours to achieve; dozens of petals were painstakingly threaded and woven throughout her hair like a floral tiara. The end result proved rewarding, in terms of the look on Xavier's face as he stood at the bottom of the steps, eyeing every inch of her; it was definitely worth all the effort.

He flipped the lights back off, clearly understanding the mood

didn't call for General Electric. She took a few steps down, standing three stair steps from the bottom, and he met her one stair below.

"Welcome home." Her voice whispered like the music. She reached out to touch his cheek, timorously; they hadn't made love in more than a month, and although she had planned this seduction, fully intending to show him exactly how much she had missed him, she suddenly felt incredibly shy. Xavier looked hesitant himself.

"It's good to be home, baby." He wrapped an arm around her waist and pulled her into him; the warmth of his hand pressed through the delicate taffeta fabric of her chemise. Gwen's arms swooped around his neck; both of his arms slipped around her waist as she pressed her body into his.

Something felt wrong.

As she pulled away, cradling his face in her hands, she said, "You OK, baby?" After all, he'd attended that funeral just a week ago; he hadn't talk about it much on the phone, but now, by the melancholy look on his face, it was obvious that it still weighed heavily on his mind.

He didn't answer immediately, just pulled her to him again, the hug transformed from gentle to powerful. "I'm fine, baby. I just missed you," he murmured into her hair. Her fingertips stroked the back of his head in circles, before moving gently down his neck. She kissed his cheek, slowly working her way to his lips. His tongue tasted of peppermint. She murmured, "I missed you too," inside his mouth. He pulled away, holding her hands up and stepping back to look again at what she had created.

"I like this." His eyes were rekindling; with the back of one hand, he swiftly traced his knuckles gently down the inside of her chemise, brushing between her legs, then drew them up gently across the front of her body. Her knees wobbled.

"Well, I didn't want to do the overdone black teddy. Thought I'd put a little color into it." She undid his tie and threw it over the banister, then began working on the shirt buttons. He remained on the stair below her, which made him easier to reach.

As she undressed him, she felt her desire expand inside of her.

She'd told herself before he arrived to be cool, but damn, all of that now seemed completely out of her control.

Xavier helped her with his cuff buttons and they kissed again, hard and fast, as the shirt floated to the floor. Xavier held her face, trying to keep her head steady as it bobbed and weaved wildly against his.

"Gwendolyn, baby..." Xavier's voice chopped at syllables, his breathing erratic.

Gwen didn't slow down. She mumbled "What" and kept tugging at his belt, feeling the prong give, then beginning an immediate assault on the trouser button.

"You want to slow down?" he asked, attempting to help her undo his pants.

"No," she said tasting the bitter mix of cologne and perspiration on his chest.

Xavier held her head as she flicked her tongue across his nipple before drowning it in full wet pucker. She heard him say, "*Damn,* baby"; the "slow down" question was pretty much abandoned.

Good thing. She wanted to be aggressive. The opportunity for her to feel that she could explore that side of her had been lost for so many years, and now Gwen wanted to go for it with the man she loved.

Her hands ran across his butt, pulling his trousers down, then traveled across his boxer-briefs to the outline of his tip, which she could feel the blood pumping into, making him harder. Not a possibility, she believed, but let it keep trying. Xavier's legs did a quick little march in place to free themselves from his pants, and he pulled her up to face him. He looked directly in her eyes, still holding her face between his hands tightly, keeping her gaze on him.

"I love you, Gwendolyn. You know that, don't you?" His eyes danced in the familiar way again, but still carried a hint of something else—fatigue, maybe sadness?

Gwen smiled. "Hmmm, yeah. I love you. My baby."

Enough talk. Gwen kissed him again, exploring his mouth with her tongue, just the way Xavier liked it. His heart beat fast against her breasts, thumping in his chest. The snaps of her chemise popped

loose, and his fingers were instantly swallowed by her opening. They worked their way out, soaked, and played gently with her clit, which Gwen could swear had been percolating all day in anticipation. But she closed her legs together and moved his hand to her hip. She knew she would come in a second and she wanted him to come first; she wanted to please him the way she had been fantasizing about for the past four weeks, four days, and nineteen hours.

"Let's go upstairs, baby." Xavier stepped onto her stair and held her hand, intending to lead her to the bedroom.

Gwen didn't move to follow; she smiled, taking his hand and kissing inside the palm, then teasing his fingers with her tongue, slipping his middle finger in her mouth, drawing it out wet, then slipping it back in, sucking on it. Xavier moaned and again attempted to lead her upstairs, and again she didn't follow.

"Uh-uh. Let's do upstairs next go-round." Gwen smiled, then added, "...or the one after that."

Xavier laughed; a laugh decorated in disbelief, but she still hadn't moved. Xavier looked at her again, she now stood a stair below him, motioning him against the railing, which conveniently had a wall behind it. She pressed his back against the wall and shook her head as he began to talk, "Baby, hmmm. Baby, we can..."

She kissed him, a light kiss, her tongue tracing the outline of his lips; his breathing fluctuated between heavy and barely there.

"Why are you still talking?"

She kissed his neck, wet kisses, then slipped his underwear down, feeling his hard-on leap forward, unrestrained, the tip rubbing against her stomach. She trailed her fingertips against it, feeling its smooth ripples, then circled her hand around it and gently tightened her grip. Xavier chanted her name, so aroused he could barely finish the "...lyn." Gwen crouched, resting one knee on a stair while her other foot steadied her on the stair below. Xavier's hard-on, unheld, rubbed against her face. She tasted him, loved him with her tongue, with her whole mouth, with all the energy and passion she owned. He said, "Gwendolyn, Baby, I love you..." as the petals in her hair dropped like

snowflakes; Xavier was gripping her hair so tightly she thought her own locks would soon be falling with the petals.

Before too long he stopped her, pulled her up to face him, and kissed her, then anxiously told her, "I need to be inside you baby." He looked so serious, so aroused; the stresses in his face dissipated, replaced by the desire to feel her, touch her, connect inside her.

Gwen allowed him to direct her; he turned her back to him, and she faced the wall. He kissed the back of her neck, giving attention to that little spot right below her hair line, while he pulled the chemise down. He whispered in her ear how beautiful she was and how perfect her body was and how much she turned him on. His tongue made magical tingles down her spinal column, kissing and teasing her butt, down the back of her thighs, then back up again. Gwen cried out. It was a true cry, not a moan, not a grunt. Where did this man come from? How could he make everything in her life so real, so pleasing, that had once seemed unimaginable?

His arms wrapped around her waist, he reached up to fondle her breasts and kissed the back of her head, the sides of her cheeks. She turned her head slightly, just enough to kiss his mouth, just long enough to lose herself in those soft brown eyes of his and tell him she loved him and she needed him and she wanted him. He was inside her quickly; their placement on the stairs, he slightly lower than she, allowed him to enter her from behind without much discomfort to either of them. He pushed her hips forward as he pulled his pelvis back, then brought her back to him, sliding himself in and out of her, urgent and strong. She was so tight, she knew he would explode quickly, which he did, and she exploded right along with him. His loud moan thundered behind hers; she held him deep inside her, and his fingers pressed into her hips.

They both took deep breaths, panting, gasping for air; neither one of them moved, their bodies meshed and dripping sweat. Xavier softly asked, "Are you OK, baby? I didn't hurt you, did I?" His baritone voice was almost breathless. She turned to face him, wiped a petal from his forehead, and kissed him. "Hmmm, hurt? Not quite, baby. Not quite."

They held onto each other; her fantasy had come to fruition, three stair steps from the bottom.

They made it upstairs to Xavier's bedroom, where they remained after leaving the stairwell. Music still played, shuffling from old-school Teddy Pendergrass to jazzy Gerald Albright to that celestial romantic, Maxwell.

Sated after two more rounds of sex, they rested in bed, kissing, touching, and talking. Gwen straddled Xavier, dressed only in his striped dress shirt, unbuttoned. Xavier sat up, resting his back against the headboard, his legs stretched out beneath Gwen. Some of the candles she had lit still burned. A few petals remained in her hair, and more were nestled in the sheets and covers.

"When was the first time you thought you were in love?" Xavier asked, moving his hands gently up and down her back.

"When I saw Taimak in *The Last Dragon*," Gwen answered quickly.

"Gwendolyn, I'm serious."

"So am I. I saw that man wearing that Hong Kong Phooey outfit and I said, 'That brother is mine.'" She giggled.

"OK, I guess I didn't make myself very clear." Xavier kissed her chin.

"Guess not. What's your favorite line—'come with it or don't come at all?' So what's the real question here, baby? When was the first time I thought I was in love, or when did I lose it?" Gwen clasped her hands behind his neck and studied him, her eyebrows flexed and her smile teasing.

"You caught me. When did you lose it?"

"This conversation is going to get us in trouble."

"Not any trouble on my end."

Gwen kissed his forehead and looked at him cautiously. She doubted his assertion, but whatever. "OK. I lost my virginity when I was sixteen."

"How old was he?"

"Uh, he was...older."

"A man or a boy?"

"This conversation *is* going to land me in trouble."

"Uh-uh, promise." Xavier pulled her down onto his chest. She stretched out beside him and snuggled between the folds, playing with the curly hairs that bloomed around his navel.

"OK, but remember—you promised." She rose to see him nod his head. She rested again. "He was...a man-boy, I guess. Twenty-one years old, a private first-class in the Army. He saw me as clay, ready to be molded, and I was primed and ready to learn."

"Learn?"

"Uh-huh. Learn. Learn how to please..." Gwen suddenly became uncomfortable with what she was saying and who she was saying it to. "...anyway, it was long time ago."

"Oh. So he was a good teacher?" Xavier's chest heaved; the question sounded strained, more serious than mere curious inquiry.

"Uh, I guess."

"Did you like pleasing him?"

Gwen rose. "Xavier..."

"You don't have to answer it." He tried to smile but couldn't fake it very well; he was jealous of kid's stuff, a forgotten affair from more than a dozen years ago.

"What kind of question was that—'Did I like pleasing him'?"

Xavier raised his hands. "Just a question. Sixteen-year-old girl, grown man. Sounds kind of perverted." Xavier's promise was clearly beginning to bust at the seams.

"Oh shit. If you're getting pissed, we can drop it."

"OK, let's drop it."

"OK." Gwen squirmed back onto his chest, hating that she fell for the promise in the first place.

Xavier didn't like the idea of her with another man. At all. She knew this, but whenever there was any discussion of past relationships—which there rarely was—Xavier always said he'd be fine, but then he ended up feeling horribly jealous. It bothered her, but the upside was that they both knew when to back off. Xavier didn't carry on like a possessive asshole; he never threw stuff back up in her face, and she never

told tell him things that she knew would piss him off. Respect was a big thing for both of them. And they almost always played by the rules.

So now this issue had been dropped. If she'd been unwise enough to continue, Gwen could have explained to him that the man in question hadn't known she was sixteen, not for a long time. She had lied and told him she was eighteen; took his sexual direction like a pro; enjoyed pleasing him; and thought sex at that time was the greatest invention since erasable ink. But that relationship fell apart. Next came Terry. End of great invention. Gwen and Xavier lay silent.

"What about you? Who was your first?" Gwen asked, wanting to turn the tables.

"Carla Faye Reardon."

"Damn, you remember her whole name?"

"Uh-huh."

"Humph, must have been good."

"It was all right." He laughed.

"How old were y'all?"

"I was fourteen and she was sixteen."

"Older woman, huh? Talk about me. What, did she have long black braids and a big old ass?"

"Nope. More like sandy blond hair and just enough ass to grab."

Gwen rose up. "She was white?"

"Something like that. Bother you?"

"Uh, no, not really." She didn't relax back, though. She sat up and crossed her legs. "I didn't think white women were your style."

"Well, Carla and I went way back. Knew each other since grade school, lived in the same neighborhood. Color didn't really cross our minds, until her mother caught us together, and let's just say that was the end of that."

"Hit the roof, huh?"

"Went through it." Xavier chuckled, halfheartedly. "Oh, she hemmed and hawed about it wasn't because I was black, it was more of the whole sex issue, period." Xavier looked at her.

Gwen looked at him before settling back down. "It was because you were black."

"Without a doubt."

They laughed. Silence took over for a while. He stroked her hair, then whispered, "I missed you, baby."

She stretched to kiss his chin, noticing the somber look had returned. "Philadelphia was rough, huh baby?" She asked.

"Yeah, but I'm all right."

"Coach Burke...that was his name, right?" Gwen asked. Xavier nodded. "He meant a lot to you, huh?"

"Yeah, he was a good guy. Family man. Only fifty-six years old, and dead. That's some shit."

"Yeah, that's sad. Want to talk about it?"

"Not really." Xavier skipped the issue, quick-paced. "What's been happening here? How are things at the office?"

"They're there. Your schedule is still terrible, but everything else has sort of tapered off for the rest of the year. Vaughn's been in and out, handling personal stuff. Some days he looks pretty shabby and other days he looks right as rain."

"Thanks to Payton?"

"Hmmm, I can't say with any kind of certainty. But I think she has a lot to do with it. They keep in touch—sometimes he'll click in from call waiting while I'm on the phone with her. She likes him, she doesn't deny that. She says they have so much in common, and that it would be just her luck to walk into the life of a forty-year-old married man with twins." Gwen sighed. "I know he's getting a divorce, but I just hope Payton doesn't get hurt. Vaughn's been married for a long time; baggage like that you just can't put down simply by signing on the dotted line. You know?"

Xavier grunted without answering.

Gwen kept talking. "Speaking of married and children and such. I saw Shay the other day. She's pregnant."

"Pregnant?" Xavier asked, surprised.

"Uh-huh."

Gwen had seen Shayla in the bathroom; her small round belly protruded like a prosthetic underneath a knit skirt not built for the bulge. Gwen asked how she was doing and she'd mumbled "Fine."

They stood side by side, fiddling and primping in the mirror; Gwen hung around waiting to see if Shayla would open up, since her condition was so obvious to the naked eye. But she left the bathroom without uttering another word. That was fine with Gwen, but she felt for her. She wondered if Tariq, the bow-legged married brother, was the father. She wondered if at night, when Shayla was alone, without make-up, her hair tied up in a scarf and all of her brash attitude and brazen sexuality tucked away for the night, she cried. If she was scared.

"It's gonna be rough. Especially if her baby daddy ain't worth a damn."

"Yeah. She's tough, though. I'm sure she'll be fine." Gwen's demeanor saddened.

Xavier rubbed her shoulder. "You OK?"

"Uh yeah, I'm good." Gwen shifted.

"Having sympathy pains for her?"

"A little."

"Do you want any?" he asked; his fingers took long, drawn-out strokes of her hair.

"Any..." Gwen careened her head back, looking at him.

"Children. Do you want any?" He lowered his gaze, his voice softened.

"Uh-huh, one day," she answered, just as softly.

"One? Two?" These questions were just as soft.

"Two, maybe three." She blushed.

"Boy and girl? For the two I mean."

Gwen shrugged, "It doesn't matter. Not really."

"With or without a husband?"

Gwen hesitated. "Uh, a husband would be nice. I guess." Marriage had never crossed her mind; she loved Xavier, but she still didn't think of marriage, mainly because she figured it would be the last thing on his mind. He didn't ask any more questions. Gwen looked at him. "Do you want more children, one day?"

"With the right woman, of course."

"A baby boy, I'm sure, huh?"

He stroked her cheek. "I'd be happy with either. A little girl who looks like her mother would be special." He kissed her lips; her face flushed. "Am I embarrassing you?"

"A little."

"Didn't mean to."

"It's OK. I…uh." Gwen stumbled, uncertain whether to reveal more of her past, but suddenly, fiercely wanting to. "I was pregnant once."

His face didn't flinch. "Really? When?"

"When I was seventeen." Gwen talked quietly; he touched her cheek, maintaining her gaze with his.

"The older man?"

"Yep."

"Abortion?"

"He wanted me to get one."

"You didn't?"

Gwen grabbed a pillow and rolled onto her back. "I didn't want to get one. I'd gone with a girlfriend once and she cried and said it felt like her insides were being scraped clean. Not me. I was ready to tell Nana, tell her I made a mistake, then beg her to help me take care of the baby. She would have. She would have been disappointed as hell, but she would have." Gwen stared at the ceiling.

"What happened, baby?" Xavier raked his fingers through her hair.

"I miscarried. Woke up bleeding and scared to death. Nana took me to the emergency room, they gave me a D&C, sent me home with some pain pills. Nana didn't ask who; didn't cry; didn't holler at me. She just told me if I was going to keep looking for ways to self-destruct, then I would either eventually achieve it or finally come away with some sense."

"And the older man?"

"He wanted to keep seeing me—wanted to keep screwing me, after it was all said and done. Said we'd have to be more careful, that's all. But after that he didn't look the same to me. It was like his compliments didn't ring true anymore; they all just sounded like words, when they used to sound like definitions. And the sex—I slept with him one more time after the miscarriage and it felt like nothing. So

he eventually got stationed overseas and I kept self-destructing for a while." She looked at Xavier and smiled wearily.

He didn't speak. He held his arms out and she climbed his lap and he cradled her like a baby. Her head rested on his shoulder.

"It looks to me like you've come away with some sense." He kissed the top of her head. She softly said "Uh-huh." They were silent again.

"Why do I tell you so much?" Gwen asked.

"Why do you?" He asked back.

"I dunno. Maybe I want you to see that I wasn't a pristine church girl; I had some pretty wild ways." Gwen flexed her fingers in and out of his chest hair.

"Or maybe you want to see if you'll say something so shocking I'll stop loving you," he countered.

"That's not true." She pulled away, enough to look at him squarely. "No?"

"No. Why would you say something like that?"

"'Cause you still have such a hard time being loved."

"That's bullshit, Xavier," she shot back, and tried to push further away; he held her tighter.

"OK, it's bullshit," he conceded. It was obvious he didn't want to get into anything major. Neither did Gwen, but when he said crap like that it was hard to ignore. Especially since in some ways it was true. He kissed her lips; she slowly began to give a little.

"I like the way you love me." Her voice was sweet.

"I like loving you."

She began kissing his neck, feeling her need for him growing again. She worked her lips under his chin, down his neck, back up around his mouth. She kissed his closed eyelids, marveling at the still portrait of pleasure his face revealed. "I love you, Xavier."

He opened his eyes and smiled, a grand smile, and said, "I love the way that sounds; the way you whisper my name, it sounds like poetry, you know that?" He fondled her breasts while she kept kissing. He moaned, "Say it again, baby. Say my name."

Say my name, bitch...

Gwen snatched her head back and jerked away from him as if he had thorns. She saw Terry. Terry, with her spit still smeared down his nose. The room, this room, was swirling; the music changed, and suddenly the rap song "Push It" was blaring in her head. Her eyes shut, tightly. The hand on her felt cold, sweaty. She slapped at it, hit without looking, felt her body fall to the floor. She pedaled her feet, trying to move back, until she felt the wall. Cornered. Again.

"Gwendolyn! Gwendolyn, baby, it's me. Dammit, stop..."

She kicked; felt her ankle being held; swung with her hands; felt her wrists being held; refused to open her eyes; didn't want to see; didn't want to see him.

"Baby, it's me, Xavier. Gwendolyn..."

Xavier...Xavier...Xavier...

The fight in her slowly calmed and she opened her eyes. Xavier knelt before her on the floor, a few feet away from the bed and looking scared as shit. "Baby..."

Gwen jerked her wrists again and he released them. She looked around; Terry Stuart was gone, the music was soft, the room stood still. She had lost control. Lost it, completely, at the sound of three words. She looked at Xavier.

How the hell was she going to explain this, or get out of explaining it?

"Gwendolyn..."

"I'm sorry. I'm fine, Xav—"

"Baby, what the hell happened?"

"Nothing." She pressed her back against the wall and eased herself up. Xavier held his hands out in front of her, ready to catch her in case she fell, or flipped out again.

"What happe—"

"Nothing. Let's drop it. OK?" Gwen moved away from him.

"I don't think so baby. You can't freak out like that and tell me it's nothing. Uh-uh, Gwendolyn."

She stood in the middle of the room, not knowing what she wanted to do—get dressed, go home, go downstairs, jump out the window.

The one thing she did know was that she didn't want to explain. She walked towards the bathroom. Xavier followed.

"Gwendolyn, talk to me." He touched her elbow. She jerked away.

"I can't, OK. I know..."He attempted to touch her again; touching wouldn't be good at the moment. She held her hands up, away from him. "...I know I need to explain what just happened, but I can't. Please, I can't."

"Another subtle reminder?" He was going to force the issue.

Gwen walked around him, heading back towards the bed, then she stopped and turned. He stood in front of her.

Shit.

"It was the college thing, right? The jock?"

Not gonna talk about this...

Gwen didn't speak, wasn't going to speak. She noticed his eye was scratched, a small scratch on the side of his face, up by his left eye. She felt bad. She had hurt the man she loved, physically, and now she was unleashing havoc on his emotions. She sat on the bed and covered her face with her hands. The bed jolted as Xavier sat down beside her.

What to do? What to say?

"You wouldn't understand?" This was her explanation. Weak— more a question than an explanation—but at the moment she felt almost lifeless. She heard him sigh. Her nose was about to drip and her eyes began to puddle. She fell back onto the bed, forcing the floods to retreat. Xavier let her be for a few minutes. She stared at his back, watched his broad shoulders rise and fall with each deep breath.

"What part wouldn't I understand?" he asked.

"I don't know." She looked at the ceiling.

"You don't know?"

"Maybe what happened." She talked in riddles.

"That a man, some punk-ass brother attacked you? Forced himself on you. Do you really think I wouldn't understand?" Now Xavier's voice began to lose its easiness.

"Maybe you'd think I asked for it. I just told you what a little fast mama I was. Screwing grown men..."

"That's bullshit, Gwendolyn. You're not saying what I would think; you're saying what *you* think. Say I'm wrong." His voice was stern; he lay on his side next to her, his head propped in his hand, waiting on her to respond.

"You're wrong."

"Am I?"

"Stop this crap, Xavier." They rose at the same time; she still didn't want to be touched, but he didn't move to touch her.

"Xavier, I know what most men think. I've heard it all, all that Mike Tyson bullshit: 'If she was in his room at two o'clock in the fucking mornin,' she knew what the deal was...' Y'all refuse to believe that rape actually happens, unless maybe some stranger jerks a woman off the street, beats her up, and fucks her. If it's a situation like mine, well, that's where the lines get blurred. Now *you* say that I'm wrong."

"You have men all figured out, don't you, Gwendolyn?"

"Don't I?"

Xavier shook his head.

Gwen crossed her arms. "We're not going to have this discussion." He looked as if he could debate well into the night, as if he planned to debate well into the night. She didn't want to—not about Terry Stuart, not now and maybe never. Xavier's eyes were heavy, studying her intently, clearly pissed that she was again trying to avoid the issue. The stare-down continued. She finally looked away.

"Were you involved with him, is that where all this is coming from?"

Gwen whipped her head around like a woman possessed, her jaw popping from the pressure of gritted teeth. "Go to hell."

"I guess that's a no."

"Let's stop this bullshit. Don't psychoanalyze me; you're not a psychiatrist, and it's a damn good thing you stuck to accounting." A low blow and she knew it.

"And you told me it was a blip on your memory, that you were over it, but you're still trippin' out. So now that we know our weaknesses, can we talk?"

"No. How about we don't?" She looked at him, too hurt to jab

again. "How about I just go home?" She stood up in the middle of the room, just stood, with Xavier's shirt twisted in her folded arms. He stood up and faced her again.

"That's how you want to handle this?" She didn't answer. She had no clue what she wanted to do, how she wanted to handle things, or where the hell she wanted to go from here.

Xavier's face melted. "Baby, how about you stay? Please." He raised a hand to touch her, hesitated, then followed through. He caressed the outline of her face with his fingertips. "Unless you really want to go."

She shook her head, shaking tears from her eyes. He wiped her tears and her arms unfolded, reached for him, and held on like a vise, smothering herself in his chest. They walked back to the bed after a few minutes and spread across it, lying on their sides, parallel to one another.

"I'm going to lose you," she said after several minutes of silence.

"Not if you don't want to."

"I don't want to."

"OK."

"Why won't I?" She asked, talking in riddles again. It sounded like a good question in her head, but out loud it sounded stupid.

"Because I love you." He said. "And in the last couple of weeks, I've come to realize just how much I love you."

"A profound epiphany struck you during your travels?" She was relieved to take the conversation away from her and her freak-out.

"You could say that." He sighed. Working his way closer to her, he slipped his hand inside the shirt she wore, his shirt, and caressed her stomach. He leaned over and kissed her, soft, then energetic, then soft again. She kept her eyes open—she felt she had to make sure he didn't turn into Terry again. He opened his eyes, too, probably to make sure she didn't flip out again. They pulled away as he began to talk.

"Gwendolyn, I believe in soul mates. I believe you're mine. Let's just say that while I was gone, missing you turned into needing you. Am I getting too serious for you?" he whispered.

"No. I need you too," she whispered back.

He kissed her again; she held the side of his face, slowly closing her

eyes, finding the rhythm they always shared, leaning forward to lend more substance to the kiss. He slowed the pace.

"Gwendolyn, you scared me tonight." Back to the rape.

"I know." She stared at him.

How different things might have been had she and Xavier first connected that night of the rape. She believed he was her soul mate, too; funny, that meant he must have been her soul mate that night as she watched him leaning against the wall, bobbing his head to the beat. They had stared at each other for a moment that night, and for that moment she had felt that he was hers. But she had a hard time believing Terry Stuart was meant to play any part in their destiny. Divine intervention he wasn't.

How could they have been best friends?

Gwen still wondered this; still couldn't quite figure out how Terry could have any redeeming qualities—any human qualities at all. She never asked. Xavier still didn't talk about Terry.

Maybe tonight was the time.

"Gwendolyn baby, you're drifting away from me. I can tell."

"Yeah. Sorry." She stroked his face. Those honest eyes of his said so much: they said that he loved her and wanted to understand her; they said talk to him.

"He was a basketball player," she started, keeping her voice regulated as if reporting the evening news. She would talk to him without hysterics or dramatics, and if he asked questions she would answer them; if he asked who, she would tell him. She continued, "I didn't know him well, we were never involved, nothing like that. I knew of his status; he was a star, but to me, that meant nothing. Back then, in my mind, *I* was a star, and if anyone was going to be idolized, it would be me first." She tried to smile; the mere crinkle of her face leaked tears, so she stopped trying. Xavier just listened, no emotion, no movement.

"It was a party, a loud, rowdy house party. I had fun, for the most part. I liked partying, getting attention, dancing close, being cute. It was a game to me, a harmless game. What was the use in being cute, if you couldn't *be cute*. Know what I mean?" she asked without expect-

ing an answer. The corners of Xavier's mouth crept upward in a tiny "I hear ya baby" smile. Gwen sucked in air and exhaled slowly. "He was in the bedroom waiting for me when I went to get my purse. My girlfriend, the girl I went to the party with, she told me everything was upstairs. My purse, the keys. She wasn't ready to go home, said she'd catch a ride. 'Cool, sister,' that's what I told her. She was having fun, had hooked up with somebody, so everything was everything. More power to her, maybe I'd get lucky next time. But I was tired and ready to go."

Gwen prolonged the rest with a long intermission. Xavier touched her cheek and she moved his hand away: not angry, just not now. Touching wasn't good at the moment. Xavier looked as if he understood, and they lay there in silence.

"I didn't think it would happen, you know? Truly. He was drunk; he looked demonic. But I really thought there was no way, in a house full of people, that he could hurt me. Scare me, yeah. Hurt me, no way. And then I think I was even more shocked when he did: when he could, in a house full of people. And he knew he could. He didn't bother to lock any doors; he didn't turn off any lights, or shove me in a dark corner, up against a wall. He took his time; he had that power. And he knew it." Another intermission.

A tear spilled; Gwen wiped it away quickly. "I screamed; for a long time I screamed. But damn if that didn't turn him on; he pushed harder, and his dick felt like it had a razor blade attached to it. I could feel him in the pit of my stomach, pushing my insides up into my throat. It burned, like when you burn your leg on the exhaust pipe of a motorcycle; I did that once, on Weldon's dirt bike when I was a little girl, and that's what it felt like. I told him that. I said, you're burning me. Please stop, you're burning me..." Gwen's face contorted and her voice choked. "He didn't stop."

She paused again, didn't cry out loud, just wiped her face with the sleeve of the shirt. She composed herself, then started talking again in soft tones. "I finally quit, you know, just said fuck it. I don't know how long into it, it seemed to go on forever, but I realized nothing was going to make him stop. He was showing me who ran the show;

he was showing me that his dick could outlast my fight, and it did. I firmly believe Lucifer was riding his dick and they were both kicking my ass. I was so pissed, so damn *mad*. At myself, not just at him. For stupid crap. Like being a nail biter, all those years when my mama used to tell me to stop. 'You gonna need those nails one day; you gonna wish you had 'em,' that's what she told me so many times. I could have scratched the hell out of him, could have scarred his face; but I didn't; I couldn't.

"I...I'm sorry, baby." She lightly touched the scratch beside Xavier's eye; his eyes closed, then opened; he held her hand and kissed it. He released her again.

"I wore a skirt that night, a tight little spandex skirt; I should have worn pants. I should have made his ass work to get it. A skirt was too easy. I never wore them again after that. Then I told myself I shouldn't have spit in his face; I shouldn't have cursed him. I should have offered him pussy. I should have given him a blow job. At least then I would have had the upper hand; I would have been *giving* something, and his power to *take* wouldn't have been shit. I asked myself how could he do this to me? He knew he was hurting me; I was crying and begging; there was my blood on his dick when he finally jacked off. My blood...*my blood*. How does someone do that? How can someone take like that and not care?" Gwen asked. Xavier shook his head, not knowing how to respond; tears rested in the corner of his eyes, glistening like ice.

"Then after that, after it was all over, I struggled with everything for months. Everything became too damn hard to do, like brushing my teeth, combing my hair, hell I didn't even want to bite my fingernails. So I took what I thought was an easy route—I tried to kill myself."

Gwen closed her eyes, remembering the pills lodged in her throat before she'd forced them down with liquor. Payton had found her that night, called 911, and saved her life. That was the real beginning of their friendship—pretty intense for two unlikely girls thrown together as college roommates. Gwen remembered the sirens, blaring like a chorus of crying babies, and the jolt of the gurney in and out of the ambulance like an old elevator settling on the first floor. A tube was

forced down her throat, and black gunk was going down and green stuff coming up. The techs were talking to her, talking around her, talking about her.

"I had a couple of years of therapy afterward and it helped a lot, but some things can't be talked away, can't be rationalized into normalcy. I could see people, women, young girls, flirting and being cute, and they seemed so *dangerous* to me, so reckless. Sometimes I feared for them and other times they pissed me off. Because they could do it and I couldn't. They could go on for years throwing their sexuality in men's faces, like Shay, and nothing would happen to them; and I couldn't. Isn't that wack of me? It took me a lot of years to see that this thinking was fucked up. To see that it wasn't my fault. To see that I didn't do anything wrong; not wrong enough to warrant that. But, baby it's been ten years, and sometimes if you catch me on a bad day, I can still switch back to that bullshit thinking in a heartbeat," Gwen snapped her fingers, "just like that. That's the worst thing he did to me, beyond anything else. He raped my mind. That's the worst. The worst." Gwen stared past Xavier with hatred.

His hand stroked across her cheek and momentarily startled her. She looked at him and tried to smile. He didn't speak. A tear trickled across the bridge of his nose and Gwen leaned over and kissed it away.

She touched his face. "You're so different. Why is that?"

"Baby, that guy was sick. Sick in the mind, sick in the soul." He rolled onto his back and Gwen carefully moved into him and rested her head on his chest, and listened to his heart beat like a drum. He rubbed her shoulder and kissed the top of her head. He didn't ask any questions—even though she was prepared to answer any questions he might ask.

They said nothing, and the sound of nothing sounded nice. Gwen felt herself drifting. Sleep would be good; good sleep would be better.

She closed her eyes and said, "I really don't want to lose you," and snuggled deeper into him. "I just want it stated for the record."

Xavier stroked her curls and murmured into her hair, "We'll be all right, baby."

Gwen nodded, hoping to God they would be.

· FOURTEEN ·

B EFORE GWEN COULD RING THE BELL, the door magically
opened, with C.J. running out of it. He gave her a "Dang, 'scuse
me, Miss Gwen," and let his basketball dribble down the driveway
while he helped her pick up her purse. Luckily she had it zipped
up, and with the force C.J. carried it was a wonder she didn't hit the
ground with it.

His boys on the curb hollered for him to come on; C.J. shooed
them with his hand, telling them to wait. They grumbled, still shouting for him to hurry up, but Gwen noticed they didn't budge from
the curb. C. J. was a natural basketball talent, from what Xavier said,
and it appeared his friends knew best to wait on him. C. J. paid them
no attention.

Gwen thanked him and he in turn told her Xavier was in the
backyard with Avery; she didn't realize Xavier was even over, she'd
really just dropped by to bring Carmen a wallpaper pattern book she'd
borrowed from Lowe's, which miraculously hadn't followed her purse
to the pavement.

Before he caught up with his friends, C.J. said Carmen was with
Cec, who was sick with a cold. It was no a wonder, with the fickle way
the weather had been. Hot one week, cold the next; Gwen assumed
that even by Christmas Day, in a couple of weeks, they still wouldn't
know whether to bundle up or strip down.

C. J. headed on his way and Gwen decided to visit with Xavier and
Avery until Carmen made an appearance from her nurse-mother duties. Besides, Gwen could never pass up an opportunity to see her man.

They had become closer than closer than close. Almost unimaginable, but they were. The day after telling him about the rape, Gwen

slept in, in Xavier's bed and still in Xavier's shirt. When she awoke, Xavier was sitting at his desk. It looked like he was paying bills. He had already showered and was dressed in jeans and a denim shirt, and hadn't noticed she was awake. Gwen sat up in bed and stretched, wondering if the entire night, beginning with the drama of her flipping out, had actually happened.

She rolled out of bed, hopped in his lap, and noticed the scratch on his face. It had happened. She had flipped out. He said, "Hey there, sleepyhead," in his usual playful tone and she said, "Hey baby," back. She went to kiss him, then suddenly realized she had sleep-breath while he had clean breath, and she pulled away. "Uh-uh, baby," he told her and kissed her and kissed her and kissed her.

All the drama and angst of her past seemed to dissolve as he kissed her; there were no more questions, no more "college thing" discussions, and for Gwen, no more doubts as to what she should do. Terry Stuart didn't exist anymore. Xavier loved her. Everything was everything.

She rounded the house and could see the backs of Xavier and Avery as they stood on the mid-level deck, leaning over the railing. Of course, she heard Avery before she saw him. Avery's voice remained at a perpetual high volume. Gwen started to shout out hello, until she heard her name in the conversation.

"Damn, Xa man, Gwen's got your nose wide open. You got it bad, my brother. You got it bad."

"Yeah, I do. Man, she's it for me. She's it, end of story, close the books."

Gwen smiled; She knew Xavier loved her, but for him to speak of her with such high praise to others—well, that was just damn special. And since he was singing her praises, she wanted to hear more.

"Yeah, man. Gwen's good people. I knew y'all would be into something at the cookout back in July. Shit, Xa, your nose was spreading then." Avery laughed.

"Yeah man, it was. I ain't gonna lie. But, hell, she's more than just good people. Gwendolyn is... Avery, man, she's so deep. Don't get me wrong now, sometimes she can be a bit spoiled..."

Gwen smirked.

"...but hell, even that's sexy." Xavier redeemed himself. Gwen smiled, proudly, listening to the rest.

"Avery man, she works hard at everything. I'm talking at the job, with her family, and with us...man with me, she..."

"She makes you feel like a natural man," Avery sang badly and laughed, "I hear ya, man. So, why you want to fuck it up?"

Excuse me?

Xavier sighed, "Hell, I don't *want* to mess it up. Avery, man we talk; we always tell each other what's going on. That's what makes *us* work. And if I don't tell her this and she finds out... look, you're right, Gwendolyn is good people, but she don't play around when it comes to bullshit."

Gwen jerked her body and contorted her face. What the hell was he talking about? It was true that their relationship thrived on good communication, and since the night they talked about the rape their relationship had seemed to soar to new heights. So what was he talking about now? She strained to listen.

"Well, Xa man, you know what I say, if the shit ain't broke don't take a hammer to it."

"Uh-huh. Maybe so..."

"Ain't no 'maybe so.' Now listen to me, brother-in-law, let's diagnose this situation..."

"Avery man, shut up," Xavier laughed.

"Naw, I'm serious. Let's diagnose it. Hell, you need my advice, 'cause apparently you don't know women like I know women."

"Is that a fact?"

"Damn straight fact. Look, Xa man, I ain't even about to argue with you on how good a woman Gwen is, but she's still a woman. And if you tell her some shit about your ex-wife, she gonna go clean off on your ass. Straight up..."

Ex-wife? Tracey...

Gwen moved closer to the side of the deck, afraid she'd be seen and screw up these true confessions.

"...so let's diagnose it. Right here and now!" Avery banged his fist

on the railing. "Avery man, keep your voice down. All I need is for Carmen to jump on my ass about this."

"Man, Carmen's in the house; she ain't thinkin' about us. And that's another thing, I know she and Gwen had lunch the other day so it's a safe bet Carmen didn't mention it in conversation. You know how she can get sometimes." Avery lowered his voice regardless.

"Yeah, well, Carmen ain't no fool. She wouldn't mention anything about Tracey to Gwendolyn anyway, not now that we're together. You know that she thinks to bring up an old flame in the company of a new flame is just rude. Thank God for southern etiquette. Plus, I'm sure she thinks I told Gwendolyn myself, which I probably should have."

"Uh-uh, my brother. There you go again. OK, let's look at it. Now think about it, were you really not forthcoming, as Johnnie Cochran would say?" Avery laughed again, getting a kick out of his own diagnostic techniques.

Get to the point... Gwen rolled her eyes.

"Man, I—"

"Ain't no 'man, I.' Of course you were. That's the answer—of course. Look, when you said you were going to Coach Burke's funeral, that was the truth. Just 'cause Coach Burke happened to be your ex-father-in-law, well that's just an extra title that don't need to be told."

Father-in-law! What the hell? Now her eyes bulged out of her head.

"...and you and Coach Burke were close, real close. That wasn't a lie either. So, I ask you again, why you want to fuck it up?"

"Because that's some stuff that could come back to haunt me."

"How you figure? I mean you saw Tracey, y'all spent some time together..."

Oh really...

"...you didn't sleep with her, right?"

"Naw man..."

"Then what's there to come back and haunt? Unless your ass did

sleep with her and she gonna be stalking you and shit. You know how women can get, and Tracey wasn't never wrapped too tight."

"Look, man. I didn't sleep with her. We just talked and...stuff."

And stuff? What stuff?

"Well, all right then. There's your answer. Talking and stuff don't mean you need to be forthcoming with any new information. I'm tellin' ya. If the crime don't fit, then don't tell shit. You know Johnnie Cochran would tell you the same thing."

"Avery man, you are full of it. I hope you don't run these 'forthcoming diagnostic' games with my sister. You know I'd have to kick your ass."

"Man, you'd have to stand in line until after Carmen kicked my ass. She can smell a lie on me like three-day funk. I'm just telling you how to handle..."

"Gwen, I didn't know you were here." Carmen rolled down the ramp that led from the kitchen and greeted Gwen, loudly.

Gwen smiled, nervously. Busted. She waved at Carmen, then looked up to see Avery and Xavier looking down at her from above. She and Xavier looked at each other. He smiled tersely, not quite sure how long she had been there. She shot him daggers, letting him know exactly how long she had been there.

"Gwen, girl, what you doin' creepin' around here?" Avery joked.

Gwen snapped her head upward. "Creeping?"

"Oh *shit,*" Avery retorted, knowing they had been straight-up busted.

"Is something wrong?" Carmen asked just as Avery leaped down the stairs and suggested they go in the house. Carmen looked at Gwen, then Xavier, and then asked Avery what mess he had drummed up. Avery said, "Ain't no mess going on. Let's just go inside." And before Carmen could ask more questions he took control of her wheelchair and rolled her back into the house. Xavier made his way down the stairs and attempted a kiss.

Oh hell, no.

Gwen jerked her head back out of the kiss's aim and stepped back.

"Look baby, don't overreact about whatever you heard..."

"*Whatever* I heard? You been hanging out with your ex-wife and conveniently neglected to tell me? So how should I react?" Gwen fought hard to keep her voice even, but she was fast losing the battle; she would use whatever answers she could pull out of Xavier as a barometer to gauge just how ignorant she should get with him.

Xavier shifted his weight. "Gwendolyn, don't twist whatever little sound bite you heard into a major deal. I didn't sleep with her. Let's just get that straight first." Xavier kept his distance. A wise move on his part.

Gwen began to pace, the wallpaper book clutched tightly to her chest. "Oh, am I supposed to pat you on the back for that, give you a medal? 'Look at me, Gwendolyn, I just spent time with my drop-dead-fine ex-wife and I didn't fuck her. Ain't I something.'" Her voice rose from even to slightly tilted. She knew she was being a complete sarcastic bitch, but she didn't really care at the moment. And by the tight expression on Xavier's face, she could tell he was beginning to lose patience, but she didn't give a damn about that either.

"Gwendolyn, it was Tracey's father who passed away last month. I should have told you that."

"Oh, that much I gathered. Why don't you just start with the 'we just talked...and stuff' part. I think that's the subject that needs further elaboration." Gwen stopped pacing and stood directly in front of him.

"Shit, this is why I didn't want to say anything to you in the first place. I figured you'd take it all wrong." Xavier shoved one hand in his pocket and shifted again.

Gwen felt herself boil. She flailed one hand in front of his face, her fingers tight against one another as if in a military salute, and hissed, "That's bullshit. Don't try to avoid the question with bullshit analysis. With all your business travel, when have I ever led you to believe I didn't trust you? When?"

Xavier didn't answer. Gwen said, "Uh-huh," and placed the wallpaper book on the steps. Then she stood in front of him again crossing her arms with a jerk and placing her weight on one hip. She was about to get ignorant. "So, let's *diagnose* this, Xavier."

"Gwendolyn, don't do this sh—"

"Oh no. If you can allow Avery to diagnose things, then please allow me the same courtesy. Let's start from the top. Were you and Tracey alone together while you were in Philadelphia?"

"This is bullshit, Gwendolyn. Let's go somewhere and t—"

"Uh-uh, this is fine, right here. Were you alone with her?" Gwen sliced the air with her hand, enunciating each word.

"Yeah, we spent some time together. Look, she was real close to her father, and so was I. She was pretty upset."

"I have no doubt."

Gwen didn't sound real sympathetic; maybe if she had known the real deal up front, she could find compassion, but now all she could see was red. Now she knew why Xavier looked the way he looked when he returned home that night, the night they made love on the stairs, the night she flipped out. It wasn't a tired look; it was a guilty look.

"Where exactly did you two spend this quality time together?"

"Look Gwendolyn, we had dinner the night before I left."

"At your hotel?"

"Uh, yeah."

Gwen shifted her weight to the other hip and her voice again changed its range, this time from slightly tilted to a mid-level growl. "Spend time in your room?"

"Uh," Xavier breathed deep, "Yeah, we talked in my room."

"Did you touch her?"

"Wha—Gwendolyn, listen..."

"Did you touch her? Just answer the fucking question."

Now Xavier began to pace. "Dammit, Gwendolyn this is bullshit. Look, if you want to know what happened, then I'll tell you. Tracey and I talked, we talked about a lot of past crap. The stuff between her and Terry, and about Kendra and all the bad blood between us. She was crying, she felt bad, she said she wished things could have been different. I told her I was to blame for a lot of it and I was sorry I put her through a lot of the shit that I did. And yeah, things got pretty emotional and we—we kissed. Look it didn't mean anything..."

Gwen's face twitched. The ignorant level had finally been reached. "You son of a *bitch*. What kind of a kiss?"

"Shit, Gwendolyn, what is this? It was a kiss, just a kiss."

"Oh, *hell* no. Was it a peck kiss or a slob kiss? Don't play this shit with me, Xavier."

Xavier looked slightly annoyed with her questions. He didn't answer. Gwen walked away from him and grabbed the wallpaper book again, pressing it hard against her chest. She needed to have her hands occupied, because she wanted to haul off and slap him. "It was a slob kiss, wasn't it? Did you touch her, grab her ass, rub her titties? Or did she suck your—"

"Gwendolyn, *stop* this shit. Look, Tracey didn't do anything to me and I didn't do anything to her. And I know we shouldn't have kissed, but we did. It happened. And if you want to know the truth, I could have fucked her if I wanted, but that's just it. I didn't want to, and I told her that. I told her there was someone in my life. Someone I was in love with, and that I didn't want to make the same mistakes I had made in the past. Gwendolyn, baby, I don't want Tracey. I don't want any other woman but you. And I don't know what else I can tell you to make you believe all this. Shit, I just don't know." Xavier moved toward her. Gwen stood still.

She looked at him, remembering the first part of his and Avery's conversation that she'd overheard. She did believe he loved her and she did believe he didn't sleep with Tracey, although the jury was still out on exactly what happened. But that still didn't lessen the hurt and anger she felt. It should have, she thought, but at the moment, it didn't.

Maybe it was because she could see Tracey's picture in her head so clearly—her rich cinnamon skin, the honey-brown glow of her thick, shoulder-length hair—real hair, not an artificial weave for effect. Her lips looked full and tulip-shaped, and her body was so petite, she was obviously a woman who wore single digits, but she was still shapely, with heavy breasts, real stand-up and teasing. Now *they* could have been artificial for effect, but whatever. The thought of her and Xavier

together, the thought of their history together, the thought of his lips on her lips. All of those thoughts pissed Gwen off.

Gwen straightened up and handed Xavier the wallpaper book, "I, um, brought this for Carmen, would you give it to her for me?" The ignorance had retreated back in her psyche and now she just sounded hurt.

Xavier took the book. "Uh, yeah. You want to go somewhere and talk or something?"

Gwen shook her head. "No. I'm going home."

"Gwendolyn..."

Gwen turned to leave and adjusted her purse strap on her shoulder. Xavier didn't call her name again, nor did he follow her. Another wise move. She needed to be by herself and sort out all of the painful diagnostic results.

Xavier left for Chicago the following Tuesday on a follow-up assignment he would be handling solo. They hadn't talked much since their fight; he called her at home a couple of times before he left, wanting to come by, but Gwen squashed his request. She simply said, "I don't want to talk."

The one time she saw him at work, he stuck his head in her office and asked, "Got a minute?" Gwen looked up and thought he was the most beautiful man she had ever seen, but she still told him, "I don't want to talk. Not about..." She left it in the air, knowing he knew what she meant. If he needed to discuss work, then they could talk. But they both knew that wasn't it.

Xavier raised his hands in surrender and said, "Fine," and then he left. He didn't ask how long she wanted to make him suffer and he didn't attempt to plead his case again. Gwen went back to work knowing Xavier was only going to put up with her pissed-off bullshit for a limited amount of time. But then, he had been the one in the wrong.

Now he had been gone almost a week. It was Monday and Gwen had taken the whole week as vacation. But her plans were anybody's guess. Christmas was on Thursday, and originally she and Xavier had planned out the entire holiday. He would be leaving Chicago

on Tuesday and flying directly to Charlotte to visit his folks. Gwen was supposed to be meeting him in Charlotte, her first meeting with his parents, and spending Christmas day with them. Then, the day after Christmas, she and Xavier were going to rent a car and drive to Augusta so he could meet Nana and Weldon. They would come back to Atlanta late Saturday night, then spend all night and the following day making up for lost time—especially since they would have been in the company of elders throughout the holidays, and lovemaking would have been difficult to accomplish. They had planned all of this four weeks ago. But now what?

Gwen did manage to get her hair trimmed. Her hairdresser's shop was all the way in Lithonia, about thirty minutes out, but it was worth the trip. She was a tiny Jamaican woman who knew just how to clip her curls without making them stick up and look crazy, and plus she was open on Mondays. She was definitely a find. Then Gwen buzzed in and out of Kroger for groceries and made it home to find her answering machine blinking with a message. It was Xavier.

He had only called once since leaving, a few days before, and took the "maybe things have blown over" approach. He didn't mention the fight, didn't apologize again, didn't act as if anything had happened at all, but only tried to make small talk: "How you doing? What's going on...." Gwen continued to play the angry role, and only grunted back at him like a true bitch. Five minutes into it, he gave up and said, "This is bullshit, Gwendolyn," receiving only a "Whatever" from her. He hadn't called again until now.

On the message his voice was rich with sincerity, sounding lonely but not pathetic, saying he loved her, saying he was sorry, and leaving his hotel room and phone number asking her to call. He missed her. She missed him too. Bad.

"Oh damn," she mumbled out loud. What the hell to do now? She wasn't as pissed off anymore, not at Xavier anyway. She couldn't really fake going through the motions either. The way she felt about him outweighed the anger she felt over a week ago. Shoot, she could barely see Tracey's face in her head any more, the way she had seen it so vividly before; now the image was all of one big blurry ball

of hair and boobs. She could only see Xavier, only wanted to see Xavier.

She picked up the phone to call him, then put it back down. No, she would go one better. She searched her Rolodex, dialed the number, gave a little information, got a little information, and jotted everything down.

Then she decided to call Payton and wish her a merry Christmas. Payton would be spending her holiday in Boston—job demands—and Gwen hated that she would have to spend it alone. Payton answered after several rings with a spirited, giggly voice.

"Well, don't you sound down and out about spending the holidays alone?" Gwen teased.

"Hey." Payton's voice dropped, "Gwen, what's up?" Background music played—Kenny G. and his one-tune-wonder wailing saxophone.

"I just wanted to wish you a merry Christmas. What are you having, a party over there?"

"Not exactly." Payton told someone on her end, "Look on the top shelf, to your left."

"Payton, you have company, you sly dog. Hope it's no one I know." It was a joke.

"Uh, OK, if you say so." Payton answered mysteriously.

Gwen's mouth dropped. "Vaughn?!"

"Uh, OK, if you say so." Payton was talking in code.

"Oooh, well I'll be damned." Gwen knew Vaughn was on vacation, but she'd had no idea he would be spending it in Boston. Which was probably because she hadn't talked to Payton in a couple of weeks.

"Uh, let's talk later. OK, Gwen?" The latter came out covert.

"OK. Wait, no. Don't hang up. I mean, let me get some juicy dirt now to pacify me. They'll require one-word answers unless you can spare more. OK?" Gwen had a little time for some silliness.

"Uh-huh." Payton sounded tickled.

"Is he in town for more than a day?"

"Uh-huh."

"Two?"

"Three."

"Oh, my, my, my. Y'all are really starting to happen, huh?"

"I think."

"Is the divorce final?"

"Almost."

"Is he staying with you while he's in town?"

"No!"

"If he wants to, can he stay with you?"

Payton giggled, "Uh-huh."

Gwen giggled too, this was fun. "OK, well, I think I'm satisfied for the moment. But just a word of advice." Finally she got to play psychologist.

"What?"

"Be careful. Take things slow. I like Vaughn, but I love you. OK?"

"Okey-dokey."

"And one more thing," Gwen chuckled, "don't hurt him," before she laughed out loud.

"Now that I can't promise," Payton snorted through her own laughter.

They wished each other merry Christmas and Gwen hung up the phone and began packing for her evening flight to Chicago.

Gwen flew Delta, first class, into Chicago's O'Hare airport. A cab delivered her safely to a suite hotel in Downers Grove, west of the city. A glass elevator sailed smoothly to the third floor. It didn't dawn on her that Xavier may not have been in his room until after she had already knocked on his door.

Damn, what if he's not alone?

Gwen rubbed her forehead, kneading her paranoid thoughts from her mind. She needed to get a grip.

Either I trust him or I don't.

"Gwendolyn? Hey..."

Gwen waved. "Hey."

"I was just trying your house again. You had me worried." He stood in front of the door dressed in a black Nike sweat suit, but he hadn't invited her inside.

"I've been in the sky." Gwen flitted her eyes upward and waved her hand in an exaggerated gesture. "I know I should have called..."

"No, you're fine, really. Come in, please." He stepped aside and Gwen walked into his suite. The television set cheered on ESPN, of course. And his wildly colorful screensaver swirled on his IBM laptop sitting on the oak desk.

"Do you have any bags...or anything?" Xavier asked.

"They're in the lobby with the concierge. I, um, made arrangements to fly out tomorrow morning for Charlotte. If the invitation is still open?" she asked somewhat innocently.

He moved closer. "It is."

She looked up at him; his demeanor still seemed uncertain as to whether he was out of the doghouse or not. And Gwen's face remained calm, but not overly receptive.

"Uh, do you have a room here, or—" Xavier left the question open.

"I was hoping I could stay with you." Gwen lowered her eyes, then slowly raised them again. "If that's OK?"

"Uh-huh. It is." This time Xavier lightly touched her cheek, his posture relaxed.

Gwen moved into him and they hugged. He held her so tight, Gwen thought she would lose her breath, but then again she wasn't sure if she had breathed since she walked into the room—hell, since she boarded the plane.

He lifted her off her feet slightly and told her he loved her.

Gwen kissed his neck and pulled her face away from his, and demanded in a whisper, "Xavier, I don't want to share."

Xavier nodded, smiling just a little. "Understood."

Now Gwen smiled a little and wrapped her arms around his neck, telling him she loved him so much. They kissed.

Then Xavier began to whisper. "Gwendolyn, I don't want to share either."

Gwen touched the tip of his chin with her lips, "Uh-huh. Understood." It was definitely understood; she didn't want anyone else, ever.

Xavier stopped kissing and held her face between his hands, "Baby, why don't we make it officially understood." He looked dead serious.

"Officially?"

"Yeah, baby. Officially."

"Uh, as in..."

"As in, all of it. The ring, the church, the preacher, you as my wife, me as your husband, to have, to hold, a couple of babies.... All of it."

She looked at him, speechless for a few moments. "Uh, you don't think it's too soon, you know, for this talk? I mean for this proposal? You know, that maybe we're rushing..."

He shook his head with determination, "Uh-uh. Gwendolyn, you're it for me, baby. We don't have to do the deed right away. If you want a long engagement, then OK. But I want you. I want everything about you."

Gwen laughed. Laughed and cried between kisses. They instinctively, on cue, began to walk together toward the bed.

Xavier still held her face. "Do *you* think it's too soon, baby?" His speech was labored, sexy and breathless.

Slow down—don't slow down—slow down—don't even think about it...

"I want you in my life," Gwen said quietly as they both fell back onto the bed. Xavier lay on top of her, fully clothed; she wrapped her legs around his waist.

"So that's a..." he asked.

Gwen smiled. She heard *slow down* one more time before she mentally shouted *shut up!*

"It's a yes, Xavier. It's an absolute yes."

· FIFTEEN ·

TERRY STUART'S PHOTO on the local evening news looked like the other shoe about to drop—in the form of a huge, black combat boot.

Gwen leaned against the door facing Carmen's kitchen. She had just finished loading up the dishwasher after another of Carmen's delicious meals. And when she noticed that face on television, she quickly pulled herself up, twisted the dish towel around her fingers, and slumped alongside the door facing the TV as if she had just been kicked in the stomach.

The news anchor, with his dark, stiff hair and grim features, couldn't be heard above the thick noise of Xavier and Avery carrying on, and Carmen on the phone with her Moms, and all the sibling chatter bouncing off the walls from C. J. and Cec, clearly restless from being cooped up in the house on a stormy March evening. But Gwen knew, without any audible commentary, that the news was bad. Terry Stuart equaled bad any day of the week.

In no time, Gwen heard someone shush the room silent and the television volume grew louder. Carmen rolled beside Gwen and began to ask, "What's going on," before looking out into the den, where Avery and Xavier stood so close to the set.

Carmen rolled away from Gwen and joined the others. Gwen didn't move; she couldn't move. She closed her eyes as the news anchor delivered the misery.

Terry had raped another woman, here in Atlanta, in his hotel. They called it assault; they called it alleged; but Gwen knew better. Terry Stuart equaled rape—vicious, brutal rape—any day of the week.

The news was brief. Comments quickly followed.

"That bitch is lying," Avery began.

Xavier shook his head, then turned to look at Gwen still standing in the kitchen doorway. "Not now, man," he told Avery, knowing rape wouldn't be a good topic to broach in Gwen's presence. Gwen still didn't move, still twisted the dishcloth around her fingers so tight she felt her fingers throb, but it felt like nothing in comparison to the rest of her pain. Xavier moved towards her.

Avery kept grumbling while picking his teeth with a ragged toothpick. "I'm just speaking the truth. Hell, Xa, you know how them hoop-ho's can be."

"Man, shut the hell up," Xavier said sternly, before approaching Gwen. Avery grunted, but shut up as ordered. Xavier reached for her hand, untwisted the dishcloth, and threw it over his shoulder. Gwen stood like a mannequin, hardly blinking.

"Don't pay attention to Avery, baby," he whispered in her ear, then asked if she was OK. She nodded. Lying.

"Poor Terry, his life just seems to keep going downhill," said Carmen. She stayed in the den with remote in hand, flipping through the channels, maybe trying to find more news.

Her statement hurt. *Poor Terry* echoed in Gwen's head. She knew Carmen knew nothing about Terry having slept with Tracey; Xavier kept that to himself, and it seemed obvious that Carmen, much like Xavier, felt compassion for Terry's battered upbringing, but those words, "Poor Terry," still hurt like hell.

They only added more fuel for Avery: "Yeah, that's cause some greedy-ass sister always tryin' to keep a brother down."

"Will you shut the hell up, Avery? Now is not the time." Xavier looked back at Avery, then again to Gwen. Avery mumbled, "What the hell is..." then fell silent. Gwen could feel their eyes on her, all of them, Xavier, Carmen, Avery. Gwen straightened up and moved away from Xavier, just as Avery said, "Uh, sorry."

They knew now. She walked past Carmen, who seemed to look at Gwen as if *she* were handicapped, physically challenged, different. Gwen knew they knew. But no one knew the truth; no one knew the real drama, the real Gwen, just like they didn't know the real Terry.

Gwen ambled toward the door; her feet felt sluggish. She grabbed her purse off the brass coatrack without grabbing her jacket. A blanket of heavy rain greeted her as she opened the door and walked into it. She ended up in the driver's seat of her car, her keys dangling off her index finger by the Infiniti key ring, her body drenched with steady raindrops dripping from her curls into her lap, before she even realized Xavier had followed her out and sat down beside her in the car.

"Let's go back inside," Gwen heard him say; she had no idea how long he had been talking, or what all he had said previously. She only stared at the steering wheel, making no move to put the key in the ignition and no move to go back inside. She finally shook her head no.

"Gwendolyn, don't pay Avery any attention. You know how he gets. He's just saying all that stuff because it's Terry, that's all."

Gwen slowly turned her head in Xavier's direction. He was drenched as well, looking concerned, rubbing her hand. But his comment, *because it's Terry...*

"You believe the same thing, don't you?" Gwen couldn't really hear her voice, so she wasn't sure in exactly what tone the words stumbled out. Everything felt numb.

Xavier ran his hand across his head, shedding raindrops, and sighed heavily. "I, uh, don't know what to believe. I'd seen women do just about anything just to get next to Terry; the brother never had to work too hard to get…" Xavier shook his head. "Damn, I don't know. Terry may be a lot of things, but…"

"But what?" Now Gwen knew her questions sounded hateful.

Xavier squeezed her hand. "Baby, let's not talk about this, OK? I know this is not an issue you and I need to talk about. Besides, there's not enough information to make any kind of judgments, so let's just try…"

"He did it." Her voice began to break through the numbness. It sounded bitter and vengeful and angry.

Xavier looked at her hard, his hand stopped its soothing rub and rested on hers. "Gwendolyn, I know all this crap with Terry makes you think of your…I mean what happened in college, but baby, we just don't know whether it's true or not."

"It was rape, Xavier. What happened to me in college was rape, and it's true. Everything about him is true." Gwen removed her hand from his and covered her mouth. Her whimpers sounded like the rain, soft and sad. Her fingers trembled against her lips.

She heard Xavier sigh, frustrated. "Gwendolyn, let me take you home. You shouldn't be driving. Let's go to your place and dry off, maybe listen to some music, curl up in bed...We don't need to talk about this, let's talk about the wedding. You keep tellin' me I need to be more involved—well here I am, involve me." Xavier laughed, halfheartedly.

Gwen stared straight ahead, looking out the window, but seeing nothing.

She and Xavier were to be married in three months, June, a few days before Xavier's thirty-third birthday.

Together they had told Vaughn a couple of weeks after they became engaged. He seemed genuine in his surprise and equally genuine in his congratulations and good wishes. He said marriage could be wonderful, although his had finally ended.

But it was obvious to Gwen that Vaughn himself was in love, and Gwen knew for a fact that Payton was, although she and Vaughn were still in what she called "the introductory phase of courtship": trying to take it not too fast, not too slow. Payton had been to Atlanta twice more since November, and Vaughn had been to visit her in Boston more often than that. They were together; Payton was happy; and Gwen thought it was wonderful how love had found both her and Payton at a time they least expected it.

Soon, other staff members found out about Gwen and Xavier's engagement—probably signaled by the blinding, one-carat pear-shaped diamond that glowed on Gwen's finger. She received whispered congratulations and a few emails of nice sentiment. Miss Mabel and Shayla caught up with her in the restroom at the same time. Miss Mabel said, "I heard the good news, darling," before she condemned the nasty bitches to toilet hell. Shayla, primping in the mirror, said, "I guess you do know a little somethin'-somethin', girlfriend," before waddling out. She was due to deliver any day.

241

Gwen and Xavier would be married in Augusta, at Nana's church, in a Methodist ceremony. They had already visited with the pastor twice for the required premarital interviews. The pastor asked about their belief in God and Jesus Christ; he asked if their union had been thought through, if they cared for one another, if they loved each other in heart and soul. Their answers had been one resounding yes after another.

Now Gwen saw it all crumbling away.

"It was him," she whispered, still staring ahead.

Xavier didn't seem to hear. "Baby, give me the keys and let me take you home." He reached for her hand again.

"It was him," she stated louder, feeling the tears rising in her eyes.

Xavier sighed again, "Baby, we don't know what the truth is; hell, maybe Terry…"

"He did it." She looked at him. "He did it to me."

Xavier started to talk again, but then brought everything to an abrupt halt. He stared at her. He didn't understand; it was so obvious he didn't understand.

"Who did what?" he asked in a collected tone.

Gwen blinked tears down her face. The moment of *her* truth had arrived. She knew she should have told it long ago: not just to Xavier, but eleven years ago, when it happened. Then maybe now it wouldn't have happened to another woman. How many had there been in between?

Oh God, oh God, oh God…

Gwen closed her eyes, then slowly opened them. Parts of her still felt numb. Parts of her didn't feel the pain flowing through her body, nor was she fully prepared for the pain she was about to inflict.

"He—him, he was the one," she gasped. She still couldn't speak his name out loud. Her keys began to jingle in her shaky grasp. "In college. It was him." Her tears stopped flowing, momentarily. Gwen waited.

Xavier said nothing; he only looked at her in disbelief. His beautiful brown eyes squinted in bewilderment, his lips parted slightly, and his body sat frozen. Gwen watched his eyes, watched them blink in rapid succession, before widening.

"Terry? Is that who you're talking about?"

Gwen nodded; a quick jut of her head.

Xavier looked away from her, sighing hard breaths. He muttered, "Shit, Gwendolyn," obviously thinking she was losing her mind.

Neither one of them spoke, not for a few minutes. The rain had lessened, yet still thumped against the windshield. The air in the car stifled; the damp smell of rain-drenched clothes built a suffocating wall between them.

"You're tired; let me take you home." Xavier sighed again and pulled the keys from her hand.

"It's true, Xavier. It was him." She couldn't hold onto her drama anymore; she had no choice.

Xavier shook his head and said, "Gwendolyn, that's *bullshit,*" then stopped, holding two fingers to his mouth as he tried to temper his tone. He took another deep breath. "Baby, I love you. You know how much I love you, but we can't seem to get past this. Why don't we go talk to someone, someone who can help us both deal with it..."

"No." Gwen shook her head. She grabbed a handful of soggy curls and pushed them away from her forehead, and sobbed, "I'm not crazy and I'm not lying." Gwen reached to touch his face; she caressed his cheek. "Baby, the rape happened in North Carolina, when I was a freshman...and you were a senior. That's where I started college—not South Carolina. He..." she stammered, then gulped hard, "Terry's the one who raped me. At the party you guys threw after the Elite Eight."

Xavier's eyes grew the size of golf balls, "What is wrong with you? Gwendolyn, do you hear how crazy that sounds? Look, just...let me drive you home." He opened his car door.

Gwen grabbed his sweatshirt, crying, "Baby, please." It was time, finally, to explain everything, reveal everything, give up all the defenses and all the barriers and all the bullshit she'd been holding out since she'd first seen Xavier appear in the halls at Talbot and Talbot.

Xavier looked at her, studied her a moment with obvious confusion, then closed the door and settled back in.

Gwen released his shirt and sat evenly in the driver's seat. She

stared at her hands as she tried to explain. Xavier sat quietly. She could see peripherally that his body was turned toward her as she told him she had attended the same college as he in 1987. She gave the street he and The Team lived on and a vague description of the townhouse—the blue-gray matted carpet, the run-down sofa with a drab-green blanket with fringes thrown over it.

Tears reappeared as she described Terry's room, the room he had raped her in, with the Kareem Abdul-Jabbar poster on the wall and the gaudy trophies that sat on the television; the aluminum foil twisted around the ends of its antenna made the trophy figures look like space aliens disembarking their rocket.

Her sobs grew louder as she told him she vividly remembered the poster on the ceiling above Terry's bed: a porno poster, a woman's naked, airbrushed body sitting with legs spread and ice cream dripping down her chin and over her melon-sized breasts, making its way to the gooey glob already formed between her legs. After that, Gwen couldn't go on. She buried her head in her hands and cried.

Xavier didn't touch her, didn't comfort her. She wiped her face with the back of her hand after a few minutes and pulled her face up to look at him. He sat, his body faced forward, his elbow rested on the arm of the door with his head dropped in his hand.

Gwen lightly touched his thigh. "Xavier..."

He looked at her. His eyes drooped, heavy, drained, and upset, and his face appeared so tight that it seemed ready to shatter from the pressure. He looked at her as if she were a stranger.

"W—will you talk to me?" Gwen asked, begged.

"You're fucking unbelievable, you know that?"

"I know I should have told you...I should have told you it was him the night I told you about the rape, about my life back then. And I planned on it, I planned on telling you everything, everything I'd been holding on to." Gwen gulped. "And I did tell you everything; things I've never told anyone. And you understood and you loved me and it seemed so irrelevant to give the monster a name...that I just didn't. I'm sorry." She reached to touch his face.

He blocked her touch, raising his hand with his fingers spread wide. "This is bullshit." He looked away.

Gwen suddenly felt cold—her teeth chattered. "You don't believe me?"

Xavier didn't answer and he didn't look at her either.

"Do you remember that night, the night of the party? The night of Carmen's accident?" she asked rapidly.

Now he looked at her again. A vein in his temple pulsed. "Gwendolyn, I'll never forget the night of Carmen's accident."

Gwen knew she had touched a nerve, but she had to continue. "And where was Terry? Did you see him that night before you left?" Her voice sounded piercing inside the car.

Xavier shook his head, as if she was still tripping. He was quiet for a moment, then he said, "Yeah, I needed his keys so I could move his car. It was blocking mine." Xavier spoke slow, cautiously, as if searching his memory of that night.

Gwen looked down. "And did you find him?"

There was a slight pause. "Yeah, I found him..." Xavier stopped. Gwen looked at him; watched him agonize over his memories of that night. He began again, speaking softly, "I, uh, took his keys off his dresser by the door. He was kickin' it with some—" Suddenly Xavier looked at her.

Now Gwen knew. Her eyes met his eyes. "That was me! You're the one who walked in and walked right back out, didn't you?" Her voice shriveled from piercing to pathetic.

Xavier blinked, kept his eyes shut for a second, then opened them again and nodded. He closed his eyes again and squeezed the lids tight before he covered his face with his hands, rubbing his forehead.

Gwen wanted to say something, but she didn't know what. She watched the feelings evident in his face go from confused to betrayed.

He looked at her. "Look, I don't know what happened to you in college, or what college or when. I don't know if it messed your head up so bad that now you're calling everything rape, or what..."

Gwen shook her head, frantically, trying to tell him no, but unable to utter a word.

Xavier kept talking, rambling, cursing. He would look away from her, then back at her again. His anger glowed. "Don't sit here and do this shit to me, Gwendolyn." Xavier held his index finger up, steadied it in front of her face, "Don't sit here, right here, with me…" Xavier pressed his finger in his chest then held it again in front of her face, "…and tell me that all this time you've known me from years ago; that you've known Terry. And now you've got this story to tell. When were you going to tell me this, Gwendolyn? Huh? When?"

Gwen reached and clasped his finger with her hand; she opened her mouth to speak, to try to give some explanation, but words wouldn't come out. Xavier removed his hand from hers and looked directly into her eyes. "So, you're saying Terry raped you?"

For some reason his question and its skeptical tone surprised Gwen. She didn't answer immediately; she had just explained that he had, but now the way Xavier asked was scaring her. He kept staring at her, hard, waiting on an answer. She wasn't sure what to make of it or what to say. She cocked her head and stammered, "What?" Xavier blurted angrily, "Did he rape you, Gwendolyn?"

Gwen blinked anxiously. "Why are you talking to me like this? It was rape. You were there, you saw him with me…" Gwen paused. "What is this, Xavier?" She shook her head; she could hear the tremble in her voice. She knew she had deceived him by withholding her truth, but it *was* the truth. She leaned closer to Xavier, their eyes locked. "What are you questioning Xavier, whether what you saw was rape or not? What do you think, I volunteered Terry a fuck?"

Xavier studied her intently before looking away and mumbling, "Did you?"

Gwen reached out of nowhere and tried to slap the shit out of him. He grabbed her wrist, but that didn't stop her from rising up out of her seat to attempt more damage. He grabbed her other wrist and squeezed so tight it hurt, then forcefully jerked her back down in her seat. Gwen cried out from the pain, the anger, the drama of everything bursting into the open. The rain began to pick up again. Gwen heard herself screaming, "That shit is not true. How could you believe that?"

Xavier held her wrists tighter; his face looked menacing, "Gwendolyn, you're the one that's been holding out all this time, telling what you want to tell, and now *I'm* supposed to know the truth. I'm not dealing with this shit, do you hear me, Gwendolyn, I am not dealing with this shit!" Xavier got right in her face, hollering at her.

She didn't speak anymore, but just wailed, wept so loud her body convulsed. Xavier jerked her wrists loose. Gwen dropped her head down on the emergency brake and screamed in tears.

Xavier slammed the door so hard on his way out that the car rocked where it sat.

Gwen made it home after Xavier left her crying in her car, how she wasn't sure. Nor was she aware of how long it took. Once home, she cried some more, still dressed in her soaked clothes, still battered from the pain that flowed freely now. She was no longer numb. Bluish-gray bruises circled her wrists like handcuffs.

She stripped out of her clothes, still crying, sometimes in soft, whimpering sobs, but most often with choked-up screams. She didn't turn the bathroom light on, just fiddled with the hot water knob of the shower, added minimal cold water, and curled up on the shower floor with her knees pulled up to her chest, and let the heat console and abuse her at the same time.

Later that night, Gwen lay across her bed, only a sheet draped over her naked body, and listened to the phone ring. She hadn't the inclination to answer it, nor the energy to talk if she did. The answering machine did all the work. Gwen just listened.

First was a call from Nana, checking to see if her Gwenny could squeeze in a visit to Miss Delilah when she came to Augusta next weekend. "She hasn't seen you since you were a young girl, and when I went to check on her today, you know make sure she was getting by all right, I told her about you getting married. You know I'm always bragging about you, and she sure would like to see the fine young woman you've turned into, said she'd like to meet Xavier too, except she called him Savior, bless her heart, you know she's almost a hundred...Give it some thought, Gwenny, and I'll see you in a few days."

Next came a call from Payton: "Uh, hi Gwen, I was hoping to catch you at home. Listen, I was just watching ESPN, um, well listen, give me a call as soon as you get this message. It's important."

Terry Stuart. Gwen already knew.

Then Carmen called: "Gwen, pick up if you're there." There was a pause; her voice sounded shaky. "...I guess you're not in. I've been trying to reach Xavier. He left here hours ago and he seemed...well, he seemed pretty upset. I don't know what's going on with you two, but I'm worried about him; I'm worried about you too. I've called his house and Avery went by there a while ago and he wasn't in. If you see him, if he comes by, will you have him call or will you please give me a call when you get in? Gwen, I'm scared, I know that probably sounds overly dramatic, but something's not right and um, I'm scared. I, uh, I love you. I'll talk to y—"

The machine cut her off. Gwen rose up slightly. Gwen had no idea where Xavier was; probably driving around trying to shake his anger...

His anger...

Gwen sat up, pulled the sheet up over her breasts. She remembered the anger in Xavier's eyes while he jerked her around in the car; the spark of hatred. She had seen that look before. *Where? When?*

Gwen pulled her knees up to her chest and wrapped her arms around them. Suddenly she bolted upright. The look on Xavier's face; the spark of hatred in his eyes was the same look she witnessed when they fought about Ellis, the night of her birthday back in August. But it wasn't about Ellis—it was the way he looked when he told her about Tracey and Terry. In a split second, while recounting the events surrounding Tracey's confession about sleeping with Terry, anger had flickered in Xavier's soft eyes like a spark from a cigarette lighter, then faded away. Gwen remembered it vividly. It scared her then, like it scared her now.

She jumped out of bed and threw on a pair of jeans and a sweat-shirt. She descended the stairs in twos, then something inside her made her turn around and run back up them.

She grabbed her gun from the nightstand drawer and shoved it in her purse.

Gwen drove directly to Xavier's condo. She knew Avery had already checked, but it seemed like a good starting point. She had a key and she'd wait for him if she had to. She'd wait all night if she had to.

She rang the doorbell first, then immediately began to use her key. She didn't have to. Xavier answered the door quickly.

"What are you doing here?" He looked surprised; his voice sounded harsh. He also wore jeans and an old, faded sweatshirt—a change from the sopping wet clothes hours before.

Gwen muttered, "I'm here for you," as she walked past him inside the house.

He grabbed her forearm and said, "Well I don't need you. How 'bout you just go." The grip on her arm wasn't as tight as before, but it still pinched.

She pulled away, wanting to cry. "I'm not leaving, not until you listen to me." She tried to sound stronger than she felt.

Xavier still stood by the door, and he held it open wider. "Leave, Gwendolyn. I don't want you here." He wouldn't look at her. He sounded so angry, and he looked like he didn't know her, didn't want her, didn't love her, anymore.

She walked up to him, grabbed the door, and slammed it shut. "I'm sorry. But I can't leave you like this; I can't leave things like this. If you don't want to believe that he—that Terry did what he did to me, then so be it. If you would rather believe that I willingly fucked that monster, then fine. But you can't believe that I don't love you; that this whole...that our entire relationship has meant nothing to me." Gwen stood closer; Xavier looked straight ahead, refusing to make eye contact. Gwen reached for his face, willing to take the chance that he might push her away. She lightly touched his cheek. "I love you, Xavier. I didn't plan on falling in love with you; I didn't plan that you would walk back into my life. I hated you...I thought I hated you when I first saw you again. Why do you think I didn't want

to have anything to do with you when you first joined Talbot? Why do you think I treated you like shit for all those weeks? *This* was why, *Terry fucking Stuart* and what he fucking did to me was why. Ten years I've hid all of this, struggled with it, and then you stroll back into my life… I thought I hated every member of The Team. For years it was as if The Team raped me, not just Terry, but The Team. Until I fell in love with you."

Xavier moved her hand. "Go away, Gwendolyn." His tone was softer, just a little, but a definite change from the hostility of a few moments earlier. He looked down at her, tears shining in the corner of his eyes.

Gwen moved closer, her own tears beginning again. She rose up on the balls of her feet and whispered, "Don't send me away. I know this will take us a long time to work through, but we love each other. Baby, please…" Gwen wrapped both arms around his waist. He seized her shoulders and lightly pushed her away.

"I don't want you here." Xavier shook his head and opened the door again.

Terry Stuart stood behind it.

"Well, I'll be damned, my man Fessor. Man, when I got your message at the hotel, I couldn't believe it. It's good to see you, man, it's good to see you," Terry crowed. He grabbed Xavier's hand and tugged and pulled on it. Xavier breathed deep and wiped the palm of his hand hard down his mouth. He looked at Gwen quickly.

Gwen began to back up away from them. Her knees were crumbling underneath her, although, miraculously, they still held her up.

There stood Terry Stuart, huge and haunting. He was grinning, which showed his crowded teeth; his dark skin looked blotchy and discolored in spots, and his eyes sunk inward, still black with evil, yet also sort of crazed. Like Weldon used to look.

Terry walked inside without an invitation. Xavier hadn't spoken. No one had spoken but Terry, and he didn't seem to notice.

"Man, I been gettin' calls left and right, my lawyers, the coach, the damn police. All these fuckin' people been on my back, but to hear from your ass, man—hell, I needed to hear from an old friend

like the Fessor." Terry paused. He slapped Xavier's shoulder. "Man, that's still a good title for you, ain't it? You know…bygones and shit." Terry grinned again, a little less exuberant, but his eyes grew large as he spoke. He was definitely buzzing from something.

Xavier sort of nodded, mumbled, "Yeah, man," which led to more verbiage from Terry: "True dat, man. Yeah, this a nice place you got. I, uh started to call you before I left, you know, get clear on the directions and shit, but I found it all right, after making a few wrong stops and shit."

Terry stopped and noticed Gwen standing there. "Uh, damn man, my ass just going off at the mouth, I ain't know you was into something.'" He beamed at Gwen and licked his ash-dry lips; his black eyes darted up and down her body.

Xavier stood slightly off to the side of Terry, fully in Gwen's view. He looked at her much the same way he had the night of her birthday, months ago. She felt immobile, yet her body began to quake. Her head began to move in little spastic shakes. She felt trapped.

Xavier squinted his eyes, studying her, then walked toward her while talking to Terry. "It's cool man. Uh, Gwend—she was just leaving." Xavier grabbed her hand, held it, felt it quivering in his. He seemed so composed.

"Why is he here?" Gwen found the energy to ask, almost in a whisper.

"Just some business." This was Xavier's explanation.

"This your lady, man?" Terry asked.

"Listen, Terry, I just thought maybe we could talk, you know clear the air about some things, you know." Xavier ignored his question and began his own agenda.

Terry muttered, "True dat, man."

Xavier pulled on Gwen's hand, heading towards the door. "Why don't you go on in the den, I'll be right there." Terry mumbled another, "True dat," and watched as they walked past him.

Gwen tried to loosen Xavier's grasp, not wanting to leave, as scared as she was. She had found herself face to face with Terry Stuart again. Her fear needed to take a back seat, not take over as it had done eleven

years ago. She had no idea what Xavier had in mind, what kind of confrontation he had planned, but Xavier would have to wait in line. Terry's ass was hers.

Terry began to walk away, toward the den.

"Terry, The Chump-Ass Man Stuart." Gwen's voice wavered, but sounded loud and clear nonetheless.

Terry stopped and turned around. "Say what?"

Xavier pulled her along, telling her, "Go home, let me handle this."

Gwen jerked away. "Handle what? Are you going to ask him if we fucked? Yeah, I'd like to hear it myself. Tell him, Terry. Tell him about us."

"Gwendolyn, stop." Xavier placed his hand on her shoulder. Gwen moved away and tightened the grip on her purse.

Terry sniffed and wiggled his index finger across his nose, then raised his hands in surrender. "Look, I don't know what's goin' on here, but I ain't up for more shit. Xavier, man, call me when you get things together." He walked towards them, heading for the door.

Xavier threw his hand against Terry's chest, stopping him. "Terry, man, we got shit to discuss."

"Shit, man." Terry threw Xavier's hands off him.

Gwen pulled her gun out, steadied it in her hands, and leveled the barrel at Terry's head, just a foot or so away. "You punk-ass..." Gwen's voice began to lose what momentary control she'd had over it.

Simultaneously it seemed, Xavier and Terry both jumped back, startled by the Glock. Terry yelled, "What's wrong with this bitch?" and kept backing up. Xavier hollered for her to give him the gun. Gwen shook her head, *No, no, hell no...*

"Tell him, Terry. Tell him how you raped me; tell him..."

"Raped your ass? Hell bitch, I ain't ever *seen* you before. Stupid-ass bitches always trippin'..." Terry kept walking back until he hit the wall. Gwen followed, keeping the gun aimed at his head, then pressed the barrel up against his neck.

"Gwendolyn, give me the gun!" Xavier's voice bellowed from behind her.

Gwen shook her head. "Uh-uh."

Terry began to sweat; beads popped up from out of nowhere and ran down his face. The smell of alcohol and some other pungent fume filled the air. Piss. Terry's piss.

Gwen moved closer, pushing the barrel harder against his jugular. "Oh, Terry, you disappoint me. I thought I would have left a much more lasting impression on you. Let me refresh your punk-ass memory."

"Gwendolyn, give me the goddamn gun!" Now Xavier stood off to the side, between she and Terry.

"No," she said, without looking at him.

"Fessor, man, get this crazy bitch off my ass," Terry stammered. The collar of his gray mock turtleneck was soaked in scare-sweat.

Gwen began to slide the gun down his neck, past his chest and stomach, before pushing it into his crotch. Terry squeezed his body tighter against the wall.

"Uh-uh. I think you better think twice who you call a bitch. Seein' as how my ass has the gun, and you're pissin' in your pants." Gwen rammed the gun harder into his crotch; his dick felt like mush. "Ooh, what's wrong? Can't you get it up for this? When you raped me you were hard as steel. Can't you get it up for this?" Gwen rammed again.

Terry lifted onto his toes; he began to plead, "Shit, look, you got me mixed up with someone else. Please, don't shoot, don't—please! Fessor, tell her, man!" He cut his eyes to Xavier.

Xavier approached Gwen. "Baby, give me the gun." Xavier touched her shoulder. "He's not worth it, baby, please." Xavier sounded so comforting and warm and scared.

Gwen shook her head no. She wanted so badly to squeeze the trigger, to blow Terry Stuart's nuts to pieces.

Xavier touched her wrist. "Give me the gun, baby..."

She began to melt; she could feel tears clouding her eyes as she looked away from Terry. Her grip on the Glock loosened and she slowly lowered it. She looked into Xavier's eyes. He believed her.

"You crazy-ass *bitch*—"

Terry's backhanded fist across the side of her head knocked Gwen to the floor, and the gun followed. Gwen could feel herself losing consciousness as she lay on the floor, watching Xavier bang Terry against the wall repeatedly. Gwen closed her eyes, then opened them again; her head pounded. There was a lot of noise, cursing, things breaking. She couldn't see Xavier and Terry anymore, but she could still hear fighting; she heard Xavier growl, "I could kill your ass for what you did to her," then there were more punching sounds, hard, fierce.

Her eyes closed and she heard nothing else.

Gwen woke up in a hospital bed. She could tell by the humming machines, the antiseptic smell, the clouds of white that engulfed her. The room was dark—it was nighttime, or maybe it was daytime, and the blinds were just closed. She tried to widen her eyes, but this made her head hurt, so she stopped trying.

Someone touched her fingers. Her eyes focused, finally, on Xavier, sitting beside her bed.

"You're OK." He looked tired, but he attempted a weak smile. His lip looked swollen and his eyes looked dull.

"What..." Gwen tried to talk. This made her head hurt. She stopped trying.

"You've got a concussion, but you're going to be OK. Nana's here. She went downstairs to get some coffee. She's been here all day, right by your side. She'll be right back."

Gwen nodded; she wanted to keep her eyes open, wanted to talk and ask questions, but she felt herself drifting again.

When she awoke again, Nana and Weldon were sitting by her bed. Xavier was gone.

· SIXTEEN ·

Nana told Gwen her lunch was ready. Campbell's soup, Chicken and Stars, with saltine crackers on the side. Gwen's favorite.

"Yes, ma'am, in a minute." Gwen never took her eyes off the book sitting in her lap. She was on page seven; yesterday she had been on page seven. The day before—page seven.

She knew Nana still stood in the kitchen, looking at her as she sat in her recliner. Nana would continue to stand there, staring at her for a while, giving her a few minutes, and would then repeat, "Come on and eat, Gwenny. Please come on and eat..." And Gwen would again reply, "Yes, ma'am. In a minute."

Minutes would turn into hours, Nana's requests would turn into pleas, and Gwen would eventually slink off the recliner and trudge upstairs to her room without saying another word, or going near the kitchen, or eating a bite of anything. This had been going on for nearly three months. When and if she ate, she nibbled, moved food from one side of the plate to the other, then abandoned the whole eating concept.

Gwen knew she needed to pull herself together. She kept telling herself,

Get a grip...

Get yourself together...

But it was as if her mind spoke to an empty audience; her body and soul had other ideas. She wanted her old life back, the one she'd had with Xavier just a few months ago. She wanted to smile again, to feel again—and yet, she still wanted Terry Stuart dead, as he had been for nearly three months now.

The night after he sent Gwen to the hospital with a concussion—

the night after Xavier had beat him like he owned him, and nearly killed him with his bare hands had it not been for a just-arrived Avery pulling the two men apart while Carmen called nine-one-one—Terry collapsed in Hartsfield International Airport.

He wasn't supposed to be leaving: the investigation into the rape for which he'd been accused was still proceeding, but Terry didn't give a shit about that. Witnesses at the airport said he looked like a beat-up madman; the Delta agent said he cursed her for not moving fast enough, then cursed the other customers, then cursed security. At that point he was detained and told to settle down, but he resisted, shoving the security guard, before running through the airport like a lunatic. He collapsed on Concourse T: a gigantic coronary, induced by huge quantities of cocaine in his system along with alcohol, painkillers, and antidepressant medication.

When she heard the news of his death, she tried to smile, tried to rally her emotions into cheer, but she couldn't. After all, she was glad he was dead, and particularly glad neither she nor Xavier had killed him and landed in trouble. But death was a good fit for Terry. She only wished it had happened before he had come to Atlanta and brought with him all of that drama.

Now that he was dead, she thought, she could go back to her old life, but better—no more Terry Stuart; no more emotional beatings; no more nightmares.

It didn't happen.

The nightmares continued, nightly and even more intense.

Xavier didn't come back to her; she hadn't seen him since the day she returned home from the hospital.

"We both need time, Gwendolyn," he had said when she saw him again at her house that day. He stood across from her as she lay upright in her bed. Her concussion had been a doozy and left her hazy for days.

Nana had been with her since the hospital, even when Gwen told her to go home. The old woman wasn't going anywhere anytime soon.

That day Gwen listened to Xavier talk, but could only hear her own interpretation. When he said, "Too much has happened, and we

both need to take the time to sort everything out," what she heard in her head was *you're losing me.* When he walked closer as she stared at him—past him, really—and said, "You need time to heal, I need time to heal, and I don't think either us is in any shape to move on as if nothing happened," it still sounded like *you're losing me.* And when he timorously touched her face and kissed her forehead without saying anything else, without telling her he loved her, without saying she wouldn't lose him, but remaining quiet as if waiting for her to speak, until he finally walked slowly out the door, Gwen whispered, "I've lost you," then curled up in her bed and cried.

Gwen had only taken a week to recover from the concussion before she went back to the office. Vaughn had been in touch, told her she could take as long as she needed, without questioning a whole lot. He knew enough, just as Carmen and Avery and Nana and Weldon knew enough.

Gwen had been in the hospital.

Xavier had been in a fight.

Terry Stuart was dead.

And she and Xavier were no longer together; their wedding had been canceled.

That was more than enough information. They could fill in the rest with whatever they wanted to. Gwen didn't really care.

But she went back to work regardless. Big mistake. She couldn't function and had a hard time even trying to look like she could. She felt the way she had felt eleven years ago. Even the simplest things seemed too hard to do.

Xavier stayed away on assignments most of the time, so having him around wasn't a problem. He called occasionally; Nana took the calls. Gwen couldn't seem to pull herself together to talk.

What more did they have to discuss anyway?

Things were in shambles.

End of discussion.

Carmen kept in touch, but neither one of them had much to say. They cried together the first time Carmen came to visit. Carmen loved Gwen as much as Gwen loved her. She didn't understand everything

that had happened, or why it had happened, but she did understand that her brother was in pain, that Gwen was in pain, and that she felt helpless. Gwen only nodded and cried.

Gwen cried all the time. All the time. At work she would go to the restroom and cry. Sometimes she wiped away tears as she sat at her desk. When she came home, greeted by Nana with a worried look, she'd lie and say that she was fine, then go upstairs, put on her pajamas, and cry.

Maybe she cried over the loss of Xavier.

Maybe she cried over the loss of herself.

Maybe she cried over the realization that she had never owned enough of herself to lose, not fully. Perpetrating a fraud, perhaps.

Maybe all of the above.

In any case, the pain only seemed to get worse. She could feel it creeping through her veins and she couldn't do a damn thing about it. The nightmares kept attacking every night. After several weeks of trying, Gwen took an indefinite leave of absence from work.

Since then she hadn't left her house, and rarely changed out of her pajamas.

When she wasn't crying, or trying to dull her pain with restless sleep, she felt angry, pissed off at anyone and everyone who came in her path.

She tried to keep it in check with Nana, but it was hard. Nana was Nana, the best woman in the world. But Gwen was getting sick and tired of her tiptoeing around her, suggesting that she eat, suggesting that she get some fresh air. Gwen wanted her to go home, leave her alone, and usually when she felt herself about to explode, on the verge of yelling at her dear Nana, Gwen would simply leave the room. Nana used to follow, hound her some more. But in the last couple of weeks she had stopped following.

Instead she brought in reinforcements.

First there was Payton. She tried to keep in touch by phone, but Gwen rarely talked. Too hard. So Payton dropped by a few weeks ago on one of her visits with Vaughn, or maybe she came specifically for Gwen. Gwen didn't know, didn't ask, didn't really care.

"Come to Boston with me, Gwen," Payton chimed, like there was some big Girl Scout convention going on in Boston.

"No."

"You need to get out of the house." Payton's voice became serious.

"I'm fine right here."

"No, you're not."

"Then I'm not."

There was a long pause, then a heavy sigh.

Gwen lay in bed, the blinds drawn, her pillow folded underneath her head. She couldn't see Payton, who sat on the other side of the bed. Gwen kept her back to her.

"You're sinking." Payton sounded as if she were about to cry.

Gwen didn't respond.

Another long pause.

"If you sink too low, it's a bitch to get back up. You know this, Gwen."

"Sinking feels good at the moment."

"That means it's working."

Gwen didn't respond.

"You know I do volunteer counseling at the Rape Crisis Center in Boston, well, really it's in Cambridge," Payton began.

Gwen said nothing.

"We do a lot of one-on-one, group sessions..."

"Don't need it."

"I'm sure there's a good one here we could get you set up with..."

"Nope."

Payton rubbed Gwen's shoulder, "Well, think about it."

"Nope."

Another heavy sigh.

Gwen closed her eyes and waited for the sound of Payton leaving.

Now today, it appeared Nana's reinforcement was Weldon, of all people.

"Nana's pretty worried about you." Weldon's voice traveled as he followed Gwen upstairs.

She had left her room to get some orange juice. She knew Nana

had gone to the grocery store to stock up on more food Gwen had no desire to eat. Gwen figured she could get to the kitchen and back to her room without a lot of hassle.

She was surprised when she found Weldon perched in her den, watching television. Not because he was there, in her house; she and Weldon had been getting along better since Thanksgiving. He had been to visit her in Atlanta a few times. He and Xavier had become OK friends. And she and Weldon had become sister and brother again, or an abbreviated version thereof.

But Gwen knew he was here because Nana had him babysitting her while she went to the store. That pissed her off.

Gwen ignored him as she walked laboriously up the stairs. She had finished her juice in the kitchen and had ignored him there, too. He kept following her, saying the same thing, "Nana's pretty worried," like a broken record. Gwen kept walking, as hard as it was.

"Gwenny, did you hear me? You got Nana scared as hell."

"So take her home." Gwen walked in her room and slammed the door. Probably in his face.

He opened it. "Why don't you stop trippin'?"

"Why don't you stay out of my fucking business?"

"Cause yo business is killin' Nana, that's why." He stood in front of her, blocking her desire to get back in bed.

"Oh, what is this—Mr. Reformed Crack-head suddenly cares about Nana?" Gwen moved to her left, but her legs felt weak. Her head still felt woozy sometimes.

Weldon moved to his right, blocking her still. "Gwenny, your bullshit don't faze me. You still the same uppity-ass Gwenny. Got your man beatin' the shit out of some other brother you was trippin' with and now he don't want nothin' to do with you. Same-old same-old, huh Gwenny? Can't have your way. Look at you, lookin' all 'Thriller' and shit. Stop being a punk-ass and deal with your shit."

Gwen backed up. "Deal with *my* shit? Weld, where the fuck have you been? *I've* been dealing with shit—my shit, your shit, for sixteen years. *I* have been the one here for Nana, while you were…*around*. I have been the functioning adult; the one who made it to work every

day; the one who made a life for myself, a damn decent life..." Gwen began crying again. "I didn't keep drowning my ass in alcohol or run and pick up a crack pipe to deal with shit, not when Mama and Daddy died, not when Terry Stuart raped me, and not fucking now! So don't you tell me about dealing with shit! I am the Queen of Shit-Dealing!"

"Gwenny!" Nana stood at the door.

Xavier stood behind her.

Gwen looked at her.

She could see Nana's pain, the helplessness in Nana's eyes. Now Nana knew she had been raped.

Now Weldon knew.

Now Xavier was hearing it again.

He stood just behind Nana in the doorway. He looked tired and like he had lost some weight. He wore one of his dark blue business suits, like he had just come from work. He probably had. Gwen realized she didn't know what day it was, or the time.

Who gave a damn?

The sight of him made her angrier.

Nana walked in and Xavier followed. They circled Gwen like an intervention.

No one spoke.

Nana began to cry.

Weldon shook his head, then dropped it.

Xavier looked at her; his sad eyes turned sadder.

Gwen knew she looked bad. She hadn't looked at herself in a mirror recently, but she knew.

"What the hell are you doing here?" Gwen posed the question to Xavier, then quickly turned to Nana. "Did you call him?"

Nana nodded. "Sweetie, we want to help you. You're not eating and—"

"So, Xavier's here to make me eat?"

Xavier moved closer. "Gwendolyn, no one is here to make you do anything. Nana's concerned, we're all concer—"

"Save it. Go away." She made direct eye contact with Xavier. "I don't want you here. I don't need you and I don't want you."

Gwen watched his throat take a big gulp. He sucked in some air through his nose; his chest inflated, then deflated as he slowly exhaled.

Gwen didn't take her eyes away from his.

Her words hurt him.

So what.

She didn't need Xavier's pity and she didn't need him for Nana's feeding patrol. He could go to hell. They all could go to hell, or at least get out of her room.

Nana approached with arms outreached.

Gwen bucked and raised her hands, not wanting to be touched, comforted, loved.

"Feel free to stay and have a party. I'm out." Gwen pushed her legs to the door and left them. She found refuge in the basement until she was sure they had gone.

That night, Gwen threw on some clothes, packed a bag, and crept downstairs into the garage.

She started the car and let it idle. She adjusted the rearview mirror and caught a glimpse of herself. Her face looked gaunt and pale; her lips, chapped and crusted; her eyes, red and puffy.

Where the hell was she going?

She stayed in the car and lowered the windows. She hadn't opened the garage door. She reached down beside the driver's seat and felt for the electronic seat recliner. She pressed it and eased herself back, closing her eyes.

Sleep would be good.

Minutes passed, and she breathed deeply and slowly.

Gwen began to drift; it didn't feel so bad.

More minutes passed.

Suddenly there was Terry. Black eyes, laughter. His face pressed against her face.

He wanted her to join him. Maybe they could get into a little somethin'-somethin', just the two of them, alone. No rescue. No escape.

Permanent sleep meant permanent Terry.

Permanent pain.

Gwen opened her eyes.

She left the garage. The next morning she landed at Boston's Logan International Airport.

· SEVENTEEN ·

THE SESSIONS AT THE RAPE CRISIS CENTER had been no picnic. Things had started out rough. It took Gwen a good week before she even decided to leave Payton's apartment and give the Crisis Center a shot. Payton didn't push; Payton was just glad to have her friend with her. Nana was glad, too.

Gwen had called Nana after she had called Payton from the airport in tears. Nana was still at Gwen's house; Nana told her she loved her, and Gwen told her she loved her, too.

There were twelve sessions total. One each week. Gwen chose the closed sessions, although there were open ones, along with individual counseling, a twenty-four-hour hotline, and tons of other kinds of support. But the closed session consisted of the same group of women—eight, including Gwen—and the sessions, conducted in confidentiality, lasted ninety minutes. Gwen saw Payton from time to time, but Payton wasn't in charge of Gwen's session.

Gwen's session leader was a young woman named Meg, a psychology intern in the grad program at Harvard, who was a petite woman with a petite voice and an incredible bedside manner. She immediately put Gwen at ease, but the sessions still scared Gwen to death.

"I want to be strong again," Gwen stated in session number three. It was the first time she had spoken at all. Tears flowed freely, as they had during in sessions one and two.

In those sessions she listened to the other rape survivors—not victims, but survivors. Some were young, others older; some had been raped by strangers, others by acquaintances, and one by her ex-husband. Some didn't share the same culture or race as Gwen, yet they all looked just like her.

Afraid.

Bitter.

Confused.

They all wanted to be whole; to feel trust again; to rid themselves of guilt and pain. They all wanted to live again by their own definition, according to a standard that was satisfactory and fulfilling for them. Slowly, Gwen's own definition began to form as the sessions progressed.

The pain no longer dominated her life. The nightmares had ended.

Gwen had returned to Payton's apartment solo after one of her sessions while Payton stayed on at the center with a client. As she exited the elevator onto the fifth floor, she noticed a familiar face walking toward her. They spotted each other at the same time.

Gwen slowed her gait as he approached.

They both smiled.

"Hey there."

"Hey you." Gwen's smile broadened.

Xavier stood tall and handsome in front of her. He wore a tailored suit, taupe and lightweight, since Boston's weather was pleasantly mild for late August.

"I hope you don't mind me showing up here like this. Nana told me how to find you."

"No, it's fine." Gwen smiled again.

Xavier smiled back, "You look good. Like the hair." Xavier reached to touch her, but stopped himself.

Gwen fiddled with her hair, which had grown out enough to be pulled into a curly ball on top of her head. "Thanks. Fooling with a hairdresser hasn't been a high priority lately." Gwen blushed. They both smiled again.

"So, are you here on business…um, I don't mean *here* here, but in…Boston?" Gwen asked with embarrassment as she struggled to remember what town she was in.

"Uh-huh, I was." Xavier paused. "My plane leaves in a few hours."

"Oh." Gwen reduced her smile to a thin line.

"I've been here all week, and, um…" He paused again. "Look, I hope you don't mind, but I check in with Nana and Payton sometimes on how you're doing and they've been giving you glowing reviews, so I didn't want to come here and…you know, mess up your flow." Xavier exhaled and looked at her.

Gwen nodded. "I understand." She smiled again.

She did understand. She hadn't talked to Xavier since their confrontation in her bedroom months ago. She thought of him often; she knew, deep down, that she still loved him deeply, but he was right. She needed to concentrate on her flow for right now. When she looked in a mirror, she was just starting to be able to bear the sight of her reflection.

Gwen and Xavier slowly walked down the corridor and stood in front of Payton's apartment. They were quiet for a spell, just wanting to experience each other's company without interruption. Oddly enough, the silence felt normal; it felt good. Gwen hesitated about asking him in, knowing that she would not want to let him go. Xavier leaned against the door with what seemed like no expectation of an invite.

"Carmen and Avery ask about you quite a bit, and Kendra too. She's with me in Atlanta again for the summer."

"Tell them I said hi. I hope your schedule has allowed you to spend some time with her."

"It has. I haven't traveled much this summer. I…um, I requested this trip."

Gwen blushed. "Oh."

"Yeah."

More silence. More smiles.

"What about you? Plan on coming home eventually, or is Boston beginning to grow on you?" Xavier drowned his hands in his pockets; his voice had found its familiar comfort zone.

"Not quite. It's a nice town, but traffic is a bitch."

They both laughed.

Gwen's voice drew quieter. "I'll be home in a few weeks. Vaughn is

expecting me back at work by the first of October. I, um, have a few more sessions here." Her voice became a whisper.

"How's that going?"

"Good."

"Yeah?"

"Yeah. Real good." Her voice strengthened "I, um, plan to continue at a center in Atlanta, for a little while at least. Until I'm one hundred percent," Gwen paused with a slight smile, "or at least ninety or so."

Xavier slowly reached for her hand. "I'm proud of you, you know that?"

She felt a warm tingle in her chest. "Thanks. But I've got a long way to go still." She tightened her fingers around his.

"But you're on your way."

"I think so."

Xavier caressed her hand before bringing it to his lips, and then to the side of his face. Tears began to well up in her eyes as he gently glided his hand across her cheek.

"You know, Gwendolyn, there are so many things that I want to say. It took a lot of restraint for me not to come see you as soon as I landed in Boston. Part of it was like I said, your flow and all, but another part of me was a little scared." Xavier shifted his gaze slightly.

The apartment door across the hallway opened abruptly. Mrs. Crabtree wrestled to break free from the entangling leash of her precious terrier, which had managed to wrap itself around her right ankle. She looked up at her audience, startled, then suspicious, but ultimately grateful after Xavier aided her in freeing herself so she could make her way to the elevators and out of view.

Gwen fiddled with her keys, asking Xavier to come inside just for a little while, so they could talk. They both needed to talk. He accepted readily. They both took a seat on the couch—Gwen sat Indian-style while Xavier sat facing her.

"This is awkward, huh," Xavier started.

"A little."

"But necessary."

"Absolutely."

Xavier loosened his tie. He gently squeezed her knee and began, "You know I've been going through a range of emotions since…you know." Gwen nodded, murmuring, "So have I." She rubbed his hand as it rested on her knee.

"I kept trying to figure out why I was so confused and upset…"

She interrupted, putting his hand toward her lips before stopping and returning it to where she rubbed his. "Xavier, you felt deceived, by me, because of my secrets. I never meant to, not consciously," Gwen paused, "well, maybe consciously, but not…maliciously. I knew I was holding back so much, so much that involved you, but to me it was about self-preservation. I didn't give too much thought to the pain I could cause, just the pain I wanted to keep to myself. It was selfish, I know," Gwen fought back tears, her voice cracking, "so selfish." She kept rubbing his hand, moving her eyes from his face back to her hand on his hand.

Xavier grabbed her hand and began fiddling with her fingers. "You know when I moved to Atlanta, I really saw it as a new start. New environment, new job, back with family. And then I met you and love never looked so real before. Ya know? And that day, that day you told me it was Terry," Xavier breathed deep then continued, "all I could think about was *my* past with Terry. And that new start began to look too much like days of old." Gwen nodded; she did understand. She should have tried to understand more then.

Xavier and Gwen sat in silence.

"Aren't we a pair?" Gwen finally asked.

Xavier moved closer and wrapped his arm around her shoulder, pulling her into him. Gwen released her legs and folded them up on the couch. She rested her head on his chest, caressing his other arm with her fingers.

He held her for hours, missing his scheduled flight but catching a later one that night. They'd see each other again, they agreed, when Gwen returned to Atlanta in a few weeks. They'd get together, talk, and try to work slowly back into their rhythm. Maybe they'd find a new

rhythm, a new level of awareness—something like that was probably required under the circumstances.

She began to hope that she hadn't, after everything, lost him; that he wasn't the price she would have to pay for losing everything else she'd finally been able to release, and what she was finally beginning to recover. But it was that—what she was recovering of herself, of the Gwen she'd been before the rape and of the Gwen she'd never quite grown into afterward, that was what made her most hopeful for the future, and that kept her going through the long, difficult days of therapy, of isolation, and of loneliness.

Lately, Gwen often remembered something she'd been told long ago by her parents and by Nana after their death and most recently by Payton—that she was a woman. Her mother had warned her not to try to rush it; not to ignore the responsibilities that came with it. There was no rushing any more, and no failure to embrace the responsibilities. Maybe she'd paid for that; maybe she'd just had bad luck. But that was all past. She knew now she was ready to live up to those responsibilities, and the grace that came with them, in the fullest way possible. She was a woman, flawed in so many ways, yet flawless in others. Just like any other woman, no more and no less. It was simple, but lately it felt like a fresh revelation every day.

The End